Making Moonta

The Invention of Australia's Little Cornwall

This highly readable account of the myth of 'Little Cornwall' traces the history of Moonta and its special place in the Cornish transnational identity. Today Moonta is a small town on South Australia's northern Yorke Peninsula; along with the neighbouring townships of Wallaroo and Kadina, it is an agricultural and heritage tourism centre. In the second half of the nineteenth century, however, Moonta was the focus of a major copper mining industry.

Philip Payton here provides some fascinating new work on life in nineteenth- and early-twentieth-century Australia, and examines the myth of 'Australia's Little Cornwall': a myth perpetuated by Oswald Pryor and others that survived the collapse of the copper mines in 1923—and remains vibrant and intact today.

Philip Payton has written widely on Cornwall and the Cornish; he is the author of *A.L. Rowse and Cornwall: A Paradoxical Patriot* (UEP, 2005, paperback 2007) and *The Cornish Overseas: A History of Cornwall's Great Emigration*. He is Professor of Cornish & Australian Studies at the University of Exeter and Director of the Institute of Cornish Studies at the University's Cornwall Campus. He has also conducted extensive research and addressed numerous conferences in Australia.

Making Moonta

The Invention of Australia's Little Cornwall

PHILIP PAYTON

UNIVERSITY
of
EXETER
PRESS

First published in 2007 by
University of Exeter Press
Reed Hall, Streatham Drive
Exeter EX4 4QR
UK
www.exeterpress.co.uk
Printed digitally since 2011
© Philip Payton 2007

The right of Philip Payton to be identified as author of this work has been asserted by him in accordance with the Copyright, Designs and Patents Act 1988.

British Library Cataloguing in Publication Data
A catalogue record for this book is available from the British Library

Hardback   ISBN 978 0 85989 795 2
Paperback ISBN 978 0 85989 796 9

Typeset in Perpetua 11½ point on 13 point by Carnegie Book Production, Lancaster

'Remembrance is Love's Last Gift'

Contents

	List of illustrations	ix
	Preface	xi
1.	'The largest Cornish communities beyond Land's End': Making Moonta's Cornish myth	1
2.	'Wherever a hole is sunk in the ground': Moonta and Cornwall's great emigration	32
3.	The cult of Captain Hancock: The man and his mines	63
4.	'Cornwall was never conquered yet': Moonta's working-class heroes	97
5.	'Moonta toil and Moonta gain': Women, Methodists and the triumph over adversity	130
6.	'Moonta's little, but she's great': The enduring myth	166
7.	'The world's largest Cornish festival': The myth revived	192
	Epilogue	222
	Notes	229
	Index	255

Illustrations

Maps

1. Northern Yorke Peninsula, South Australia — xiv
2. Moonta and Moonta Mines — 2
3. Mines and settlements around Moonta — 4

Illustrations

1. Moonta Mines in 1897 — 10
2. George Street, Moonta, looking west in the late 1860s — 11
3. Hughes engine-house, Moonta mine, c.1864 — 13
4. Cornish miners assembled at Hughes's Shaft, Moonta mine, in 1894 — 16
5. The jetty at Port Wallaroo, c.1870 — 29
6. Moonta Mines Brass Band, c.1874 — 55
7. Kadina Salvation Army Band, c.1919 — 56
8. Kadina Primary School Band, c.1913–15 — 58
9–12. Cartoons illustrating the complex relationship between Captain Hancock and his workforce — 64
13. The New Cornwall mine, sketched by W. Wyatt, c.1862 — 72
14. The Kurilla mine, near Kadina, sketched by W. Wyatt, c.1862 — 76
15. The Moonta mine, sketched by W. Wyatt, c.1862 — 77
16. Hancock's team, c.1865–66 — 78
17. One of the northern Yorke Peninsula mines, showing a horse whim — 79

18.	Richman's plant, the Moonta mine, in 1908	87
19.	Loveday Maria Hancock in later middle age	93
20.	Conditions underground in the Peninsula mines	104
21.	A 'telescope' rock drill in use, Wallaroo mine, c.1914	109
22.	Moonta and Wallaroo delegates during the 'Great Strike' of 1874	113
23.	The smelting works at Port Wallaroo, c.1910	145
24.	The dangerous paraphernalia of mining at surface	147
25.	Children at play outside John Rowe's cottage, East Moonta, 1883	148
26.	A miner's cottage of the better sort at Wallaroo Mines	150
27.	Two little girls at Wallaroo Mines, c.1916	152
28.	The Bible Christian chapel at Moonta	159
29.	Robert Street Methodist Church, Moonta	160
30.	'Honest' John Verran, South Australia's first Labor Premier	171
31.	VIP visit to the Wallaroo mine, October 1910	175
32.	New investment at the Wallaroo mine: Office Shaft, c.1900–10	183
33.	Moonta Mines Methodist Sunday School in 1911	185
34.	New electric pumps underground at the Wallaroo mine, 1905	188
35.	'Scatterin the bal': removal of equipment from the Wallaroo mine	193
36.	Excursion train at Moonta for the 'Back to Moonta' celebrations, 1927	195
37.	Pickey boys in the ore-sorting plant at the Moonta mine, about 1913	200
38.	The Cornish Furry Dance being performed at the first 'Kernewek Lowender' festival, 1973	216
39.	Moonta's myth on the eve of the new Millennium: the largest Cornish festival in the world	219

Preface

As a small child I attended primary school in South Perth in Western Australia. Looking back, I remember it as an idyllic moment in my life. On balmy days, we would have lessons on the grass outside, the air heavy with the scent of eucalyptus, and Mr Greep – our headmaster – would lead us in singing 'Click Go the Shears', 'The Wild Colonial Boy', and all the other essential ballads and folk-songs of an Australian childhood.

In grade four we learned about Kalgoorlie, with its dusty roads 'wide enough to turn a bullock cart', and to my astonishment I heard about the 'Cousin Jacks' – the Cornish – the miners who had done so much there, we were told, to dig the gold from deep underground. Why was I astonished? Because the Cornish were my people, and Western Australia seemed a world away (as indeed it was) from the damp and often rainy granite-grey Cornwall that I had known only so recently. Yet, even at such a tender age, I had come to love Cornwall (in our family, we had little choice), and that classroom revelation in South Perth of a link between Cornwall and Australia was profound. Things would never be quite the same again.

Much later, back in the UK and at grammar school in Sussex (of all places), I chanced across a slim volume in our local county library branch, with the intriguing title *Australia's Little Cornwall*. On closer inspection, the book turned out not to be about Kalgoorlie and the Western Australian goldfields, nor even (as I had suspected) about the island State of Tasmania, with its own Launceston, River Tamar and County of Cornwall. Rather this was a book about South Australia, of which State I then knew very little, and thumbing the pages proved to be another revelation: for here in words and pictures was the evocation of a community and a landscape that was strikingly reminiscent of Cornwall itself. The author, Oswald Pryor, had caught in prose all the essentials of Cornish life and manners, and the photographs – of tell-tale Cornish engine-houses and Methodist chapels – depicted a place that for all the world looked just like Cornwall.

This was something that I had to act upon, and not many years afterwards I found myself at the University of Adelaide, working on the Cornish in the history of South Australia and visiting the many places of Cornish association in that State – not least Moonta and environs, the 'Australia's Little Cornwall' that Oswald Pryor had illuminated so perfectly and with such skill. My research had found a rich vein – a 'keenly lode', as the Cornish miner would say – and I duly produced my thesis on the social, economic and political impact of the Cornish in South Australia. In subsequent years, I have returned time and again to the grand themes of the Cornish in Australia, in America and all the other places across the globe to which have they ventured, chiefly (though not exclusively) as miners, and principally in the nineteenth century.

And yet, for all my immersion in this, my favourite subject, there remained an intriguing conundrum, an enigma, that continued to worry away at the back of my mind. Why, I asked myself ever more insistently, was Moonta so self-consciously such a place apart? How had it been able to proclaim its status as 'Australia's Little Cornwall', and over time to defend that title so successfully against all comers? How was it that Moonta, though in many ways an exemplar of the overseas Cornish communities created by Cornwall's 'Great Emigration', also such a visible exception? What was it that lay behind Moonta's Cornish myth, what had allowed it to take root and grow in the first place, and then to endure, seemingly so effortlessly, over the years and now into the twenty-first century.

This book, then, is an attempt to answer those and other questions. It is principally a book about Moonta. But it is also a book about Cornwall and the wider theme of the Cornish overseas, and demonstrates yet again – if further demonstration be needed – that the Cornish were (and are) a distinct people with their own transnational identity. Moreover, this is a book about Australia more generally, and contributes to the way in which we now read and write about Australian history. For many years a conventional wisdom insisted that Australia in the colonial period, and indeed up until the 1950s, was remarkably homogenous, its people largely the descendants of immigrants from Britain and Ireland, any differences between them ironed out by the shared experiences of emigration and settlement. When, in the 1950s, the eminent Australian historian Manning Clark attacked this cult of 'sameness' (as he dubbed it) and called for a new focus on 'differences', his was a lone voice.[1] Even in the 1980s, as Australians grew used to becoming a 'multicultural' society, Geoffrey Blainey – another distinguished Australian historian – had to remind observers that 'Australia before 1950 was a multicultural society because the cultural differences between Irish Catholics and Scottish Presbyterians and Cornish Methodists and many other groupings was intensely felt, at times too intensely'. Moreover, Blainey added, 'These differences permeated politics, culture, education, sport, business, the public service and every branch of national life'.[2]

Today, there is greater recognition of this diversity, and *Making Moonta: The Invention of Australia's Little Cornwall* is a contribution to the further elaboration of 'difference' and to grasping the fact that, from the first days of European settlement, Australia was in many ways a decidedly pluralistic country. The book is, I hope, a contribution to both Cornish and Australian studies.

A great many people in both Cornwall and Australia, and elsewhere, have helped me in this project. Alas, many of those who offered sage advice and readily shared their own research years ago when I was at Adelaide, have since passed on. Notable amongst these were the late Ian Auhl, Jim Faull, John Playford and John Tregenza. Here in Cornwall, the late Leonard Truran was likewise a great source of encouragement, as were John Rowe, A.L. Rowse and A.C. Todd. Happily, so many of my other friends and colleagues are still very much with us! It would be impossible to list all those who have helped with this book. But those deserving special thanks, in Australia, include Peter Bell, Mary Callaghan, Liz Coole, Mel Davies, Greg and Lynn Drew, David Dunstan, Charles Fahey, David and Kay Gill, Lillian James, Richard and Diana Hancock, Jim Harbison, Edwin Jaggard, Keith Johns, Pat McCooey, Neil and Roslyn Paterson, Eric Richards, Paul and Kathryn Thomas and Suzette Worden. In Cornwall, I should thank especially Bernard Deacon, Alan M. Kent, Charles Thomas and Garry Tregidga. Further afield, there are Gage McKinney and Ilka Weber in California, and Bill Jones in Wales. And at University of Exeter Press my thanks are due to Simon Baker, Anna Henderson and Vicky Owen, who have so professionally steered this book from concept to production, and with whom it has been a delight to work.

More generally, I should like to thank the British Academy, which provided a grant for me to attend the Australian Mining History Association's conference at Kadina in July 2006, where I spoke on the subject of 'Making Moonta' and was able to complete research for this book. I should also thank the Cornish Association of South Australia, which has on several occasions allowed me to speak 'on location', as it were, at their biennial seminars, scheduled to coincide with the Kernewek Lowender festival. Other institutions deserving of particular thanks include the University of Adelaide Library, the State Library of South Australia (which has given permission for illustrations from its collection to be reproduced from its collection), the National Trust of South Australia, Moonta Branch (for permission to reproduce Pryor cartoons), the Cornish Studies Library at Redruth, and the Courtney Library at the Royal Institution of Cornwall.

And finally, I should say thank you once more to my wife, Deidre, who has so readily accompanied me to far-flung destinations across Australia, and who remains my best critic as well as my best friend.

Philip Payton, Bodmin, Cornwall. 11 April 2007

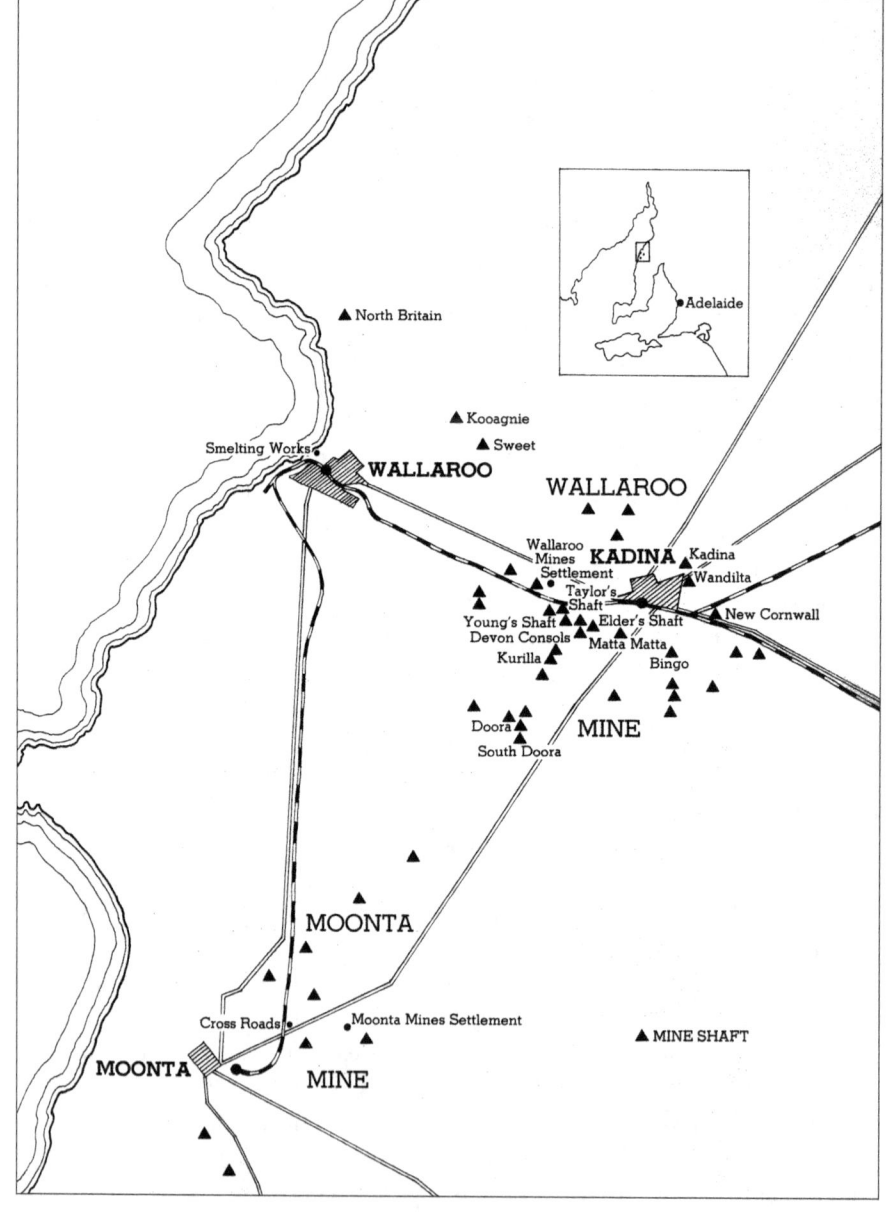

Map 1 Northern Yorke Peninsula, South Australia.

CHAPTER ONE

'The largest Cornish communities beyond Land's End'
Making Moonta's Cornish myth

'To the Cousin Jacks and Cousin Jennys who made
Moonta "Australia's Little Cornwall"'.[1]

This was Oswald Pryor's solemn and deliberate dedication in the preliminary pages of his book, *Australia's Little Cornwall*. First published in Adelaide in 1962, and still in print today, *Australia's Little Cornwall* is celebrated routinely as a delightfully insightful portrait of the lives and fortunes of Cornish emigrants on South Australia's northern Yorke Peninsula from the early 1860s until the years just after the Great War.

The son of a Cornish mine captain (manager), Oswald Pryor had been Surface Manager ('grass captain' in earlier Cornish parlance) at the world famous Moonta copper mine from 1911 until its closure in 1923. But he was by then also a cartoonist and journalist of note, as well as a budding local historian who was already collecting material for the book he was to produce almost forty years later. Many of his cartoons were political commentaries, appearing in the Sydney *Bulletin* and elsewhere, but a considerable number was devoted to the Cousin Jacks and Cousin Jennys, the emigrant Cornish, capturing their ways, manners, prejudices and preoccupations. There was an 'authenticity' in these depictions that struck those who knew the Cornish as 'extraordinarily true to life',[2] a sense that Oswald Pryor, who after all was Cornish by descent, had got under the skin of the emigrant Cornish in their Australian home. Pryor 'knew' the Cornish of 'Australia's Little Cornwall', in just the same way as – the saying goes – the Cornish 'knew tin', a peculiar intimacy and intuition that underscored all he produced. He wrote with authority and persuasion, articulating in prose what many had known all along – that Moonta had long since cultivated a distinctive, superior identity – and in so doing he served to perpetuate, reinforce and to a degree explain the myth that lay behind 'Australia's Little Cornwall'.

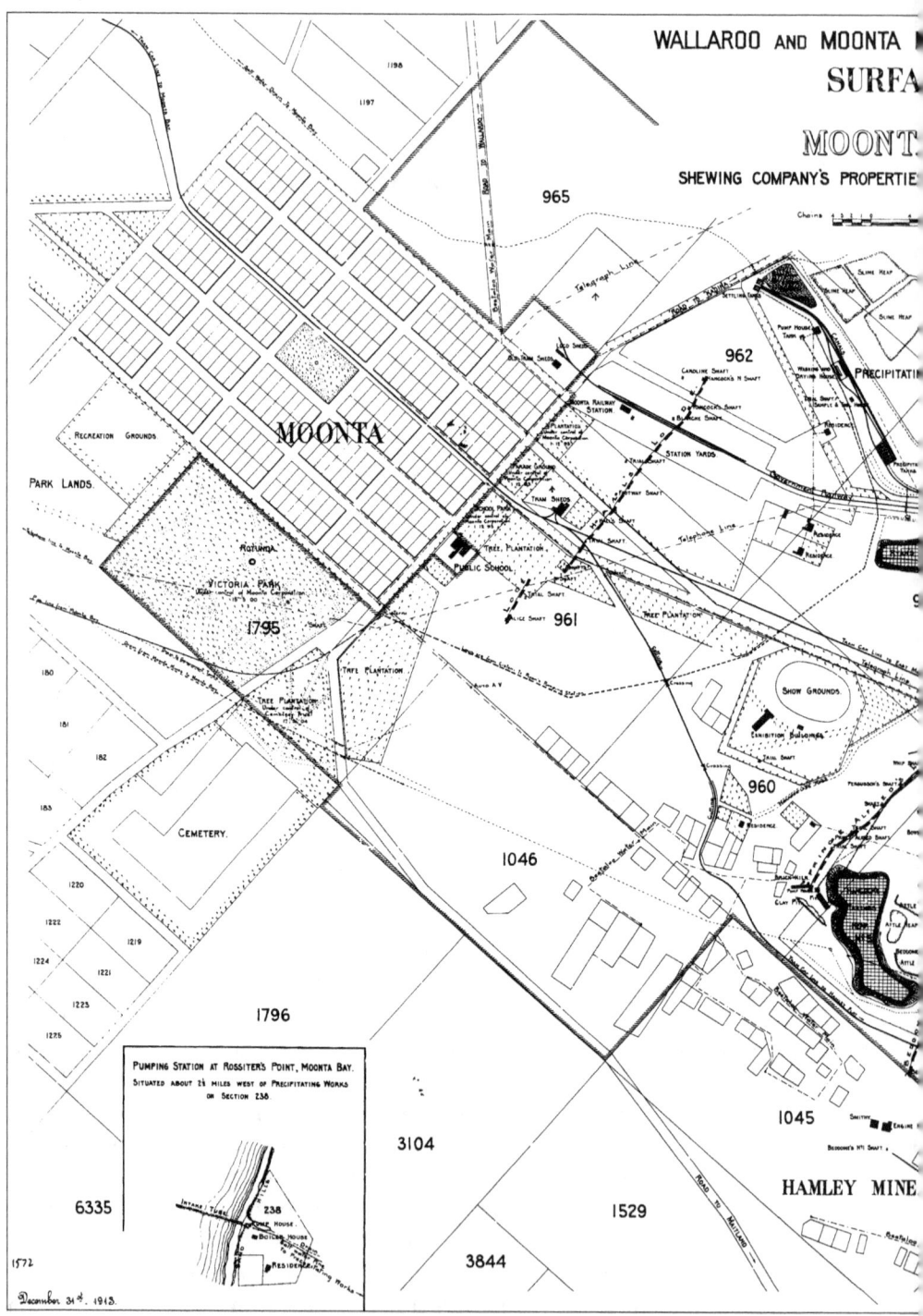

Map 2 Moonta and Moonta Mines.

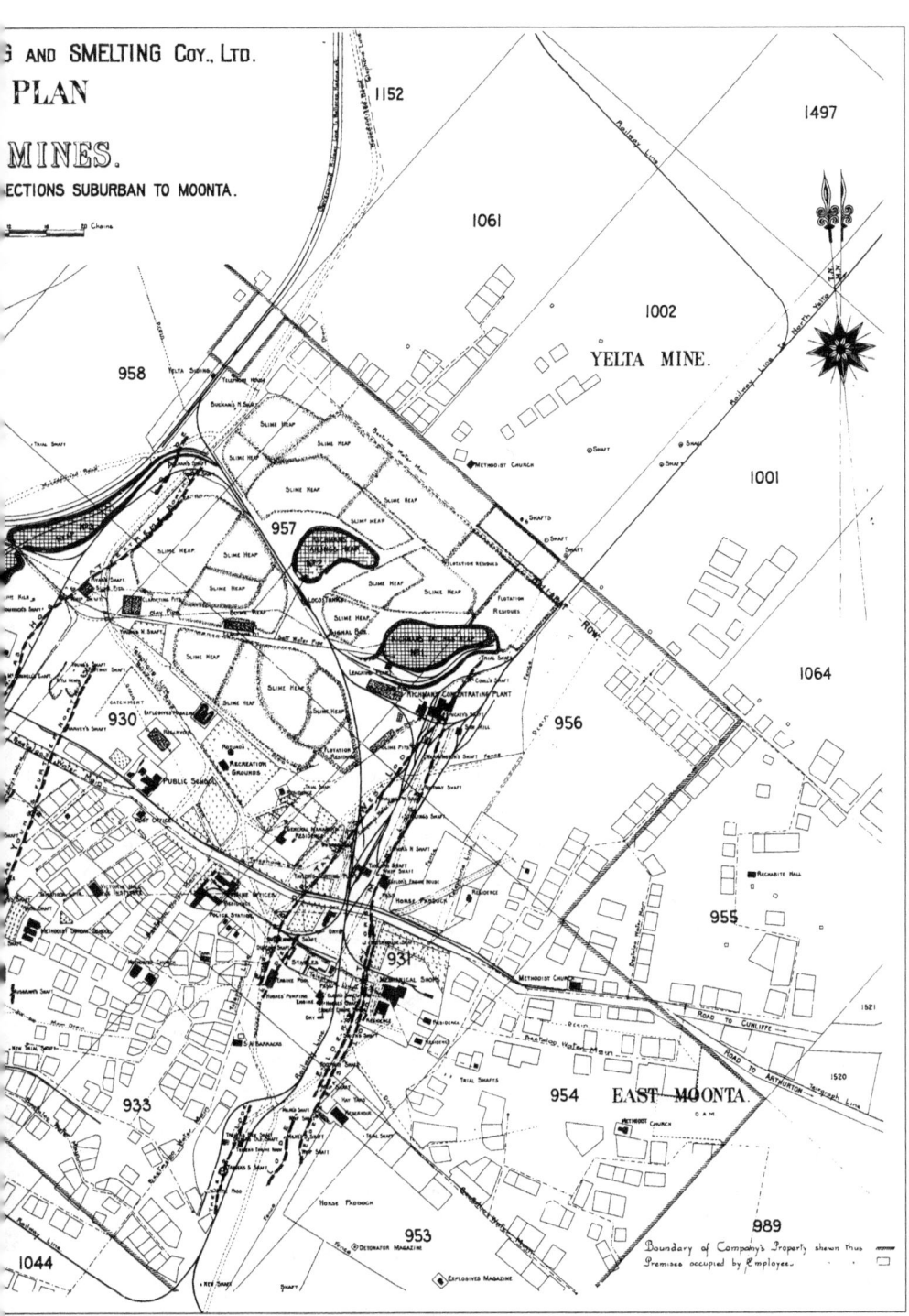

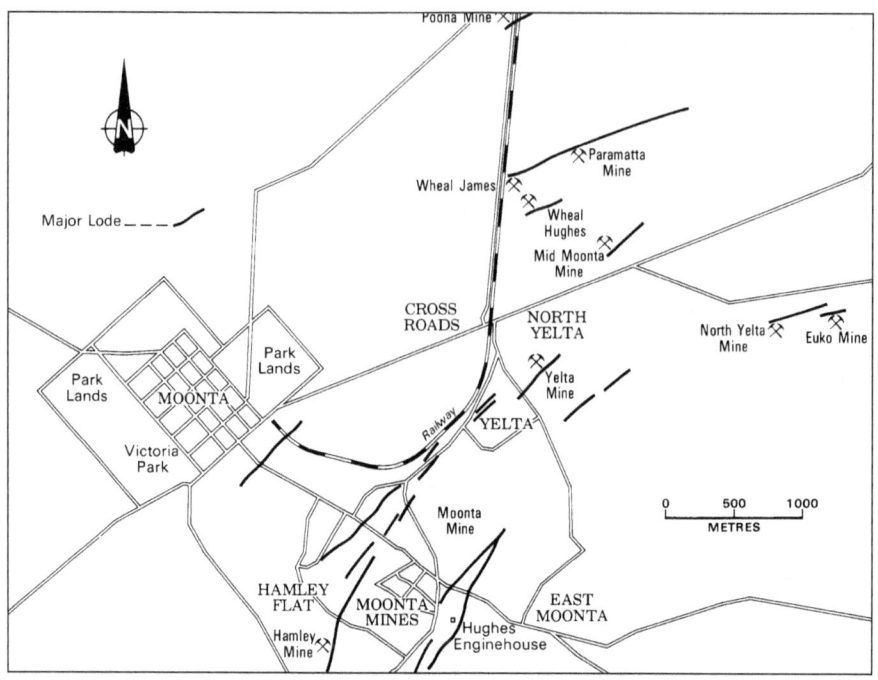

Map 3   Mines and settlements around Moonta.

This book picks up where Pryor left off, returning once again to 'Australia's Little Cornwall' but this time with the more explicit intention of seeking to understand just how and why Moonta was able to construct, and sustain, its particular mystique. This chapter is the first step, an attempt to identify those mechanisms – cultural, topographical and, above all, institutional – that helped mould Moonta's myth. To the district's ethnic composition and relative isolation from other peoples and places in South Australia, was added a maritime and peninsular location that also begged comparisons with Cornwall. So too did the physical appearance of the mines and adjoining settlements, with an abundant use of local stone for all manner of buildings, and an architectural style drawn straight from Cornish practice. Cornish practice underpinned much else that made the place distinctive: from mining methods, technology and terminology to the system of remuneration in the mines and the 'cult' of the 'captains' who managed every aspect of these activities and wielded enormous social power in the wider community.[3] Most powerful of them all was Captain Henry Richard Hancock – a man of immense international reputation in mining circles – and his charismatic leadership did much to enhance Moonta's myth.[4] But his relationship with his workforce was ambivalent (he was, after all, a Devonian), and the increasingly vocal trade union movement that emerged at Moonta was overtly 'Cornish' in the way it articulated its demands and fashioned its own cohesive identity. The trade unionists were also Methodists, a religious conviction that gave moral content and strength to their activities but which was also overtly 'Cornish' in the way it was conceived and expressed.

Over time, the links with 'home' became less close – not least as de-industrializing Cornwall lost its once unassailable place at the forefront of deep, hard-rock mining – but Moonta's Cousin Jacks successfully re-invented themselves as 'Moontaites'. It was an enviable status that provoked jealousy and even hostility in other communities near and far, and was one that wedded itself to an emerging Australian national consciousness in the Great War. 'Moontaites' were respected wherever they ventured – in Australian mining fields such as Broken Hill in the 1880s and Western Australia in the 1890s, and overseas in America and South Africa – and they were much sought after by mining companies which recognized their skills. But this superior status rankled, as indeed it still does today: even in the early twenty-first century Moonta still manages to project itself effortlessly as the principal centre of 'Cornishness' in the Australian continent, the biennial 'Kernewek Lowender' on northern Yorke Peninsula marketed unashamedly as 'the world's largest Cornish festival'.[5]

'The hub of the universe'

Moonta, as Oswald Pryor made plain, was the focus of a Cornish identity that was already writ large across South Australia, the distillation (in his opinion) of all that was inherently and characteristically 'Cornish' in the state's copper-mining districts. More than a dozen years before payable copper was discovered on Yorke Peninsula, first at Wallaroo Mines in 1859 and then at Moonta in 1861, the Cornish had already played a major role in the development of mining – and the creation of 'Cornish' communities – in places such as Kapunda, Burra Burra and the Adelaide Hills. Indeed, in 1857 one South Australian newspaper had proclaimed the hill country around Mount Barker and Callington 'the Cornwall of Australia',[6] such was the supposed Cornish ambience of the local mines and villages. More modestly, the previous year Callington and neighbouring Kanmantoo had been dubbed 'the Cornwall of the colony',[7] for much the same reasons.

But such pre-eminence was relatively short-lived, as once promising mines were at length abandoned, their miners moving on to pastures new, and even the mighty Burra Burra – in the mid-1840s the pride of South Australia – was closed and derelict by the late 1870s. Moonta, by contrast, lived on, a magnet for Cornish folk from elsewhere in South Australia as well as from Cornwall itself, its expansion and its consolidating sense of 'Cornishness' fed by the continued arrival of Cousin Jacks and Cousin Jennys from near and far. Even today, Moonta is still hailed as the epitome of the Cornish experience in South Australia, on occasions subsuming and eclipsing other localities in the state that might plausibly describe themselves, at least in part, as 'Cornish'; so much so that one scholar in neighbouring Victoria – with an evidently hazy grasp of South Australian topography – could write innocently of 'Moonta and Burra, a copper mining area which was to earn the appellation of "Australia's Little Cornwall"'.[8]

Moonta's mystique was not confined to South Australia. 'Moontaites', as they were known universally across the continent, turned up wherever there was mining to be done in Australia. At Peak Downs in Queensland, Cobar in New South Wales, Coolgardie and Kalgoorlie in the far West, and at Broken Hill, Moonta folk were often perceived as 'different' – sometimes even congregating together in separate 'Moonta camps' and 'Moonta towns'.[9] Here they took the 'myth of Cousin Jack' to new extremes. They insisted, as did their compatriots the world over, that the Cornish were innately equipped above all others as expert hard-rock miners. But to this myth – as familiar in California, Nevada and Michigan as it was in Victoria, New South Wales or Western Australia – the Moontaites added their own dimension. They reasoned that, if Cornishmen generally were to be preferred above all other classes of miners, then within Australia it was the Moonta Cornish who were at the forefront of the continent's mining industry.

In time, Moonta itself, rather than distant Cornwall, became the principal focus of Cousin Jack loyalty and identity. Second-generation Moontaites, born on Yorke Peninsula, could assert their credentials with confidence and authority – their local birthplace enhancing rather than eroding their Cousin Jack status in Australian eyes: they were, as one report in 1873 dubbed them, 'Moonta Jacks'.[10] Moreover, as the industrial prowess that underpinned the Cousin Jack myth faltered in Cornwall during the closing decades of the nineteenth century, when Cornish claims to superiority seemed increasingly hollow, so the continued celebration of Moonta, with its still active mines and vibrant communities, was a sensible strategy for those Moontaites intent on stressing their enduring worth.

As Pryor observed, Moonta was trumpeted regularly as 'the hub of the universe', the humorous bravado scarcely concealing the profoundly serious belief that lay behind what Pryor called 'Moonta patriotism'.[11] To illustrate his point, he told the tale of 'Billy Bray from Moonta'. This was, perhaps, an apocryphal story – Billy Bray was a famous name in the annals of Cornish Methodist history, possibly adopted by Pryor as a deliberate literary device to impress and convince the Cornu-Nonconformist *cognoscenti*. But it was also a story that made plain the global pretensions of an assertive Moonta identity: to emphasize in the wider world, at a time of profound upheaval and change, that 'Moonta's prosperity was expected to continue indefinitely'. As Pryor recalled, it was a 'veteran of the 1914–1918 war' who had first spun him this yarn. 'One evening,' explained the veteran, 'I was drinking in France with a cobber, Billy Bray from Moonta. He was small in size but big in heart, and Moonta was his theme.' Some drink had been spilt at the table at which Billy and the veteran were sitting. As the young waitress approached, Billy dipped his finger in the liquid and drew a circle. 'Mamzelle you compree the world?' he asked in Australian *franglais*. She nodded. '"Then", said Billy, dabbing a finger in the centre of the circle, "this is where I come from – Moonta!".' As Pryor added, confirming the underlying authenticity of the veteran's story and, to a degree, expressing sympathy – if not quite common cause – with the boastful Moontaite: 'To thousands of people like Billy Bray, Moonta *was* the hub of the universe'.[12]

The time and place of the story are important. The choice of name – Billy Bray – may well have been made to chime with Cornish sentiment. During the Great War hundreds of Australians of Cornish descent, Moontaites included, made the point of journeying to Cornwall when in Britain on leave or recovering from wounds, seeking out the former homes of their parents or grandparents and making contact with Cornish relatives. But, as Pryor was careful to note, the Billy Bray of his story was also a 'cobber', quintessentially Australian, part of an Australian army that was to distinguish itself in its own right on the Western Front and which already had done much to create the 'Anzac myth' at Gallipoli. For all his possible 'Cornishness', Billy Bray was an Australian and it was Moonta – not Cornwall – that was the centre of his world. As Pryor's story implied, the battlefields of northern France were not, despite first appearances, incongruous places in which to articulate 'Moonta patriotism'; its relevance and purview were truly global.

'If you haven't been to Moonta'

Moreover, notwithstanding the brief revival in Cornish tin mining before the First World War – and despite the importance of tin as a strategic metal during the conflict – the inexorable decline of Cornwall's copper and tin industries had been apparent since the 1860s and 1870s. Ironically, Australian output, including South Australian copper and Tasmanian tin, had played a major role in the overseas production whose competition had eroded and finally put paid to Cornwall's pre-eminence. Cousin Jack loyalty and identity altered and shifted as a result. At Grass Valley in California, a gold-mining town in the foothills of the Sierra Nevada mountains, where the Cornish had once fiercely defended both their 'superiority' as miners and the boundaries of their ethnic identity, it was possible now for individuals from a variety of backgrounds – Irish, Norwegian, even black – to become what were known as 'galvanized Cousin Jacks'.[13] Although not possessing a full set of Cornish credentials, their association with the locality and its culture – together with their connections with the mining industry itself – were enough for such people to invite or attract the sobriquet 'Cousin Jack', a term no longer so jealously guarded as before, or as ethnically exclusive. At Moonta, where the population was more homogenously Cornish, or of Cornish descent, there may have been a similar assimilatory mechanism at work. But if there was, it was hardly noticeable. The boundaries of Cornish Jack identity were not subject to renegotiation in the way that they were at Grass Valley; rather, they were now merely reversed: Moonta had become their principal foundation.

However, as Oswald Pryor had recognized in setting his Billy Bray story in war-torn France, 'Moonta patriotism' might be Moonta-centric but it was also global in its aspirations. This singular sense of place was mirrored in another telling aphorism recorded by Pryor, the insistence that 'If you haven't been to Moonta, you haven't travelled'. For Pryor, penning his book on-and-off in the decade or two before publication in 1962, this was a familiar 'old wheeze', a well-worn saying well known 'all over Australia, and in many other parts of the world'.[14] It was the stock in trade of after-dinner speeches, sermons and music-hall jokes; of politicians, clergymen and stage comedians. Always calculated to raise a laugh – or at least a wry smile, and sometimes a jealous grin – the phrase would invariably play well with any informed audience which understood (or thought it understood) Moonta's peculiar claims. Moonta devotees loved it; detractors were happy to see Moonta being made fun of.

Pryor imagined the saying to have arisen at Broken Hill – the silver-lead-zinc mining district just across the South Australian border in outback New South Wales – in the early 1880s as miners from across the continent arrived to participate in Australia's latest mineral boom. Among them were 'Cousin Jacks from Bendigo [in the goldfields of Victoria], and others from Moonta', wrote Pryor, and 'A lot of bantering went on between these two groups, the Bendigonians stating that the Moonta-ites knew nothing of mining methods outside of those used in the South Australian copper mines'. One of the Bendigo miners, emphasizing his breadth of experience in mines in many of the countries to which the Cornish had ventured, boasted extravagantly: 'I've travelled. Been everywhere – Californy, Boliv'a, Peru, South Africa, New Callydon'a.' But as he spoke, one of the Moonta miners cut him short: 'Hast 'ee been to Moonta?'. The other's hesitation betrayed the answer. 'No? Then 'ee's never travelled, boay!'[15]

In fact, the saying had been heard well before the 1880s – in North America and in Cornwall itself – and it survived long after the hey-day of Broken Hill. Pryor's book, of course, perpetuated its currency into the closing decades of the twentieth century, further popularizing the aphorism to the extent that Mandie Robinson deployed it to great effect as a literary device in her semi-fictional biography of Captain Henry Richard Hancock, long-time manager of the Moonta mine, published in 1978. This time the setting is early 1950s Cornwall, with Mandie Robinson's husband a student at the famous Camborne School of Mines. One day she encounters 'a world-travelled Cornish miner down Trelowarren Street in Camborne ... propping up Tyack's Hotel and watching the world go by'. She tells the miner that she has just returned from a holiday that has taken her and her husband right across France and Switzerland: '"Oh", I swank, "we've been everywhere"'. The miner stops her mid-sentence: 'Ah! But 'as 'ee ever bin to Moonta?' She admits that she has never even heard of the place: '"If 'ee 'asn't bin to Moonta, missus, 'ee 'asn't travelled". And he grins, triumphantly. He has put me in my place.'[16]

Robinson's re-telling adds something new to the story. As well as being Moonta-centric it is also Cornu-centric, no longer merely the bantering between Cousin Jacks from different parts of Australia but integral now to a Cornish transnational identity that privileges Moonta over and above all the other destinations to which the Cornish had travelled. That the story is told in Cornwall somehow authenticates Moonta's pretensions: that there is a wider international Cornish consensus which agrees Moonta's special status and raises it above the level of a parochial internecine dispute between 'Bendigonians' and 'Moontaites'. Robinson was not the first to witness this elevation – as noted above, the saying was current in Cornwall and America before the 1880s – but, even if prompted by Pryor, her skilful use of the story served to demonstrate its enduring strength. Even in post-Second World War Cornwall, Robinson would have us believe, people could still assert that 'if you haven't been to Moonta, you haven't travelled'.

'Bendigo versus Moonta'

Nonetheless, Pryor's identification of the 'Bendigo versus Moonta' context in 1880s Broken Hill was important. The Cornish had played a major role in the development of the Victorian goldfields, from the early gold-rush days of the 1850s through to the 1870s and beyond when their skills as deep, hard-rock miners had helped to solve the difficulties of dealing with the quartz reefs encountered at depth.[17] Many were world-travelled, and had already toiled in the mines of South Australia, California and elsewhere before ending up in Victoria. At Bendigo, the Cornish settled into a variety of occupations, as they did elsewhere, but at least a third of them worked as gold-miners, dominating the town's extractive industry. In 1881 no fewer than 46.9 per cent of fathers in Bendigo – and 41.4 per cent of mothers – had been born in Cornwall: nearly half of the town's reproductive population. Almost one in four of Bendigo households was headed by a Cornishman, and at the 1881 census the Cornish-born element of the population stood at slightly over 3,000 souls.

This did not include those of Cornish descent – children born at Bendigo or as far away as Mexico and Brazil – and so, given the generally large families characteristic of the period, it is likely that the number of those who might have been deemed 'Cornish' by any wider definition stood far in excess of the 3,000. At the same time, it seems possible that the total number of Cornish householders at Bendigo outnumbered the combined strength of their Irish and Scottish counterparts, again emphasizing Cornish dominance.[18]

And yet, this strong numerical presence did not translate into the cultural supremacy of the type exhibited at Moonta, though in many respects the two towns were comparable. By 1870, for example, the population of Moonta township and the adjoining Moonta Mines mineral leases stood at about 10,000, of whom some 6,000 lived on the leases – their cottages scattered apparently randomly amongst the engine-houses, crusher-plants and other paraphernalia of heavily capitalized mining.[19] The 6,000 were overwhelmingly Cornish but there were also a great many Cornish people among the population of the township itself: miners and their families, and those who had settled into other occupations – cobblers, blacksmiths, shopkeepers and so on. More generally, the Cornish in Victoria seemed never to have been as culturally 'visible' as their counterparts in neighbouring South Australia. Paradoxically, it is possible that during the nineteenth century Victoria played host, either temporarily or permanently, to larger numbers of

1. A classic view of Moonta Mines in 1897, taken from the ridge on Hamley Hill and looking across to Hughes's engine-house in the distance. Dotted all around are the 'Cornish cottages' typical of the locality. Note too the abundance of picket fencing.

2. George Street, Moonta, looking west in the late 1860s. This view, conveying something of the town's frontier atmosphere, shows – left to right – Solomon's Store (known as the 'Nimble Ninepence'), Chappell's cobbler's shop, and the Moonta Institute.

Cornish immigrants than did South Australia. But the *proportion* of Cornish amongst the South Australian population remained consistently higher than it did in neighbouring Victoria, the latter with its much larger and more diverse population.

However, as the Bendigo miners sensed at Broken Hill in the 1880s, the comparisons with Moonta, and between Victoria and South Australia, were not about numbers alone. There were qualitative differences too. As Pryor saw, the Bendigo Cornish smiled patronizingly at the way in which the Moonta Cornish had clung to their traditional mining methods, not yet embracing the new techniques developed elsewhere in the continent – or overseas. Copper was pre-eminently the Cornishman's metal, even more so than tin, and although there were important geological differences between Cornwall and South Australia, the latter was viewed by many in both places as an Antipodean extension of the Cornish mining industry. It was not surprising that the Moonta Cornish seemed set in their ways. But although sometimes criticized for their apparent conservatism, the Cornish were not always averse to drawing upon their reservoir of mining skill – some of it Old World, some acquired in the New – to help solve new problems in mineral extraction and processing. In Victoria they helped solve the quartz problem, and at Broken Hill they tackled the 'sulphide problem', the difficulty of separating the silver-lead deposits from the sulphides in which they were increasingly found at depth. Taking their cue from a newly arrived generation of American mine managers – Cousin Jacks among them, from the Comstock silver-lead fields of Nevada – the Cornish also quickly embraced the practice of 'square-set' timbering at Broken Hill, a method of supporting underground workings pioneered in the United States and thought appropriate to local geological conditions.[20]

In South Australia, by contrast, while there was certainly innovation – notably the 'Hancock jig' in the processing of copper ores – the standards and practices of the mining industry were overwhelmingly 'Cornish'. From terminology and technology to methods of employment and remuneration, South Australian copper mining remained resolutely Cornish in character until the early twentieth century. As R.K. Johns, one-time Director of the South Australian Department of Mines and Energy, observed in 1986: 'The Cornish influence during the formative years of the Colony of South Australia was profound ... In South Australia, mining methods, haulage and processing of ore and pumping of water from the mines were based on Cornish technology which remained in vogue until World War I.'[21] Architecturally, too, South Australian mine buildings, especially the distinctive engine houses and their Cornish beam engines (most of which had actually been built in Cornwall), were more than reminiscent of their Cornish counterparts. The most famous of these was Hughes' pump house at Moonta, its engine built at Hayle in Cornwall, which worked day and night from its installation in 1865 until the mine's closure in 1923.[22] The local limestone from which such engine houses were built was in quality and texture not unlike Cornish 'killas' – metamorphosized clay slate – and lent itself to the construction of mine, civic, religious and private buildings in the district, complementing the appearance of the mines themselves to produce a landscape that was unmistakably and distinctively 'Cornish'. Although the occasional Cornish engine house might be encountered elsewhere in Australia – as at Cadia in New South Wales or at the Duke of Cornwall mine at Fryerstown, Victoria[23] – the mining landscapes of South Australia, and Moonta in particular, stood in marked contrast to those elsewhere in the continent. The Bendigo miners had been right to point to what they saw as the profound and unbending influence of Cornish copper-mining methods at Moonta and environs.

'The Cornish captain ... a rare master of many skills'

There may even have been a hint of envy in the Bendigonians' criticisms. As Charles Fahey has noted, despite the prevalence of the Cornish as managers and in other positions of responsibility, only infrequently in Victoria did they rise to become major capitalists in the gold-mining industry.[24] In South Australia, much the same was true, although there was certainly more

3. Hughes engine-house, Moonta mine, c.1864. This engine-house contained a 60-inch pumping engine, manufactured by Harvey & Co. of Hayle, Cornwall. It worked twenty-four hours a day until the mine's closure in 1923. The house was built by John Beaglehole, builder of Ryan Street, Moonta, who was born in Cornwall in 1831 and had worked at Burra Burra and on the Victorian goldfields before taking up his trade at Moonta.

than a sprinkling of Cornishmen who made the transition from manager to entrepreneur, their shrewd dealings in shares in the continent's mining companies allowing them to retire in relative comfort to the spacious villas of Adelaide's seaside suburbs. However, there was one major difference. In nineteenth-century Victoria, the term 'captain' to describe a mine manager had been actively discouraged by the industry's entrepreneurs – notably the mining magnate George Lansell – as old-fashioned and out-of-date, not least because (it was argued) it encouraged an atmosphere of deference based on respect for rank alone rather than professional merit. Victoria's managers were admired because they did their job well, not because the mine-workers doffed their caps to them as 'cap'n'. In South Australia, by contrast, (and again, most especially at Moonta) the mining industry was structured in strictly hierarchical fashion, each mine with a team of 'grass', 'underground', 'first', 'second', 'third' and other captains, and a 'chief' captain as head of them all. They demanded respect – and by and large they got it, not least because there was a degree of socio-occupational mobility, so that the forelock-tugging miner of today knew that with luck he might become the much-revered captain of tomorrow.

The cult of 'captain', of course, was an integral part of the Cornish mining culture transplanted in South Australia. Although in Cornwall there was sometimes criticism – as the *Mining Journal* put it – of the 'pride or superciliousness which abound in a good many upstart captains', especially those who had been 'never a working miner',[25] the traditional respect for 'captain' (and the expectation of eventually joining and enjoying his rank) was widespread. There was also the strict hierarchy. At Camborne in the 1870s, for example, the celebrated Captain Josiah Thomas was known locally as 'the field marshal of Dolcoath', such was his authority in Dolcoath mine and his standing in the community. He had a large team of captains and under-captains working beneath him: Captain Tonkin was his second-in-command, with Captain Provis 'almost equal in station'.[26] The term 'captain' was greatly prized – in maritime Cornwall a mine was indeed akin to a ship, its master enjoying the same commanding status – something to be striven for and, once achieved, to be guarded jealously. As D. Bradford Barton put it: 'the Cornish captain had worked his way upwards from the lowest rank of buddle boy, and was a rare master of many skills'.[27]

In South Australia the same was true, especially at Moonta where there was an army of captains comparable to that of Dolcoath. The experience of Christopher Faull, originally from Trenoweth in the parish of Crowan in Cornwall, stands as an exemplar. Having arrived in South Australia in 1864, Faull had worked at both Moonta and Peak Downs in Queensland, returning to the former and working his way through the ranks until in 1883, at the age of 39, he was appointed captain. As his biographer, Jim Faull, has observed: 'Henceforth he expected to be addressed as Captain and woe betide any of his underlings who overlooked the courtesy'.[28] The tangible benefits of a captaincy at Moonta 'included a company house, free firewood, excellent wages, the right to recommend hirings and firings to Captain Hancock and, for underground Captains, special distinctive clothing provided at company expense'. As Jim Faull concluded, the Moonta captains 'were an elite group in the community, a privileged class of management personnel that were the undisputed decision makers in the daily operation of the mines'.[29]

Some of these captains may, in turn, have become successful share-dealers, making handsome profits from their investments in mines in Australia and overseas. But most, like their counterparts in Victoria, did not. And yet, for many, this did not matter – acquisition of the coveted rank of 'captain' was more than enough to crown a successful career – and here was a distinction that may have rankled among those Bendigonians at Broken Hill. 'The privileges of the Captains of the Moonta Mines in the early 1880s had changed little since the 1860s':[30] this was part of the apparently unchanging Moonta scene sneered at by the Bendigo men – it was also the source of their envy. As well they knew, those Bendigonians who had tried against the odds to maintain their title and status as 'captains' had sooner or later fallen foul of their employers.

In 1864, for example, George Lansell had engaged Richard Williams, originally from St Blazey, to run his Cinderella mine at California Gully, near Bendigo. Williams had toiled in mines in the United States and Canada, as well as his native Cornwall, and took enormous pride in his status as a Cornish captain. It was a personal title that he did his best to perpetuate and cultivate in Victoria. As Ruth Hopkins has noted: 'As "Cap'n Dick", one of the few it seems to be honoured with the Cornish title for a mine Captain in the Bendigo district, Williams became a legendary if sometimes controversial figure'.[31] At first Lansell turned a blind eye to Williams' individualism and eccentricity, admiring his undoubted abilities and putting him in charge of a string of other mines in and around Bendigo. But at length Lansell appeared to tire of Williams' attempts 'to command the same patriarchal style Cornish mine Captain status, as seen at Moonta', and the two men fell out: 'Family legend has it ... that Lansell drove Williams to the point where he arrived home for lunch one day and told his wife he could no longer stand to work for him'.[32]

The world of 'H.R.H.'

Turning their envy on its head, Oswald Pryor's Bendigonians scorned the way in which the Moonta Cornish stood in thrall of their captains, a stupefying awe, as critics saw it, that stifled individual initiative: '"Theece d'only know what Cap'n 'Ancock taught 'ee", scoffed a man from Bendigo'.[33] The case was no doubt over-stated – the Moonta Cornish generally were not known for their impaired imaginations or for lacking self-confidence – but the reference to Cap'n 'Ancock was telling. Henry Richard Hancock was, as the subtitle of Mandie Robinson's biography has it, 'Ruler of Australia's Little Cornwall', chief captain of the Moonta mine for thirty-four years: from appointment in 1864 until his retirement in 1898.[34] If the cult of 'captain' helped underpin the wider Moonta myth, then that of Captain Hancock – or 'H.R.H.' as he was often known – was critical in elaborating it over time. A legend in his own day, Hancock had ruled his mine with a subtle blend of iron discipline and sensitive understanding. It made for an individual style of leadership whose impact was felt far beyond the mine. Hancock was a pillar of the local community, not least the Wesleyan chapel at Moonta Mines. His fame reverberated around the international mining world, mirroring and accompanying that of Moonta itself: 'A South African mining engineer even heard Africans unemployed underground on the Rand say that they wouldn't do something, "not even for Cap'n 'Ancock'".³⁵

The Moonta mine was 'Cap'n 'Ancock's white cow' ³⁶ – rich and bountiful – and the Moonta miners' maxim, the recipe for success or at least a quiet life, was said to be: 'When Cap'n says thing is so, it is, even if it edden'.³⁷ The unquestioning loyalty of Hancock's under captains reinforced his authority and reputation, a solidarity shot through with a strong streak of nepotism which groomed his son, H. Lipson Hancock, as his successor at the Moonta mine. Hancock also created a position at the mine for his son Edwin. Another son, Leigh, managed the Paramatta Mine, north of Moonta, and went on to run the Burnie Copper Mine in Tasmania (of which his father was conveniently a director) as well as the Boulder Central in the Western Australian goldfields, for which position his father had recommended him.³⁸

This was dynastic control reminiscent of Cornwall, not least that of the Thomas family at Dolcoath. Josiah Thomas, the 'field marshal', had been groomed for the position by his father Charles. Captain James Thomas, Charles' elder brother, had cut his teeth at Cooks Kitchen mine – also in Camborne – before acquiring a supervisory position at Dolcoath. His three sons all became captains, including one prominent in the copper mines of Ireland, and Josiah's sons, Ernest and J. Arthur, became mine captains on the Rand. Ernest later became a mining consultant in Western Australia.³⁹ One of these men was certainly the 'Captain Thomas', an 'eminent tin miner' ⁴⁰ from Dolcoath, who in 1888 had been engaged by the New South

4. Cornish miners assembled at Hughes's Shaft, Moonta mine, in 1894.

Wales government to report on the scope and prospects of the Euriowie tin fields some fifty miles north of Broken Hill. The Thomas influence was felt in Broken Hill itself. Captain John Warren was one of those Cornish captains who, at the Block 10 mine, helped solve the 'sulphide problem'. He had come to Australia (initially to work at the Kurilla mine, near Moonta) armed with first-class testimonials from Captain Charles Thomas of Dolcoath and Captain Josiah Hitchins at Devon Great Consols.[41] Hitchins was another great Cornish mining character who – in another dynastic twist – had probably known and encouraged the young Henry Richard Hancock before his emigration to South Australia. At any rate, if Cap'n Hitchins and Cap'n Thomas said a thing was so, then it was; and with such recommendation, Warren's career had prospered.

Such dynastic influence had a momentum of its own, which could sometimes produce surprising results. For example, H. Lipson Hancock, though carefully nurtured by his father, had strong ideas of his own. He had, moreover, been educated at the Ballarat School of Mines, acquiring the Victorian disdain for 'old-fashioned' copper-mining methods. He was now a 'book-learned' mining manager (as the Cornish would say, somewhat critically), and on acquiring the Moonta reins from his father in 1898 set out to change much of what he now disapproved. Foremost among the undesirable baggage inherited from earlier days was the term 'captain' itself – now, on the eve of the twentieth century, a seemingly anachronistic term hardly redolent of the image of a modern, go-ahead industrial plant that H. Lipson Hancock strove to create. As Oswald Pryor noted with wry satisfaction, H. Lipson Hancock 'soon announced that he and the sub-managers would no longer be known as captains; all officers were to be plain "Mister". But it didn't work; to the Cousin Jack all bosses were still captains.'[42] Such was the enduring influence of 'H.R.H.' and the wider tradition of which he was so prominently a part.

A further twist was that Henry Richard Hancock was not actually Cornish. In fact, he had been born in 1836 at Horrabridge, a few miles east of Cornwall's River Tamar border, a village set in the midst of what was in effect an eastward extension of the East Cornwall copper-mining district. Although in Devon, it was a district dominated by Cornish mine names – many with the characteristic prefix 'Wheal', a working, such as Wheal Anna Maria, Wheal Elizabeth and Wheal Jenny – and indeed by Cornish miners. Following the copper discoveries on the eastern bank of the Tamar in the early 1840s, the Cornish flocked across the border to work or manage the new mines: men such as Captain Clemo at Devon Great Consols and Captain Phillips at Bedford United.[43] Although as a youngster Henry Richard Hancock would have rubbed shoulders routinely with such individuals, it seems that the Hancocks were genuine Devonshire people and not numbered among the Cornish interlopers.

They were an old Horrabridge family, and the Lipsons into which they married had been yeoman farmers in those parts for at least three generations. At Moonta, however, as Pryor explained, the Cornish were prepared, by and large, to overlook these impressively Devonian credentials and to agree that Captain Hancock, if not exactly a Cousin Jack, was 'near enough to one'.[44] This did not prevent them from remembering, however, when they thought it necessary to do so, that 'the manager of the Moonta is a Devon Dumpling'; a whiff of ethno-territorial superiority that asserted itself from time to time, despite the apparently all-pervasive deference to 'Cap'n'.[45]

'Strikes and rumours of strikes'

This apparent chink in Hancock's armour did not negate his cult but it did reveal its sometimes contradictory, and deeply enigmatic, nature. So upright – even straight-laced – was his reputation, that 'for some reason best known to themselves' (as Pryor put it) the miners would insinuate that in his private life he was a rake: 'a dreadful libertine'.[46] In one such tale a miner pointed out a colleague working at a distance, explaining to a visitor that this other man was 'brother-in-law to Cap'n 'Ancock, in a manner o' speakin'. The nonplussed visitor asked how this could be. '"Well", he was told, "'s wife did have first child by Cap'n"'.[47] Pryor declined to ascribe a reason to the miner's impish behaviour – was it the enjoyment of 'taking-in' the visitor, or the harmless fun of gently ridiculing Captain Hancock with hilariously absurd untruths? Or was there something deeper? For behind the façade of faultless deference, there was sometimes – in addition to the uncomfortable fact that Hancock was not 'really' Cornish – a grudging quality to the respect the miners showed their captain. Hancock's power seemed absolute but increasingly it was counterpoised, if not exactly challenged, by the organized strength of the Moonta Miners' Association: the embryonic trade union movement on northern Yorke Peninsula which eventually became part of the great Amalgamated Miners' Association of Australia. Here, then, was another paradox in the Moonta myth: the schizophrenic relationship between Captain Hancock and his men, and the manner in which it compounded rather than undermined the fabric of the myth.

The budding trade unionists – John Prisk, Reuben Gill, John Visick and so on – were, as their names betrayed, Cornishmen, portrayed at the time as typical Cousin Jacks. Methodists all, they spoke in Cornish idiom and couched their rhetoric in biblical allusions that their union brethren would readily understand.[48] They made a virtue of their Cornishness – and the Cornish motto 'One and All' – and built their union's solidarity around the ethnic homogeneity of the workforce, so much so that on one occasion the Moonta directors thought briefly to obtain '200 Miners or Pitsinkers of other than Cornish nationality'.⁴⁹ Hancock had come to power in the aftermath of a bitter three-month strike in 1864, and had enjoyed an extended honeymoon period as he listened to the miners' grievances and generally put the mine on a secure footing, employing labour rather than laying it off.⁵⁰

However, ten years later, and conditions had altered. Although the Moonta mine – incredibly rich, and with deposits near the surface – had been able to weather the low international copper prices of the late 1860s and early 1870s, by the mid-1870s things were beginning to change. The mine was deeper now, and more costly to work, and there was a sense that the early bonanza days were gone for good. There was, consequently, a general 'belt-tightening' in an effort to reduce costs – and one measure was a general reduction in wage rates. This was not only for the salaried staff and day labourers but for the skilled underground miners too – the 'tributers' and 'tutworkmen' who performed part of the entrepreneurial function themselves and were paid according to the value of ore won (tribute) or the amount of ground mined (tutwork). These miners, especially, believed that their efforts had contributed significantly to the early success of the Moonta mine and its international reputation, and understandably felt aggrieved. To date, they had worked hand-in-glove with Captain Hancock; there was a sense of partnership, albeit one within an unequal power relationship.⁵¹ Now, however, the partnership had been compromised. Put another way, the miners had already done their bit to help forge Moonta's myth, complementing the efforts of Captain Hancock as he set about creating his own mystique. But now this tacit alliance had become strained – and with it, the Moonta myth itself was made all the more complex.

A further paradox was that although the miner's union at Moonta was seen, both by the miners themselves and by external observers, as being thoroughly 'Cornish' in all respects, the prevailing view of the Cornish miner then (and indeed, until very recently) was one of an individualistic 'quietism' which did not lend itself to collective action. Writing in 1891, L.L. Price remarked upon 'the contrast between strikes and rumours of strikes in other parts of the country and the peaceful condition of Cornwall', a situation that would prompt even 'the dullest observer' to conclude that 'Strikes are unknown'.⁵² Price attributed this apparent state of affairs to the beneficial effects, as he saw them, of the system of employment prevalent in the Cornish mines – tribute and tutwork bargaining – where the miners competed amongst themselves for the right to work parts of the mine, and where the miners (who were paid by results, and invariably supplied their own tools and materials) were in several respects entrepreneurs themselves. This was a view echoed by A.K. Hamilton Jenkin in 1927 in his classic study *The Cornish Miner*, where he noted that 'Foremost of all ... among the reasons for the peaceableness of the Cornish miner was the peculiar system of wages under which he habitually worked'.[53] To this, Jenkin argued, was added 'the racial characteristics of the Celt, whose clannishness rarely embraces anything wider than his immediate neighbours', along with the relative socio-economic mobility and lack of class consciousness also characteristic of Cornwall, and the deferential relationship between the miners and 'the older Cornish landowning families who drew their incomes from the mines'.[54] More recently, John Rule has also identified the system of employment in Cornish mines as a contributory factor to this 'quietism', while also emphasizing the influence of Methodist theology, a religious perspective which encouraged a certain fatalism in this world and anticipated the rewards to come in the next.[55]

However, in marked contrast to L.L. Price and other nineteenth-century advocates of the Cornish wages system as 'perfect', Rule also demonstrated the negative, socially deleterious features of tribute and tutwork. There were miners who were forced to steal ore from one another, and others left with little or no remuneration to feed their families after an apparently promising piece of ground had failed to live up to initial expectations.[56] And, as Mel Davies has shown, the prevalence of tribute and tutwork did not in itself create either conditions of harmoniousness or a reluctance to strike. In 1848 at Burra Burra in South Australia, for example, the mine's largely Cornish workforce participated in a major strike 'that denies the stereotype picture that has previously been drawn regarding the inability of Cornish miners to act collectively before the late 1860s'.[57] The caveat is interesting. Davies recognized that in South Australia the Cornish miner had indeed developed a propensity to strike by the 'late 1860s'. But more than this, he also acknowledged that the 'quietism' thesis was already under pressure in Cornwall itself. In a major revision of Cornish labour history, Bernard Deacon had demonstrated that the apparent 'peaceful condition' identified by Price and echoed by later writers was in reality a chimera.

In fact, by the mid-1860s miners in Cornwall were becoming increasingly restive – especially in the relatively new copper mines of East Cornwall where the workers proved more ready to question 'traditional' attitudes, practices and deference. During 1866 hundreds of miners throughout the district clamoured to join a new Miners' Mutual Benefit Association, with meetings held at Liskeard, Gunnislake, Callington and across the Devon border at Tavistock. There were strikes at several of the large Caradon mines north of Liskeard and at Wheal Trelawney lead mine in neighbouring Menheniot. At Drakewalls and other mines near Gunnislake, the employers took pre-emptive action, locking out Association members, and at Devon Great Consols 181 soldiers and special constables were hurriedly brought in to protect the mine from a feared 'invasion' from across the Tamar. Concerted action by the employers brought the unrest to a speedy halt. And 1866 – the year of the great 'copper crash' – proved disastrous for the Cornish mining industry, with many mines forced to close and their workers likewise scattered overseas (to destinations such as Moonta) as they emigrated in search of jobs. Many of the striking miners had in any case signalled that they would rather emigrate than bow to the employers, and many did just that – taking with them their new experiences of unionism and industrial action to destinations as diverse as the Isle of Man, the North of England, and South Australia.[58]

As Deacon noted, the failed action of 1866 mirrored the first faltering steps of the South Wales miners in their unsuccessful strikes of 1863. But while the Welsh coal industry continued to expand – spawning an increasingly confident and well-organized trade union movement, 'the Fed' as it was known – Cornish copper mining was already in swift decline and proved no basis for the development of a corresponding Cornish movement. Tin, however, outlived copper. In the early 1870s there was a brief rise in the fortunes of the Cornish tin-mining industry, and a similarly brief upsurge in collective action. There were two main issues: the generally low levels of remuneration – especially the 'artificially low' levels set for tribute and tutwork bargains – and the infrequent payment of wages: the 'five-week month' in which miners would receive no greater remuneration than during a shorter, 'normal' month.[59]

At the end of 1871 and in early 1872 there were protest meetings against the 'five week month' at St Blazey in mid-Cornwall, at the Caradon mines, and at St Just-in-Penwith in the far west. As a result, many of the Cornish mines decided to abandon the 'five week month' altogether. However, the price of tin began to fall, and against the background of increasingly deleterious economic conditions many of the mines determined in early 1874 to re-introduce the 'five week month'. This provoked a series of strikes in the Camborne, Helston and St Just districts. They culminated in stoppages at Wheal Basset and South Condurrow, both in the Camborne–Redruth mining district, where the re-introduction was defeated and steps taken to form a trade union structure. But Cornish tin mining was already in decline, with the continued emigration of the would-be leaders of men, and the union forged with such enthusiasm soon came to little. As Gill Burke has concluded: 'The diminution of the Cornish industry during these years was most certainly one important factor in the delayed advent of Trade Union organization on any scale in Cornwall'.[60] It was not that the Cornish were innately or temperamentally resistant to trade unionism. Rather, economic conditions, especially early de-industrialization, militated against its development in Cornwall.

A.K. Hamilton Jenkin's portrayal of the Cornish miners as passive and deferential – 'though frank and independent in their ways and speech',[61] as he admitted – is, then, one that requires, at the very least, strong qualification. In this light, Oswald Pryor's contention that the trade union movement and industrial action at Moonta were somehow typically 'Cornish', and so integral to Moonta's myth, no longer seems surprising. Indeed, just as emigrant Cornishmen became what R.E. Lingenfelter called 'the leaders of the mining labor movement in the West' [62] of America, so they had brought their new ideas and ambitions to Moonta. In the aftermath of the 1874 strike, the Moonta Miners' Association turned its attention to the 'the five-week month' – one of the many features of Cornish mining practice transplanted in South Australia – and in February 1877 one newcomer wrote home in dismay: 'no doubt you will be surprised when I tell you that the system of five weeks' pay which the miners not only in our mine but of almost every mine in Cornwall fought so valiantly to crush is in operation in this far-off land'.[63] It cannot be entirely accidental that brief upsurges in collective action in Cornwall in the mid-1860s and 1870s coincided with those at Moonta in the same years – nor, for that matter, that in 1872 Cornishmen had led similar strikes at Calumet and Hecla and other copper mines on Michigan's Upper Peninsula, another major destination for the emigrant Cornish.[64]

In Victoria, the Cornish had likewise participated in the emergence of organized labour in the mines. In the summer of 1871–72 – a time of discontent in Cornwall, as we have seen – the Bendigo Miners' Association was formed, the first of its kind in Victoria. It was immediately successful, attracting many miners to its ranks and engaging in fruitful negotiations with mine owners. Its most enduring victory was the achievement of the eight-hour day, and it also influenced the Regulation of Mines Act in 1874. Thereafter, it courted continued popularity by pandering to anti-Chinese prejudice, arguing – as Europeans, Cornish included, did the world over – that the presence of Chinese workers had a generally depressing effect on wages and conditions, 'coolies' taking the jobs that by rights belonged to white men.[65] Similarly, the tell-tale motto – 'One and All' – was deployed in the usual way as an appeal to Cornish sentiment and for workers' solidarity, an indication as ever of Cornish influence. In 1883, for example, the *Bendigo Advertiser* published just such a call to arms:

> United may we stand,
> Guarding throughout the land
> Right against wrong.
> Justice we seek for all,
> Ready at duty's call,
> Our motto 'One and all'
> We shall be strong.[66]

The rhetoric was matched by activity on the ground, the Bendigo Miners' Association in 1882 sporting Cornishmen in all its leading executive positions. This was a dominance maintained for many years – the roll call of Association Presidents is littered with unmistakable Cornish surnames (such as Dunstan, Grigg, Rowe, Laity, Treleavan and Trewartha) – and the Cornish remained visible in the Association's ranks until at least the Great War.[67] Elsewhere in the Victorian goldfields, the Cornish were also active as trade unionists. Creswick, in the heart of the goldfields, became the centre of an Australian-wide federation, the Amalgamated Miners' Association (AMA), as localized Associations such as those at Moonta and Bendigo forged links in the spirit of 'unity is strength'. One of its most notable activists (banned for a time from employment in the mines in neighbouring Clunes) was John Sampson, grandfather of the Australian Prime Minister Sir Robert Menzies, a Cornishman who had been the first President of the Creswick branch of the AMA.

Not surprisingly, there were Cornish mine mangers in Victoria who – like Captain Hancock and his team of Cornish captains at Moonta in South Australia – opposed the activities of the trade unionists, viewing any attempt to influence the management of the mines as unacceptable interference and an affront to their authority. Oddly, Ruth Hopkins takes this to be evidence 'that makes something of a mockery of the oft expressed viewpoint of the Cornishman as a radical liberal'.[68] This is hardly a sophisticated analysis but it does hint at a wider point – that the 'Cornish' political culture underpinning trade unionism that was so readily visible in South Australia, manifest most noticeably in the intimate relationship that was to develop in the Yorke Peninsula mines between the AMA and the United Labor Party (ULP), was far less an influence in Victoria. Integral to the political culture so visible in South Australia, was the link between Methodism, especially Primitive Methodism and the Bible Christians, and the activities of trade unionists and the ULP. By contrast, argues Hopkins, in Bendigo – and by implication elsewhere in Victoria – 'the experience appears to differ from that of Moonta'. Here, she says, 'one would be hard put' to find links 'between religion and unionism'. That is not to say that there were not Cornish unionists who were not also Methodists, nor 'that unionists in Bendigo were a completely irreligious lot'. Rather, 'the different experiences of those on the goldfields [compared to those at Moonta] had moulded them into a more hard bitten company'.[69]

There may well be some truth in Hopkins' assessment. But, even allowing for the contrasting experiences of Moonta and Bendigo, what is even more striking is the *perception* of difference. For Oswald Pryor, trade unionism – and the attendant connection with Methodism – was identifiably 'Cornish' and central to the Moonta myth that he had elaborated so carefully. For Ruth Hopkins, not only was trade unionism 'not Cornish' (despite the presence of Cornish miners in the AMA ranks) but, in Victoria, 'Cornishmen were conservative in their politics',[70] with no discernable link at all between politics, trade unionism and religion. While Pryor had highlighted what he saw as an integrated, coherent and highly 'Cornish' political culture at Moonta, Hopkins pointed to cultural fragmentation and admitted a high level of assimilation in Bendigo – and in Victorian society generally – where 'Cornishness' had had little direct influence upon political behaviour or events. It was a telling comparison. Pryor may well have done much to elaborate the Moonta myth, but, in her paradoxical way, Hopkins was complicit in its perpetuation. She acknowledged the Cornish particularism inherent in Moonta's story but failed to find – or construct – something remotely similar in Bendigo or in Victoria as a whole. By implication, Moonta's special status was thus confirmed.

'The Holy Land of Moonta'

Methodism as a central strand of this particularism was apparent from the first. John Prisk, one of the early trade unionists, was secretary of the Moonta Miners' Association for many years. He was also a Bible Christian local preacher, a fitting qualification, his contemporaries suggested, for such a leader of men.[71] Here, as one local newspaper put it, was 'the Holy Land of Moonta under the able leadership of their modern Gideon, Mr J. Prisk'.[72] Reuben Gill, his colleague, was likewise a Bible Christian – renowned as 'the Billy Bray of South Australia', an indication of both his individualistic preaching style and the esteem in which he was held in Methodist circles.[73]

Periodic religious 'revivals' swept Moonta and environs, led by men such as Reuben Gill, moving and re-enthusing a populace for whom religious affiliation was already important. These revivals had profound and lasting effects: in 1965, for example, a *Centenary* booklet – published to celebrate a hundred years of the Moonta Mines Methodist Church – recalled vividly that 'An outstanding feature of church life at Moonta Mines was the revivals that took place'.[74] In August 1875, the booklet remembered, Phillip Phillips, 'the singing pilgrim', had delivered his song sermons to packed congregations at Moonta. In March 1886 Mr T. Houston, 'the blind Evangelist', held a series of fervent singing services, as did the evangelical Barrett brothers in 1905. The passage of the years had not dimmed remembrance of these remarkable events, which even in 1965 still seemed as wondrous as those days early in the twentieth century when observers could exclaim: 'Glory! Glory! Glory! Glory be to the Father, and to the Son, and to the Holy Ghost! Yes, we have had the Barrett Brothers on the Mines and have had a glorious time. If you don't believe it, come and see. Oh, such a revival!'[75]

The sense of ownership that 'the Holy Land of Moonta' felt for Methodism – in its Bible Christian, Primitive Methodist, Wesleyan and other guises – mirrored that in Cornwall itself where, as D.H. Luker has put it, 'an increasingly articulated regional sensitivity on the part of the Cornish ... fuelled an exaggerated identification of Methodism as "theirs"'.[76] As in Cornwall, at Moonta this 'Cornish Methodism', as it was known routinely, manifested itself in all sorts of ways; from the activities of local musicians who composed 'Cornish carols' and conducted male voice choirs, to the Sunday school 'tea treats' with their Cornish fare of pasties, saffron cake and splits, and their parades led by the district's brass and silver bands. The social cohesion encouraged by such activity was reinforced by the tendency for Methodists to marry within their own ranks. Indeed, marriage 'outside' was not only frowned upon in the community but discouraged officially by Methodism's governing bodies. At Moonta, where the Methodists were often also Cornish, this stricture had the effect of perpetuating the Cornish–Methodist nexus and encouraging a deep sense of ethno-religious exclusivity.[77] Indeed, in the 1891 census an extraordinary 80 per cent of the population of northern Yorke Peninsula was recorded as Methodist.[78] It is a mistake to read religious affiliation uncritically as a proxy for ethnic identity (there were many English Methodists in South Australia's 'Paradise of Dissent') but the figure is impressive nonetheless, suggesting as it does the all-pervading influence of the Cornish.

There was also the spirit of 'self improvement' which motivated the Methodists in their daily lives. In many Methodist homes at Moonta, and in the Miners' Institute and the chapel libraries, could be found 'improving' literature such as the novels of Walter Scott, Charles Dickens and the Bronte sisters, or the poetry of the Brownings, Tennyson and Longfellow, or the complete works of Shakespeare.

The 'Cornish stories' of Mark Guy Pearse were likewise popular at Moonta, bringing to bear a peculiarly Cornish dimension to this literary repertoire. Born in Camborne in Cornwall in 1842, Pearse became 'one of British Wesleyanism's leading ministers',[79] as Arnold Hunt described him, and he produced a steady stream of literary works underpinned by Methodist themes designed to guide the lives of his readers. He was especially aware of the Cornish overseas, and was sympathetic to the privations and the pangs of homesickness suffered by Cornish emigrants on the mining frontiers of the New World. He had toured California and other parts of North America, meeting the Cornish there, his lectures and sermons drawing large crowds of eager listeners. 'Lor, Maaster Pearce,' exclaimed one sentimental Cousin Jack in Canada, 'It's like being down to home again to hear 'ee spaik.'[80] In 1891 Pearse also visited South Australia, among other things laying the foundation stone in Adelaide for the Malvern Wesleyan Methodist Centenary Church.

The Hocking brothers, Silas and Joseph, born in St Stephen-in-Brannel in Cornwall, in 1850 and 1860 respectively, were also hugely popular in Moonta and in South Australia generally, the Methodist morality of their novels (many set in Cornwall) finding a ready appeal in homes, chapel libraries and miners' institutes from the 1890s onwards.[81] Some of these novels dealt with the Cornish overseas – such as Silas Hocking's *The Lost Lode* and Joseph Hocking's *What Shall It Profit a Man?*, both stories about an emigrant's return to Cornwall – but others pursued a distinctly anti-Catholic theme. In December 1899 the Adelaide *Christian Weekly and Methodist Journal* wrote approvingly of Joseph's novel *The Scarlet Woman*, welcoming it as 'a scathing exposure of modern Popery'.[82]

Such popular literature – 'pulp Methodism',[83] as Alan M. Kent has described it – was read widely and did much to perpetuate the spirit of Cornish Methodism in the everyday lives of Moonta people, combining Methodist morality and theology with tales of the Cornish at home and abroad to create a profound sense of belonging and togetherness. Like their compatriots in Cornwall, Moonta folk saw Methodism as 'theirs': particularly the Bible Christians, who were keenly aware that their denomination had had its origins in Cornwall and adjoining North and mid-Devon. Moving out from their Cornish and Devon heartlands, the Bible Christian missionaries had sought to evangelize other places ripe for their attentions: the newly opened-up agricultural expanses of Wisconsin and Ontario, where many of their members had settled, or (nearer to home) the coal-mining districts of Kingswood (near Bristol), Monmouthshire and the Forest of Dean.[84] But South Australia remained the denomination's principal focus beyond Cornwall and Devon, and Moonta was its base: in 1875 the Rev. W.H. Hosken, a Bible Christian minister from Victoria, visited northern Yorke Peninsula and was 'persuaded that I have never seen a finer field of labour anywhere in our Connexion'.[85]

'A simple but stout-hearted woman'

One of the distinctive features of the Bible Christian Connexion was its widespread use of women as preachers. The Wesleyans were reluctant to employ women, the Primitive Methodists less so, and it was only the Bible Christian denomination that saw the use of females as a positive virtue: 'We believe God can enable a woman as well as a man to speak to edification, and exhortation and comfort'.[86] There were no ordained women in South Australia, but the Bible Christians in the colony used female local preachers to good effect – notably Serena Thorne.[87] She was the offspring of Mary O'Bryan (daughter of William O'Bryan, the denomination's Cornish founder) and the Rev. Samuel Thorne, one of the Thorne family of Shebbear in North Devon which had played an important part in establishing the fledgling movement after its foundation in 1815. The Rev. John Thorne, another of the family, became a much respected minister at Moonta, further enhancing

Moonta's place in the Bible Christian world and creating a direct link with the denomination's centre at Shebbear. Shebbear was actually in Devon but for many at Moonta it was always 'Shebbear, Cornwall'.[88] Serena Thorne was, after all, half-Cornish.

Already renowned as 'the girl preacher' of North Devon, Serena Thorne was sent as a missionary to Queensland in 1865 by the Bible Christian Conference. From there, she moved on to Victoria, and thence to South Australia, establishing missions in several country circuits and remaining the colony's leading woman preacher until her death in 1902. Others were less well known but their work was valued, not least by women who saw in gender equality the manifestation of God's Word. When, towards the end of the nineteenth century, there were moves towards Methodist Union in South Australia, there was a strong body of Bible Christian opinion at Moonta opposed to union on the grounds that it would undermine this equality. In 1896, when a ballot on the subject was held among the Methodist denominations, one Moonta resident wrote to the local *People's Weekly* newspaper, complaining that: 'in Christ Jesus there is ... neither male nor female ... Bible Christian women are now asked to vote in a new order of church life, where they are basically ignored; and in the constitution of which they are not named!'[89]

This was an echo, perhaps, of the feisty reputation Moonta women had earned some twenty years before, when they had played a remarkable role in the strike of 1874. Then, at the instigation of the Moonta mine's directors, the engine-men had been persuaded to stay at their posts in the engine-houses. Had they struck with the other men, the pump engines would have been stopped, and the mine workings swiftly inundated – a disaster that the employers wished to avoid at all costs. John Prisk, one of the strike's leaders, and a Bible Christian, was equally determined that pumping should cease. Addressing a strike meeting, he encouraged a novel solution, exhorting the miners' wives, mothers and daughters to take direct action themselves in support of their menfolk. 'There's a rumour,' Prisk is reputed to have said, 'that you're going to sweep all the nuisances out of the engine-houses.'[90] The women needed no second bidding, so the story goes, and marched from one part of the mine to the next, vigorously applying their brooms to the engine-men and other blacklegs they encountered during their sweep. Their action helped to expedite negotiations, bringing the strike to a successful conclusion – at least as far as the miners were concerned. As one of the defeated directors was reported to have observed with wry insight: 'We can be damned thankful that women don't usually unite for a common purpose. Those Cousin Jennies up at Moonta showed us what can happen if they do.'[91]

Pryor retold the story in his *Australia's Little Cornwall*, enshrining it as part of Moonta's myth, and establishing a particular place for 'strong women' in the iconography of the district. Somehow it comes as no surprise to learn that it was Moonta that produced Kate Cocks, the daughter of a Cornish miner, who in 1915 became 'the first woman police constable in the British Empire'.[92] Tough but compassionate; loyal, resourceful and courageous – this was the image of Moonta women encouraged by the likes of Oswald Pryor. It was also the image of Cousin Jenny. For if there was a 'myth of Cousin Jenny' to match that of Cousin Jack, then it was this: that Cornish women were somehow equipped above all others for the rigours of life on the frontiers of Australasia or North America or South Africa, able to match the 'superiority' of their menfolk and to play a key role in the establishment and survival of frontier communities.[93] At Moonta, the myth was co-opted and internalized – just as that of Cousin Jack had been – so that Moonta women were more than archetypal Cousin Jennys: they epitomized the type.

This special status was reflected in the novel *Not Only in Stone*, written by Phyllis Somerville (who had three Cornish grandparents) and published in 1942. Still in print today, the novel tells the story of Mary Elizabeth 'Polly' Thomas, a Cornishwoman who emigrates to South Australia with her husband Nathan, a copper miner, and their son, who has been born at sea during the voyage. They settle briefly in Adelaide, the colonial capital, but then move to northern Yorke Peninsula where Nathan finds work in the mines. But Nathan falls ill and, as his health deteriorates, Polly finds herself having to fend for her family in the harsh environment of the mines: 'courageously [she] assumes the responsibility of raising four children by herself. A simple but stout-hearted woman, she stands fast in the face of many tragic set-backs.'[94] Today, the story still rings true, an authentic remembrance of the stoicism and tenacity of frontier women. Such is the novel's continuing resonance that it is recommended as essential reading on a website devoted to Moonta and the promotion of the district as a tourist destination. According to the site, it is 'A novel based on a family who emigrated from Cornwall to the Moonta Mines, it's a good story of hope, tragedy and human endurance'.[95] But, while capturing the spirit of the book, the recommendation is not quite accurate: Polly and Nathan Thomas live not at Moonta Mines but at Wallaroo Mines – a different settlement, some half-a-dozen or more miles away.

The Copper Triangle

This is no doubt an unwitting error. But the slip serves to illustrate the all-pervading power and presence of Moonta's myth. It also reflects a sleight of hand, made plain by Oswald Pryor but by no means of his making, in which Moonta can have it both ways. Moonta can be its own place, the 'hub of the universe', exhibiting a quiet – and sometimes not so quiet – superiority over other places near and far. At times of such exclusivity,

5. The jetty at Port Wallaroo, c.1870.

it is Moonta alone that is 'Australia's Little Cornwall': as the 'Welcome to Moonta' sign proudly proclaims today as the motorist enters the town. But at other times 'Australia's Little Cornwall' is geographically, and culturally, more inclusive. Moonta retains its status and authority as the district's spiritual centre, and yet the whole of northern Yorke Peninsula combines to assert its Cornish identity, most overtly in the region's biennial 'Kernewek Lowender' Cornish festival, first staged in 1973 and held subsequently thereafter in every 'odd' year. Here Moonta stands shoulder to shoulder in regional solidarity with Kadina and Wallaroo – the other towns of the 'Copper Triangle' (to give the district its alternative name) – and is at the head of a complex series of satellite settlements that, even in the early twenty-first century, reflects so visibly the pattern of nineteenth-century ribbon development. As the mines spread, so to did the settlements, spawning 'suburbs' such as Moonta Mines, East Moonta, Cross Roads (or Wheal Hughes), Yelta, Wallaroo Mines, and long forgotten precincts such as Newtown, Portreath, Jericho and Menadue. There was also Port Hughes and nearby Moonta Bay, furnishing a maritime dimension that gave further opportunities for comparisons with sea-girt Cornwall. Like Cornwall itself, Yorke Peninsula was the 'ill-shaped leg'.[96]

Moonta, Kadina and Wallaroo (or Port Wallaroo, as it was known at first) were government townships, laid out in orderly fashion as the surveyors dictated. The satellite settlements were, by contrast, *ad hoc* affairs in which hurriedly erected miners' cottages existed cheek-by-jowl on the mineral leases with the mines themselves. As one astonished visitor wrote in 1873: 'There is no attempt to form streets here, but houses have been built in every direction, with [water] tank and fence ... To the visitor this all presents a novel and pleasing appearance'.[97] The entire district was contained in and around a tract of land – with the coastline of Spencer's Gulf to the immediate west – that formed an isosceles triangle with 'sides' (Moonta–Wallaroo and Moonta–Kadina) measuring some ten miles and a 'base' (Wallaroo–Kadina) of approximately six miles. Moonta Mines was the largest of the constituent settlements; and when Pryor and others wrote or spoke of 'Moonta' implicit in this was the inclusion of 'Moonta Mines'. When people said Moonta they meant not only the government township but also the larger, sprawling district immediately to the east where the Moonta mine was situated and where the majority of the miners and their families lived. Occasionally, they also meant northern Yorke Peninsula as a whole; after all, in 1875 some three-fifths of the district's 20–25,000 population lived in and around Moonta and Moonta Mines.[98]

Moreover, the whole district exhibited a certain topographical coherence – it was 'the Moonta mining field' – which enabled Pryor to adopt his deliberately hazy definition of 'Australia's Little Cornwall'. Most often, as we have seen, he meant Moonta, or Moonta and Moonta Mines, but, when it suited his purposes, he could also insist upon a 'Little Cornwall on Yorke Peninsula, South Australia, made up of Wallaroo, Kadina and Moonta'. It was a convenient blurring, for in practice it made little sense to consider Moonta in isolation from the neighbours with which it was so intimately connected, and in any case it was a construction that privileged Moonta's place within the whole. It is a privilege that survives today. During the Kernewek Lowender festival, for example, the organizers are careful to present a balanced programme of events in which Wallaroo, Kadina and Moonta feature in equal measure. But the Gorsedd of the Cornish Bards in Australia – the most solemnly symbolic 'Cornish' part of the festival's proceedings – has usually been held in Moonta, an unspoken but universally understood acknowledgement of Moonta's special place in the pantheon of things Cornish.[99]

It is a privilege that can still rankle. 'It concerns me that Wallaroo Mines has always been the "poor second cousin" to the better known Moonta Mines',[100] wrote Keith Bailey in 2002 in his history of the Wallaroo mine and the settlement to which it gave its name. There were reasons for this secondary status, Bailey thought. Moonta's ores had been much richer than Wallaroo's in the early years, and when in 1889 the Moonta and Wallaroo mines were merged, Henry Richard Hancock – the general manager of the combined concern – continued to live near Moonta and to run the amalgamated company from his offices at Moonta Mines. Moreover, Bailey observed, 'Moonta has been better promoted in the years since closure',[101] a reference, no doubt, to Oswald Pryor's pivotal role in popularizing and perpetuating Moonta's myth.

Further afield, Moonta's status also continues to rankle. In a fascinating echo of the rivalry between Moontaites and Bendigonians in 1880s Broken Hill, Ruth Hopkins complained a hundred years later in her history of the Cornish in Bendigo that 'too much emphasis has already been placed by certain historians on the role played by South Australia in Cornish migration'.[102] Later, returning to her theme, Hopkins went on to express her indignant 'belief that it was Victoria, rather than South Australia, which became the main destination of Cornish people'.[103] The Cornish in Victoria had hitherto simply 'not been taken into account', she insisted crossly, and this was because they had been spread across many mines in many districts, mingling with numerous other ethnic groups in an overall population much greater than South Australia's. By contrast, she said, 'Much has been made of the Cornish presence in South Australia ... it has been more noticeable because of mining being confined to a relatively small area on the Yorke Peninsula'.[104]

It was a paradox that irked, and Hopkins was determined to do something to redress the balance. But, as she recognized reluctantly, Moonta's visibility and status reflected the reputation that 'Moontaites' had enjoyed throughout the Antipodes. Moonta's captains, tributers and tutworkmen had taken their skills to all corners of Australia and New Zealand. And yet, despite this apparent ubiquity, Hopkins discovered to her delight that in nineteenth-century Bendigo only three Cornish mine managers – John Ennor from St Cleer, Sam Bartlett and John Truscott – had actually 'passed through the mighty Moonta' before ending up in Victoria. Moreover, she added with undisguised glee, 'despite Ennor's obvious aptitude in mining matters, Moonta is unlikely to have affected him as he left there when only five years old'.[105] So much for Moonta's much vaunted reputation and influence! But Hopkins protested too much. She objected to Moonta's myth but in her attempts to refute it, was complicit in its perpetuation, her attempts to play down Moonta's superior status a tacit recognition of its existence. Not much had changed, it seems, since those days a century or more before when Ruth Hopkins's forebears had been put in their place by the self-satisfied interjection of Moonta patriotism. 'Hast 'ee been to Moonta?', the tiresome Bendigonian would be asked. 'No?' Enough said.

CHAPTER TWO

'Wherever a hole is sunk in the ground'
Moonta and Cornwall's great emigration

Moonta may have been exceptional but it was also an exemplar. For all its attempts to construct and project its own myth, Moonta can only be understood fully in the context of its comparative place in the vast panoramic story of Cornwall's 'Great Emigration', that huge movement of Cornish people overseas in the century between the years after 1815 – the end of the Napoleonic Wars – and the outbreak of the Great War in 1914. Long before lonely shepherds on the arid expanses of northern Yorke Peninsula had noticed that their campfires burned bright with curious green flames, or that burrowing wombats had turned up small piles of strangely attractive deep-green stones, Cornish miners had already been drawn to extraordinarily rich mineral discoveries the world over: from neighbouring Devon and Somerset to the far-flung reaches of Peru, Mexico and Chile.[1]

These Cornish miners took with them their highly developed sense of superiority – an identity drawn from the culture of 'industrial prowess' that pervaded Cornwall until at least the mid-1860s – and re-invented it abroad as the myth of 'Cousin Jack': the self-belief that insisted that the Cornish were innately qualified above all others as skilled hard-rock miners. At root, as we have seen, this self-belief was the foundation of Moonta's own developed sense of special identity. But by the time copper was discovered at Moonta in 1861, the Cornish had been at the forefront of the expansion of the international mining frontier for half a century already, honing in distant lands their developed sense of self. Founded on the eve of the crash of Cornish copper – and the consequent faltering of Cornish pride – in 1866, Moonta had thus emerged at the high point of this process. Insofar as the phenomenon may be divided into two periods – 'before' and 'after' the pivotal year of 1866 – the rise of Moonta seems like the culmination, the apogee, of the first half-century of Cornwall's 'Great Emigration'. It was not quite the end of an era, nor exactly the beginning of a new one, but the making of Moonta did coincide with a profound shift in the nature of Cornish emigration.[2]

A transnational Cornish identity

Of course, the emigration of mining folk from Cornwall continued long after Moonta's appearance on the global Cornish map. But, as the century drew on, this was an emigration designed increasingly to support the informal welfare system that had grown up in Cornwall, where the remittances sent home, especially from South Africa, were ever more important in supporting large sections of the community. The emigrants themselves were no longer, perhaps, the intrepid adventurers of earlier years but were now more often reluctant escapees from wholesale unemployment. In earlier decades, ambitious would-be emigrants from Cornwall had responded to the enticements of high wages in places like Cuba or Colombia or assisted passages to Cape Colony or New Zealand. But now, as the Cornish economy faltered, so the emigrants took refuge from growing dislocation and impending de-industrialization, many of those departing for distant shores in the closing decades of the nineteenth century hoping one day to return, as, eventually, some did. As one observer wrote of the Cornish in the Transvaal in 1900: 'They looked prosperous but not happy'.[3]

Moonta, then, sat centre-stage in the story of Cornwall's 'Great Emigration'; temporally and, in its own estimation, culturally too. Its loudly proclaimed identity represented the high water mark of Cornish self-confidence overseas, and laid the foundations, as we shall see, for a formidable regional culture on northern Yorke Peninsula. But Moonta was also inextricably entwined in a sophisticated Cornish transnational identity.[4] In a very real sense, it owed its existence to that identity, for in the half century preceding Moonta's foundation, all the building blocks that were to facilitate its rapid development had already been put in place.

The Cornish had come to view the world as their oyster, with Cornwall the epicentre of a complex international information network. People at home in Cornwall had ready access to remarkably accurate intelligence about the relative fortunes of different potential destinations on the ever-expanding international mining frontier. They came and went, as individuals and sometimes as families, moving within and between continents, responding to the growth of the frontier and the demands of its attendant international labour market. Sometimes they went back to Cornwall, temporarily or permanently, but more often they stayed abroad. As individuals, they maintained links with friends and relations in Cornwall, or in other parts of the globe where the Cornish had settled, and sometimes they sent home money to swell family or community coffers, or wrote to give advice and encouragement on where and when to emigrate. Often they clustered together in 'Cornish communities' overseas, both consciously and unconsciously transplanting in the new lands the cultural habits of home. When newcomers arrived from Cornwall, they were welcomed into these communities, given shelter and advice and pointed in the direction of jobs. By the mid-nineteenth century, the Cornish had become used to seeing themselves as a transnational people, with links – community as well as personal, sentimental as well as economic – to a 'greater Cornwall' beyond the seas. It bred a particular sense of familiarity, intimacy and cohesion.[5] For many Cornish people, for example, the United States of America was merely 'the next parish after Land's End'.[6]

Central to this transnational identity was the notion that the Cornish were to be found, quite literally, wherever there was mining to be done. In 1927 A.K. Hamilton Jenkin recalled in the pages of his classic *The Cornish Miner* what was then already a well-worn adage: 'wherever a hole is sunk in the ground ... no matter in what corner of the world – you will be sure to find a Cornishman at the bottom of it, searching for metal'.[7] It was a truism, he said, acknowledged the world over. For example, he explained, 'not many years since ... A seasoned traveller' of his acquaintance had observed in his journeyings the global extent of this Cornish diaspora. 'From Nova Zembla to New Zealand, from Cape Horne to Korea, from Klondike to Cape Town', exclaimed the explorer, 'the Cornish miner may be found at work'. The Cornish turned up everywhere, he said, 'frozen in the Artic snows, dried to the bone in tropical deserts, burnt out with fever in equatorial swamps, and broiled thin under equatorial suns – in every country of the New World and the Old'.[8]

An 'emigration trade': a 'culture of mobility'

As Hamilton Jenkin also acknowledged, there was 'a constant coming and going between Cornwall and the new mining camps' abroad, a trait observable 'from the very start of the overseas movement'.[9] In this way, the 'Great Emigration' had been from the first a complex phenomenon. The majority of emigrant Cornish miners did eventually settle abroad permanently – many after several temporary sojourns in different parts of the world – requiring or persuading their families to join them in the distant lands. Many married men had in any case taken their wives and children with them, especially to those British colonies anxious to create in the new territories a stable society based on a proper balance of age and gender. Free or assisted passages, designed to achieve this balance, drew the Cornish to Cape Colony, New South Wales, New Zealand and other destinations in the British world. Fortuitously, many of these, in a sudden string of bonanza mineral discoveries, soon proved important additions to the burgeoning international mining frontier that had emerged after 1815. To this 'formal' or 'official' emigration trade – directed by British colonial settlement policy and managed on the ground by a small army of emigration agents – was added its 'informal' or 'unofficial' equivalent in which mining companies overseas, especially in North and South America, liaised directly with mine captains in Cornwall to secure the Cornish workers that they required.[10] In September 1831, for example, an advertisement in the *West Briton* newspaper sought fifty miners and three blacksmiths for the Gongo Soco gold mines in Brazil, advising would-be applicants to report to the count-count at Wheal Damsel mine, Gwennap.[11]

Where the menfolk had gone abroad alone, many were careful to send 'homepay' to their relatives and friends in Cornwall, a habit observed in the earliest days of Cornish emigration but of especial significance towards the end of the nineteenth century. After the copper crash in 1866 and the faltering of tin in the mid-1870s, overseas money provided crucial support for the Cornish economy, and numerous Cornish families were increasingly dependent on the funds sent home regularly by loved ones toiling abroad. But, long before that, homepay had been an important element of the emigration experience, part of the cement that bound Cornwall to its international community. Sometimes overseas mining companies managed homepay arrangements for their employees, deducting monies at source and transferring these directly to Cornwall as remittances. In this way, for example, in March 1867 the Real del Monte silver mine in Mexico sent £4,619 to Cornwall, £633 of which went to Redruth to be administered by Messrs Williams & Co.[12]

At other times, individuals managed their own remittance transfers, such as the 'foreign money orders' organized through the US Post Office at Sutter Creek in California's 'Motherlode' gold-mining district in the period 1898 to 1907. Here, for example, M. Venning, a Cornish miner, arranged for part of his hard-earned wages to be forwarded to one 'Mary Jane' at Torpoint: his wife or fiancée, perhaps, or possibly his mother or daughter or an elderly relation. Likewise, Lewis Kempthorne sent money home to 'Martha' at St Agnes, as did James Berryman to 'Beatrice' at Ponsanooth.[13] The rise of South Africa as a major destination for the emigrant Cornish at the end of the nineteenth century provided an important new source of such remittances. By the mid-1890s Redruth alone was receiving a weekly sum of £1,000 to £1,300, while every mail was bringing home to Cornwall remittances of between £20,000 and £30,000. As Gary Magee and Andrew Thompson have concluded, 'South Africa's constant flow of money orders back to the UK provided a lifeline for Cornwall until at least the 1920s'.[14] In this way, Cornwall managed to cling on to vestiges of its role as the epicentre of a transnational Cornish identity, a role that lingered into the early twentieth century, even after Cornwall had long since lost its status as the centre of the hard-rock mining world and was no longer a major source of new emigrants for the international mining economy.

Despite this longevity, much of what would characterize Cornwall's 'Great Emigration' had been established early in the nineteenth century. Even before 1815 the Cornish, a quintessentially maritime people, had constructed lasting conduits of contact and movement between Cornwall and overseas destinations, especially America and Australia. Many had served in the Royal Navy or as merchant seamen – or even as deep-sea fishermen off Newfoundland – ensuring in Cornwall's ports and harbours an easy familiarity with New World names and places. Others had been amongst some of the first settlers in North America – from the failed Roanoke colony off the coast of Virginia in the mid-1580s to the later, successful Puritan enterprises of Massachusetts, West New Jersey and Pennsylvania – and there was a sprinkling of Cornish amongst the first convicts transported to New South Wales. Others were in Australia as soldiers, sailors, administrators and, before too long, free settlers as well. Such contacts created a 'culture of mobility' in Cornwall, an attitude of mind in which long-distance journeys and sojourns – if not yet exactly commonplace – were seen as normal, and where a network of linkages with overseas lands was already in place.[15]

After 1815, as new opportunities for emigration presented themselves in Cornwall, this culture of mobility was important in smoothing the way overseas for increasing numbers of Cornish people. Methodism, too, with its emphasis on 'self-help' and 'individual improvement', advocated emigration as an 'improving' cause, as did Radical newspapers such as the *West Briton*.[16] Indeed, the Liberal–Nonconformist character of nineteenth-century Cornwall became an increasingly important element of the culture of mobility, lending it ideological content and civic approval. By the 1820s and 1830s, emigration was accepted in Cornwall as an entirely legitimate response to hard times at home or new opportunities abroad. By the middle of the century chain migrations to parts of the Americas and Australasia had established 'Cornish communities' overseas, many of them now ready recipients for further waves of emigrants from home. The emigration trade in Cornwall had itself become ever more complex, with a whole range of private and public practitioners – emigration agents, shipping agents, shipbuilders, clergymen, merchants, publicans, provisioners, newspaper editors, journalists, printers, coaching operators, solicitors – becoming involved with what was now a lucrative economic activity. In this way, emigration pervaded Cornish life, so much so that when economic disaster overtook Cornwall in 1866 and again in the mid-1870s, there was in place already an impressive repertoire of potential destinations for would-be emigrants, alongside well-tried mechanisms to ease their departures. The 'exodus of the seventies',[17] as Hamilton Jenkin dubbed it, was to that extent well managed, avoiding the worst excesses of want that wholesale unemployment might have visited upon Cornwall.

The 'rage for emigration'

But not all Cornish emigrants were miners, or miners' families, and across Cornwall there was an intricate pattern of micro-emigrations, certain localities becoming linked to particular overseas destinations. This was true of the mining communities – for instance, individuals from the 'central mining district' of Camborne–Redruth–Gwennap were statistically more likely than those from other Cornish mining areas to emigrate to Latin America[18] – but it was especially true of the non-mining districts. For example, the large tract of North Cornwall running from the Camel estuary to the North Devon border (and beyond) had emerged as an important emigration sub-region as early as the 1820s, gripped by a 'rage for emigration' (as the Cornish press called it) which lasted into the 1830s, 1840s and even the 1850s. High rents and agricultural depression left swathes of North Cornwall relatively depopulated. During the 1840s the population of Stratton hundred, nearest the Devon border, decreased by ten per cent as many of its inhabitants departed for pastures new. Many of these emigrants were Bible Christians – a Methodist denomination founded in the North Cornwall parishes of Week St Mary and Launcells in 1815 – who sought to recreate their ethno-religious communities overseas. Bible Christians from Bude, Jacobstowe and St Minver settled together in parts of Pennsylvania, while those from Warbstow, Poundstock, St Gennys, Egloskerry, Boyton, Tresmeer and half-a-dozen other North Cornish parishes tried to rebuild their Cornish agricultural communities anew in south-eastern Wisconsin. Others founded similar settlements in Ontario and Prince Edward Island. Padstow, situated on the Camel estuary, was – along with Bideford in North Devon – the principal emigration port for these folk, and a particular North Cornwall variant of the emigration trade emerged, local ships sailing for Canada and the United States full of emigrants and returning laden with North American timber.[19]

Agricultural depression was but one factor that persuaded emigrants to leave Cornwall. Religious considerations could also be important, as the Bible Christians had demonstrated, and Cornish Methodism was suffused with resentment at the legal requirement to pay tithes to the Established Church. Many sought Reform at home but others decided to find religious freedom overseas, whether in the United States or (for example) in South Australia, the very first British territory to eschew the link between Church and State. To this religious radicalism was added a wider desire for socio-economic mobility and civil liberty, the Liberal–Nonconformist nexus that underpinned a great deal of Cornish attitudes and behaviour prompting many to look overseas to fulfill their desire for personal opportunity and political freedom. This was especially so during the 'Reforming Thirties', when the

Reform movement was strong in Cornwall and when Cornish emigration was beginning to assume some of its 'mass' characteristics.[20]

The 'Reforming Thirties' were followed by the 'Hungry Forties'. The potato blight struck in Cornwall, as it did in Ireland and the Highlands and Islands of Scotland, bringing in its wake much distress and near starvation. In 1758 William Borlase had observed that in Cornwall the potato was 'a more useful root'[21] than the turnip, and in West Penwith it was found to be an excellent preparatory crop for growing barley on heath or boggy ground. In North Cornwall, before the blights of the 1840s, the potato was said to have been 'the principal staff of Cornish life'.[22] But the Cornish potato crop failed in 1845 and again in 1846, hitting both the rural poor and the population of the mining districts whose rapidly expanding populations had become dependent upon the potato. There were food riots across Cornwall as angry mobs of miners and agricultural workers attempted to force 'fair prices' for flour and bread, and to prevent the export of wheat from Cornish ports. In this desperate situation, emigration proved to be the safety-valve, existing conduits allowing the continued movement of individuals abroad to familiar destinations. Moreover, several important new destinations for the Cornish had emerged during the 1840s. By the end of 1844 hundreds of Cornish were arriving in the Keweenaw district of Michigan's Upper Peninsula, following the recent development of copper deposits along Lake Superior, and before long hundreds more were clamouring to emigrate to South Australia, where copper had been discovered at Kapunda in 1843–44 and Burra Burra in 1845.

Destinations

The rapid exploitation of copper in Michigan and South Australia in the second half of the 1840s represented a significant expansion of the international mining frontier. This was a 'coming of age' at a time when Cornwall itself was changing, moving decisively – as Bernard Deacon has shown – from a proto-industrial to a fully industrial society by the late 1840s.[23] Recovering swiftly from the worst ravages of the 'Hungry Forties', Cornwall continued to experience economic growth – Cornish copper achieved its maximum annual output in 1855–56 – and began in its social and economic make-up to look increasingly like other provincial industrial regions in Britain. As in the North of England, for example, there was in Cornwall a confident middle class, a strong sense of territorial identity, a vibrant provincial culture, and a robust set of religious, civic and professional institutions. But there was one significant difference. In Cornwall, economic growth had been accompanied by the emergence of mass emigration, the particular industrial skills of the Cornish workforce perpetually in demand overseas.

In the first two decades after 1815, Latin America had established itself as an important destination for the emigrant Cornish, the high salaries that Cornish skills could command there proving a significant enticement for those who had been unsettled by the post-Napoleonic vacillations in the fortunes of mining at home.[24] As Latin American countries, one by one, wrested themselves free from Spanish and Portuguese rule, so they were opened up for penetration by British capital. Richard Trevithick, inventor of the locomotive and champion of high-pressure steam, had sailed for Peru in 1816 to supervise the operation of Cornish beam engines in the high-altitude Andes, and spent the next ten years in Latin America, travelling through Costa Rica, Colombia, Nicaragua and elsewhere, acquiring various mineral rights along the way.

Meanwhile, by the early 1820s Cornish miners had begun arriving in Mexico in considerable numbers, many having been engaged to re-work the ancient Real del Monte silver mines.[25] The *Western Luminary* newspaper noted in February 1825 that 'Several captains, we understand, have lately accepted situations in the Mexican Mines at salaries from £700 to £1,000 per annum'.[26] Similarly attractive remuneration awaited the enterprising Cornish miner in Cuba, where extensive copper workings were opened during the 1830s, although the price of high wages was often, in Mexico and elsewhere, debilitating illness and disease, with more than a few Cornish succumbing to yellow fever, malaria and other tropical ailments. Brazilian independence in 1822 had paved the way for British capital and Cornish technology to unlock the deep gold deposits of Minas Gerais, and in Chile in the 1820s copper mining was developed rapidly with the help of Cornish know-how. The initial boom had spent itself by 1827 but the full potential of Latin America was by now already understood, so much so that Cornish copper production was soon considered to be under more or less permanent threat from overseas competition. British commitment to free trade encouraged the import of foreign ores, and in September 1845 one newspaper – reflecting on this paradoxical state of affairs – opined that 'The copper of Chili and Cuba is at present the great bugbear of Cornwall'.[27] Cornish copper would not face its ultimate crisis for another two decades but the changing nature of the international mining economy, and the implications for Cornwall, were already being understood by those who cared to observe this complex scene. Behind the façade of continued economic growth, and Cornwall's apparent convergence with other British industrial regions, was the spectre of international competition.

The United States, cherishing its freedom from European rule and determined on economic self-sufficiency, had also sought to develop its mineral deposits in this early period.[28] In the 1820s and 1830s there had been a sprinkling of Cornish in the goldmines of the southern Appalachians – in

Georgia, North Carolina and Virginia — and in the same decades they were found working for copper in Vermont, Connecticut, New Jersey, Maryland and Kentucky. By the late 1820s, some — like Captain Francis Clymo, originally from Perranzabuloe parish in Cornwall, who had already worked in these eastern districts — had turned up at Galena in the northwestern corner of Illinois. This was on the southern tip of what was shortly to become the important Wisconsin (or Upper Mississippi) lead mining region, a major resource for American industrialization. By the mid-1830s the Cornish were arriving in droves. Mineral Point, in south-west Wisconsin, became the focus for their activities in this region but they were also to be found in strength in neighbouring Linden and in Dodgeville. As John Rowe observed: 'by 1850 there were nearly six thousand Cornish people in the three Wisconsin counties of Grant, Iowa, and Lafayette, and perhaps two or three thousand more in the neighbouring counties of Jo Daviess, Illinois and Dubuque, Iowa'.[29] In 1898 it was estimated that there were still some ten thousand people of Cornish birth or descent in the region, though by then many had dispersed, a considerable number joining the Wisconsin Volunteer Infantry — the 'Miners' Guard' — which fought with distinction for the Union during the Civil War in the 1860s. Others had left for other hard-rock mining localities, as in 1844 when Cornish miners from Wisconsin were among the first on Michigan's Upper Peninsula, joining those who had been brought down from the Bruce iron and copper mines in Ontario.

The Keweenaw Peninsula, jutting out from the main body of the Upper Peninsula into Lake Superior, was the focus for these Wisconsin Cornish. They were joined shortly by many more arrivals direct from Cornwall. By 1844 there were two mines operating on the Keweenaw, with a stamp mill erected at Eagle River to crush and dress the ore. Less than twenty years later, there were more than twenty thousand settlers in the Upper Peninsula or 'Lakes' counties of Keweenaw, Houghton and Ontonagon, of whom at least three thousand were Cornish. As one observer wrote of Houghton in 1866: 'Cornwall has emptied her army of miners among these hills'.[30] Mines such as the Cliff, the Central, the Pewabic, and the Minsesota [sic] — together with the mighty Calumet and Hecla, which came to dominate the locality — were manned and managed by Cornishmen: T.A. Rickard, the well-known mining historian of Cornish stock, reckoned that at one time just about every underground captain on the 'Lakes' was Cornish. The Cornish remained prominent in the Upper Peninsula mines until the eve of the Great War, increasingly the skilled 'labour aristocracy' among an ever expanding multilingual, multiethnic workforce of Finns, Swedes, Italians, Croats and others. By then, however, they had already spread to innumerable other destinations in North America, from the nearby Marquette Range and the iron mines of neighbouring Minnesota to a whole new mining frontier on the far side of the Rocky Mountains.

The Californian goldrush in 1849 proved an extraordinary magnet for Cornish miners the world over. Some were already in the territory, mining quicksilver in the cinnabar hills of New Almaden. Others came north from Mexico as soon as they heard news of the gold discoveries. Still others were enticed from the gold and copper mines of the Appalachians, with many more from Wisconsin and Michigan – and, of course, from Cornwall itself. The Cornish were active all along California's Motherlode but they came into their own as mining operations moved from the alluvial 'placer' deposits to deep-quartz hard-rock mining. Grass Valley, especially, in the foothills of the Sierra Nevada mountains, became known for its concentration of Cornish miners and their families. By 1861 it was 'the Cornwall of California', according to the *Grass Valley National* newspaper, for 'mining is for the most part carried on by Cornishmen'.[31] By 1884, the Cornish had settled into many other occupations in the locality, the *West Briton* noting that 'Cornishmen here are not engaged exclusively in mining. The signs over almost all the stores bear Cornish names, and several of the business men hold responsible positions in the county and State.'[32] But Grass Valley was not homogeneously Cornish. As Ralph Mann has shown, by the 1860s the town sported distinct and mutually antagonistic 'Cornish' and 'Irish' precincts, with a fair sprinkling of other ethnic groups. 'Their prickly sense of self had helped involve the Cornish in ethnic brawls from the first days,' argues Mann, 'and their pugnaciousness did not diminish as their numbers grew.'[33]

Rivalry between the Cornish and the Irish, often institutionalized into conflict within the emerging trade unions, became a feature of mining life west of the Rockies. From California the western mining frontier spread northwards and eastwards, from British Columbia and Montana to Utah and Arizona, and with it spread the Cornish–Irish antipathy. It was apparent in Nevada – where the silver deposits of the Comstock Lode had been discovered in 1859, leading to the growth of famous Virginia City – and in Colorado in the 1880s when Leadville and Central City were said to be 'full of Cornish'.[34] In this burgeoning frontier, with its profusion of ethnic groups, the Cornish fostered their 'clannish' reputation, deploying the myth of Cousin Jack to assert their superiority over the other groups and to retain their advantage in the employment market.

Just as the Californian goldrush had precipitated first an influx of Cornish onto the Motherlode, and then an expansion of the western mining frontier into neighbouring territories, so it was an important impetus to the gold discoveries of Australia in 1851: first in New South Wales and then, even more importantly, in Victoria.[35] The Victorian goldrush drew Cornish settlers from neighbouring New South Wales and South Australia, as well as from California and Cornwall itself. They helped put the gold towns of Ballarat and Bendigo on the mining map of the world, along with places such as Creswick, Forest Creek and the Ovens River. From there, there were rushes to New Zealand, to Queensland and – eventually, in the 1890s – to Western Australia where the rise of Coolgardie, Kalgoorlie and Boulder brought prosperity and self-confidence to this often marginalized, far-flung colony. Other important mining districts had by then emerged in Australia, each with a visible Cornish component, notably the silver-lead fields of Broken Hill and the Barrier Ranges, while further overseas the Cornish participated in the yet wider search for gold and other mineral wealth, most obviously in South Africa.[36]

The 'copper kingdom'

By the time South Africa was at its zenith in the late 1880s and 1890s as a destination for the emigrant Cornish, Moonta had been in existence for a quarter of a century and more. Founded before the crash of Cornish copper but some fifty years after the first stirrings of the 'Great Emigration', Moonta was at the cusp of Cornwall's global emigration experience. It also represented the full flowering of the Cornish experience in South Australia. From the moment of its foundation in 1836, the colony – with its early reputation as a 'Paradise of Dissent' and its explicit adherence to Utilitarian notions of settlement – had caught the imagination of Cornwall, attracting large numbers of would-be Cornish emigrants.[37] In the period between 1836 and 1840 some ten per cent of all applications for assisted passage were lodged in Cornwall, establishing a pattern which by the end of the century had ensured that perhaps as much as ten per cent, maybe more, of South Australia's population – about 35,000 people – were of Cornish birth or direct descent. The first Cornishmen in the colony noted the highly mineralized character of the hills surrounding the capital, Adelaide, and by April 1841 Australia's very first metalliferous mine, Wheal Gawler, was in operation at Glen Osmond, producing silver-lead ore for the British market. In 1843 it was joined by a second mine, Wheal Watkins.

In the same year, Francis Dutton and Charles Bagot made separate discoveries on their leases at Kapunda, north of Adelaide, of what at first appeared to be 'beautiful green moss'.[38] It was malachite – copper – and by 1844 a mine was being sunk. As Bagot later recalled, 'the result of our first trial was encouraging, and induced us at once to prepare for opening the mine in a regular and permanent manner. To effect this, I agreed with Robert Nicholls, a Cornish miner, for a twelve month to work on tribute.'[39] Dutton observed that 'Among the general population of the colony were some few Cornish miners who were quietly following pastoral and agricultural pursuits'. When the workings commenced, 'the pickaxe was quickly resumed by them, and we gave them a liberal tribute (3s. 6d. per £) to set the thing going'.[40] The successful development of Kapunda prompted an atmosphere of 'coppermania' which prevailed in South Australia until Victorian gold stole the limelight in 1851. In the vicinity of Kapunda itself copy-cat mines sprang up – South Kapunda, North Kapunda, Wheal Gundry – and in the Adelaide Hills, nearer the capital, copper was soon discovered at Montacute. Other finds followed in the locality, Francis Dutton opining in superior tones that the prospects of such properties 'will undoubtedly be furthered by their engaging, as soon as possible, the assistance of practical Cornish mining captains, as the proprietors of the Kapunda mine have done'.[41]

Kapunda had been a spectacular discovery; Burra Burra was even more so.[42] In June 1845 two shepherds made separate finds of copper, malachite and azurite, along the Burra Burra creek, one hundred miles north of Adelaide. Alert now to the potential mineral wealth of the colony, investors in the capital clamoured to become involved in developing this latest discovery, leading to the foundation of the South Australian Mining Association (SAMA). Thomas Roberts, a Cornish mine captain, was enticed from Montacute by SAMA and sent north in charge of nine other Cornish miners to begin work at 'the Burra'. Incredibly rich, the Burra mine – the 'Monster', as it was known colloquially – acted as a magnet for the Cornish already in the colony, and precipitated a new wave of emigration from Cornwall to South Australia. As we have seen already, the discovery of copper in the colony in 1844–45 had come at a significant moment, coinciding with the failure of the potato crop in Cornwall and providing an important new destination for would-be emigrants. It was, indeed, a major element in the further expansion of the international mining frontier and its increasingly global labour market, the rise of Kapunda and Burra Burra adding Australia very firmly to an extra-European world metal mining map hitherto dominated by Latin America and (more recently) the United States. South Australia was now – in its own estimation, but in Cornwall's too – the 'copper kingdom'.

Captain Henry Roach, who had worked at the Tresavean mine, near Redruth, in Cornwall, and who had also been out in Colombia, was appointed chief captain at the Burra mine in January 1847. His senior colleagues were all Cornishmen. Captain Matthew Bryant was engaged as second captain in June, and in March of the following year Richard Goldsworthy from Bodmin was appointed to the third position. William Mitchell was appointed fourth captain in 1849. S. Penglaze became 'grass captain' in charge of surface operations, and his chief ore-dresser was Samuel Osborne. Philip Santo, from Saltash, became Clerk of the Works in September 1849, and his administrative assistant was a Mr Boswarva. Peter Spargo was chief engineer from 1848 to 1851, when he was replaced by John Congdon from the Caradon Mines in East Cornwall. The tributers and tutworkmen, the skilled miners, were also overwhelmingly Cornish, as their surnames attest: Trevorrow, Bosanco, Andrewartha, Tremewan, and so on. It was reported in September 1845 that the 'greatest excitement has been produced in Cornwall'[43] by the copper discoveries, and in January 1846 SAMA urged the Colonial Secretary to make special arrangements for the procurement of Cornish miners for the colony. By then, almost every emigrant ship arriving at Port Adelaide was carrying its Cornish contingent: thirty in the *Isabella Watson* in 1845, thirty in the *Rajah* and sixty-six in the *Kingston* in 1846. The *Britannia* and the *Hooghly*, two other arrivals during 1846, carried mainly Cornish miners and their families, while in the November the *Princess Royal* was reported bound from Plymouth for South Australia, its passengers 'chiefly from Cornwall'.[44] John B. Tregea, 'a very superior miner', and James Rundle – 'a good wheelwright, miner, carpenter and excellent character' – were amongst Cornish emigrants dispatched in the *David Malcolm* in 1846,[45] and in the following year and into 1848 the stream of Cornish arrivals continued unabated. By 1849 it had become a flood: half of the 366 passengers aboard the *William Money* were Cornish, as were half the 266 in the *Pakenham*. The *Prince Regent* arrived with sixty Cornish emigrants, the *Eliza* with forty-two, the *Himalaya* with fifty-three, and so on. The majority of these new arrivals made their way swiftly from Port Adelaide to the 'northern mines', as they were known: 'Oh! Richard', enthused one Cornish miner in a letter home, 'it would make your mouth water to see the Burra Burra Mine'.[46]

Emigration agents had been appointed in Cornwall and Devon to assist the selection of Cornish miners and to manage their dispatch, along with their families, from Plymouth. J.B. Wilcocks, based at the Barbican in Plymouth, was one such agent. He developed a close relationship with SAMA during those years, and throughout the early 1850s maintained the steady stream of Cornish emigrants to the colony. When, in 1852, the Cornish had left the Burra and other South Australian mines in their droves to try their luck at the Victorian goldrush, Henry Ayers, the SAMA secretary, wrote to Wilcocks to demand 'a thousand hands consisting of Miners, Smiths, Engineers, Carpenters and others employed at Copper Mines'.[47] A few months later he added dramatically that 'We are thirsting for labour',[48] and in 1854 offered Wilcocks a personal bounty of £2 per head for every Cornish miner he could find. Wilcock rose to the occasion: during 1854 and 1855 he sent over 1,600 Cornish people, mainly miners and their families, to Port Adelaide. A Cornwall and Devon Society had also been formed in South Australia, designed to encourage emigration from Cornwall and the adjacent mining district of West Devon, and to promote the interest and welfare of Cornish (and Devon) emigrants in the colony. Although, like much else, it fell victim to the impact of the Victorian goldrush, it had proved an important lobby, raising the profile of the Cornish in official eyes and emphasizing the importance of Cornish emigration to the sustainability of the South Australian mining industry.

Alongside the arrival of Cornish emigrants had been the importation of mining machinery from Cornwall. Cornish beam engines, for winding and pumping, were obtained from Harvey & Co. of Hayle and the Perran Foundry, together with a vast array of ancillary material from pitwork (pump rods and pipes) to iron nails, crucibles and emery paper. Especially important was the giant 80-inch pump engine built by Perran Foundry which was installed at the Burra during 1852, and started triumphantly on 16 September by John Congdon, the chief engineer. Cornish engine-houses were built to accommodate such machinery, their distinctive outlines lending an unmistakably 'Cornish' ambience and appearance to the mine site at Burra Burra, their lofty bulk an enduring and defining feature of the South Australian mining landscape.

The Burra townscape also had more than a hint of Cornwall, not least the use of buff-coloured stone, visually so similar to Cornish killas or clay-slate, as the preferred local building material. The SAMA company township of Kooringa sported the grandest edifices. But of the several other Burra suburbs, 'Redruth' was probably the most 'Cornish': in ethnic composition, in appearance – with its single-storey 'Cornish cottages' – and in the telling nomenclature of its streets. There was Fore Street, as there was in just about every town and village in Cornwall, and the others were all named after places across Cornwall: Sancreed Street, Mevagissey Street, Helston Street, St Just Street, and so on. In addition to the 'Redruth Arms' and the 'Cornish Arms' there was also in Redruth the 'Ancient Briton' public house, a reminder that the Cornish thought themselves descendants of 'ancient Britons',[49] a badge of distinction that marked them off from the Anglo-Saxon English and made them – according to the Wesleyan minister at Kooringa – 'the real descendants of the Celts'.[50]

As predominantly Wesleyans, Bible Christians and Primitive Methodists, the Cornish also brought their 'Cornish Methodism' to the Burra, as they had to Kapunda and other mining settlements in the colony, its physical presence evidenced in the large number of plainly built Nonconformist chapels, its religious and cultural influence felt in any number of activities from the annual 'tea-treats' to the Revivals that swept the mines from time to time. At Kapunda the miners marked the Duke of Cornwall's birthday as a public holiday, and at Burra in the earliest days the Cornish observed 5 March, the feast of St Piran, patron saint of Cornish miners. Cornish wrestling, 'the favourite amusement of Cornwall'[51] as one South Australian newspaper put it in 1848, was a popular pastime at the Burra, contests conducted 'in the real Cornish style'[52] as up to a thousand spectators gathered to watch the proceedings. There were brass bands at both Kapunda and the Burra, the

Northern Star noting at the former in 1861 that the bandsmen were 'all Cousin Jacks with the exception of one'.[53] Midsummer bonfires, lit traditionally in Cornwall on St John's Eve (24 June), were also a feature of Burra life. Held in the Antipodean midsummer, they were no less popular for that, the *South Australian Register* explaining to its readers in June 1863 that it was 'a red-letter day in Cousin John's [sic] calendar ... celebrated by diverse juveniles who lighted up numerous bonfires'.[54]

Kapunda and Burra Burra, then, were added swiftly to the repertoire of international 'Cornish communities'. They had attracted hundreds of Cornish emigrants, with their distinctive cultural attributes, and the mines themselves were archetypically 'Cornish', managed according to Cornish custom and employing Cornish technology as well as manpower. All this was the 'Cornish' foundation in South Australia that had given the colony its particular place in the Cornish transnational identity, and which Moonta was soon to inherit. Yet even in those days neither Kapunda nor Burra Burra was represented as homogeneously Cornish – in marked contrast to the myth that Moonta was shortly to elaborate – and from the beginning there was a sense of both communities being a kaleidoscopic multicultural mix. While the Cornish provided the 'labour aristocracy' at the mines and dominated mining methods – the myth of Cousin Jack saw to that – there were representatives of other ethnic groups in a variety of occupations. At Kapunda, for example, there was a strong Irish-Catholic element in the population, and when many of the mine's Cornishmen left to try their luck on the Victorian goldfields in the 1850s, the Irish became correspondingly more important, so much so that when Michael Davitt, the Irish Land League agitator, visited the locality in the 1890s it felt as though 'Kapunda was somewhere in Connaught [Ireland] instead of being fourteen thousand miles away'.[55] At the Burra, there was also a sizeable Irish community, and Cornish–Irish rivalry became a feature of local life. There were also several other important ethnic groups. After all, this was 'Burra of the Five Towns', as it became known, a topographical straggle of several satellite settlements beyond the company township of Kooringa. Although many of the Cornish lived in dug-out homes along the Burra creek, others lived at Redruth, as we have seen, giving it and the other 'Cornish' suburbs of Copperhouse and Lostwithiel a distinct ethnic identification. Other suburbs had similar ethnic connotations. Llwchwr, where many of the Welsh smelters and their families lived, was thought to be 'Welsh', while Hampton and Aberdeen mirrored the presence of English and Scottish workers in the district. Chilean muleteers and German mineworkers added to Burra's cosmopolitan mix.

'A considerable number of Cornish on board'

For all that, Kapunda and Burra Burra – together with other mining towns in the colony, such as Callington, Strathalbyn and Truro – acted as important reservoirs of Cornish manpower in the early days of Moonta and Wallaroo. Although a great many of South Australia's smaller mining 'shows' had succumbed to the influence of the Victorian rush, never to work again, the fortunes of Kapunda and Burra Burra had revived as their miners trickled back from the goldfields and as new hands were recruited from Cornwall. However, the glory days of the 1840s were not easily restored, and both Kapunda and Burra Burra faced increasing difficulty as their deposits became less rich and more costly to work, and as international copper prices fell in the 1860s. To this was added the enticement of the new, and it was hardly surprising that already hard-pressed Kapunda and Burra should find their workforces haemorrhaging in the direction of northern Yorke Peninsula. Both mines struggled on to the end of 1877, after which they were at last abandoned, the remaining miners heading for Moonta and Wallaroo or destinations in the Far North of the colony.

When Tom Cowling arrived at Yelta, near Moonta, in the late 1860s, he found that most of the inhabitants 'were natives of Cornwall who had come to this country before the opening up of the peninsula mines. Several of them had come from the Burra, others from the Kanmantoo and Callington mines, and a few from Kapunda.'[56]

Others had come across from Victoria, and during the 1860s both the Moonta and Wallaroo companies made strenuous efforts to recruit Cornish miners on the Victorian goldfields. But Cornwall itself remained the greatest reservoir of skilled labour. Responding to public opinion in the wake of the partial failure of the wool and wheat crops, the South Australian government had in the late 1850s put a brake on immigration. Only six shiploads of government migrants arrived in 1859, and by 1861 immigration had ceased altogether, albeit only temporarily. There was, however, an excellent harvest that year, which combined with the excitement of the Yorke Peninsula copper discoveries to create a new mood of optimism. One petition circulated at Kapunda called for 'a thousand miners'[57] to be brought out to the colony. Other petitions followed suit, and in response the colonial government allocated £25,000 to finance the resumption of immigration. At the end of 1862 this was followed by the 'Sutherland Act' (the Waste Lands Sales Act) which provided for one-third of annual land sales to be put into an immigration fund to finance assisted passages to the colony. This act, coming at a time of deepening crisis in the Cornish copper industry, precipitated a new wave of Cornish emigration to South Australia.

In the period 1862 to 1870 over thirteen thousand immigrants were recorded in South Australia's shipping passenger lists.[58] No fewer than a quarter of these was from Cornwall. The occupations of a thousand Cornish males immigrants were also recorded in these same lists for the years 1862–67. More than a third were miners, with others in ancillary trades such as blacksmiths or recorded simply as 'labourer'. The influx from Cornwall began in 1863. In 1864, a year of heavy immigration, over sixteen per cent of all immigrants were from Cornwall – 150 from the Marazion district alone – and in 1865 an extraordinary 43 per cent of arrivals were Cornish. Each of the fourteen ships dispatched from Plymouth for Port Adelaide that year sported a huge Cornish contingent: 211 out of 315 in the *Queen Bee*, 214 out of 358 in the *Lady Milton*, 242 out of 388 in the *Gosforth*, and so on. This stream continued into 1866 and 1867, relieving Cornwall of many of its skilled workers at the moment its copper industry collapsed.

Those arriving at Port Adelaide had strongly mixed feelings, no doubt, shocked by the experience of industrial failure and mass emigration that had overtaken Cornwall but thankful that they at least had escaped those grimmest of years. For many, it was a memory that they carried for the rest of their lives, and decades later some looked back with those same intense emotions. A sense that whole communities in Cornwall had been torn apart as family after family upped and left, was tempered by the fond memory of those same folk who all those years ago had been thrown together by circumstances, forging new relationships during the long sea voyage to South Australia. Moreover, it was these very same people who, in the aftermath of their fortunate escape, had helped to build the vibrant new Cornish communities that, phoenix-like, were already rising fast on the arid and inhospitable plains of northern Yorke Peninsula. It was a cathartic experience – or so it seemed with hindsight – and at the time it gave substance to Moonta's already emerging myth, the sense that a way of life under threat at home was being successfully replicated abroad. The *Canterbury* had arrived at Port Adelaide from Plymouth on New Year's Day, 1867, full of Cornish emigrants. Sixty years later one of its erstwhile passengers recalled the event with a nostalgic whimsy in which we glimpse fleetingly something of those complex emotions of long ago:

> There was a considerable number of Cornish on board, and not a few of these afterwards became Peninsula residents. The Stockers, a musical family settled at Wallaroo Mines; while John Opie, his wife, son, and two daughters (Temperance and Prudence), made their new home in what was then known as Pomeroy Street (Moonta) ... The late Fred Hancock was another of the *Canterbury* passengers ... George Treais and Tom Worth, single men, as soon as they reached Moonta found work at Wheal Hughes mine. They were natives of St Dominick, overlooking the Tamar, in the Royal Duchy.[59]

As early as 1864 the Moonta company had taken steps to recruit direct from Cornwall. The Warmington crisis that year (see Chapter Four), when the miners had come out on strike in protest against the managerial regime, prompted the Moonta company to write to its agents in London, Messrs A.L. Elders. 'You will learn from the Adelaide papers that the miners at Moonta and Wallaroo Mines are now out on Strike', wrote the company secretary. As he further explained: 'this circumstance coupled with the fact that considerable difficulty has been experienced hitherto in getting really good hands, has induced the Directors to send to Cornwall through you for fifty men to be brought out under the Assisted Passage Regulations of the Government'.[60] Shortly after, Henry Richard Hancock was appointed chief captain at Moonta, and he carried out his own review of manpower requirements. One element of this was a request to Elders for a further two hundred Cornish miners. The Wallaroo company made a similar request, and by the end of 1864 parties of miners recruited in Cornwall were already beginning to arrive at the mines.

Moonta and Wallaroo, with their still rich ores readily accessible from what were, by Cornish standards, relatively shallow workings, were able to weather the economic crisis of 1866 when world copper prices were sent plummeting. Nonetheless, there was belt-tightening at both mines, with measures to recruit additional workers put on hold. This was reflected in a more restrictive immigration policy from 1867 until 1871, when fewer assisted passages were offered. When a more liberal Immigration Act was passed by the Adelaide Parliament 1872, the Cornish remained a significant proportion of 'government emigrants' arriving in South Australia: almost seven per cent of the 25,000 recorded in the shipping passenger lists. By now, the Moonta mine had recovered from the economic downturn after 1866 and was experiencing an acute labour shortage. In September 1872 the directors toyed with idea of bringing out 5,000 miners from Cornwall, at the expense of all the dividend-paying mines in the colony, a policy that was only abandoned when it became clear that most of the cost would fall on the Moonta company.[61]

The emergence in November 1872 of the Moonta Miners' Association, the fledgling trade union movement, meant that the workers were now in a position to take a view on the supply and demand for labour. A scarcity of labour would lead to higher wages, which was all to the good the miners thought, but if there were too few workers the development of the mines would be impaired. It was, the trade unionists acknowledged, a difficult balance to strike. Moreover, each of them had relations back in Cornwall, many of whom wished to join the emigrant throng. When the demand for labour on the Peninsula was high, it was unreasonable to dissuade them from coming out. But when times were hard, it was unfair to entice them to a destination where they might be met with unemployment and perhaps resentment. The Moonta Miners' Association wrestled with such issues. In August 1873 it decided to send a deputation to the Adelaide Parliament to call for tighter controls on immigration. Yet there remained a vocal minority in the Association which opposed any restriction on those coming out from Cornwall. But in 1874 the Association was alarmed to find that, although the demand for labour had fallen on the Peninsula, Cornwall – by now suffering from a downturn in tin mining – had become the subject of a renewed South Australian recruiting campaign. Letters in the Peninsula press warned increasingly of the dangers of bringing out more miners indiscriminately. Drought in the late 1870s added to the atmosphere of economic difficulty. One 'new chum' expressed his dismay at what he had found in South Australia. Although Adelaide was 'a fine little town, very little inferior to Truro at home', Yorke Peninsula itself was 'one of the most barren places I have ever seen'. He felt deceived by the emigration agents – 'Is this the beautiful country we heard so much about at home?' [62] – and others criticized the proselytizing zeal of those Nonconformist ministers who had adopted the cause of emigration as their own. One critic had 'heard a new chum cursing that Bryanite [Bible Christian] preacher, called [the Rev. John] Thorne, as he had said there was plenty of work in South Australia for miners, and they need not fear about getting work'. According to Thorne, 'the captains of mines would come on board ship and put them straight to the mines'.[63]

In the heady days of 'coppermania', and in the early years of Moonta and Wallaroo, the captains had indeed met the emigrant ships, vying with one another to secure the best workers. By the 1870s, however, such practices were largely a thing of the past; although as late as July 1876 it was reported that Captain Sanders of Burra Burra had 'secured nine Cornish miners from [the] late arrival in Adelaide' [64] in a desperate attempt to revitalize his flagging mine, and those making their way to Yorke Peninsula found sometimes that getting a job could be hard. In September 1879 John Prisk, the miners' leader, argued that the men should 'be writing home to their friends in Cornwall ... to give them a truthful account of how things are here ... it would keep others from coming out to swell the numbers of unemployed here.' [65] His Association continued to lobby the colonial government, and by 1880 there were again restrictions on immigration.

The attitude of the Moonta Miners' Association reflected rational self-interest. There was also sympathetic regard for the sometimes complementary, sometimes competing, interests of kith and kin back home in Cornwall. But when there appeared to be an economic conflict of interests between the Peninsula miners and their compatriots at home, there was no doubt, as John Prisk made plain, where the Association's duty lay. This demonstrated, perhaps, the limits of Cornish transnational identity, and offered a hard-headed alternative to the more sentimental notions of creating a Cornwall in the Antipodes. But it was also evidence that Moonta itself was already a strong focus of loyalty and identity, and a hint that the trade union movement on the Peninsula was in the years ahead to become a powerful institutional embodiment of that identity. When, in the early 1880s, Captain Hancock recommended the vigorous re-working of the old Great Devon Consols mine – by now subsumed as part of Wallaroo – there were those who were suspicious of his plans to recruit new miners to support the project. In November 1882 the Wallaroo directors sent Captain Richard Piper to Cornwall to select, as his advertisement in the *West Briton* put it, 'Fifty good miners, including steady young men, also married men with their families, to proceed to the Wallaroo Copper Mines, South Australia'.[66] In the March the Moonta directors decided that they too would recruit a hundred miners from Cornwall, and at both Moonta and Wallaroo the companies began to build cottages to receive the newcomers. Local gossip asked: 'Where is Captain Piper? And is he going to bring coolies or Cornishmen? And supposing the Dolcoath Mine stops working will he engage all the miners in a mass to come out here?'[67]

Piper arrived eventually with 408 'new chums'. The majority went to live in the 'New Chums' cottages', as they were known, at Wallaroo Mines, the rest going to Moonta. Captain Hancock did his best to make the newcomers feel welcome. But, as before, there were those who felt that the charms of Peninsula life had been exaggerated unduly. One claimed that he had been told that the companies had built them 'five-storeyed houses, such as adorn the streets of Plymouth', and wrote with bitter irony of 'the fertile plains and ... shady woods of Wallaroo' where 'the noble horse roamed, awaiting his new chum master's hand'.[68] In fact, Piper's recruitment drive was to prove the last great movement from Cornwall to northern Yorke Peninsula. Although it had been greeted with suspicion at the time, with many of the newcomers disappointed with what they had found, it was an event that passed into local lore. It was a convenient temporal benchmark, for example, referred to routinely by those measuring the passage of time and locating themselves within it: 'I came to Moonta in 1883, just after the famous Captain Piper had returned from Cornwall with his hundreds of immigrants', wrote W. Lamshed in 1935.[69] But it also represented a significant infusion of 'new blood' from Cornwall. More than forty years since the arrival of the first Cornish miners in South Australia, and twenty since the first influx attendant on the rise of Moonta and Wallaroo, Piper's immigrants represented a new generation of Cornish men and women. Their arrival did much to re-establish a sense of intimacy between Cornwall and northern Yorke Peninsula, reinforcing the transnational identity at a time when Moonta had already created a fierce identity of its own.

'Cousin Jack loves his holiday'

It was this Janus-like identity that characterized the regional culture of northern Yorke Peninsula in the nineteenth century, one that continued to look back to Cornwall but which was increasingly self-sufficient, drawing its strength and self-confidence from the growing myth of Moonta itself. In the early days at least, there were practical as well as sentimental ties with Cornwall. Homepay was important, as it was elsewhere, many of the miners sending part of their earnings to dependants back home. Captain Thomas Cowling, for example, had arrived on Yorke Peninsula in 1862 to work at the New Cornwall mine, near Kadina. Earlier, he had been out in both Wisconsin and Michigan, sending remittances to his family at Calstock. From the United States he returned briefly to Cornwall before moving on to South Australia, leaving his wife and children at home but arranging for some of his salary to be paid directly to a bank in Tavistock for their benefit. The arrangement worked well, keeping the family supplied with adequate funds until Captain Cowling sent for Sarah and their three sons to join him in the colony in 1867.[70] Cowling was conscientious, dependable and relatively well paid. For the feckless and the poor, however, homepay could sometimes be difficult. On occasions, families in Cornwall lost track of their kinfolk overseas, letters from abroad no longer arriving with the latest news and remittances drying up. Sometimes relations wrote to Captain Hancock at Moonta, enquiring as to the whereabouts of certain individuals. In such cases, Hancock encouraged errant husbands to make contact with those at home. The more pathetic stories must have been repeated around the Hancock dinner table, for on one occasion Hancock's daughter sent £1 to a poor woman near Redruth whose husband had disappeared in South Australia.[71]

Cultural habits often reflected those of Cornwall. In 1865 the *Wallaroo Times* newspaper observed that 'Of all the people in the world Cousin Jack loves his holiday'.[72] And so it seemed. Survey-day, when the skilled miners, the tributers and tutworkmen, negotiated or renewed their contracts was a time of general merrymaking. The Duke of Cornwall's birthday was observed as a general holiday, and Whit Monday was reckoned to be a more important celebration than the Queen's birthday, as indeed it was at home. On midsummer's eve – 'as Cousin John still persists in calling it'[73] – scores of bonfires were lit on the Peninsula 'according to the Cornish custom'.[74] In 1867 there were fifty bonfires at Moonta Mines alone, it was said, and at Wheal Hughes there was a terrific conflagration when an abandoned bough-shed was set ablaze as part of the festivities. The spectators, meanwhile, were kept supplied with a steady flow of 'swankey [home-brewed beer] and saffron cake'.[75] 'Shooting' – the liberal use of explosives – was an integral part of the 'midsummer' fun. In 1881 it was alleged that 'the amount of powder, dynamite and other explosives used by the youngers [sic] was almost enough to bombard a town'.[76] The following year, 'from early morning crackers and other fireworks were being set off almost without limit'.[77]

Observed as a general holiday, 24 June had also become the occasion for other community events: football matches, band concerts, chapel tea-treats and parades. In 1886 more than a thousand people marched in an impressive Wesleyan jubilee demonstration at Moonta.[78] Equal numbers, it was said, also attended the Cornish wrestling bouts held at 'midsummer'. By then, the Methodists had long since given up attempting to suppress Cornish wrestling as a 'pagan' pursuit, embracing it now as a manly sport – or at least recognizing the need for peaceful co-existence in a community where passions were not restricted to religion alone. Cornish wrestling was a popular means of expressing rivalries – personal, between individuals; local, between Moonta and the other settlements; or even wider, between Moonta and Ballarat, for example – and competitions were held at festivities throughout the year, especially 24 June, Easter and Christmas. On such occasions, the matches were extraordinarily well managed; sometimes the bouts were spread over four or five days, with as many as fifty people participating in the final play-offs. The 'wrestling rings' were formed adjacent to public houses in each of the three main towns – such as the 'White Lion' at Port Wallaroo, the 'Miners' Arms' and 'Wombat Hotel' at Kadina, or the 'Royal Hotel' and 'Miners' Arms' at Moonta. Each town had its local champions, as in Easter 1869 when John Doney – the 'Moontaite' – met William Mitchell, Kadina's hero, in the final: 'after a sharp tussle Doney threw his man over his head and landed him in true Cornish style amid great cheers'.[79] Even more memorable was the clash in 1868 between Moonta's John H. 'Dancing' or 'Dancer' Bray and the Ballarat champion. As Tom Cowling recalled, it was a tense contest in which the Ballarat man seemed to be getting the better of his Moonta opponent. But then, all of a sudden:

> like a flash of lightning, he [Bray] brought off the 'Flying Mare' trick. It was said that 20 captains who were there had not seen anything equal to it in Cornwall. Now when a man has had 'The Flying Mare' trick played on him, he generally admits he has been beaten, but on this occasion the Victorian claimed another round. But it had been better for him had he given in at the first throw, because in less than 10 seconds he was on the broad of his back 'flat as a flounder'. There followed a shout such as might have been heard when Sebastopol was captured.[80]

Elias Nankivell was another who remembered the legendary John H. Bray, and how eventually he was beaten by W. Renfry of Wheal Hughes:

For many years wrestling was the chief sport, and great struggles have been witnessed at Moonta. I have forgotten many of the old wrestlers' names. I will just mention a few of them. I will start with the Moonta Cup, held by Billy Curnow of Kadina. The cup had to be wrestled for at Moonta. So Billy journeyed to Moonta fearing only one man, and when he threw him he ran to the post office and sent the following wire to big Jim Curtis, publican at Kadina – 'Threw my man, am now sure'. But it was not to be, for Dancer Bray, of Moonta, threw him, so the cup was at Moonta again. Dancer walked with a stiff back for a while and thought he was secure, but when it came to the final in the next wrestling, he had to meet a very quiet young man from Wheal Hughes, by the name of W. Renfry. This man had been coached by Ned Nankivell, of Moonta, who was at that time considered very smart with the toe. Renfry threw Dancer, and the cup went back to Kadina. This cup was finally won by John Whinen of Wallaroo Mines.[81]

The starting of new engines at the Peninsula mines was also an excuse for holidays and merrymaking. When the famous 60-inch Hughes pumping engine was started at Moonta in 1865, Captain Hancock together with 'most of the notabilities of Moonta'[82] and a local brass band were perched on the bob-platform high up on the engine-house, with the cheering crowds far below. When the 80-inch engine was started at the New Cornwall mine in 1866, Captain East invited all the local captains to the festivities, for 'It was a good old Cornish custom to meet together on occasions like the present, and to show a friendly feeling, although engaged on different mines'.[83] There was a similar ceremony at the Yelta in 1871, and at the starting of the Paramatta mine engine in 1869 'a plentiful dinner ... [was] provided for every miner or other person in connection with the mine. In the new smith's shop, three tables were laden with good things to be eaten. Around these tables a pretty considerable number of persons sat – the mine employing about 150 miners.'[84]

Christmas was also, of course, an important holiday; a universal Christian festival but one with a Cornish dimension which, like much else, was transplanted on the Peninsula. In December 1873 the *Yorke's Peninsula Advertiser* observed that at Moonta Mines 'the miners' cottages were profusely decked with evergreens ... it is well known that Cornishmen, wherever they may be, delight in keeping up the good old custom of decorating their habitations at this season of the year.'[85] They also kept up the Cornish 'caroling' tradition, singing the Cornish carols they had known at home but also participating in the great upsurge in carol writing that swept the Cornish transnational world in the second half of the nineteenth century and beyond. Between 1890 and 1925 several collections of local carols – from Polperro to Johannesburg – appeared, and amongst these was *The Christmas Welcome: A Choice Collection of Cornish Carols*, published at Moonta in 1893.[86] The Moonta collection mirrored the now almost obligatory Cornish form – 'a florid air, frequent word repetitions and a large flowing bass'[87] of the type exemplified by the compositions of Thomas Merritt of Illogan – but its contributions were original compositions, written in South Australia by an accomplished, although essentially amateur, group of musicians dedicated to sacred music. Typical of the group was James 'Fiddler Jim' Richards, born at Perranporth in 1828, who arrived in South Australia c.1857 and joined the Primitive Methodists, first at the Burra and later at Moonta Mines.[88] At the latter he became conductor of the Primitive Methodist choir, well known for his musical compositions – including his solemn 'Rapture', a firm favourite at funerals when set to the words of Isaac Watts' hymn 'Thee We Adore'. Among his several contributions to *The Christmas Welcome* was the carol 'The King of Glory', its opening verses so characteristically typical of the *genre*:

> The King of Glory sent His son,
> To make His entrance here on earth,
> Behold the midnight bright as morn,
> And heav'nly choirs proclaim his birth.

6. Moonta Mines Brass Band, c.1874. 'Fiddler Jim' Richards, the bandmaster and local carol composer, is in the back row, extreme right.

7. Kadina Salvation Army Band, c.1919.

> About the young redeemer's head
> What wonders and what glories meet
> An unknown star arose and led
> The eastern sages to His feet.[89]

By the 1890s, when *The Christmas Welcome* was compiled, male voice choirs – an increasingly popular feature of amateur music making in late nineteenth-century Cornwall – had also exerted their transnational appeal on northern Yorke Peninsula. One adherent was Leslie Davey, already known locally as a carol composer, who was founder member of the Moonta Mines Male Voice Choir; in October 1907 crowds hurried to the East Moonta Literary Society's meeting to hear Davey's rendering of 'Lead, Kindly Light', the popular Methodist hymn that for a time almost supplanted 'Trelawny' as unofficial Cornish national anthem.[90] Similarly, brass bands, also typical of Cornwall in this period, had been popular from the earliest days of European settlement on the Peninsula. 'Bargwanna's Band', founded by George Bargwanna at Moonta in the early 1860s, was soon in constant demand for chapel anniversaries, Sunday-school tea-treats, temperance marches and the like. The 'Moonta Mine Band', composed entirely of miners (with 'Fiddler Jim'

Richards as bandmaster), was in existence by April 1865, while 'Mr Rickard's Kadina Brass Band' was appearing regularly by September 1875. In 1876 E.G. Tregonning set up his 'Cross Roads Fife and Drum Band', and in 1895 the most celebrated band of them all – the 'Wallaroo Town Band' – was formed.[91] Its founding member was Arthur Chynoweth, a Cornishman who had come from the Burra to work in the Port Wallaroo smelting works, and its conductor for many years was Henry May, a member of the well-known local engineering family (see Chapter Three). May championed northern Yorke Peninsula as the natural centre of the growing 'banding' tradition in South Australia, and in 1904 the Peninsula played host to the embryonic annual South Australian Band Association Contest. It was a pivotal moment, attended by some eight thousand people, confirming Henry May's stature in the banding movement and reinforcing the Peninsula's already impressive musical credentials. When May died aged only 49 years he was honoured as local hero: his funeral cortège was led by his beloved Wallaroo band, the mournful strains of 'Abide With Me' and 'Nearer My God To Thee' echoing across the town as the people of Port Wallaroo paid their last respects.[92]

'A people ... distinct from the ordinary population of the colony'

The transplantation and subsequent development, even metamorphosis, of Cornish cultural attributes was both conscious and unconscious: unconscious, in that people were only doing what they had always done at home; conscious in that on occasions individuals and organizations deliberately replicated former behaviour or adopted 'Cornish' rhetoric as a means of asserting community or institutional identity in their new land. This conscious assertion was, as we shall see in later Chapters, a device routinely deployed by both the Methodist churches and the miners' trade union. At times, such assertion could be surprisingly aggressive. In November 1883, for example, one local resident wrote to the *Yorke's Peninsula Advertiser* to complain about the impact of non-Cornish incomers in the district. 'And shall Trelawney die/Then twenty thousand Cornishmen/Will ask the reason why', he thundered: 'Sir – So essentially Cornish are we that we would think not only our habits and national amusements would prevail, but that our Mayor, magistrates, and leading men would be chosen from among them, and that our church music would be sung in places of worship, and funeral anthems at our burial services.'[93] Non-Cornish ministers were introducing novelties in chapel services, he complained, while allowing traditional standards to slip. Local choirs, he fretted, now 'compare unfavourably with Cornwall, with its hundred sonorous voices, or even with Kapunda or Burra Burra'. The ministers were not troubled by this worrying decline: 'but then they are not Cornishmen'.[94]

8. Kadina Primary School Band, c.1913–15. Such cultural activities were important vehicles for the perpetuation of Cornish identity on northern Yorke Peninsula.

Likewise, there was some concern when local schoolchildren were warned that they 'must not make use of any Cornish expressions'[95] in their writing or speech when at school. But assertion of identity was not always so defensive. Overseas, the Cornish had used Freemasonry and other 'Masonic' or friendly societies as a means of creating ethno-community cohesion and solidarity; vehicles for the myth of Cousin Jack and a helpful way of introducing new arrivals to new friends and potential colleagues and employers, as well as sometimes offering medical and funeral insurance. On northern Yorke Peninsula, there was a profusion of lodges and societies – some forty-four in all at their height. Most of the locality's mine captains were Freemasons, with lodges at Moonta, Port Wallaroo and Kadina. At Moonta there was also the 'Loyal Moonta' lodge of the Independent Order of Friendly Societies, established in 1863, the 'Life of Moonta' lodge of the Independent Order of Rechabites, founded in 1865, the 'Loyal Daly' of the Grand United Order of Oddfellows, set up in 1874, and the 'Star of Moonta' Druids' Lodge which first met at the 'Royal Hotel' in 1876. Other lodges of various hues were established at Moonta over the years, with still more at Moonta Mines, East Moonta and the several other townships and settlements of northern Yorke Peninsula.[96]

The prominence of the Rechabites pointed to the importance of the Temperance movement on the Peninsula. In April 1873 the Moonta 'Band of Hope' could boast some three hundred members, its blend of evangelical fervour and anti-drink rhetoric appealing to many local Methodists.[97] Others found a home in the Orange Order – by 1905 it had seven lodges in the locality – which was anti-Catholic as well as anti-drink. There was certainly a sprinkling of Roman Catholics in the district, not least pockets of Irish, such as those who had gathered at the squalid 'Irish Town' beyond Wallaroo Mines, their existence provoking the by now familiar hostility of the Cornish. There was trouble when the foundation stone for a Roman Catholic church was laid in Moonta – 'The Cornish men ... declared there were would be no Catholic church in their town'[98] – although there appeared to be relatively little antagonism thereafter. Nonetheless, as late as 1904 the Rev. D.C. Harris could tell his Methodist congregation at Moonta Mines that 'The work of Protestantism would not be finished and the Orange Institution would not survive the need of its existence until the Church of Rome came back to the New Testament and the sway of the Papacy was at an end'.[99]

On occasions, expressions of a local Cornish identity could be deliberately self-conscious. For example, humorous but telling 'Cousin Jack yarns' appeared in the Peninsula press from time to time, many in dialect form which included any number of Cornish words – some inherited from the old Celtic language of Cornwall – from 'motts' for tree roots and 'clidgy' for toffee to 'louster' (physical work) and 'nuddick' (the nape of the neck).[100] 'Jan Rogers', from Horse Downs, near Camborne, was author of numerous such yarns during the 1870s, many set in 'Cornwall, near England',[101] but the *genre* was still going strong in 1902 when the development of the cementation process at Moonta for the re-treatment of mine wastes was an opportunity for one dialectician to offer comparisons with techniques in Cornwall:

> tes jes like e was ome – down East Wheal Rose way. Ef they lef their shovels overnight in the water, wen the forenoon shif men come nex day the shovels was turned to solid copper. Wan day Cap'n Josiah Thomas, down Dolcoath, was standin talking to another cap'n about the quarterly meetin', and they got talking and talking fer purty near an our, an wen e got up top he appen to look down to es boots, an all the nails was turned to copper! Es, sure nuff![102]

Such discussion was light-hearted and colloquial. More erudite was the debate in the pages of the *Yorke's Peninsula Advertiser* during 1873 concerning the origin and usage of the Cornish words 'wheal' (a working, usually employed as a prefix in a mine name) and 'bal' (a mine). It was an exchange that revealed both a deep-seated cultural commitment to Cornish practice and a high level of educated, informed opinion. One correspondent, for example, argued passionately for the adoption on the Peninsula of the original Cornish-language spelling 'huel' in mine names, instead of the commonplace but 'corrupt' form 'wheal'. J. Anthony, Inspector of Mines in neighbouring Victoria, joined the discussion, writing in to say that – although possibly tautological and involving the use of two languages – the rendering of names such as 'Wheal Hughes Mine' (his example) should not necessarily be considered incorrect. It was an intervention that provoked a fierce retort from one 'Cornubia', who insisted that only 'Wheal Hughes' would do. Anthony, he declared, had an imperfect knowledge of Cornish usage.[103]

The assertion of 'Cornish' identity was not always, then, a homogeneous process likely to promote consensus and agreement. Inevitably, there were differences of opinion between those with ostensibly similar aims and attitudes, such as those who took offence at Cornish dialect stories, thinking their quaint style demeaning and considering that such pieces 'could never be written by a Cornishman'.[104] Moreover, as the Peninsula itself became increasingly the focus of Cousin Jack identity, so the superior role that Moonta had carved out for itself became all the more irksome for other settlements in the district – and a source of potential conflict. As early as 1875 one newspaper contributor observed wearily that it was always 'Wallaroo and Kadina versus Moonta', another correspondent in the following year complaining that 'Everybody says that a good feeling does not subsist between Wallaroo, and Kadina, and Moonta'.[105] People from East Moonta were known locally as 'Copper Tails' while those from Moonta township were 'Silver Tails', reflecting the supposed social superiority of the latter over the former, while fights between rival gangs of youths from the different settlements were not unknown. Sometimes this was institutionalized in sporting events – such as Cornish wrestling competitions – and the creation in the 1880s of the Yorke's Peninsula Football Association provided a new medium for such rivalry. In 1888, for example, a serious dispute broke out during a match between the Moonta Mines Young Turks and Wallaroo teams, leading to the resignation of an umpire and a re-play on neutral ground at Kadina.[106] And things did not improve with the passage of time. An editorial in the Moonta *People's Weekly* in November 1904 expressed its frustration at the negative effects of the suspicions and hostilities that continued to exist between the settlements. 'Our local watchword "One and All", stands not for boastful braggadacio,' wrote the editor, 'but for beneficial brotherhood.' Nonetheless, he continued, 'its contents have surely undergone a narrowing process ... No more excellent motto could be conceived, but when its use becomes only a weapon of irony, it is time to rescue it from its degradation.'[107]

And yet, for external observers, there were strong unifying characteristics that drew the northern Yorke Peninsula settlements together, lending them a common identity and marking them out collectively as distinct from the rest of South Australia. Paradoxically, this collective identity was often described as 'Moonta', despite the intention of including all the local settlements, a confusion that tacitly recognised the superior position of Moonta in local identity formation. Oswald Pryor explained this neatly, noting that when an excursion train left Moonta for Adelaide, it picked up additional passengers along the way: 'More passengers joined the train at Wallaroo and Kadina, but once aboard all were classified as "Cousin Jacks from Munta [Moonta]"'.[108] Certainly, external commentators played an important part in the creation of Moonta's myth, projecting the Peninsula as geographically remote and culturally 'different'. As early as 1868 one report could insist that 'Under the shadow of the two great companies, the Moonta and Wallaroo, lives a people in manners, customs and social habits distinct from the ordinary population of the colony'.[109] By 1875 the Peninsula had become an 'Australian Cornwall',[110] and when W.G. Spence visited the district in 1889 he discovered that the locals 'lived isolated from the rest of the colony, remaining more Cornish than Cornwall itself'.[111] People in Adelaide, it was said, thought that 'Cousin Jacks ... had long tails'.[112] When one of their number moved to the Peninsula c.1900, he was amazed by what he found: 'My first impression of Moonta Mines was – what had I let myself in for? It was soon made clear that I was a foreigner with habits and opinions to be viewed with suspicion.'[113]

Indeed, the people of northern Yorke Peninsula had their detractors in the colony, many actively disliking or disapproving of their aura of 'difference'. 'Sacred dramas' were popular on the Peninsula, played out not only by children in Sunday schools but also adult members of Methodist chapels who found in such activities important moral or improving lessons. Their audiences thought likewise, and renderings of sacred dramas such as 'David and Goliath' – performed at Wallaroo Mines in March 1876 – drew large crowds. To visitors from outside, however, such plays seemed gauche and naïve to the point of embarrassment. 'The sacred drama or miracle play has had its day,' scorned the critic of one performance, though conceding sarcastically that 'It is true that, in some remote villages in England (and then almost confined to "Cornwall, near England") the story of "Moses", groping its way for the first time finds admirers in village girls, and a rehearsal for the delectation of those to whom the story is new.'[114] The critic was not alone. In 1877 another visitor to the Peninsula was horrified to find the locals 'the slaves of superstition'. Their 'minds are the miserable abodes of superstition', he declared, the daily routine of Peninsula people governed by marks and signs and omens.[115] But for those for whom this presumed 'difference' was not a threat, the way of life on northern Yorke Peninsula often seemed attractive. The Rev. John Thorne, a Bible Christian minister from North Devon, had worked among the Cornish before he had emigrated to Australia. 'He felt very much at home on the Peninsula,' he said, 'it was more like Cornwall, almost surrounded by the sea and insulated in position.' Moreover, 'the miners preserved the same rugged characteristics that marked them in Cornwall, and preserved their independence. Wherever they went they never forgot themselves as Cornishmen.' Indeed, he added, 'they carried their principles and convictions with them and never failed to give them expression and effect'.[116]

External opinion was divided, then: supporters applauded the transplantation of Cornish 'independence', 'principles' and 'convictions'; detractors regretted the survival of rustic custom and 'superstition' that 'has had its day'. But, as the nineteenth century drew to a close, most would have agreed that a formidable regional identity had by then been forged on northern Yorke Peninsula. On 21 February 1890 the Cornish Association of South Australia was inaugurated at a glittering banquet in Adelaide Town Hall, when all the capital's grandees and literati strove to marshal their Cornish credentials and to celebrate the intimate link between Cornwall and South Australia. Branches of the Cornish Association soon sprung up elsewhere in the colony – Gawler, Clare, Kapunda, Burra – but representatives of the parent Association hurried from the capital to northern Yorke Peninsula in an anxious bid to ensure that no feathers had been ruffled and to show that Adelaide did not intend to steal the limelight. Branches were duly formed in the Peninsula towns but that the Adelaide enthusiasts had come perilously close to offending local sensibilities was evident in the remarks of one local observer: 'We should think Moonta not only a good place to establish a branch,' he snorted, 'but that it could not be bettered.'[117]

CHAPTER THREE

The cult of Captain Hancock
The man and his mines

Captain Hancock was not, strictly speaking, a Cornishman. And, despite his humble origins, he had an air of natural superiority that, even sometimes to his own chagrin, opened up something of a gulf between him and his overwhelmingly Cornish workforce. Nonetheless, as we shall see in this chapter, the cult of 'Cap'n 'Ancock' – which he himself had created, both deliberately and unwittingly – was central to the myth of Moonta and the invention of 'Australia's Little Cornwall'.

'Ssh! Caan't 'ee see I be talkin' to Cap'n 'Ancock?'

'Ssh! Caan't 'ee see I be talkin' to Cap'n 'Ancock?'.[1] So exclaims the anxious Cousin Jack who, in a self-conscious display of nervous deference, has removed his headwear to talk on the telephone to Captain Hancock. He is speaking on an extension from a stores shed, no doubt a considerable distance from Hancock's office, but nonetheless due form must be observed – and so the Cousin Jack is mortified when, just as the conversation with Hancock has commenced, another miner bursts noisily into the shed and interrupts the proceedings. This is the amusing scene in Oswald Pryor's collection of cartoons *Cornish Pasty*, a telling commentary on the relationship between Captain Henry Richard Hancock and his employees at the Moonta mine. Rank is important in this relationship. The joke, however, is about more than mere rank. It provides a penetrating insight into the character of Hancock's managerial regime at Moonta: it is more than a clue to the myth and mystique that had grown up around the extraordinary 'H.R.H.'.

As Pryor was well aware, Hancock's mystique extended beyond the mine and into the wider community, not least the Wesleyan Methodist chapel at Moonta Mines where H.R.H. was a local preacher. Hancock's reputation as a preacher on northern Yorke Peninsula was almost as formidable as it was as a mine captain. He was constantly in demand to preach at other chapels in the locality. Thus in another of Pryor's cartoons, a frock-coated gentleman of obvious standing in the community stares enigmatically at a volunteer at one

'Ssh! Caan't 'ee see I be talkin' to Cap'n 'Ancock?'

'We'll be wantin' seats in the aisles, Mister Tresize, Cap'n 'Ancock ez takin' the service.'

9–12 These four cartoons show Oswald Pryor's interpretation of the complex relationship that existed between Captain Henry Richard Hancock and his workforce.

'I called Cap'n 'Ancock all the rotters in the world but I said it to meself.'

'Sack Cappen Ancock.'

such chapel who is cheerfully carrying a long wooden form into the building, explaining as he goes: 'We'll be wantin' seats in the aisles, Mister Tresize, Cap'n 'Ancock ez takin' the service'.[2] Here the message is ambivalent. There is obvious pleasure that Hancock is due to preach at the chapel, and the expectation of a full house is indicative of the congregation's desire to hear the captain speak. But Mr Trezise's expression of stern surprise is an indication, perhaps, that the ubiquitous Captain Hancock is not always welcome, while the expectation of a large turn-out may also reflect the locals' anxiety that they *ought* to be seen in chapel when Hancock is preaching.

Pryor's ambiguity is deliberate. He is aware that alongside the genuine deference afforded Captain Hancock there was also a weariness, even reluctance, about having continually to conform to expectations as to how to behave and about how he should be treated. As we shall see (Chapter Four), this reluctance became increasingly prickly as the local miners' trade union – later formally incorporated into the Amalgamated Miners' Association of Australia – emerged to challenge the management at both Moonta and Wallaroo. Here, although the veneer of deference remained, there was also a subversive resentment that was expressed quietly but continually and firmly by the miners. Only occasionally, during periods of unusually taut industrial tension, was this resentment articulated publicly. More often, as Pryor knew, it was confined to murmurings and grumblings, and little acts of defiance. In one cartoon, two miners are having a beer after work. One explains: 'I called Cap'n 'Ancock all the rotters in the world but I said it to meself'.[3] In another cartoon, a miner surreptitiously slips an anonymous note into the suggestions box outside the mine office: the note reads 'sack cappen ancock'.[4]

Even the ostensibly strait-laced Methodists were not above having a laugh at Captain Hancock's expense. In 1889 the Wesleyan chapel at Moonta Mines installed an impressive two-manual pipe organ, largely through a generous financial gift from Captain Hancock. The pedal notes afforded tremendous reinforcement to the bass singers of the chapel choir, who, reflecting the competitive spirit that existed between the different denominations, now felt that they were considerably ahead of their rivals in volume and range. However, they had not reckoned with the Primitive Methodists, the 'trade unionists' chapel', who were not impressed by Hancock's gift. The Primitives had in their ranks one Samuel Browning, a big powerful miner with a huge voice, and they insisted 'that a chapel which had Sammy didn't want an organ with a box of whistles'.[5] Manly attributes, it was insinuated, were more than a match for Hancock money.

Others remembered with wry amusement the benefits that could accrue from adherence to the Wesleyans, the 'bosses' chapel', where Hancock was local preacher. Ephraim Major recalled a typical anecdote:

The story goes that once a new arrival [at Moonta Mines] went one Monday to Mr [sic] Hancock, and asked for a job. The reply was 'no opening'. The man replied, 'that was a lovely prayer you made at the meeting last night, Mr Hancock'. 'Oh, call in again tomorrow morning. I will see in the meantime what can be done for you,' said H.R.H. The man got a job.[6]

Behind the humour, of course, was a sense of latent conflict — whether at prayer or in the workplace. Hancock's purview was vast, his influence felt in seemingly every institution across the Peninsula, and this in itself could provoke resentment and jealousy. Sometimes this hostility would exhibit a strong democratic element — when the trade unionists strove to build an alternative source of authority in the mines, or when civic institutions emerged to complement the hitherto all-embracing presence of the mine companies — but it could also be very personal. For despite his reputation as firm but fair — reasonable, balanced, even kindly and understanding — Hancock also had his detractors. The trade unionists, of course, as we shall see, were inevitably opponents. But within the workplace, as we shall also see, there was in addition a deep-seated suspicion that Hancock was sometimes prepared to abuse his apparently all-seeing absolute power. He would be accused of favouritism and nepotism: giving plum jobs to cronies and relations, and dismissing or freezing out those whose faces did not fit. Worse still were the accusations that surfaced from time to time, claims that Hancock had appropriated as his — and for his own financial gain and professional prestige — technical innovations that had in fact been developed by mechanics on the mines. Oswald Pryor dubbed these unsung mechanics the 'local Trevithicks' of Moonta and Wallaroo. They were 'Trevithicks' — like Richard Trevithick himself, the 'Cornish Giant' who had invented the steam locomotive and had experimented so successfully with high-pressure steam — in that they could demonstrate remarkable ingenuity and an innate aptitude for mining engineering. But they were also 'Trevithicks' in the sense that, like their namesake, they often died penniless and without due recognition in their own time for the significant technical contributions that they had made to their industry.[7]

To the workers underground or in the machine-shops, Captain Hancock did indeed appear all-powerful: the public face of the Moonta and (later) Wallaroo mine companies. Behind the scenes, however, Hancock's authority was conditional and often contested — for his detractors numbered not only the grumbling miners and mechanics so visible to Pryor but also those more shadowy directors who were often irritated by Hancock's self-confidence and superior attitude. Perversely, when Hancock was proved right in his tussles with the directors, as he so often was, this won the momentary gratitude of the board but also fuelled the long-term lingering resentment felt by some of his critics. Here was a love–hate relationship as complex as that between Captain Hancock and his men. It was also another of life's battlegrounds. In time, his international reputation increasingly assured and his financial situation more than secure, such conflict would become of less personal importance to Hancock. But the wrangles remained. When the Cornish Association of South Australia was formed in 1890, Hancock – a 'Devon dumpling', as everyone knew – was not invited to join its leading luminaries despite the fact that the Association's inaugural Vice-President was Sir John Langdon Bonython, a Londoner by birth, albeit of Cornish parentage. Nor did Hancock join the Moonta branch when it was established.[8] Later, when Hancock achieved his life-long ambition – retirement to his native village in Devonshire – he was greeted not as local-boy-made-good but rather as a social upstart who had arrogated to himself the unwarranted airs and graces of 'H.R.H.'. Not surprisingly, Hancock soon returned to South Australia: where social standing was not linked so resolutely to birth, and where social mobility was accepted – even applauded.[9]

Devonshire days

Henry Richard Hancock sprang from modest Devonshire stock: artisans on his father's side, yeomen farmers on his mother's. He was born on 1 April 1836 at Horrabridge, near Tavistock, the son of George and Sarah Hancock. George was a Wesleyan local preacher, whose peripatetic work in the Tavistock circuit took him from the heights of Dartmoor in the east to the Bere Ferrers peninsula – the strip of land on the western edge of Devon formed by the confluence of the Tamar and Tavy rivers – where he ministered to the local Bere Alston silver-lead miners. George had a good understanding of the ways of the miners, both the local Devon men and, increasingly, the large numbers of Cornish copper miners who crossed the border to work in the locality, especially after the opening of the Devon Great Consols mine on the eastern bank of the Tamar in 1844. For, in addition to his role as local preacher, which had given him intimate contact with the mining population, George was also a blacksmith, wheelwright and coachbuilder – a partner in his father's business at Horrabridge: Robert Hancock & Sons. As well as building and mending vehicles and making implements for the local agricultural community, the firm was increasingly employed in the manufacture of components for the burgeoning mines of the district, and in this way George became ever more closely involved in the affairs of the Tamar Valley mining industry.[10]

George Hancock married Sarah Lipson, of Leigh Farm in the parish of Bere Ferrers, in 1830. Their first two children died in infancy. Henry Richard Hancock, their first surviving child, came along in 1836, and was brought up in the cottage alongside the family business premises in Horrabridge. In this way, the young H.R.H. was exposed to practical mining engineering from an early age, and his formative teenage years corresponded with the spectacular rise of the local copper mines. Mines with Cornish names, worked by Cornish hands from across the Tamar, sprang up across the district. Mighty Cornish beam engines, installed in massive engine-houses, dominated what had become in effect an eastward extension of the Cornish mining landscape. It was a phenomenon remarkably like that experienced at Moonta and northern Yorke Peninsula a decade or so later. By 1850 Devon Great Consuls, the largest mine in the district, employed a total of 1,024 persons, its constituent workings – Wheal Maria, Wheal Fanny, Wheal Anna Maria, Wheal Josiah, Wheal Emma – spread the length of Blanchdown Woods on the Devon bank of the Tamar. Nearby was another important copper mine, Devon Great United. Near the town of Tavistock itself were mines such as Wheal Crowndale and Wheal Crebor, and further north on the edge of Dartmoor was Wheal Friendship – second only to Devon Great Consuls in importance in the locality – and a string of other workings such as Wheal Betsy and Wheal Hope. In the vicinity of Horrabridge was the Sortridge group of mines – Great Sortridge, Great Sortridge United, Great West Sortridge, East Sortridge, North Sortridge, Sortridge Consuls – which developed swiftly in the 1850s.[11]

George Hancock had died in 1848, aged only forty-five, and his father Robert followed him to the family grave in 1852. Sarah then took the dramatic decision to sell the family business. One consequence was that young Henry had to find employment elsewhere. Inevitably, perhaps, he made his way into one of the local mines. This, it appears, was Sortridge Consuls, situated half a mile north of Horrabridge on the site of an earlier working, West Wheal Robert. When it opened in 1853 copper ore was encountered a mere five feet below the surface, and in only a few months £3,200 worth of ore had been extracted. By 1854 the mine was down to thirty fathoms, with the copper ore still incredibly rich. Like many other mines in Cornwall and West Devon, Sortridge Consuls fell victim to the plunging copper prices in the crisis of 1866. But in the intervening period it had been astonishingly successful, with a new beam engine installed in 1855 amid great celebrations. It was during these heady years that Henry Richard Hancock had learned to be a mine manager. Already sixteen or seventeen years old when he joined the mine, he rose rapidly – learning assaying, mineral-dressing, surveying and book-keeping as well as underground mining methods – and within five years he was already a captain, working under the supervision of a superintendent who visited the mine but once a week to keep an eye on things. H.R.H. was already on his upward trajectory.[12]

Wheal Ellen

Notwithstanding the rapid development of the Tamar Valley mines after 1844, the attention of almost every able and ambitious man in the Cornish mining industry at that time was drawn overseas. Only rarely was the interest academic. Even if an individual had decided that he would not (yet) venture abroad, he would have any number of colleagues, friends and relations already resident in localities overseas who would be eager and willing to furnish detailed descriptions of the opportunities that awaited the emigrant Cornish on the frontiers of the New World. Equally, emigration agents toured the Cornish and West Devon mining districts to identify suitable potential emigrants, while overseas mining companies enlisted the help of local mine captains in Cornwall to try to find the recruits that they needed. Horrabridge – no less than Calstock, St Blazey, Redruth or St Just – was immersed in this transnational contact, and it was no surprise when in late 1858 Captain Hancock was hired by the Wheal Ellen silver-lead mine in South Australia. He arrived in 1859, aged only twenty-three.[13]

Wheal Ellen was situated at Strathalbyn, about thirty miles from Adelaide and a handful of miles down the Bremer River from Callington. In the late 1840s and early 1850s three copper mines had been opened near Strathalbyn but by 1854 these had each fallen victim to the Victorian goldrush, when the miners abandoned their work to try their luck in the neighbouring colony. These mines were reworked briefly in 1857, in an attempt to turn from copper to silver-lead, but attention had by then turned to adjoining Wheal Ellen. The mine was opened in 1857 and fully operational by 1860. Experienced mining men were engaged to come out to South Australia to run Wheal Ellen: John Cornish from Helston, William Arundel Paynter from Hicks' Mill, Gwennap, Joseph Jolly from Ladock, Thomas Nicholls from St Austell, and Henry Richard Hancock from Horrabridge.[14] Of these, Captain Paynter had worked in mines in Cornwall, Wales and Cumberland before emigrating to South Australia, and it was in Cumberland that he had first heard of Wheal Ellen. He wrote to his wife Sophia in Cornwall, mentioning that 'there is a cornishman [sic] here about to leave for Australia on tuesday or wednesday next, his name is Vial from Chacewater'.[15] A few weeks later, in February 1859, he told her that 'I have had a little information as to the mine in Australia'.[16] By the September he was at Wheal Ellen, saving hard to bring out Sophia, and working as the mine's chief ore-dresser and engineer. He stayed until 1861, then moving on to the Moonta district.

H.R.H. was already making his mark. In 1860 Wheal Ellen purchased a 60-inch Cornish pumping engine, its components manufactured jointly by the Perran Foundry and Messrs Nicholls, Williams of Tavistock.[17] It had arrived by 1862, where it was observed to be in pieces on the ground, about to be erected in the engine-house built for the purpose. The choice of the Nicholls, Williams foundry smacks of Hancock's influence and his in-depth knowledge of the West Devon mining scene. But the joint construction suggests an unusual compromise — perhaps the resolution of opposing wills? — because the Perran Foundry lay close to the Gwennap mining district and would have been familiar to Paynter, and was no doubt his preferred choice. Interestingly, Paynter had resigned his position before the engine was installed and working. Hancock stayed on. But not for long, for when his contract expired in 1862 he refused the offer of renewal and made instead for northern Yorke Peninsula where he had been invited by the Wallaroo mine directors to 'gather information and particulars relative to the Mines and the Wallaroo District generally'.[18]

The rise of Wallaroo and Moonta – and Captain Hancock

Like Paynter before him, Hancock had realized that Wheal Ellen was small beer when compared to the extraordinary potential of northern Yorke Peninsula. When Hancock had first contemplated emigration to South Australia, the Peninsula hardly featured on the colony's mining map. Early copper finds were dismissed as too meagre to be worked with any success in such remote and difficult country, although the Scottish sea-captain, Walter Watson Hughes, on whose pastoral leases the discoveries had been made, knew well enough that there was any number of interesting mineral deposits on the Peninsula. Campfires sometimes burned bright with an unusual green flame, and burrowing marsupials occasionally threw up small piles of curious green and blue stones. Specimens of copper could in those days be 'picked up freely' on the beach at Port Wallaroo, it was said, and it was in this vicinity that the Peninsula's first mine, Wheal Mixter, was worked. Located on one of Hughes' runs, Wheal Mixter was in operation 'long before the discovery of the [neighbouring] Wallaroo Mine',[19] but it was never really a going concern and was numbered among the colony's numerous marginal and insignificant 'shows'. In December 1859, however, came the major discovery that Hughes had been waiting for. James Boor, one of his shepherds, chanced across the deposits several miles inland that would shortly become the magnificent Wallaroo mine. Hughes swiftly engaged the services of four Cornish miners from Burra Burra: Walter Phillips, from Bokiddick, near Luxulyan; Richard Truran, from St Agnes; William Pascoe; and Richard Walter. In Cornish fashion, one of the miners whirled his pick around his head and then let go. The others began to dig where it had landed — breaking the ground for what would be the first shaft of the new Wallaroo mine.[20]

A little over a year later, in 1861, an equally spectacular discovery was made at neighbouring Moonta, where Patrick Ryan, another of Hughes'

13. The New Cornwall mine, sketched by W. Wyatt, c.1862.

shepherds, had observed a wombat's diggings. Hughes brought some of his Cornish miners across from the Wallaroo mine, and soon operations were under way at Moonta. Before long, countless other claims were appearing in the locality. In January 1861 the prospectus for the Wandilta mine, to be opened near Kadina, was published, and in the February the commencement of the New Cornwall mine – again, near Kadina – was announced. Captain George Vercoe, originally from Marazion, was hired by several companies to examine the worth of their claims in the area. In September 1862, Captain Goldsworthy was engaged to open the Wilkawat (or Nalyappa) mine near Moonta. The Karkarilla, later to become part of the successful Hamley mine, was opened on the southern edge of the Moonta leases in July 1862. The Doora mine was discovered in November 1862, Wheal Hughes was opened in 1865, as was the Paramatta in 1866, and petroleum shale was detected in the Old Cornwall mine in 1867. In early 1866 the South Wallaroo mine, shortly renamed Great Devon Consols in imitation of its near-namesake on the Tamar, was being developed under the guidance of Captain Williams. Soon there was a Wheal Fortune and a Wheal Prosper – almost obligatory mine names back in Cornwall – and before long the Wandilta had spawned a North Wandilta. Likewise, the discovery near Moonta of the Yelta mine had led in no time to a North Yelta, while there was any number of hopeful copy-cat Moonta derivatives in the locality: the Moonta Consols, the Mid-Moonta, the New Moonta, and so on.[21]

This was a period of feverish speculation and expansion very similar to that Hancock had observed as a youth and young man in the Tamar Valley. In the little time he had been at Wheal Ellen, northern Yorke Peninsula had emerged from nowhere to become far and away the most promising mining field in South Australia, and one of the most exciting in the continent as a whole. Now experienced as well as shrewd and ambitious, Captain Hancock observed all the signs, read them correctly, and acted accordingly. It was a calculated risk, for the Wallaroo appointment was only short term. But Hancock had enough confidence in his own abilities, and in the potential of the new mining field, to recognize that it would be only a matter of time before he would secure a permanent position. It seemed at first that he would be employed at the Bingo and Wandilta mines, but the directors reluctantly decided otherwise, considering that the workings were not yet sufficiently developed to warrant such a senior appointment. The Wallaroo directors, in a rare display of guilt, felt embarrassed by Hancock's apparent inability to land a job – they, after all, had been responsible for enticing him to the Peninsula – and offered to pay £50 towards his fare to Plymouth, should he decide to seek work in Cornwall or Devon.[22] They need not have worried. In October 1863 Hancock was employed on a three-month contract at the Moonta mine as assayer, his term later being extended until the following June when John Bennett, already appointed as the company's permanent assayer, was due to arrive from Cornwall.[23]

Hancock had been sure to make his mark at Moonta; just as he had at Wheal Ellen. On the expiry of his assaying contract, he moved across to the Yelta mine as captain. But the Moonta company has been impressed by his energy, abilities and bright ideas, and re-engaged him on a part-time basis to prepare plans of their mine's underground workings and mineral deposits, intelligence which, paradoxically, was also very useful to Hancock's masters at the Yelta. For a fee of £100 Hancock was to draw longitudinal sections of the workings at Elder's and Taylor's shafts – a course of action he had himself previously recommended – and for a further £50 he was to do the same for Young's, Dominick's, McDonell's and Buchan's shafts.[24]

In June 1864, following the demise of the unfortunate Captain James Warmington (see Chapter Four), the Moonta directors in an inspired act of faith decided to employ Henry Richard Hancock as their Chief Captain (in preference to Captain Trestrail, the other candidate they had considered seriously). As their Minutes put it, Hancock was 'named as the most suitable person for the appointment'.[25] At the same time they appointed Samuel Sandoe Bice as underground captain. Interestingly, Bice came from Bere Alston in Devon – not a million miles from Horrabridge – and already the Hancock touch was being felt on the Moonta tiller. Not long after, Samuel's brother Henry Bice – born in St Blazey, Cornwall, in 1830 – arrived at Moonta from Callington (South Australia) and secured a senior position before later moving on to become captain of the Matta Parra and South Hamley mines.[26] A pattern of appointments was being established at Moonta that would set the tone for the regime that H.R.H. wished to create. In short, Hancock intended to establish a patriarchal style in which he would appoint to key managerial positions only those whom he knew, either personally or by reliable reputation, and on whose loyalty he could count without question. It would also be a paternalistic regime, where everyone knew his place, and where mutual responsibilities and obligations were clearly understood. Virtue in the workplace mirrored religious conviction and personal morality, Hancock argued, and this too was a significant consideration in making appointments. Methodists, especially Wesleyans, would be particularly welcome to apply.

Later, in the aftermath of the 'Great Strike' of 1874 – when he had been made to feel a Devon dumpling 'other' by the men with whom he had hitherto claimed common cause – Hancock began to rue the ethnic solidarity he had created on the mines, suddenly feeling the cultural distance between Devon and Cornwall and beginning to mistrust his Cornish workforce. But that mood passed – in 1883 he sent Captain Piper to Cornwall on a massive recruiting drive – and for the most part Captain Hancock was gratified to have secured so successfully what he had set out to achieve: the creation at Moonta, and later at Wallaroo too, of what was essentially a large Cornish copper mine in the Antipodes. This was a Cornish mine worked by Cornish hands according to Cornish practice, dependent on Cornish technology and shot through with the culture, habits, mores and terminology of the Cornish copper mining industry. In Cornwall itself, the great crash of 1866 tore the heart out of copper mining, with many mines abandoned for good and others having to turn to tin, but Moonta weathered the storm. In this way, strangely, Captain Hancock's 'white cow' – the Moonta mine – survived as a model Cornish copper mine long after its prototypes in Cornwall had disappeared or metamorphosed. This did much to elaborate Captain Hancock's own myth and mystique, and it contributed enormously to the consolidation of Moonta and environs as 'Australia's Little Cornwall'.

Building the team

Hancock's starting salary at Moonta was £350 per annum plus 'the usual allowances'[27] (including free accommodation), a reasonable sum in those days, and he was permitted to continue to hold his Yelta appointment concurrently for a further twelve months.[28] He applied himself immediately with his customary vigour and enthusiasm. As he explained to the board of directors, H.R.H. now foresaw a period of rapid development. He had accepted his appointment on condition that he be allowed to initiate a bold recruitment plan, aimed at dramatically increasing the number of Cornish miners employed at Moonta. He also demanded the right to dismiss any of the existing officers and to replace them with Cornish captains of his own choice. The directors agreed, although they insisted on retaining 'Captain Osborne – who has been specially appointed by the board'.[29] Shortly after, however, Samuel Osborne decided that Moonta under Hancock's management was no longer the place for him, moving across to the Wallaroo mine and from there taking up a position as captain of the Belmont Copper Mine in New South Wales in 1867.

In the same year Osborne was engaged as recruitment agent for the Peak Downs copper mine in Queensland. Ironically, he looked to Moonta and Wallaroo as the potential source of the skilled copper miners he required. Here was an interesting example of a paradox that would continue to bedevil Captain Hancock's recruitment plans. Hancock was to prove enormously successful in enticing Cornish miners to Moonta, projecting the mine as a bastion of Cornishness where Cousin Jack's skill would be acknowledged and rewarded, and yet this very success had the effect of encouraging every other hard-rock mining company in Australia to cast its eyes enviously at this pool of skilled labour. 'Moontaites' were increasingly sought after throughout the continent. In the heady days of rapid expansion on the Peninsula they played hard to get, demanding the highest remuneration before they might be persuaded to move on, but in later lean years – in the 1880s and 1890s – they were only too keen to be admitted to the enthusiastically welcoming embrace of places such as Broken Hill and the Western Australian goldfields. As it was, Osborne had managed to lure sixty miners to Peak Downs in 1868, with a further sixty following in 1872.[30] As Hancock no doubt reflected, he would not have expected or experienced such 'disloyalty' from men he had appointed himself.

In addition to Osborne, Hancock had also allowed Captain John Rapson to remain on his staff. It was a mistake. Born in St Ives c.1828, Rapson had toiled in mines in America, Victoria and New Zealand before arriving at Moonta to work as second captain under the erstwhile Captain Warmington. Rapson reckoned that he knew a thing or two about mining, and confrontation with H.R.H. was inevitable. Rapson was a proud man but he was also sensitive, and easily took offence. He spoke with a stutter and was very conscious of this supposed disability. On one occasion, it was said, a stuttering man approached Rapson to ask for a job: Rapson thought he was being made fun of, and sent the poor man away with a flea in his ear. Increasingly at loggerheads with Hancock, Rapson was soon moved on, leaving H.R.H. with his hand-picked team.[31]

First amongst Hancock's officers was his chief underground captain, Malachi Deeble. A ring-leader of the 1848 Burra strike (see Chapter Four),

Deeble was the scourge of the trade unionists at Moonta, and Hancock's principal ally in maintaining his authority in the mines. Born in St Austell c.1820, Deeble had arrived in South Australia in 1846. After the Burra strike, he farmed briefly on newly opened-up country near Clare, as did many other miners-turned-farmers from the Burra, but later made his way to northern Yorke Peninsula to become captain of the Kurilla mine. It was there that he caught the eye of Captain Hancock. He was moved across to Moonta, where he worked until his retirement in 1888. Oswald Pryor thought Deeble the archetypal Cornish captain: 'Captain Deeble had a typical Cornishman's beard. He shaved his upper lip and chin and grew a monkey-fringe beard.' More importantly, he was a stern disciplinarian who ensured that Captain Hancock's will was done: 'He was a local preacher and always wore a belltopper to chapel. Also, he was a J.P. and didn't let anybody forget it.'[32] Deeble's colleague underground was Captain James Barkla, another of Hancock's early appointees, who was born in Bodmin in 1827. Like Deeble, he had worked at the Burra, before going on to manage or report on various mines on Eyre Peninsula and in the Far North of the colony. Near Mount Remarkable, in the north, Barkla had run the Spring Creek copper mine, a promising property with 'magnificent ore'[33] – as he reported to the *Mining Journal* in 1863 – but like many such far-flung enterprises it suffered from inaccessibility and the consequent high cost of transportation. For an adventurous man like Barkla, this was frustrating. But Hancock recognized Barkla's tenacity and his ability to sniff out high grade ore in the most unlikely of places, and Barkla was invited to join the Hancock team.

14. The Kurilla mine, near Kadina: another of Wyatt's sketches, c.1862.

15. The Moonta mine, again by Wyatt, c.1862.

Captain Joseph Jolly, whom Hancock had first met at Wheal Ellen, was also asked to join, and was appointed mine accountant at Moonta. Hancock had chosen wisely. When not busy balancing the mine's books, Captain Jolly was fulfilling his role equally conscientiously at Moonta Mines Wesleyan chapel as local preacher, class leader and Sunday-school superintendent. Jolly had been born in 1809 and was then already well into middle age, a decade or two older than most of Hancock's other appointees and considerably senior to H.R.H. himself. His task was not physically taxing, so age was not an issue, and Hancock was no doubt attracted by Jolly's long experience in Cornish mine accountancy. Jolly's meticulous attention to detail was certainly reassuring, and perhaps Hancock saw him as something of a father figure. At any rate, Joseph Jolly became Hancock's father-in-law in 1872 when, following the death of his first wife in 1870, H.R.H. married Loveday Maria Jolly, a strategic union that helped cement the Hancock dynasty in Australian mining lore.[34]

Joseph Jolly's son Joe, destined to become Hancock's brother-in-law, replaced Captain Bennett as chief assayer at Moonta. William and James Datson, both of whom had worked for Hancock at the Yelta, were recruited as under captains, as was Captain C. Mitchell. John Trewennack was appointed head blacksmith, and Bennett Opie became head carpenter. Hancock's team was almost complete. But there were two further senior appointments, both of which proved to be of considerable significance. The first was Frederick May, born in Cornwall in the parish of Perranzabuloe in 1840, who had arrived in the colony in 1858 to work as an engineer at the Burra mine. His

16. Hancock's team. Captain Hancock and his entourage of Cornish captains at the Moonta mine c.1865–66.
Back row: Captains Rapson, Davies, France, Knowles, Barkla, Paynter, Phillips, Neales, unknown, Jolly, Bice.
Front row: Captains Datson, Osborne, Deeble, Hancock, Wyatt, Bennetts, Mitchell.

reputation was swiftly established, and in 1864 – when only twenty-three years of age – he was engaged by Captain Hancock as chief engineer at Moonta, a position he was to hold for eleven years. The other important appointment was William Arundel Paynter, who had preceded Hancock to the Peninsula, where he was employed in one of the other mines (possibly Wallaroo) before H.R.H. secured his services for the Moonta. Later, other key appointments were also made – Captain James Pryor from Wendron, Captain Christopher Faull from Crowan, Captain Joshua Skinner (whom Hancock had also known at Wheal Ellen), and so on – but it was this initial team that put the Moonta mine on its secure footing, managing a decade of rapid development, despite uncertain copper prices, and running the workings true Cornish style in just about every respect.[35]

'Cornish miners indifferently employed'

His team thus assembled, Captain Hancock arranged for further miners to be recruited from Cornwall (see Chapter Two). Recognizing that this would be inevitably a lengthy process, he also took steps to hire Cornish miners in neighbouring Victoria. As Hancock was aware, many Cornish copper miners had gone from South Australia to Victoria in the early days of the goldrush, while still others had been enticed directly from Cornwall – or even California, where a large number of Cornish had participated in the rush of 1849 and were eager to test the next bonanza. Subsequently, the development of deep quartz mining in Victoria had depended to a considerable degree on the hard-rock mining skills of Cornish immigrants. But as Hancock also knew, there was great interest in Victoria in the prospects of the new mining field on northern Yorke Peninsula. In April 1861 the Adelaide *Register* had noted that 'The news of the Wallaroo Mines having reached the diggings in Victoria, we find that several Cornishmen have left their gold-diggings to come here and work at their old occupation [copper mining]'.[36] Indeed, the Wallaroo directors had already placed advertisements in the principal Victorian newspapers, calling for experienced copper miners, and Hancock was keen that Moonta should do something similar. The board of directors agreed, echoing Hancock's belief that in many areas of Victoria would be found 'Cornish miners ... indifferently employed'.[37] As the directors put it: 'Your proposal for increasing the number of Hands and extending the Works at the Mine has the approval of the Board'.[38]

Hancock's recruitment plans were ambitious. In August 1864 S.R. Wakefield was sent to Victoria as Moonta's representative, with instructions to engage 'some 200 to 300 miners', and to persuade others to follow 'on their own account'.[39] These recruits were to be 'from the Mines of Cornwall and Wales, and it is only to be experienced and respectable miners':[40] no

17. An early photograph of one of the northern Yorke Peninsula mines, showing a horse whim, a device for hauling ore from underground.

Irish, Chinese or others need apply. At first, Wakefield had difficulty in locating sufficient numbers of the right sort of men, and he was reminded firmly that he was to seek 'Copper Miners and not to engage Gold diggers'.[41] Wakefield persevered, and by 30 September 1864 some 150 miners and their families had already arrived at Moonta from Victoria, more than seventy of these having travelled directly to Port Wallaroo in the steamship *Coorong*. The plunge in world copper prices put the process on hold, like much else at Moonta, but by May 1868 Captain James Datson was in Victoria at Hancock's behest to recruit a new wave of miners. Datson knew the goldfields well, having spent some time there with his father Hugh, gold-seeking in the early 1850s. He dispatched '35 Cornish Miners' in the *Coorong* on 22 June, considering them 'smart looking fellows', with another party of fifty departing in late July. Further contingents sailed in the *Kangaroo* and the *Aldinga*, with another batch said to be making its way across to Moonta by the overland route.[42]

Moonta had now become something of a Cornish Mecca, as Hancock had hoped it would, a beacon of Cornish mining practice in the continent where, so the story went, Cornish miners would be assured of a friendly welcome and preferential treatment. This was, as Hancock no doubt understood, the myth of Cousin Jack writ large, institutionalized in the great copper mines of northern Yorke Peninsula. At any rate, further groups continued to arrive from Victoria on their own initiative in the late 1860s and early 1870s. One party arrived from Ballarat in February 1873, and the cluster of cottages that the newcomers built for themselves at Moonta Mines was still remembered as 'Ballarat Row' when May Vivienne visited the Peninsula in the early 1900s.[43]

'Prudence and true economy'

In June 1865 Henry Richard Hancock's position as chief captain at Moonta was confirmed, with a substantial pay rise to £850 per annum on the understanding that he gave up his parallel post at the Yelta.[44] This was the impetus, if any was needed, to press ahead with his bold development plans. A large 60-inch pumping engine – the celebrated 'Hughes'' engine that worked all the way through to closure in 1923 – had been ordered in February 1862 from Harvey & Co of Hayle, Cornwall. It was erected by Frederick May on its arrival, and started amid great ceremony at 3.30 p.m. on 27 August 1865. Captain Matthew East, who during the Warmington crisis in 1864 had been loaned to Moonta on a temporary basis from the New Cornwall mine, had recommended the purchase of a further 22-inch rotary beam engine. This was to be complete with crusher, crusher rolls, whim [winding] chain, brasses, kibbles [mine buckets], and plans for an engine-house and crusher-house.

East hailed from Calstock, on the Cornish bank of the Tamar, not far from Horrabridge, and his preference, like Hancock's, was for machinery made by Messrs. Nicholls, Williams at their Bedford Foundry in Tavistock. Hancock, with his own territorial prejudices, was happy to confirm the order and to agree that the acquisition was sensible. Other equipment, from rope and chain to rivets and pressure-gauges, was obtained direct from Cornwall. In 1866, a set of theodolites, costing sixteen guineas apiece, was purchased from the well-known Cornish firm of William Wilton of St Day.[45]

Hancock began the construction of a railway system around the mine, and planned the erection of a 'cookhouse and dining room for the single men'.[46] He secured the directors' approval for a scheme to extend the developmental work in Bower's shaft, and persuaded them to offer a reward of £50 to anyone discovering a payable lode on the Moonta property. Unfortunately, even as Hancock pressed ahead with his ambitious schemes, the price of copper was dropping on the international market. The directors detected what they imagined to be a parallel drop in the cost of living on Yorke Peninsula, and in September 1865 determined to reduce wages accordingly. Inevitably, the miners expressed strong disapproval, although the sting was taken out of their complaint when it was explained that each of the mine's captains, with the exception of Captain Hancock, had has his salary reduced too. Hancock's remuneration may have been spared but in other areas he was now under pressure. Several of the directors, including Walter Watson Hughes himself, began to complain loudly that Hancock was incurring higher costs at a time of declining profitability. This was reckless behaviour, it was alleged, and Hancock was summoned before the board to explain himself. Persuasive as ever, H.R.H. was able to justify his expansionist policies, with even the most sceptical directors giving their grudging approval. Nonetheless, despite expressing its confidence in him, the board told Hancock in no uncertain terms that, whatever else happened, 'the cost of production of ore *will* be reduced'.[47]

During 1866, the year that was to prove so catastrophic for the Cornish copper-mining industry, the directors noted that they had 'heard with concern of the serious Commercial Panic that has taken place in England and of the heavy pressure on the Money Market'.[48] The pressure was again on Hancock to cut costs – in a fit of pique when annoyed the board refused him permission to become a director of the neighbouring Bald Hill Mine – and he was instructed to reduce operations 'without producing distress' in the area.[49] He was also told to introduce another round of wage cuts, and the board resolved that 'Captain Hancock will abstain from taking on new hands and offer no opposition to the withdrawal of any old hands who may be discontented'.[50] There was a hint here that the directors considered Hancock sometimes unduly sympathetic to the miners. When economic conditions began to pick up a little during July 1867, H.R.H. was soon requesting permission to re-employ those whom he had so recently been forced to let go. Anxious not to lose their reservoir of skilled workers, the board agreed, writing to Hancock: 'The board approve of your letting the old Tribute pitches ... to the Old Hands out of employment whose families reside on the Mines'.[51] In fact, by April 1868 a shortage of good hard-rock miners had become apparent, and Hancock was again taking steps to recruit further supplies.

Over the next few years, Hancock applied his innovatory skills with determination. He developed his own design of pneumatic drill, for instance, which was manufactured in the machine-shop at Moonta, and he introduced new large-sized kibbles to increase the amount of ore hauled from underground, at the same time phasing out the older standard Cornish kibbles. By the early 1870s, however, Hancock was again routinely at loggerheads with the directors. In July 1871, for example, the board had decided to abandon Buchan's shaft, and asked Hancock's advice on how best to achieve this. Hancock failed to see the logic of the move, and sent a reply that was considered evasive and 'not sufficiently explicit'.[52] Somewhat irritated by Hancock's response, the directors agreed to proceed with the abandonment, and instructed Hancock to make it so. But Captain Hancock refused, insisting that 'he could not at present undertake the responsibility of recommending a course involving so much risk'.[53] Remarkably, the directors backed down, deferring to Hancock's superior credentials as a practical miner. It was a measure of the extent to which they had become dependent upon him, for behind the tetchy responses to rising costs or falling profitability, when Hancock was periodically called to account, was their increasing reliance upon H.R.H. for strategic leadership. Subsequently, they readily agreed to his various schemes for the acquisition of a traction-engine, a coasting schooner, a steam-hammer, and the erection of a brass foundry at the mines.[54]

In April 1877, as we shall see below, Henry Richard Hancock became chief captain of the Wallaroo mine, on the resignation of Captain Samuel Higgs, thus further increasing his power, prestige and authority: locally, and on the continental and international stage. But it was the events of June 1877 that really demonstrated how dependent upon him the Moonta directors had become. The continuing low price of copper threatened the continued viability of the Moonta mine, and encouraged the directors to look for desperate measures. They resolved, therefore, that all work should cease at Moonta, except that of an exploratory nature. Hancock was horrified. A cessation of operations would put the mine in an even more parlous position. As it was, he said, the supply of low-grade ore was currently so vast that the stamps were in operation twenty-four hours a day in a bid to crush it for processing. If the stamp batteries were stopped, he explained, then the backload of ore could never be cleared in the event of a copper price rise. Moreover, he argued, the proceeds of this low-grade ore, when sent to the smelters, would finance exploratory work to locate high-grade deposits which could be left untouched until copper prices revived. It would also be disastrous to lose Moonta's much-prized pool of skilled labour by dismissing tributers and allowing them to disappear elsewhere. His own plan, he re-emphasized, was to treat as much low-grade ore as possible, while leaving the high-grade ore in the ground – a pragmatic policy of resource conservation which, the directors were forced to acknowledge, was the only realistic course of action.[55]

During 1878 and 1879, while the directors were dismayed by the sudden loss of profitability, Hancock was still looking to the future. He acquired redundant plant from Wheal James and the Paramatta mine, and visited Kapunda and Wheal Barton (near Truro, at the northern end of the Barossa Valley) to observe new techniques in ore-dressing. In the early 1880s he purchased a diamond drill for exploratory work, and began the importation of durable Oregon timbers to secure the workings underground.[56] In 1884, recognizing their due to the courage, single-mindedness and foresight of Captain Hancock, the directors granted him six months' paid leave. He returned rejuvenated, pushing through new work to such an extent that the unsettled directors had yet again to caution him, requiring him to exercise greater 'prudence and true economy'.[57] But there was no hesitation in confirming H.R.H. as General Superintendent of the combined Moonta and Wallaroo mines when at last they amalgamated in 1889, a position he was to hold until 1898, when he was succeeded by his son, H. Lipson Hancock.

'Higgs ripped out everything'

Before their amalgamation in 1889, the Moonta and Wallaroo mines had worked in close co-operation, especially when Hancock had become chief captain at the latter in 1877. When Eneder Warmington had been dismissed, like his brother James at Moonta, Captain East had also taken temporary charge at Wallaroo. He was replaced by Captain Edward Dunstan, who had arrived from Cornwall in January 1865 and was chief captain at Wallaroo until 1869. Like Hancock at Moonta, Dunstan immediately applied himself with vigour, ordering a vast array of materials and equipment from William West's foundry at St Blazey: kibbles, dialing [surveying] equipment, six jigging machines, four Cornish boilers, and 400 fathoms of whim [winding] chain.[58] However, an atmosphere of mutual antipathy had already grown up between Dunstan and Paul Roach. Although Roach, from Ludgvan, had already been at Wallaroo for several months, he was second captain and therefore subordinate to Dunstan, a position he resented. In February 1865, Roach complained to the Wallaroo directors about Dunstan's alleged bad management. Although the board agreed that the accusations 'were substantial' and that Dunstan had shown 'a certain degree of laxity', it ruled that Dunstan's behaviour was not serious enough to warrant censure or dismissal, and that Roach should take care to treat him 'with the deference due to his superior office'.[59]

In the following November, Roach and Dunstan were warned 'to act harmoniously together in order that the interests of the mine may not suffer through the disagreement of two of its chief officers'.[60] Several months passed without further trouble, but in early 1867 James Harvey, manager of the smelting works at Port Wallaroo, accused Dunstan of continually inaccurate assaying of the Wallaroo ores. This time the allegations were considered important enough to invite independent investigation, a task carried out by Captain Hancock of Moonta and Captain Thomas Bryant of Burra Burra. Dunstan was reprimanded but clearly did not learn his lesson: in February 1869 he was finally dismissed on account of his 'improper sampling of the Tributers's ores' which had resulted in a large loss to the company.[61]

Following Dunstan's summary dismissal, Captain Hancock was brought in from Moonta to provide temporary management of the Wallaroo mine. The Wallaroo directors, however, were not anxious for Hancock to stay. They wanted, they explained, 'a person of Education, and scientific as well as practical knowledge'.[62] Hancock, in their estimation, was none of these things: he was a rustic Devonian of humble origins, and largely self-tutored. The type of person they had in mind would be someone from one of the celebrated dynastic Cornish mining families, who would bring to Wallaroo great learning, exceptionally high standards and instant international prestige. They found just such a man in Captain Samuel Higgs, Jun., FGS, FGSC, Honorary Member of the Imperial Society of Arts and Sciences of Lyons, late Secretary to the Royal Geological Society of Cornwall. A member of the distinguished Penzance dynasty that had made its fortune from Wheal Providence and Wheal Margery, Higgs was a son-in-law – so it was reported breathlessly in the South Australian press – of Sir Humphry Davy, of miner's safety-lamp fame.[63] He seemed ideal.

Samuel Higgs arrived during 1870, and by 1872 was on a salary of £850 per annum. At first, the Wallaroo directors were delighted with their catch. However, as the decade wore on, they began to reflect that their mine was increasingly unprofitable, especially when compared with the apparently more dynamic Moonta mine almost next door. The relative inferiority of the Wallaroo ores was part of the explanation. But the directors felt, not without justification, that management played a major role in determining performance, and by now they were beginning to wish that they had secured the services of H.R.H. Accordingly, in April 1877 the board did the unthinkable: it wrote to Captain Samuel Higgs, requesting his resignation. As the board explained politely: 'The reason for this decision is that the Mines are at present working at a heavy loss and rather than close them altogether at once, the Directors wish to try if under other management more successful results can be obtained'.[64]

The door was opened for Henry Richard Hancock to extend his rule to Wallaroo, and now he really did seem to be omnipresent. The Wallaroo mine, for its part, appeared resigned to its subordinate role as a satellite of H.R.H.'s Moonta empire. As it happened, even Captain Hancock was unable fully to revitalize the mine, although there remained the feeling that Higgs had somehow ruined the Wallaroo workings. Hancock, with his emphasis on ore conservation, went underground to inspect recent operations. He exclaimed that 'Higgs ripped out everything'[65] of value, 'picking the eyes out of the mine' by ransacking all the high-grade ore when a more prudent policy would have been in order. Hancock reported that it would take twelve months of exploratory and developmental work to put the mine on a secure footing. Higgs, his reputation dented, found alternative employment with the fire brigade. Tragically, he died in 1879 when he fell from a horse.[66]

Doing 'the Hancock jig'

Hancock was now at the height of his powers. His appointment to Wallaroo was something of a personal moral victory, and he had also stood up to the Moonta directors – and won. The 1870s had been in many ways a formative decade (Hancock had also had to deal with the 'Great Strike' of 1874, as detailed in Chapter Four). But it was during that period that the 'Hancock jig' conundrum emerged: the veiled accusation that Hancock had claimed as his own – and patented for his own benefit – an important technical innovation made by his subordinates.

As the Moonta mines had expanded rapidly and had become more capital-intensive and productive, so more sophisticated and efficient ways of processing the ores were sought. Mechanical 'jigs' had existed in Cornwall as ore-dressing devices for generations but at Moonta there was a new mood of experimentation and improvement. Captain William Arundel Paynter was one of the innovators, and it is said that he had 'invented' – or at least developed – the basic structure of what would later be patented as 'the Hancock jig'. As Mandie Robinson explained: 'Paynter, ... a conscientious man, painstakingly perfected and patented a mechanical jig'. This, however, was 'the cause of some heart-ache later when Henry [Hancock] added his own modification and patented the Hancock Jig, his chief claim to fame in the international metal-mining world'.[67] Hancock had introduced several important refinements to this machine, as Robinson observed, and so it would be unfair to imagine that he had merely 'stolen' Paynter's original design.

Nonetheless, Hancock did patent the jig as his own in 1871, and it was known thereafter as simply 'the Hancock jig'. Paynter did not contest the patent, 'at any rate publicly', and, the jig's provenance now seemingly unambiguous, his own contribution to its development rather disappeared from view thereafter.[68] Hancock grew rich on the royalties of the jig – in 1900 it was said that he was earning £5,000 a year – and his reputation grew accordingly. *The Wallaroo and Moonta Mines*, a pamphlet published in 1914, explained that 'The Hancock jig ... is the invention of Mr H.R. Hancock. It has been the subject of a series of improvements and has not only been extensively used in Australia, but is now being widely adopted in America.'[69] The jig's principal advantage, it was added, was its 'immensely greater capacity' when compared to earlier appliances: a single machine could process up to 800 tons of ore in every twenty-four-hour period. Hence its world-wide popularity.[70]

Captain Paynter appeared not to be disappointed by this turn of events. Given the hint of rivalry that had existed between him and Hancock years before at Wheal Ellen, this was perhaps surprising. But maybe Paynter subscribed to Oswald Pryor's resigned view of such things, where the 'local Trevithicks' developed new ideas and Captain Hancock patented them as his own. Pryor recorded a Cousin Jack yarn which later, in modified form, found its way into his book *Australia's Little Cornwall*. As told originally, it was about a 'Typical incident involving a fitter called John Hockin who was building a mechanical contraption. "Some funny old thing theece got there" remarked a miner, "Oo's idee ez 'ee?" "S'like this", replied the fitter, "if ee d'work, tez Cap'n 'Ancock's, and if 'ee doant, tez John 'Ockin's".[71]

But if Paynter did not mind, there were others who did. For there were those who saw in Hancock's jig not merely Paynter's innovations but those of other practical engineers active at Moonta. According to Tom Cowling, in an autobiographical note penned in 1922, the Hancock jig was a modified form of the 'Warren-May jigger' developed for use at Richman's plant at Moonta and further improved by the 'Cowling's plunger'.[72] All Hancock did, it was alleged, was to patent this device. The Cowling in question was Tom's father, Captain Thomas Cowling, originally from Baldhu in Cornwall, who on northern Yorke Peninsula worked first at the New Cornwall mine before moving on to Wheal Hughes. Warren was Captain John Warren, who had worked in Devon Great Consols before emigrating to South Australia, and who on the Peninsula managed the Paramatta and Hamley mines. He later became one of Broken Hill's great mine managers, at the Block 10 mine successfully developing with Frederick May a jig for the mechanical separation of sulphide ores. This was the May mentioned by Tom Cowling, the chief engineer at the Moonta mine.

It seems likely that Frederick May felt slighted by Hancock's patent, and thought that he should have had some recognition or reward for his role in the

18. Richman's plant, the Moonta mine, in 1908.

development and application of the Hancock jig. At any rate, in 1873 Frederick and his younger brother Alfred suddenly left Moonta to join James Martin's foundry at Gawler. They were looking for a fresh start in a new environment, perhaps as a result of continuing ill feeling over the jig controversy. James Martin, their new host, was a Cornishman (he hailed from Stithians) and he eagerly welcomed the May brothers and the mining engineering skills they brought with them. His business had developed rapidly as he manufactured mechanical devices to support the expansion of both the agricultural and mining frontiers in the colony. Later, the Mays developed their own highly successful foundry business, first at Gawler and then at Port Wallaroo.[73] But the Hancock issue continued to rankle, and a sense of continuing bitterness has come down to our own time. In a recent (2002) biographical note, the issue is dealt with with delicate diplomacy, allowing us to read between the lines. During Frederick May's time at Moonta, we are told, 'he worked on the concentration of ore by mechanical (instead of chemical) means. The automatic jig was first put into operation under May's direction.' Slightly more explicitly: 'Fred May was the archetypal "quiet achiever". He carried out many of his projects while in the employ of others, who therefore enjoyed the resulting fame and success.'[74]

When W.G. Spence, the Amalgamated Miners' Association leader, visited Moonta in 1889 to adjudicate in an industrial dispute between men and management (see pp. 126–7), he heard all sorts of stories about Captain Hancock – as well he might, for feelings were running high and the miners were in the mood for a fight. Some of the accusations were scandalous, and Spence quickly saw them for what they were: cheap attempts to blemish Hancock's record, based on hearsay. He had no hesitation in saying so, and 'Captain Hancock sent his second in command all the way to Kadina to thank us for clearing his name'.[75] Spence also found Hancock a reasonable man, and open to suggestions: Hancock asked 'our advice on a certain matter connected with the mine and the men. He honestly carried out our recommendation'.[76] But Spence was a tough trade union negotiator, and there was no question of Hancock pulling the wool over his eyes. He found 'In the detail of the Moonta trouble several instances ... of what will be found in all industries where men are not [properly] organised'.[77] For example, he alleged:

> We found in charge of pattern-making in the foundry a first-class tradesman working for 7s. per day. He was a very superior tradesman, with considerable genius for invention. He was of the type who take a keen interest in their work for work's sake, and but little in what they receive for it. Quiet and unassuming, and content with a living wage, his only ambition was to excel in the quality of his workmanship. At an exhibition in Adelaide the manager [Hancock] of the mine had been accorded great credit for a rock drill with improved jacket. The drill was the unacknowledged patent of a Victorian, and the improved jacket the invention of the workman paid 7s. per day, whilst his market price anywhere else was at the lowest 12s. per day.[78]

As Spence explained: 'Naturally, we made a good deal of this man's case, and ... it came under the notice of a big firm in Gawler, whose manager was waiting on the railway station at 6 o'clock in the morning to intercept us and offer the man 12s. to come to their firm'. In the end, the tradesman in question went not to Martin's or May's at Gawler but to a mine at Waukaringa, in the Far North of the colony, where he earned 'double the wages he had been paid at Moonta, and, of course, [was] more highly appreciated'.[79]

Spence had found Captain Hancock 'a rather nervous, elderly gentleman'[80] – hardly the usual stereotype – and there was a sense that, if not exactly losing his touch, Hancock after a quarter of a century in the job had lost sight of much of the detail. For example: 'We found grown-up young men working for 2s. 6d. to 4s. 6d. per day, and in more than one case they were married. Starting as boys, it was apparently forgotten by all concerned that they had grown older as time went on.' As Spence noted, 'As their producing power increased, so their share of wealth decreased'.[81] Such situations were often, as Spence acknowledged, the result of imperfect unionization. But at Moonta,

Spence intimated, there was now something surprisingly lackadaisical about aspects of Hancock's management style. Rather like the Moonta directors, who had admonished Hancock from time to time, Spence seemed to detect in Hancock a fixation on the bigger picture at the expense of scrutiny of detail, a preference for strategic thinking rather than mundane facts, a desire to constantly press forward instead of being detained by trifles.

This, in the end, may help to explain the 'Hancock jig' conundrum. Like Paynter and his generation of Cornish miners and engineers, Hancock appeared to see the development of machinery as an organic, evolutionary process. Improvements were made on an incremental basis, a result of trial and error and experience as well as innate skill and ingenuity, and their adoption and application – a critical part of the whole process – was sanctioned by the management. In this way, no one person took the credit for innovation, although responsibility for its application – and whether the machinery in question actually worked – rested firmly with the captain who had decided to adopt it. As Mandie Robinson has observed, 'as far as the Moonta mines were concerned, and apparently as far as Captain Hancock was concerned too, the Hancock Jig was merely an advance upon previous movable-sieve jigs'.[82] For Hancock, the detail of who might legitimately lay claim to have 'invented' the jig was far less important than the strategic aim of treating ore more efficiently – and therefore maximizing profit – by applying the improved machinery in timely fashion. Indeed, Hancock had not considered patenting the jig – another lapse in detailed thinking, perhaps – until prompted to do so by the board of directors, which worried that the Moonta company would be severely disadvantaged if a rival concern was to patent a similar device first. In this way, Hancock was prodded into belatedly patenting 'his' jig. The subsequent handsome remuneration and international reputation were, to that extent, quite unplanned and unexpected. But it was not surprising that some should have looked askance at the manner in which this had been achieved, nor that in a more professional (and democratic) age the 'local Trevithicks' were no longer content to be seen merely as lowly cogs in a developmental wheel.

'The promotion of social and moral welfare'

For all the weaknesses identified by Spence, Hancock was genuinely concerned for the well-being of his workforce and the local community; sometimes, in the opinion of the directors, excessively much so. Here again was the force of religious conviction, together with an affinity with the working-class mining men of Cornwall and West Devon which, for all his elevation as 'H.R.H.', Hancock never quite lost sight of or forgot. The inhabitants of the mineral lease settlements, especially, were seen by Hancock as 'his' people

— women as much as men, children as well as adults. It was a concern that was paternalistic rather than democratic, and Hancock as much as the directors would have seen the advantages of maintaining strict paternal control over the local community. For example, the conditions under which employees might be allowed to erect cottages on the leases had been carefully regularized. The mine company retained the right to refuse an individual's request to build, and could insist on the immediate departure from the leases of anyone who had caused their displeasure. But the directors also issued a general disclaimer: they would 'not acknowledge any claim upon them for any building erected on the mine'.[83] Should any difficulty arise from the erection of cottages on the leases, it was no business of theirs.

Hancock, however, was keen to develop a more proactive welfare policy at Moonta. When local representatives of Methodist denominations came to see him to request permission to build chapels on the mineral leases, Hancock was happy to oblige. As well as improving the moral climate of the locality, a 'respectability' much to the mine company's advantage, the erection of places of worship would also enrich the lives of local people and promote a sense of community. In April 1865 the Wesleyans were given the go-ahead to extend their chapel on Moonta Mines, and in the June a request from the Rev. James Trewin for permission to build a Bible Christian chapel was readily agreed to.[84] Hancock was also keen to found an Institute on the mine as a vehicle for mutual improvement. In November 1864 the directors wrote to Hancock to say that they were 'greatly pleased to hear of the good conduct of the Workmen, and they agree with you as to the advisability of adopting any reasonable measure for the promotion of the social and moral welfare of the men'. Accordingly, 'they approve of the proposed expenditure of £100 on a Reading Room Library'.[85] Hancock was concerned that this Institute be properly stocked with educational volumes, as in March 1871 when he spent £25 on reference books in geology, surveying, mechanics, mineralogy and mining, together with a new encyclopedia and dictionary.

Similarly, Hancock was anxious to support proposals for the opening of schools and the development of educational provision. In August 1865 Mrs Magill was given permission 'on the recommendation of Captain Hancock'[86] to erect a schoolroom on the mineral leases, and Miss Emma Matthews was given similar permission a year later. When Hancock suggested an evening school for boys employed on the mine, the directors expressed their 'warmest sympathy' for the idea and asked him to make the necessary arrangements. Half a dozen years later Hancock was insisting that no boy under fourteen years of age be employed on the mines unless he had attended day or night school at least three times a week. He also persuaded the board that it should pay for those boys who could not afford the fees.[87] When, in 1873, the Adelaide Parliament took steps to introduce universal education,

Captain Hancock addressed a meeting of 1,000 people at Fergusson's shaft. He admired, he said, 'the enlightened manner in which the inhabitants of Moonta and neighbourhood had rejoiced at the action of the Legislature in introducing measures to promote education in the colony'. Moreover, 'he was glad also that the people were readily signing memorials in favour of a free, compulsory and non-sectarian system'.[88]

Earlier, when Hancock had advocated the formation of a brass band at the mine, the directors voted £50 for the purpose, and Captain Mitchell was sent down to Adelaide to buy the necessary instruments. When a Youth Club was constructed on Moonta Mines, Hancock provided the labour free of charge. As in the larger mines in Cornwall, a 'club & doctor' fund had been established at Moonta, with medical treatment made available to anyone injured in the mine and financial assistance provided to those off work on account of illness or injury. Hancock also secured a deal in which, for an annual subscription of £10, the Moonta company was given access to the Adelaide Hospital for the treatment of its employees with more serious medical problems. When a miner named Tresise was badly injured in an underground accident in Bower's shaft, Hancock recommended the authorization of £25 to pay for an artificial leg for the unfortunate man.[89]

This was not just good industrial relations. It was also evidence of Hancock's humanity. Indeed, behind the public façade of 'H.R.H.' – the deference demanded of his men, the air of superior knowledge sometimes paraded before the directors – was a private humility. Hancock knew that he had to wield his considerable power wisely, and to recognize it limits, especially if the conflicts with which he was confronted were to be resolved satisfactorily. Each day he prayed privately for wisdom and humility. It was a prayer that he had written himself, and which he kept to himself:

> O gracious Lord, forgive my sin,
> My will into submission bring;
> Remove from me all guilt and stain,
> And every evil thought restrain.
>
> Through my redemption, free for all,
> Help me obey Thy loving call;
> From bondage grant me sweet release,
> Through faith in Thy abundant grace.
>
> O, help me always choose the right,
> And serve thee fully with my might,
> While seeking with humility,
> To lead the life of purity.

O, grant me richly of Thy love,
Prepare me for Thy home above,
And on mankind Thy grace bestow;
O, that the world Thy love may know.[90]

Hankering for Horrabridge

Captain Hancock's faith may well have assisted him in his work. It also helped him in his private life. In April 1866 he had married Sarah Annie Maynard, a Methodist who had lived in Yorkshire before emigrating to South Australia. Their first child – Henry Lipson Hancock, much later to succeed his father at Moonta and Wallaroo – was born on 5 March 1867. A second child, Leigh, was born in 1868, and a third, Annie Allen, in 1869. Alas, less than a year later their mother was dead, for the typhoid, no respecter of rank or station, that swept the mines periodically, had claimed the wife of Henry Richard Hancock. Sarah had died 'triumphantly', as Methodists were expected to do (see pp. 161–2), and there is no doubt that Hancock was sustained in this sudden and terrible loss by his religious faith.[91] He was also sustained by the handsome Loveday Maria Jolly, the buxom young daughter of his friend and ally, Captain Joseph Jolly. There is a story that as Sarah lay dying, she 'took Loveday Jolly's soft hand, placed it in Henry's, and whispered that she would like Loveday to be the mother of her children'.[92] Henry took Sarah's advice, and on 28 August 1872 Captain Hancock – the Devon dumpling – famously married a Cornishwoman, Loveday Jolly. Loveday did indeed become mother to Sarah's children; she also became mother to another ten of Henry's.

Henry and Loveday's progeny arrived in quick succession – almost indecent haste, some said – provoking a new round of smutty Cap'n 'Ancock jokes.[93] Hancock was certainly an ardent family man, as the evidence suggested. But his enthusiasm was not merely sexual. Although he sometimes ran his family as he ran the mines – Henry Lipson and Leigh were packed off to the Ballarat School of Mines as soon as they were of an age – there was also the sense that in his family life he sought an alternative existence: the privacy he was denied in his working environment, and the intimacy of his relationship with Loveday. To some extent, he had achieved this alternative being at his homestead at Nalyappa, outside of Moonta, and, later, at Cliff House on Moonta Bay. On his retirement from the mines in 1898 he purchased a further property, Ivymeade, in the foothills near Adelaide. But in 1907 he sold Nalyappa and announced that he was to return to Horrabridge. It was a mistake. Since leaving the district, almost all the mines had been abandoned, the heady days of the 1840s and 1850s a distant memory. Horrabridge had

19. Loveday Maria Hancock (née Jolly) in later middle age.

settled back into its village existence. There were some, of course, who remembered Henry Richard Hancock, the blacksmith's boy, but few could connect him with the superior, almost aristocratic, gentleman who had suddenly come to live in their midst. There was some friction with the locals: there were objections when H.R.H. replaced his parents' gravestones with more ostentatious memorials, and there was offence when he offered to fund the building of a new Wesleyan chapel entirely from his own pocket. In 1911 Henry and Loveday decided to return to South Australia, settling once more at Ivymeade.[94]

As Henry no doubt now realized, 'Cap'n 'Ancock' was a South Australian phenomenon. Despite his international reputation, he was in his native Devon no more than a retired colonial gentleman – and rather an insensitive one at that. In South Australia, by contrast, his name was everywhere associated with the mines that had made such a vital contribution to the State's economic development. He was seen not as a colonial upstart but as a man who, through hard work, determination and clean living, had risen from modest beginnings to the towering heights of personal success. He had made Moonta what it was, and Moonta had made him.

Sir John Langdon Bonython, the newspaper magnate of Cornish descent who was said then to be 'the power behind the throne' which had dominated several South Australian governments, had – like Hancock's hankering for Horrabridge – long nurtured the idea of retiring to his beloved Cornwall. But, unlike Hancock, he had accurately weighed the situation before making any decision. In the words of John McConnell Black, whose diaries are a shrewd commentary on Adelaide life in the early twentieth century, Bonython eventually 'concluded that it was better to be the most powerful personage in South Australia than to become a Cornish country gentleman'.[95] It was not merely a question of being a big fish in a small pond. Like Hancock, Bonython had acquired an international reputation of sorts. But it was a reputation that could only really be lived in South Australia where, again like Hancock, he had become a legend in his own lifetime.

'When men talk of the mining wealth of South Australia'

Henry Richard Hancock died on 14 January 1919, aged eighty-two, almost three decades after the amalgamation of Moonta and Wallaroo, and two decades since his retirement. Perhaps fortunately, he did not live to see the rapid demise of his mines thereafter. Under his stewardship, those mines had dominated the colony's mining scene, and had become major players on the international stage. As Anthony Trollope had observed as early as 1873: 'when men talk of the mining wealth of South Australia they allude to Wallaroo and Moonta'.[96]

During its independent existence, the Wallaroo mine had been at its most productive in the years 1866–75, before Hancock had taken over, in which time most of the easily accessible high-grade ore had been extracted. Hancock took control during 1877, when the mine was already making a loss, and it was not until 1880 that the mine was back in full production. But the Wallaroo mine remained an indifferent property thereafter, certainly in the remaining years before amalgamation. Profitability had fluctuated wildly, ranging from a surplus of £49,000 in 1872 to a loss of £45,000 in 1878. The average number of employees in the period before amalgamation had been 580; the greatest number was 1,003 in 1872, the lowest a mere 43 in 1878 when Hancock was striving to save the mine. The Wallaroo mine was a marginal concern after 1876 but it remained in production, if somewhat erratically, to help feed the voracious appetite of its hugely profitable smelting works at Port Wallaroo.

In those decades before amalgamation, the Moonta mine was consistently stronger than its Wallaroo counterpart, and dominated northern Yorke Peninsula. By 1875, when the copper-mining industry in Cornwall had all but disappeared, it was asserted that the Moonta mine in its short life thus far had already outstripped the performance of even the mightiest of the once-great Cornish copper mines. In the period October 1861 to July 1875, it was said, Moonta had raised 236,160 tons of ore, worth some £4,000,000. In Cornwall, Consolidated Mines had raised the comparable amount of 230,296 tons. But this had been over the forty-year period, from 1815 to 1856, and the value had been a 'mere' £2,893,482. Dolcoath, Tresavean, Fowey Consols, United Mines and other Cornish properties all similarly fell short of the Moonta performance. Even Devon Great Consols, whose astonishing rise Henry Richard Hancock had witnessed in his early days, had in the years 1844–56 managed to raise ore to the value of 'just' £1,402,807.[97]

Three years after the commencement of operations, the Moonta mine was employing 1,000 hands, a figure that had risen to a maximum of 1,700 by 1877. Thereafter, the total workforce declined, as did profitability, although the number of underground miners grew, as the ore became increasingly inaccessible and difficult to extract. The common problems facing both Moonta and Wallaroo led to their amalgamation in 1889–90, it being argued that the mines would be then better placed to benefit from economies of scale. Thereafter, the combined company initiated a 'bold and enterprising policy' of renewal, led initially by H.R.H. but pursued with single-minded vigour by his son and successor, H. Lipson Hancock, which paved the way for a new era of prosperity in the early twentieth century.

It had been the ingenuity and tenacity of Captain Henry Richard Hancock that had kept both mines, Moonta and Wallaroo, going during the lean years as well as those of plenty. As we have seen, Hancock was a complex man, some of whose failings and vulnerabilities were common knowledge in the public domain, and yet whose inner strengths, as well as desires, were often intensely private. To that extent he was an enigma. This prompted the gossip, tall stories and controversies that surrounded him, and sometimes forced people to take sides: 'for' or 'against'. During his time, the Moonta mine had become an institution – in South Australia, and internationally – and 'Cap'n 'Ancock' was likewise an institution in his own right. Hancock had acquired 'cult status' in mining circles at home and abroad, and had become integral to the making of Moonta's myth. He was seen as personification of the fame and glory of the Moonta mine: it was Captain Hancock's 'white cow'. But his independent-minded stubbornness and determination was also read as emblematic of Moonta folk as a whole, typical of that breed of people who stood apart from the rest of the colony's population. Cultivating an air of superiority that demanded due deference, Hancock had deliberately placed himself above 'ordinary' mortals. Yet he was indisputably a 'Moontaite' – his charismatic aura tied inextricably to people and place – the celebrated face and voice of what one commentator called 'your Australian Cornwall'. But, enigma to the last, this did not mean that he was Cornish – though he was certainly more than an honorary Cousin Jack, and had married a Cousin Jenny and fathered a string of children who were proud of their Cornish descent. He was, according to one who knew him well in later life, 'a benign, white bearded patriarch with an old-world courtesy, and I came to the conclusion that the numerous stories about him ... were myths. That he was a masterful man, there is no doubt.'[98]

CHAPTER FOUR

'Cornwall was never conquered yet'
Moonta's working-class heroes

In May 1873 an angry letter appeared in the pages of the *Yorke's Peninsula Advertiser*. Exasperated by the antics, as he saw them, of the recently formed 'Moonta Miners and Mechanics Association of South Australia', the letter's author announced that he – and no doubt other sensible like-minded people – 'would now seek refuge in some place where Cousin Jack has no existence'.[1] Opposition to the first signs of organized labour, in Australia or in Britain, was hardly rare among those who felt their interests threatened by this incipient trade unionism. To that extent, the letter was commonplace.

But what was distinctive and new was the identification of 'Cousin Jack' as the object of hostility. The point was, of course, that just as the Cornish dominated the locality as a whole, so now they had established a new institution – the Moonta Miners' Association, as it was generally known – through which to exercise their regional hegemony. From the first, this embryonic union was seen, by detractors and supporters alike, as quintessentially 'Cornish', part of the repertoire of Moonta's assertively Cornish institutions that moulded the cultural identity of northern Yorke Peninsula. It was an exclusivity and dominance that could sometimes alarm: 'as Britain is represented by England, Ireland, Scotland, and Wales', wrote one critic, 'I consider a mistake was made ... in forming the [Association] committee by selecting all Cornishmen'.[2]

The Association had been launched in November 1872, prompted in part by the arrival of radicalized emigrants from Cornwall who had witnessed the strikes of the mid-1860s and, more recently, the unrest over the 'five week month'. Founded upon 'the principles of Christian equity and charity',[3] the Association betrayed the Methodist – especially Bible Christian – allegiances of its activists, the practised eloquence of the local preachers making them natural leaders of men. At first unsure of its tactics, let alone its long-term strategic goals, the Association vacillated as it moved from one issue to the next. Some members complained about the high price of meat at the butchers, and wondered what the Association might do about it, while others argued for the creation of a co-operative store to be run in the interests of the miners and their families. Such was the level of interest in this suggestion that an article from the *West Briton* newspaper (published in Cornwall) on the subject was reprinted at length in the *Yorke's Peninsula Advertiser*.[4]

'And shall Trelawny die?'

Those who hoped for more aggressively militant industrial action were heartened by a brief strike at the Blinman mine, in the Far North of the colony, over the method of setting tribute pitches. There were those who saw the Association as the precursor of a fully fledged trade union movement.[5] As one miner wrote:

> We invite the young and old
>   To join our miners' band;
> Come and have your name enrolled,
>   And join us heart and hand.
>
> Cornwall was never conquered yet,
>   By men of mighty powers;
> And shall we all in silence sit
>   And show ourselves like cowards?
>
> We have the motto 'one and all';
>   This coat of arms is ours;
> Then let us rise both great and small
>   To carry out our endeavours.[6]

Behind the call for workers' solidarity was a pronounced Cornish consciousness. As well as the usual appeal to the Cornish motto – 'One and All', tailor-made for the aspirations of trade unionism – there was a yet more powerful expression of Cornish sentiment: the notion that 'Cornwall was never conquered yet'. Deeply engrained in the Cornish psyche, this belief reflected the wider sense that Cornwall was not really part of England. But it also enshrined a characteristic individualism and independence. This insisted that not only had Cornwall never been conquered – not by the Romans, the Anglo-Saxons, the Danes, the Normans, or indeed the English – but also that the Cornish were not about to give in now.

This was not a new thought. In 1646, as Cornwall was subdued by the Roundhead army in the Civil War, Hugh Peter had warned the Parliamentarian victors that 'there was a common muttering among [the Cornish] that their country was never conquered'.[7] Mark Stoyle reads this as evidence that the Cornish 'saw the Civil War as a fight between England and

Cornwall as much as a conflict between King and Parliament'.[8] But it also hinted at a more enduring intransigence, something that was observed eighty or so years later in the correspondence between the Cornish antiquaries William Borlase and Thomas Tonkin. In November 1730, Tonkin had written to Borlase about some ancient remains in Wendron parish that he took to be Roman. In his reply, Borlase warned Tonkin that this interpretation 'will incur the severe censure of some Antient Britons [Cornish] who value themselves above all things, like their brethren in Wales, upon their never having been overcome by the Romans'.[9] This remembrance the emigrant Cornish took to South Australia, surfacing, as we have seen, at Moonta in 1873. Almost forty years later, in February 1901, John Langdon Bonython voiced identical sentiments in an address to the Cornish Association in Adelaide. Over the centuries, he said, Britain had witnessed several waves of invaders: 'They conquered England, but they never conquered Cornwall (cheers)'.[10] Oswald Pryor thought the same, writing in the Moonta *People's Weekly* in 1954 that 'Cornwall boasts that it was never conquered and not without reason'.[11]

Other echoes from the conflicts of early modern Cornwall had been heard at Moonta as early as 1868. This was some years before the Association's foundation but was a time of uncertainty, when the international slump in copper prices that had almost obliterated Cornwall's copper-mining industry threatened redundancies and when legal disputes concerning the mine's ownership were dragging on. The unsettled miners, worried about their jobs, objected angrily: 'Here's five thousand Cornishmen will know the reason why'.[12] They were expressing a catch-cry that had emerged in Cornwall some 200 years before, when in 1689 James II had incarcerated Bishop Trelawny in the Tower on the grounds of 'seditious libel'. It was a defiant slogan that in the early nineteenth century Robert Stephen Hawker had formalized into a patriotic Cornish ballad, almost overnight transforming it into an unofficial Cornish national anthem. As shown elsewhere (see p. 58, p. 153, pp. 168–9), 'Trelawny', as the song was known popularly, was readily adopted by the overseas Cornish as a badge of separate ethnic identity, deployed at Moonta whenever a collective Cornish voice needed to make itself heard. In October 1873, for example, as the Moonta Miners' Association gained in confidence and the rumours of labour troubles rumbled on, the *Yorke's Peninsula Advertiser* thought it timely and politic to publish the ballad in its entirety. The message – and warning – was unmistakable:

> And have they fixed the where and when?
> And shall Trelawny die?
> Here's twenty thousand Cornishmen
> Will know the reason why! [13]

The budding Moonta trade unionists drew upon the cultural capital of 'Trelawny' and the powerful myth of unconquerable Cornwall. There was also the legacy of the recent strikes in Cornwall itself, and among those who had sworn to leave Cornwall rather than bow to the bosses' demands were several militants who had found their way to northern Yorke Peninsula, bringing with them their new ideas on collective action.[14] To this was added the experience of those Cornish miners who had participated in earlier strikes in South Australia itself: at Moonta and Wallaroo in 1864, and much earlier at Burra Burra in 1848.

The Burra strike

As Mel Davies has observed, the Burra strike was an early repudiation of the 'quietist' thesis (see Chapter One), and in the South Australian copper-mining industry it set an important precedent that would not be forgotten.[15] It was a strike that lasted, on and off, for a period of three months and involved a total of some 600 miners – mostly Cornish. The Burra Burra mine was managed on Cornish principles, including the 'Cost Book' system of shareholding and accounting, and the tribute and tutwork system of employment for underground miners. Such arrangements met with the general approval of the Cornish immigrants. In 1846, the Burra's first full year of operation, the *South Australian News* observed that miners in the colony 'are no longer satisfied to work on "owner's account" [a day labour form of tutwork] for less than 30s. per week, especially at any distance from town [Adelaide]'. Instead, the newspaper explained, 'the prevalent wish of this class is to be placed on "tribute" or "tutwork", which is natural enough when they know that some of their brethren are earning such splendid remuneration at the Burra Burra Mines'.[16] A few months later, the same newspaper could add that 'the Cornish system of "tutwork" and "tribute" ... will doubtless prevail' in South Australia's rapidly developing mining industry.[17]

When industrial conflict broke out at the Burra in 1848, the bone of contention was not the system of employment, with which the miners were well pleased, but rather the results of the assay analysis performed by the South Australian Mining Association (SAMA, which ran the mine) in determining the value of the tributers' ore. The value of a particular pitch (an area of the mine) was calculated by the comparison of three assays – those conducted by miners who had worked the pitch in the past or wished to in the future, that of Thomas Burr (then the mine superintendent), and that made by Mr Elphick (a chemist hired by SAMA). SAMA considered that Elphick's more conservative estimates were accurate, that Burr's were too liberal and invariably in the miners' favour, and that the tributers themselves – or rather their representative, James Hosken, who performed most of the assays on their behalf – generally made the assay results 'greater than they really were'.[18] The Cornish miners were incensed, and reacted angrily – especially to the insinuation that assays would be made more stringent in the future – by mixing their ores together and by striking. Embroidering their grievances, some of the miners added that SAMA had left their ore lying around for months before settling their accounts, and others complained at the level of bal-bill charges levied on the men for candles, powder and the Club & Doctor Fund.

The disturbance caused considerable alarm in the colony. The *Register* newspaper noted gravely that 1848 had been a year of European Revolution. SAMA meanwhile, in characteristic over-reaction, arranged for the despatch of a detachment of police troopers from Adelaide to keep the peace, though there was little violence at the Burra save for the pinning of blacklegs to wheelbarrows and their being carried shoulder high through the town – 'exposing them to the gaze and ridicule of 1800 laughing souls'.[19] Burr was dismissed by SAMA as a convenient scapegoat, and the tributers were persuaded to return to work. However, in an inept move, SAMA decided that it would now seek to reduce the wages of day-labourers. The tributers and tutworkmen again downed tools, in 'solid consideration' of their colleagues, and in a memorial presented to the Association demanded the restoration of existing rates of pay for all 'miners, labourers, carriers on the mine, whim boys, and ore-pickey boys'.[20] Among the signatories of the memorial were James Hosken, the miners' assayer, and the outspoken agitator Malachi Deeble from St Austell: the latter the same Malachi Deeble who later became Captain Hancock's right-hand man at Moonta and a virulent anti-trade unionist.

SAMA reacted, again characteristically, by offering at the next survey-day only seven tutwork bargains and fourteen tribute pitches (instead of the usual 70 or 80), with the direction that the other skilled miners would now have to toil as day-labourers should they wish to return to work. Cracks in the strike were appearing already. Some of the miners had, in any case, left for New Zealand (for the new copper mine on Kawau island) and SAMA's teamsters, who had struck in sympathy with the miners, had decided to return to work. Meanwhile, SAMA had drawn up a list of 'Obnoxious men'[21] (including Malachi Deeble) it would no longer employ in the mine, and it prepared to evict some of these (including James Hosken) from the cottages that it owned. In Adelaide there remained considerable sympathy for the strikers – 'here's Five Guineas for your cause my old friends Cousins Jackey',[22] wrote one supporter in the local press – but at the Burra economic necessity was forcing the miners back to work. By January 1849 it was all over. SAMA presented this outcome as a victory but in reality it had been shaken by the sustained opposition of the miners and the fact, as Davies put it, that 'Cornish miners refused to scab on fellow countrymen ... the directors ... underestimated the solidarity among the Cornish immigrants'.²³ Thereafter, there was a noticeable change in attitude, with SAMA far more ready to consult its skilled employees on a range of matters relating to the mine's management.

At Kapunda, another copper mine manned largely by the Cornish, the miners had demonstrated the 'proof of their unity in the common cause' by being prepared to send £100 or more to 'our brethren' at the Burra.²⁴ The implications were not lost on observers elsewhere in South Australia, one writing to the Adelaide press to express his view that 'one thing is certain, that to a great extent, a species of "Trade Union" has been established amongst the miners of several mines'.²⁵ In fact, this was hardly the case. The Cornish miners at the Burra had demonstrated their capacity for collective action – as had many in Cornwall during the food riots of the mid-1840s, the 'Hungry Forties', when they had forced 'fair prices' for wheat and bread at places such as Helston, Wadebridge and Callington.²⁶ Moreover, Cornish people elsewhere in the colony had expressed their sympathy for their fellow countrymen at the Burra. But none of this yet amounted to 'trade unionism' in the sense that the miners had embraced collective action as a prelude to permanent combination. It would be some years to come before the Cornish miners in South Australia sought to establish institutions through which to defend their interests and voice their aspirations. For the moment, they relied upon ethnic solidarity in the face of perceived injustice.

'The two tyrants'

The same was true at Moonta and Wallaroo in 1864. In the early months of that year there was growing dissatisfaction with the managerial regimes at the two mines. This unrest, combined with impatience at the delay in introducing tribute contracting, provoked northern Yorke Peninsula's first taste of industrial action.²⁷ The managerial regime was that of the Warmington brothers: William and Eneder – together with James, who in October 1862 had already lost his job as chief captain at Moonta as a result of his 'misconduct'.²⁸ The Warmingtons were mine captains with considerable experience in both Cornwall and America, and had been appointed to positions on the Yorke Peninsula mines in the early 1860s on the recommendation of Captain Henry Roach, chief captain of the Burra. But their sojourn on the Peninsula was not a happy one. They failed to win the confidence of their subordinates – not least by being slow in introducing Cornish methods of employment and remuneration – and their relationship with the mines' directors also was often tense.

James Warmington had been engaged by the Moonta mine proprietors in April 1862, on the not inconsiderable salary of £250 per annum, together with a rent-free house, free firewood, free water for domestic use, and a further

£25 for miscellaneous expenses. Two months later to the day, however, he resigned on 16 June on the grounds of 'ill-health'.[29] The stunned proprietors accepted the resignation reluctantly, only to be further surprised when just a few weeks later an apparently recovered James Warmington asked for his job back. The directors accepted the resignation's withdrawal but expressed their 'dissatisfaction at the inconsiderate way in which he [Warmington] has acted', and placed on record their disapproval of his 'hasty manner'.[30] But their trust had been dented, and less than three months later James was sacked and replaced by his brother William. The directors' minute book recorded that: 'Captain William Warmington had been appointed Chief Captain at the [Moonta] Mines in place of his brother James who had been discharged in consequence of misconduct'.[31] William, however, did not settle easily into his new post, and by May 1863 an atmosphere of hostility had grown up between William Warmington and Captain Osborne, recently brought out from Cornwall at great expense, a potentially explosive situation which the Moonta directors did their best to smooth over.[32]

Meanwhile, at the Wallaroo mine, Eneder Warmington was also in trouble. He had been offered a financial interest in mining claims elsewhere on northern Yorke Peninsula. Although persuading the Wallaroo directors that the claims were of little value, and not worth their investment, he had nonetheless acquired them himself. This was disloyalty on the grand scale, and at least one Wallaroo director threatened to resign from the board as a result of 'the impropriety of Captain Warmington's conduct'.[33] Warmington was advised that he should relinquish his holdings immediately, and if that he did not he would be dismissed. Needless to say, he did as he was told.

At the same time, there was widespread disquiet among the underground workers that neither William nor Eneder, despite their obvious Cornish credentials, had introduced the tribute system at their mines. As early as December 1862 the Adelaide *Register* had explained that Cornish miners, who had only recently left the Burra for the new enticements of Moonta and Wallaroo, were on their way back again as a result of the Peninsula mines' failure to introduce tribute contracting. 'A few of the miners at this place [Moonta] are returning to the Burra', the newspaper observed, 'and a great many who are practical miners urge that the tribute system should be introduced into the workings of the mines of the Peninsula'. Echoing more general criticism of the Warmingtons' regime, the same report concluded that if tributing was to be introduced, then the mines would become altogether more efficient: 'doubtless, in the case of the Moonta, hundreds of pounds would fall to the share of the men, [and] thousands would go to the proprietors more than the present yield would admit of'.[34]

A little more than twelve months later a contributor to the same newspaper could complain, in the unpleasant racist metaphor commonplace at the time,

20. Conditions underground in the Peninsula mines: Cornish miners emptying loads of ore into shaft ore bins, whence it gravitates into skips for haulage to surface.

that the unimaginative but bullying Warmingtons were capable of little more than 'nigger-driving'. Cornish aspirations were being ignored, it was claimed: 'An intending Cornish mining emigrant would, on looking at our public reports of mining, suppose that its miners were paid according to the mining usages of Cornwall. But have the lessees of Wallaroo and Moonta so paid their men? Yes and no.'[35] 'Yes', in that some short-term development work had been done on tutwork, but 'no' in that successful tutworkmen were soon moved on to work as day-labourers, and – most especially – because not one tribute pitch had yet been offered. Not only were miners returning to the Burra but, in a more worrying development, they were, it was alleged, writing home to Cornwall to advise friends and relatives not to come out until such issues had been resolved. By early 1864, further miners were returning to Kooringa (the principal Burra township) from Moonta and Wallaroo. They were 'dissatisfied with the wages' and the treatment that they had received at the hands of the Warmingtons. Later, others 'returned disgusted' to the Burra from Moonta, protesting against 'the annoyances they had to suffer from the captain [Warmington], who was a short time ago one of themselves'.[36]

Things came to a head in March 1864 when miners at both Moonta and Wallaroo came out on strike. At the Wallaroo mine a group of timbermen had been instructed by Eneder Warmington to repair some shaft work over the Easter weekend, so that the shaft would be fit for haulage after the holiday break. Ephraim Major, a Cornish miner who witnessed the turn of events, explained what happened next: 'the men refused to do it, and when they returned to work on Tuesday there was a notice on the dry [changing room] door to the effect that the [eighteen] men who had refused to repair the shaft would be fined'. An impromptu meeting was held: 'they decided to petition the directors to dismiss the manager, they then formed in a line and marched to Moonta Mines'.[37] The Wallaroo men reasoned that the workers at the larger Moonta mine would be equally keen to plot the demise of their equally unpopular chief captain, and that acting in concert the Wallaroo and Moonta miners would together present the proprietors with an ultimatum they could not refuse. The Moonta men readily agreed. A strike committee was formed, with one of the Moonta contingent, Richard Collingwood Kitto, appointed chairman. Mr Knowles, another Moontaite, was appointed to draw up a memorial calling for the Warmingtons' dismissal.

Thereafter, the Moonta and Wallaroo men met regularly, holding 'monster meetings'[38] – as they were dubbed in the press – at Bald Hill, a locality between Moonta and Wallaroo Mines, which were attended by upwards of 300 miners. As well as demanding that the Warmingtons be expelled, they called for a general rise in levels of pay and for the introduction of the tribute system. Feelings ran high as new grievances were added to the list. The Warmingtons were condemned as 'two tyrants',[39] and William was accused of savagely flogging a young lad. At Moonta, as attitudes against the Warmingtons hardened, there was some intimidation. Outside of William Warmington's office, the men kept themselves amused by beating tattoos on empty kerosene drums and firing pistol shots into the air. The local sergeant of police asked Warmington if he needed protection: 'Mr Warmington replied that the Cornish people were law abiding and would do no harm to him or the mine'.[40]

'Captain Warmington could write, but very little'

His calculation was broadly correct, for the strike had by now acquired a strong moral and religious dimension, and the Bald Hill meetings concluded each time with hymns and prayers. Among the leaders was Reuben Gill, a Bible Christian local preacher. Later to become a ringleader of the 1874 strike, he had cut his teeth a decade earlier in the Warmington affair, when he had proved both an effective negotiator (he and Collingwood Kitto met with the Moonta directors to discuss grievances) and a skilful orator. He was a favourite speaker at Bald Hill: 'Mr Gill's style of speaking was extraordinary. Jumping upon the platform as though propelled there by a catapult, he would jerk his head from side to side, and instantly let loose his eloquence at a tremendous rate.'⁴¹ He also had a moderating effect on the men, it was said. According to one observer: 'In his advocacy of the working-men's claims, though very zealous, he was much more moderate than others who took part in the proceedings'. Indeed:

> when the miners were wrought up to take extreme measures, Reuben, by his good-natured addresses and jocular remarks, caused them to be less unreasonable in their demands. He was a good tempered and earnest speaker. His rough eloquence would fall from his lips in rapid stream, and apt metaphor and racy contemporaneous rhyme follow each other with lightning-like rapidity, while the attention of his audience would remain enchained throughout his speech.⁴²

Reuben Gill and the other strike leaders also took their grievances to Adelaide, holding public meetings at which the Warmingtons' inadequacies were described – 'Mr Tresize said Captain [William] Warmington could write, but very little' – and at which they sought support from the capital's citizens. Generally, the miners were well received, and they won an important political ally when James Penn Boucaut, a local Member of Parliament, and a Cornishman, expressed his 'entire sympathy' with the miners, an opinion that was greeted with 'loud cheers'.⁴³ Back on Yorke Peninsula, the strikers lobbied the local business community, which stood to lose much if there was an extended strike, and the merchants and storekeepers of Moonta and Kadina duly submitted their own memorial to the mine proprietors, supporting the miners in their cause.

Meanwhile, the Moonta and Wallaroo directors had not been inactive. They thought the miners' demands unacceptable, and although they resisted the temptation to sack the ringleaders, they determined to ease them out quietly when once the difficulty was resolved. They also tried – without success – to recruit strike-breakers from mines elsewhere in the colony, and – anticipating a lengthy dispute – decided to acquire a new batch of miners direct from Cornwall. Accordingly, the Moonta directors wrote to their agents in London, instructing them 'to send to Cornwall ... for fifty men to be brought out under the Assisted Passage Regulations of the Government'.⁴⁴ The directors also let it be known that they had full confidence in their managers, and would not admit any complaints against them. But public opinion had already turned against the Warmingtons, and soon the directors began to relent, their first concession being an agreement to inquire into the conduct of the two brothers. Then suddenly Eneder Warmington announced his resignation. This was due, in part, to ill-health (he died a few weeks later, poor man, from stomach cancer) but the jubilant miners saw it as an admission of guilt. Sensing victory, the Wallaroo men indicated their willingness to return to work. The demise of Eneder having diffused the situation considerably, the Moonta men thought that it was only a matter of time before William would be forced out too, and also decided to return to work – under the temporary management of Captain Matthew East, who had been seconded from the New Cornwall mine, near Kadina. At the same time, Collingwood Kitto was appointed captain at the nearby Yelta mine; 'probably to keep him out of the way'.[45]

As the Moonta men had calculated, William Warmington's position was now untenable. In the face of considerable public hostility, on Yorke Peninsula but also in Adelaide, and under investigation by the mine company, his opponents were no longer confined to the ranks of the striking miners. He had, he felt, little choice but to tender his resignation. The Moonta directors thought it wise to accept, the company secretary writing to William Warmington to explain that 'although they [the directors] believe that you have served there [Moonta] faithfully and to the best of your ability, they have reluctantly come to the conclusion that it would be expedient to accept the resignation which you have placed in their hands'.[46] The next day – 28 June 1864, some three months since the trouble first broke out – Warmington was given one month's pay in lieu of notice, together with an *ex gratia* payment equivalent to three months' salary. Salving their collective conscience, the Moonta directors thought they had 'dealt liberally with him.'[47]

The Moonta miners thought that Warmington had been humiliated, and had got his just desserts, and with their Wallaroo colleagues planned a major celebration at Bald Hill.[48] They were also delighted when the directors, following the recommendations of two Cornish mine captains – Captain Prisk of Kanmantoo and Captain Trestrail of Magill (near Adelaide) – who had been engaged to sound out the mood of the miners, announced the extension of tutwork contracting and the introduction of tributing.[49] At the Wallaroo mine, a similar decision was made. By February 1865, the mine was offering 72 tribute pitches and 107 tutwork contracts at survey-day, with the expectation that the number of tributing pitches would increase in future. In December 1866, the Wallaroo directors paid for Captain John Tredinnick to come out from the mighty North Downs copper mine in Cornwall to take charge of underground contracting. Recommended by his brother-in-law, Captain Dunstan, who was already in the Wallaroo mine's employ, Tredinnick was said to be 'especially conversant with Tribute work'.[50]

The initial reluctance to adopt tutwork and tribute is difficult to explain – especially in the light of their apparent popularity at Burra Burra and their general adoption at other mines in the colony: including the Wandilta, near Kadina, on its opening in 1861.[51] It may have been simply, as the strikers had averred, that the Warmingtons saw their priority as maximising profits during the early developmental stages at Moonta and Wallaroo. One tactic to help achieve this would be to keep wages as low as possible through the use of day-labour – even for underground work. If this was their aim, then it had failed spectacularly, for the Warmingtons had not reckoned with Cornish aspirations and the expectations in a colony already steeped in Cornish mining practice. Writing years later, Oswald Pryor observed that the Warmingtons 'were good, practical miners but not over tactful'.[52] Ephraim Major, who had witnessed the events of 1864, thought that 'Captain Eneder Warmington was a very conscientious man and liked a fair days work for a fair pay'.[53] But whatever their simple qualities, the Warmingtons had proved indifferent managers, failing, despite their own Cornish credentials, to understand the motivations of their workforce. Both men were desperately ill with cancer, so perhaps their failure was inevitable. The Moonta and Wallaroo directors realized all this but slowly. Yet when, however reluctantly, they had accepted the Warmingtons' resignations, they had paved the way for a new regime at Moonta and Wallaroo. This involved the consolidation of tribute and tutwork contracting at both mines, together with a programme of vigorous expansion, and opened the door – first at Moonta, and later at Wallaroo too – for the reign of Captain Henry Richard Hancock.

'The present depressed state of the copper market'

For the miners, this represented a considerable victory. They had secured the Warmingtons' departure and had successfully demanded their preferred system of employment and remuneration. The mines were also about to embark on a period of development, with the attendant prosperity that this appeared to imply: as early as August 1864, for example, Captain Hancock had announced his attention of recruiting a further 200 or 300 Cornish miners – from Cornwall itself or from neighbouring Victoria.[54] It was for these reasons, perhaps, that the rapid growth of Moonta and Wallaroo after 1864 was not punctuated by continuing industrial action of any major consequence. It was not until a decade later, in 1874, that the mines were again brought to a standstill by striking workers. But that is not to say that there were not periods of uncertainty, tension and even conflict.

The downturn in international copper prices in the mid-1860s had deleterious effects in South Australia, as it did elsewhere, and these jitters were felt at Moonta and Wallaroo. In August 1864, only a few weeks after the Warmington crisis had been resolved, there was talk of forming an Anti-butchers Association to tackle the high price of meat locally. This smacked of incipient trade unionism, and in the October the Moonta directors were worried that the men might 'fully persist in going on with this Union'.[55] In August 1865 the Wallaroo miners submitted a memorial calling for a Saturday

21. Conditions underground: a 'telescope' rock drill in use in a stope (underground cavity), situated near either Young's or Taylor's shafts, Wallaroo mine, c.1914.

half-holiday; but by then the low copper prices were beginning to bite. Instead, there was to be a general lowering of wage rates at both mines. At Moonta a notice was posted to the effect 'that in the present depressed state of the Copper market the Directors find it necessary to reduce the rate of Wages on the Moonta Mines from and after 1st October next'.[56] The miners countered immediately with a memorial demanding higher tribute rates. But the wind was taken out of their sails when it was announced that the new team of captains – all recommended by Captain Hancock – appointed at Moonta to manage the proposed expansion plan had agreed to lower salaries than had been promised originally. The directors had 'been reluctantly compelled to adopt this step in consequence of the low price of copper',[57] they said, and the men felt that they had little option other than to follow the example of their captains. A potential crisis had been averted.

However, the price of copper did not improve. Two years later considerable distress was reported among the 'labouring classes' at Moonta, a result of the continued low levels of remuneration, and a movement of miners to Victoria and Queensland in search of higher wages was noted.[58] Events took a turn for the worse when an anonymous notice threatening Captain Hancock with physical violence was posted at the mines, and in August 1867 the miners met to compose a memorial to the Moonta directors insisting upon improved levels of pay. Inevitably, the directors refused to accede, explaining that 'The price of copper is now lower than it has been for many years; and in consequence of the existing depression numerous mines (amongst these the Burra Mine) have recently been closed'. There was also the less than veiled threat that the miners' demands might damage the interests of their colleagues at neighbouring Wallaroo: 'Any advance of wages now must have the immediate effect of closing The Wallaroo Mines, upon the working of which so large a body of Workmen depend for their daily bread and for the maintenance of their Wives and families'. Indeed, 'if the Directors had consulted only their own interests they would long ago have largely reduced the number of hands employed at Moonta'. Moreover, they 'would have brought the operations at the Wallaroo Mines to such a point as must, in the present circumstances of this Colony, have entailed great distress upon the Mining populations of Yorkes Peninsula'. Not only that, but the 'average payment at last "Take" at Moonta was Tutworkmen 35/– to Tributers 42/– ... these rates are better than wages paid at other Mines in the Colony'. And, 'Flour and meat are unusually cheap'.[59]

The Moonta directors also explained that the low copper prices were largely a result of competition from Chile, something they were powerless to respond to, and on a more conciliatory note assured the miners that they would 'always be ready to listen to reasonable suggestions of their Workmen on any subject'. However, they added, 'the good feeling which ought to exist between employers and employed is only weakened by threats of violence by recourse to which no good result can under any circumstances be obtained'.[60] The directors had snatched the moral high ground. The bewildered workers – who did not know that the directors had been greatly alarmed by the leaching of miners to Victoria and Peak Downs, fearing a shortage of skilled labour – dropped their demands: 'the threatened strike may be considered at an end'.[61] Skilfully, meanwhile, Captain Hancock had sought the approval and continued loyalty of the workforce by re-engaging Reuben Gill, who had found work elsewhere on the Peninsula after 1864, taking him on as an underground miner at Moonta. There was a sense of reconciliation in the face of perceived mutual adversity.

However, there was another small reduction in wages in 1870, and in 1872 Reuben Gill annoyed the directors by suggesting in a letter to the Adelaide *Register* that they had unduly influenced the casting of votes in recent elections for the colonial Parliament.[62] But by the end of 1871 the worst of the price slump was over, ushering in a renewed period of prosperity at Moonta and Wallaroo that would last until 1874. The Cornish miners reflected that, broadly speaking, they had got what they desired: a large and generally prosperous copper mining field, worked by Cornish hands according to Cornish practice – including the much prized tribute and tutwork system that they had fought so hard to achieve – with a corresponding social, cultural and religious life that was also reassuringly 'Cornish'. Moonta's myth, in the active making during the preceding decade, was already maturing, Moonta and environs having become (in the estimation of one newspaper report) 'like villages from Cousin Jack's country dropped in South Australia'.[63]

'One and All, stick to it, my men'

A civic sense of place had already developed. In April 1872 a public meeting at the Moonta Institute advocated the formation a Moonta Corporation, a desire for municipal local self-government that was emulated soon after by both Kadina and (Port) Wallaroo. A few weeks later and the locality's sights had been raised even higher, another meeting at the Moonta Institute resolving to petition the Adelaide Parliament for a separate constituency to represent the 'mining interests' of northern Yorke Peninsula. These demonstrations of collective civic will brought swift results. The Corporations of Moonta and Kadina were proclaimed in early August 1872, and in the October the electoral district of Wallaroo was created: the much anticipated 'mining' constituency in which the region would be directly represented in the colonial Parliament for the first time.[64]

These democratic developments were not lost on the working people of northern Yorke Peninsula. It was in the spirit of these civic advances that a meeting was held in the Globe Hotel at Moonta in October 1872, attended by some 70 miners, to discuss the possible formation of a Moonta Miners' and Mechanics' Association.[65] A few weeks later, as we have seen, the Association was born. One of its early duties was to elect the Moonta mine's new bal-surgeon (mine doctor) in December 1872, a responsibility devolved to the

Association by the directors, though soon reclaimed when they realised that they had unwittingly legitimized the embryonic trade union. But they need not have worried yet, for the process of legitimization in the community would inevitably take time. At the 'ring meeting' held for the election, for example, one miner objected that 'he would sooner be attended by an old dear Cornish woman than by doctors (Hear, hear)'[66] – a prejudice that represented at least in part a grassroots suspicion of the Association's alleged desire to manage peoples' lives and intrude upon their privacy.

Nonetheless, little by little the Association won the workers' confidence. John Visick, originally from Kea in Cornwall, a Wallaroo miner, was appointed President of the Moonta Miners' Association in March 1873 – a deliberate attempt by the Moonta men to open their organization to others within the wider Peninsula but also to ensure that Moonta remained the centre of trade unionism as the movement developed. Likewise attracted was John Prisk, recently a beam-engine driver at the Bingo mine (near Kadina), who though a Bible Christian was invited in the April, in the spirit of interdenominational solidarity that characterised the current mood, to preach at the Moonta Wesleyan Anniversary.[67] Twelve months after the Association's launch, it was apparent that the organization was beginning to exercise considerable influence on the Peninsula, a cautionary note in the *Yorke's Peninsula Advertiser* in December 1873 warning unwary locals where all this might lead. It recalled the 'damaging effects' of the 1864 strike, and of recent strikes in Britain and America, and – in a direct reference to the new Association – opined that 'Hitherto our isolation alone has prevented us from experiencing, except indirectly, the baneful and demoralising influences of these impolitic movements'. A few days later, a lengthy report in the same newspaper on the recent 'Camborne riots' back in Cornwall served to emphasize the dangers of 'impolitic', hasty and violent action.[68]

Perhaps the *Yorke's Peninsula Advertiser* had sensed a change of mood in the locality; the prevalence of infant disease at Moonta Mines that year, especially diphtheria, had taken its toll, and a more sombre atmosphere was everywhere apparent. To this was added renewed financial difficulty at the mines, notice of which was served perfunctorily when, without prior warning, the Moonta directors announced on the morning of 2 April 1874 an immediate reduction of pay levels. There was a simultaneous announcement at the Wallaroo mine. In scenes reminiscent of a decade before, over the next few days hundreds of miners converged regularly on Bald Hill to hear the latest news. At Moonta a 'ring meeting' of some 1200 men had already agreed to strike – Reuben Gill had 'mounted the buggy amidst vociferous cheering'[69] – a decision that was delivered gravely to the board of directors by Captain Hancock. The strikers' action was swift. The women had promised 'to do their best with their mallee poles' – brooms made from

22. The Moonta and Wallaroo delegates – an alliance of trade unionists and local business and civic leaders – who successfully represented the miners' case to the Moonta and Wallaroo companies during the 'Great Strike' of 1874.

sticks of mallee scrub – and in their famous action at Moonta swept the blacklegs from the engine-houses, bringing the pump engines to a halt. As the *Yorke's Peninsula Advertiser* put it:

> The women went vigorously to work with their brooms, charging in all directions ... The females attached to the sweeping regiment numbered about a hundred strong ... carrying, many of them, brooms, poles and pine branches. Never before, perhaps, was such an extraordinary spectacle witnessed as here presented itself. The space between Bower's and Ryan's [shafts], an area covering acres of ground, was alive with people of all classes, miners, mechanics, tradesmen and travellers, boys and girls, women (some with children in arms) excitedly talking, shouting, laughing and hurrying towards the engine house.[70]

News travelled fast. At the Wallaroo mine, despite the desperate pleas of Captain Higgs that no-one should take actions 'for which they would suffer to their dying day', engine-men were similarly driven from their posts by enraged women. They marched first on the nearby Matta Matta mine, whose engine-house was nearest the 'meeting ring' at Matta Flat, ejecting the drivers, firemen and boiler-tenders, and then proceeded one by one to the other pump engines in the area. At one engine-house a driver was threatened that he would have his 'brains knocked out', his hat sent flying by a mallee broom, and at another one of the women was reportedly wrestled to the floor by the cornered engine-man.[71]

Events were unfolding rapidly, and John Prisk, chairman of the hastily convened Strike Committee, thought it politic to approach the Moonta directors to request a meeting. The directors declined, considering that the men (and women) had gone beyond 'the legitimate course of striking' in 'forcibly stopping the engines [and] expelling the Mechanics from the Workshops'.[72] The confrontation seemed insoluble. Another 'monster meeting' at Bald Hill – attended, it was said, by some 5,000 people, a 'grand sight' – signalled its determination to defeat the directors, the brass bands thundering out the strains of 'Cheer Boys, Cheer!'.[73] Addressing the striking miners, their Primitive Methodist minister urged them to: 'One and All, stick to it my men; you have principle and right on your side and angels look down upon you men who are longing to do right'. Be fearless, he said: 'The God of nations will defend you, trust in God; nothing will harm you, you will come out on the right side presently. God bless you!'[74]

However, at the same time that the men were being reassured that God was on their side, so their leaders were marshalling support elsewhere. As in 1864, they ensured that the local business community lobbied the mine directors in their favour. They also took their demands to Adelaide – winning the approval, as they had done in 1864, of the prominent politician, James Penn Boucaut – where the directors had at last agreed to meet them.[75] Distinctly rattled, the Moonta directors, who had taken the precaution of securing from the colonial government the promise of military support to protect life and property should the strike drag on, capitulated in the face of what they saw as unbreakable solidarity. Sheepishly, they announced that 'In deference to a generally expressed opinion that the Miners were taken by surprise by the absence of previous Notice of the intended reduction in wages, the Directors will pay the late rate for the next two months, after which, unless the price of Ore should improve, a reduction will take place'.[76] The latter was an important caveat. But the strikers' delegates – John Prisk, Thomas Rodda, John Anthony, J. Uren, John Visick and Martin Edwards, Cornishmen all – returned to the Peninsula in triumph, the cheering crowds at Bald Hill welcoming them home as the bands played 'See the Conquering Hero Comes', the celebratory bonfires lighting up the night sky from Moonta Mines to Port Wallaroo.

The men had begun to return to work at Moonta on 20 April 1874. But Captain Hancock reported dissatisfaction with the rates offered at next survey day, and he was handed a note by John Prisk in which the Moonta Miners' Association demanded that in future one month's notice should be given for any planned reduction in wages. The directors retorted angrily that they would give only a fortnight's notice.[77] It was a predictable exchange but it highlighted the situation as it now stood: an embryonic trade union, the Moonta Miners' Association, determined to capitalize on its recent advances, and a beleaguered board of directors anxious to reassert its authority. The scene was set for a new era of industrial relations in the copper mines of northern Yorke Peninsula.

'United in the grand old Cornish motto'

To begin with, the 'Great Strike', as it was now known, was already passing into local lore, the ringleaders elevated to the status of superheroes: another strand of the Moonta myth was in the making. An epic poem was written in the strike's aftermath to commemorate and immortalize the struggle, its melodramatic style adding further lustre to the legend. Full of classical allusions to Achilles, Priam and the Amazons, this lengthy work explained how 'Bold Cousin Jack, with skilful hand/Soon cleared the scrub from off the land/King Copper lost his virgin crown/And soon a shaft was driven down'. Further meandering doggerel described the vicissitudes of life on the Peninsula in the early days of European settlement, and how the wicked Warmingtons had been deposed back in 1864. But the greatest eulogizing was reserved for the heroes of 1874:

And soon they met at Elder's Shaft;
The 'Ring' was form'd, the glor'ous ring,
Where Cousin Jack stands like a king;
And freely to each thought gives vent,
As to his brain each thought is sent,
In eloquence, that's all his own,
He thunders forth in manly tone;
States his opinions quick and clear,
Nor will he yield to force or fear,
Nor will he back from anything
He states when standing in the 'Ring'.[78]

Hand-in-hand with the romanticization of the 'Great Strike' was the new attitudes it had created. In the early days of the strike, the miners were at pains to make clear their continued deference: 'We have not anything against our Managers or Captains (hear, hear) but on the contrary we respect them'.[79] Yet the mood altered swiftly. One observer was surprised to note 'the threatening attitude of the Cousin Jacks lately', and at one 'ring meeting' at Moonta Mr Tonkin – an enthusiastic striker who hoped now to perpetuate the atmosphere of confrontation – proposed that 'men will not work again under Captains Hancock and Deeble'. The motion was defeated (Hancock and Deeble were tougher nuts to crack than the Warmingtons, as the miners well knew) but the hostility was genuine. At another meeting one miner had ventured that 'Sometime since in a parish of Devonshire there was an old cripple' – an allusion to Captain Hancock that was immediately recognized by the others, amidst hoots of laughter and great cheering.[80]

On another occasion, Hancock and Deeble were accused of being un-Christian and irreligious (though some of the men thought this going too far) and John Prisk was alleged to have said that 'The best news I have for you is that Mr Higgs [Captain of Wallaroo mine] is spitting up blood'. Hancock was, Prisk said, 'Warmington No. 2'. By 1879 the Association's attitude to the captains in general, and Hancock in particular, had hardened to the extent that John Prisk could claim that if 'Captain Hancock knew how much the men spoke against him ... he would be ashamed to look the men in the face'. The Moonta captains would be long remembered, he said, for their 'dirty tricks and new-fangled schemes'.[81]

Integral to the new attitudes was the desire to professionalize the Moonta Miners' Association and to further its influence and prestige. Although even in 1878 one frustrated trade unionist could complain that 'a portion of the [Association] members have been aiming to make the Union a mere Co-operative store affair' – and that 'Cornish men do not understand the true principles of Unionism and never will during the present generation' – the miners became active and organized in way that they had not been before.[82] For those who needed persuading, there was always the appeal to Cornish patriotism. At a 'ring meeting' held soon after the strike to discuss ways of projecting trade unionism, for example, John Anthony reminded colleagues that their influence had already been felt as far away as the colonial capital. 'The people of Adelaide were united with them', he said, 'in the grand old Cornish motto "One and All"': and this was something to nurture and build upon.[83] As another unionist put it:

> Tell me not, ye horrid grumblers,
> That unity's an idle dream;
> If we firmly stand united,
> We are stronger than we seem.
>
> Let us all, then, be united,
> Be our motto – 'ONE AND ALL',
> Firm as rocks when bound together,
> But divided, down we fall.[84]

J. McArthur was appointed secretary of the Moonta Miners' Association in May 1874. His view was that, given the recent upheaval, there could be no better opportunity 'for the establishment of an union on a firm basis ... it was necessary that they would do so if they would resist tyranny and oppression'. An anonymous letter had already appeared in the press, 'urging immediate steps ... be taken to form a trades Union embracing the whole of the Peninsula having Moonta for its centre'. Such an opinion reflected Moonta's by now well-developed sense of place, a 'superiority' that had been evident before the strike when the Association had taken care to co-opt John Visick, leader of the Wallaroo miners. But now, having played their own role in the Great Strike, the Wallaroo miners wished to form their own Association. The Moonta men had little choice but to acquiesce, though John Visick was visibly angry when it was insisted by the Moonta Miners' Association that its rules should be adopted by the new Wallaroo organization. Reuben Gill pleaded with the two groups not to squabble; the bosses would take advantage – they would 'analyse, tantalise, scandalise and pulverise them if they could'.[85]

'I contemn and despise mere money shoddy aristocracy'

Such fallings out were not always easily resolved as the fledgling union movement on the Peninsula struggled to organize itself and motivate its members. McArthur, looking for political support elsewhere in South Australia, turned for guidance to James Penn Boucaut, the Adelaide politician who had spoken up for the miners in their strikes of 1864 and 1874. Born at Mylor in Cornwall in 1831, and educated at Saltash, Boucaut was, according to one contemporary commentary, a 'proud son of Cornwall ... [as] he has more than once boasted ... on public occasions'. He came to South Australia when still a youth but not before he had 'received those delightful impressions found in quaint legend and hoary tradition so dear to the heart of every true Cornishman'.[86] Although an Anglican, he was at pains 'to express my sympathy towards the Nonconformist churches, partly from my own natural feelings and greatly from old family associations'.[87] His sentimental aim in life was to return to Cornwall to become a Radical MP at Westminster but it was not to be: perhaps just as well, for when he visited his homeland in 1892 he was saddened as he travelled through 'miles of mining country with the mines deserted ... giving a melancholy tinge to the country'. As he reflected: 'Australia and America, with their richer mines, have beaten poor old Cornwall, which now seeks amends by growing vegetables for the Londoners'.[88]

It was in South Australia that Boucaut built his career, becoming Premier of the colony and, eventually, a Supreme Court Judge. He was knighted in 1898. He first entered the Adelaide Parliament in 1861, gaining invaluable support during the campaign from the working-class Political Association – the latter an early indication of an emerging labour consciousness – and having won his seat formed an immediate personal alliance with another Radical member, Philip Santo from Saltash in Cornwall, whom he considered a 'liberal nonconformist'.[89] Santo was also a political ally of James Crabb Verco, originally from Callington in Cornwall, the two men enjoying parliamentary reputations in the 1860s as 'great lovers of political and religious freedom'.[90] In the fluidity of the Adelaide Parliament, before the emergence of clear party politics, Boucaut was a natural partner in such a grouping. He went on to become Premier of South Australia in 1866–67, a position he was to hold twice again during the 1870s, and among his achievements in the latter period was a bold plan to roll back the agricultural frontier of the colony, facilitated by a network of new railways to penetrate the far-flung country districts, and the introduction in 1875 of universal secular state education.[91]

Boucaut was at the zenith of his powers in the mid-1870s when McArthur first wrote to him. Boucaut explained to the miners' leader: 'I have always stood by my counties motto "One and All" and contemn and despise mere money shoddy aristocracy'. He had, he said, been persuaded to enter politics by 'friends who knew my democratic sympathies'. He was himself a 'Cousin Jackey' – as he wrote proudly to his sons, encouraging them to remember their Cornish inheritance – and he impressed upon McArthur that: 'I wish you to believe that I do not profess liberal sentiments in order to gain power. I should have far more power if I were to hold contrary sentiments'. His political opponents had branded him a 'Red Republican'. Boucaut countered that: 'I have been accused of setting class against class. That is absurd. Class was against class long before I came into the world. Such an accusation is a very common thunderbolt launched by capital.' But he had never heard of capitalism setting class against class, he told McArthur: 'This is because capital is true to itself while labour is too often true neither to itself nor to its friends who become marks for sneering until few men have courage left to face it'. Yet times were changing: 'A great struggle between capital and labour is commencing all over the world. Labour was once enslaved. It now demands liberation, and that labour shall no longer be considered as so much animal clay.' For the future: 'There is no reason why the man whose industry makes the article should not look forward to the time when he will be on a perfect equality in every respect with the man whose capital aids him in doing so.'[92]

Responding to McArthur's call for guidance, Boucaut explained that 'I differ from those who think the Union should be dissociated from politics'. But he criticized the Moonta Miners' Association because it exercised its power 'in fits and starts which is bad both for the country and yourselves'. Moreover, the Association 'had no settled principles and no cohesion'. He urged the Cornishmen not to be divided by sectarian feeling: 'if a Wesleyan vote against a Bible Christian because he is of a rival Church both suffer'. He also advised the Moonta unionists to forge links with like-minded groups in Adelaide, recognizing that organized labour in the colony needed to co-ordinate its efforts if it was to maximize its potential. His principal recommendations were that the Association should concentrate on the political education of its members, so that in argument and debate they would be able to compete on equal terms with their capitalist adversaries, and on the achievement of payment of parliamentary members. As soon as Members of Parliament received a salary for their parliamentary duties – rather than performing without financial reward, as they did at present – it would be possible for labour candidates without private means to stand and be elected. As Boucaut concluded: 'everything comes back to payment of members and education. These are your two great necessities.'[93]

'The iron heel the Hancocks had for the Unionists'

All this was good advice. But at the same moment that McArthur saw his opportunity to put the Moonta Miners' Association on a more professional footing, so the directors thought to stifle the emerging trade union before it could entrench itself more fully in the life of the Peninsula. They were encouraged by press reports critical of the miners, some of which had adopted a distinctly anti-Cornish tone. References to 'Cousin Jack's childishness' and 'despised Cousin Jack' indicated that the Association had not monopolized public opinion, and there was also the insinuation that the Cornish – being Celtic, like the Irish – were incapable of managing themselves in a measured or responsible manner. One newspaper correspondent observed loftily that, 'about 1900 years ago', a 'clever man' had written *'at sunt Gallorum subita et repetina constitia'*. In 1874, the correspondent added, this could be rendered freely as '"the councils of Cousin Jack are hasty and sudden". The Galli were Celtic,' he noted, 'and Cousin Jack is their lineal descendant.'[94]

This identification of the Moonta Miners' Association as an essentially 'Cornish' movement encouraged the directors to seek ways of undermining the miners' ethnic solidarity. The Wesleyans were seen sometimes as belonging to 'the bosses' chapel' – Captain Hancock was a Wesleyan Methodist, as was Captain Christopher Faull – and this distinction was unobtrusively but firmly encouraged, so much so that an exasperated McArthur warned his members against religion getting 'mixed up with copper and wages'.[95] There was also an attempt to recruit workers of other than 'Cornish nationality', and in early 1875 the directors had decided to try to find Scottish and Irish miners. At the same time, they sought to erode the predominance of the Cornish by reducing the number of tribute pitches and tutwork bargains offered on survey day – a strategy that would also allow them to get rid of 'undesirable' characters and to achieve the savings that they had hoped earlier to make through wage reductions.[96]

As early as June 1874, in the immediate aftermath of the strike, Captain Hancock had told the directors that he could easily discharge 200 'or more' men at Moonta, 'without damaging the Mine to any parlous extent'. A week later and Hancock was having second thoughts, reporting that achieving such an extensive cutback would be difficult, and that to dismiss any of the 50 miners regarded as Association ringleaders (one of the aims of the discharge) would provoke a strike. A month later, and the directors were complaining to Hancock that 'the number thrown out of employment is only 15 as yet'. Accordingly, at next survey day some 50 or 60 miners were dismissed. Hancock reported nervously that 'great excitement and anxiety prevailed at the Mine', with John Prisk asserting that the discharges were done to create dissension in the Association ranks. At the Wallaroo mine, where there were similar cutbacks, the directors rejected similar accusations put to them by the miners' representatives, David Edyvean and Stephen Spargo: 'they most distinctly repudiate the allegation that they have been in any way instigated by motives or feelings of retaliation'.[97] At both Moonta and Wallaroo, the captains bore the brunt of the miners' complaints. Hancock, especially, was increasingly the focus of the workers' ire: years later Stanley Whitford, a Labor politician brought up at Moonta, could still write of 'the iron heal the Hancocks had for Unionists'.[98] As a precaution, the directors had notices posted at Moonta, pointing out that the sackings were not Captain Hancock's fault but were a consequence of the current economic situation.

The rumblings continued, and Hancock decided that 'certain leaders of the Union will never settle down contentedly to work as long as they remain at the Mine'. The directors agreed the 'advisability of getting rid of rowdy characters', adding that they would 'not retain in their service men who attempt to interfere with the Management of the Mine'. Accordingly, Messrs Tonkin (who had expressed explicit hostility to Hancock and Deeble), Sleep and the ironically named Strike were immediately dismissed. Soon Hancock could also report 'that the better class of Men were withdrawing from the Union'.[99] One of these was J. McArthur, author of the correspondence with James Penn Boucaut, who had been discharged from the Moonta but had written a pleading letter to the directors 'requesting to be reinstated in the Company's employ as a Miner'. He considered, he said, that he 'had committed a grave mistake in joining the Union and had therefore determined to shake free of it'.[100] The directors were happy to re-employ McArthur as an example to the rest of them. Reuben Gill condemned him as a 'Judas' and a 'traitor'.[101] But Gill was another of those eased out eventually by Hancock and the Moonta directors. He found employment for a time at the Hamley mine, an independent working near Moonta, but ended his days in Adelaide – first as a mechanic, and then trying to sell insurance.

'And eke he was a Citizen/Of famous Moonta town'

Despite the dismissals and the defections, the Moonta Miners' Association was determined to make progress. It aimed to achieve a 'closed shop' at the mines – full unionization of the workforce – and, in the manner advocated by Boucaut, began to formulate a clear political strategy. Remembering Boucaut's exhortations, it sought free and compulsory education for all and demanded the payment of Parliamentary members. Betraying its Methodist leanings, the Association called for a prohibitory liquor law. It also called for an end to immigration, an attempt to control the supply of labour and thus achieve high wages, despite the misgivings of those members who were loath to see the door closed on friends and relatives from Cornwall. Significantly, the Association lobbied for land laws to be liberalized, anticipating the opening up of northern Yorke Peninsula for agricultural purposes and staking a claim for those miners who might wish to turn to farming.[102]

Although payment for members was still only an aspiration, there was much debate as to who might best represent the miners in parliament. Earlier, at Burra Burra and Kapunda, the Cornish miners had aligned themselves with the Political Association, which demanded payment of members and freedom of speech and the press, believing 'that the happiness and well-being of the mass is paramount to the aggrandizement of the few'.[103] It had lent is support to politicians such as Boucaut, who was invited to stand for Burra Burra in 1868. Similarly, at Kapunda in 1862, John 'Mochatoona' Rowe, nicknamed after a mineral discovery in the colony's Far North, was elected 'largely owing to a solid miners' vote'. Born in St Agnes, Cornwall, in 1816, Rowe was said to be 'a tolerably good speaker and deeply versed in Scriptural history'. He was also in favour of 'reimbursement or remuneration of members', and argued that 'Yorke's Peninsula must be developed by the poor man, Yudnamutana [in the Far North] was discovered by a poor man'; his point being that while mines were found generally by humble prospectors, the profits from their development invariably went into the pockets of wealthy capitalists.[104]

This was a political inheritance of which the Moonta Miners' Association was well aware. It was also alive to a wider Cornish radical tradition, the 'Liberal–Nonconformist nexus', that had come to play an increasingly important part in the political life of Cornwall itself – especially after the Great Reform Act of 1832. This was a political culture, rooted in Cornwall and honed in South Australia, that helped mould the attitudes and activities of the Moonta trade unionists as they developed their own political strategy. At the end of 1874, indeed, there was talk of the Association selecting its own candidate for election to the Adelaide Parliament. John Prisk let it be known that he would be happy for his name to go forward, a suggestion which immediately divided the Association into his supporters and detractors. Prisk was, as one anonymous local poet acknowledged, a man of some standing in the community:

> John Prisk, the Union President
> Of credit and renown,
> And eke he was a Citizen
> Of famous Moonta town.

Certainly, there would be those happy to support his elevation to parliament:

> Then up jumped Reuben Gill,
> And he stanked on the floor
> To send John Prisk to Parliament
> He'd beg from door to door.
>
> And Brother Strike would do the same,
> (Bold Rodda cried 'hear, hear')
> The Union would support the cause,
> Of that there was no fear.

Yet others were not so keen:

> Then up jumped bold John Anthony,
> And he swore by his word
> To send John Prisk to Parliament
> Was really quite absurd.
>
> Then there were words of fierce debate,
> And voices loud and high,
> Till 'Junius' moved for peace's sake
> Adjournment *sine die*.[105]

The verses were an amusing insight, perhaps, into the petty politicking and jostling for position characteristic of such organizations. But they also reflected deeper animosities and wider structural difficulties. John Visick blamed Prisk's Moonta-centric stance, with his desire to subsume the Wallaroo miners, for the still-birth of the proposed sister body: 'through his mismanagement the Kadina Union is defunct'.[106] Plainly, the Moonta Miners' Association was not yet mature or sophisticated enough to begin to adopt its own candidates, and it settled down – as had the erstwhile Political Association – to lobbying and vetting other candidates. In February 1875, for example, the Association declared 'in favour of Mr Richards', because he supported Boucaut's railway scheme, defended the mining interest, advocated payment of members, and was in general agreement with the principles of trade unionism.[107] The fact that John Richards was Cornish, born in Helston in 1843, was also important: a mine captain who had contributed to both the Adelaide *Register* and London *Mining Journal* on mining matters. He was elected a member for Wallaroo in 1875 but stepped down in 1878. Similarly, the Association supported William Henry Beaglehole, born in Helston in 1834, who was a local member from 1881 to 1887.

Two years later, in 1889, the Moonta Miners' Association, by now firmly entrenched in Peninsula life, joined the Amalgamated Miners Association of Australia (the AMA), a continent-wide trade union based in Victoria. Sister branches were established at Kadina (for the Wallaroo mine workers) and at Port Wallaroo for those employed in the smelting works there. These were significant developments that reflected both the maturing of trade unionism on Yorke Peninsula and the wider consolidation of the labour movement across Australia. It was not only the miners who were organizing. A 'United Trades and Labour Council' (UTLC) had been formed in Adelaide in 1884, and new unions were emerging while others were becoming better organized and more vocal. The strike of the 400-strong Bootmakers' Union in South Australia in 1885 demonstrated a new spirit of militancy – interestingly, its ringleaders bore the Cornish surnames Trenwith, Tregilgas and Hosking – while the rise of Broken Hill just across the New South Wales border in the 1880s gave Australia a new and vigorous centre of trade unionism.[108]

One result of this new mood was the birth in 1891 of the United Labor Party in South Australia, the brainchild of the UTLC. Instead of merely supporting sympathetic candidates, as the Moonta miners had done, the aim now was to launch a party organization capable of nurturing its own parliamentary candidates, and of contesting and winning elections. The achievement in 1890 of the much sought after 'payment of members' suddenly made all this seem possible. On Yorke Peninsula, the several branches of the AMA responded by sponsoring Richard 'Dickie' Hooper as their own Independent Labor candidate in a by-election in the Wallaroo constituency in May 1891. Born in Cornwall in 1846, Hooper was a past President of the Moonta branch of the AMA. In the election, he topped the poll, winning more than twice the number of votes cast for his nearest rival, in the process becoming the first Labor member of the Adelaide Parliament.[109] His victory heralded the growth of the United Labor Party (ULP) as a force in South Australian politics, and paved the way (see Chapter Six) for the Premiership in 1910–12 of John Verran – the Cornish-born Moonta miner and Primitive Methodist local preacher who had made his way, via Presidency of the Moonta AMA, to election for the seat of Wallaroo and (ultimately) leadership of the ULP.

'Labor is brought below a nominal figure'

All that, however, remained in the future. For the moment – despite the euphoria of Hooper's election – the AMA faced considerable difficulty in its relationship with the Moonta and Wallaroo directors. In the aftermath of the 1874 'Great Strike', as we have seen, the local trade unionists had weathered a period of confrontation – in which ringleaders were sacked, eased out or persuaded to repudiate their colleagues – which had led to a general hardening of attitudes. One result of this was that the sense of partnership evident in the 1860s, following the departure of the Warmingtons, in which the proudly 'independent' tributer could justly claim entrepreneurial status alongside the directors and shareholders, had diminished considerably. The miners felt increasingly that, for all their much-prized skills as hard-rock miners, they had been reduced in the directors' estimations to little more than labourers. The method of remuneration – tribute and tutwork contracting – had likewise, they argued, shifted from being a means by which the enterprising miner might earn a more than decent living, to the mechanism by which the bosses were able to keep wages artificially low. In a remarkable reversal of the position generally adopted by Cornish miners in the early days of copper mining in the colony, the Peninsula trade unionists were now arguing for the abolition – or at least radical restructuring – of the tribute and tutwork system.

In fact, there had been some criticism of the system as early as the 1860s, voiced in the *Wallaroo Times* and other local newspapers.[110] But these were grumblings about the way contracts were set rather than hostility to tribute and tutwork. After 1874 these criticisms became more frequent – including discontent over the 'five week month' adhered to by the directors in determining pay periods. Moreover, attacks on the system itself became more common. Although, as in Cornwall, a tributer working an apparently indifferent piece of ground on a favourable contract might suddenly uncover a 'sturt' – a hugely rich ore deposit – and thus make a considerable amount of money during that particular 'take' (contract period), the reality was that the disadvantages of the system were as prevalent in South Australia as they were at home. In 1865, for example, the Moonta directors had been forced to dismiss two tributers for stealing ore, while just weeks later a further group was dismissed for the same offence. And the system did not improve with age: in 1889, for example, two tutworkmen – Simmons and Trebilcock – were suspended for six months for failing to adequately timber their workings. They were, of course, responsible for purchasing and supplying their own materials, and in an effort to save money were skimping and cutting corners.[111]

In 1879 came the first major signs of discontent with the system, voiced by the trade unionists. Largely in response to this pressure, the Moonta and Wallaroo companies replaced 'open bidding' – in which groups ('pares') of miners competed openly for tribute pitches or tutwork bargains – with 'private tendering'. This new method required miners to tender for their preferred work by submitting their offers on pieces of paper. Although this reduced the overt competitiveness – and sometimes outright hostility – between pares as they fought to secure a particular contract, it did not really address the unionists' grievances. As one observer wrote knowingly in April 1880:

> Cornishmen are generally of an envious disposition, the characteristic principle being a dislike to see a neighbour advance a step ahead, and so with tendering. I have heard a remark passed when a miner has heard another is tendering for the same job. 'Ef 'ee d'get un 'ell have tew tender some law', hence they all tender low and labor is brought below a nominal figure.[112]

Others began to agree. One 'old miner, what do belong to Cornwall' wrote to complain that tribute and tutwork were 'good for the company, but not so good for the workman'. Another considered that 'The fact is we miners cut each other, hence we bring down the price of labor, and it is to be feared that our price is often far below the captain's price [the guide price for a particular pitch or bargain, set by the relevant underground captain], which is cutting wages with a vengeance'.[113] There was a brief strike in protest at the system in 1884, and in 1886 there was further trouble following the abolition of 'subsist' – an advance of earnings – for long-term contracts (the latter had been introduced in 1877, and could span several months). 'Subsist' was now replaced by a 'percentage retained' policy. Instead of applying for subsist when their funds ran low, the miners were now paid a weekly rate – the amount being calculated as a weekly average of the estimated total earnings over the contract period. However, a percentage of this weekly rate was retained by the companies in case the miners did not realize their estimated earnings, the retained money being paid out on the expiry of the contract. By March 1888 the percentage retained had reached 25 per cent, and the miners – considering this unacceptably high – came out on strike. The directors agreed to reduce the percentage retained to 12.5 per cent but the men did not return to work until Captain Hancock had also promised a general increase in the weekly rate. Later it was also decided, in deference to union pressure, that a percentage would only be retained if average weekly earnings were above £2 2s. 0d. per week.[114]

By this time, however, the miners had become heartily sick of the whole principle of contracting. In February 1889 a memorial was submitted to the Moonta company demanding the abolition of the system, the miners insisting that 'we have borne with the evils too long already for the comfort of our homes and our own peace of mind'.[115] When this was rejected, a more moderate proposal was submitted by Messrs Peters, Pascoe and Rowe, 'requesting the Board's assent to a list of rules dealing with underground contracts'.[116] The directors were again unmoved, setting the stage for several years of hostility and conflict. During 1889, as we have seen, the Moonta Miners' Association became a branch of the Australia-wide AMA, with similar branches established at Kadina and Port Wallaroo. The mood of the moment was 'unity is strength', and as W.G. Spence recalled in his book *Australia's Awakening*:

> The Cornish miner is generally a man who can do his share of grumbling, and frequently reckons he knows how to run a mine better than the manager, so when Unionism caught on they realised that many injustices might have been remedied years ago had they been organised and pulled together, instead of merely growling as individuals.[117]

With growing tensions at Moonta and Wallaroo in 1889, a strike seemed inevitable. The Moonta directors having refused any changes in the system of employment, and the Wallaroo company having announced a general lowering of wage rates, the Peninsula AMA branches had little choice to but to threaten industrial action. The men stopped work on 13 May but to try to smooth the situation AMA representatives from Victoria – W.G. Spence among them – travelled to the Peninsula. Their suggested 'sliding scale' of wages – to be related to the price of copper, and replacing contracting – was rejected by the companies but they were successful in winning a number of concessions for the miners. They were also allowed to inspect the companies' accounts to satisfy themselves that the present economic situation would allow neither a rise in wages nor a major upheaval in the system of employment. The AMA representatives explained this to the striking miners, who grudgingly returned to work.

However, 'Nothing ... could convince the Primitive Methodist radicals that the Moonta mine was now working at a loss'[118] and the agitation continued, with local union personalities such as 'Uncle Joe' Goldsworthy, John Prisk (hero of 1874) and Jimmy Peters (the Moonta Branch secretary) calling for a renewal of the strike. During July and August of 1889 they demanded further concessions from the companies, and in the December there was a brief but successful strike by moulders and fitters demanding 'closed shop' conditions. In the following February, the union forced the directors to honour their 'percentage retained' agreement, as the antagonisms continued into 1890. Finally, in March of that year, 500 men at the Wallaroo mine struck – without official sanction from AMA headquarters – and stayed out until winning yet further concessions from the newly amalgamated Wallaroo and Moonta company. But the basic grievance – the system of employment – had not been addressed. There were further negotiations in July and August 1891 but little progress was made. Accordingly, in the September, the Moonta Branch of the AMA declared a strike, the stoppage soon spreading across the Peninsula.[119]

The Primitive Methodist minister told the miners he could see 'victory' in their eyes but the strike was characterized by the extreme hardship it caused. As much as £8,507 was sent to the Peninsula – by sympathetic miners at Broken Hill, Bendigo and Charters Towers, and by UTLC colleagues in Adelaide – but still the AMA found it difficult to maintain its strike payments. Eventually, after eighteen gruelling weeks, the strike was broken by desperate miners going to the mine office to apply for work. The AMA conceded defeat, and in return the company promised what it termed 'substantial modifications' to the employment system.[120] The unfortunate men whose desperation had caused the strike to collapse were ostracised by the local community and branded '92ers' – the strike ended in February 1892 – a prejorative label which they carried and were known by wherever they went; even on the

Western Australian goldfields, where many Moontaites went to try their luck in the 1890s.[121] And despite the defeat, agitation against tribute and tutwork continued throughout the 1890s. In March 1895, for example, one militant unionist tried to rally the miners to the cause: 'Cornishmen, my advice to you is to be true to each other; and let your motto be "One and All" ... let the spirit of your fathers animate you on to freedom and justice.'[122] Partly in response to this continuing unrest, numerous adjustments were made to the letting of contracts. The most significant was in 1903 when the time-honoured practice of 'captain's prices' was replaced by a 'sliding scale' – based on changes in the price of copper – in which the contractor participated directly in the company's profits.[123] Ironically, this had been what the AMA representatives had recommended back in 1889.

Towards Federation – maintaining the myth

The miners' union at Moonta and Wallaroo survived the trauma of 1891–92. It became even more firmly entrenched in the life of the Peninsula community, aligning itself closely with the local United Labor Party – setting the stage for John Verran's Premiership in 1910–12 – and maintaining its intimate links with local Methodism, especially the Primitive Methodists. This, like the frequent appeals to 'One and All', was evidence of the continuing influence of the Cornish background, although – despite the union's overtly 'Cornish' reputation in South Australia – the experience on Yorke Peninsula had by now diverged significantly from that in Cornwall. Moreover, as John Prisk had intended, Moonta had established itself as the focal point of trade union activity on the Peninsula, assuming a leadership role which survived the formation of the Kadina branch of the AMA and the amalgamation of the two mining companies in 1898.

Significantly, despite the growth in hostility to tribute and tutwork contracting, the Peninsula miners retained their proud sense of self as 'independent' and 'individualistic'. In the press and in poetry such as Shelley's 'Great Strike', they had been elevated to the status of working–class heroes, an essential ingredient of which was their ethnic identity as Cousin Jacks. To this was added the developed sense of place – with Moonta at its heart – complementing separate identity. Distance from Adelaide, the colonial capital and focus of metropolitan trade unionism, reinforced this feeling of being apart. Despite their supposed close links with the UTLC in Adelaide, the Peninsula miners were in fact far more intimately aligned with AMA branches elsewhere in Australia, not least at Broken Hill, just over the New South Wales border, where many Moonta and Wallaroo men had gone to find work in the 1880s. In the same way, just as Yorke Peninsula had ostensibly led the way in the foundation and growth of the United Labor Party, in fact the local party was completely autonomous of the metropolitan organization. Its formal status was that of 'ally' of the ULP proper.[124]

This institutional independence slipped easily into independence of action. In the debate that preceded the Federation of the Australian colonies in 1901, for example, the Peninsula miners adopted their own strategy – in direct opposition to the official policy of the Labor movement in Adelaide. The Labor position was that Federation was not in the interests of the working class. The proposed Federal Senate was dismissed as 'undemocratic', while the additional tier of government made necessary by Federation would mean – it was asserted – an increase in taxation. South Australian manufacture would be hit, it was argued, by the removal of inter-colonial tariffs, while the lucrative Broken Hill trade – so important to South Australia – would be siphoned off by New South Wales. None of this impressed the Peninsula miners. They believed firmly that inter-colonial free trade – a fundamental principle of Federation – would be a dramatic boost to the region's copper industry. In the Federation referendum in 1898, the Peninsula voted accordingly, producing an overwhelming endorsement of the Federation Bill.[125] In distant Adelaide, ULP and UTLC officials shook their heads in disbelief: as ever, Moonta and environs were going their own way. But they did things differently up at Moonta, it was admitted, a certain puzzlement and dismay tempered by the knowledge that Moonta remained a place apart: 'where class and regional interests clashed, the latter triumphed'.[126]

CHAPTER FIVE

'Moonta toil and Moonta gain'
Women, Methodists and the triumph over adversity

>Com'st thou here from distant country?
>　　Over land and over sea?
>There beneath the Moonta minings
>　　Subterranean wealth you see.
>
>From far countries strangers share in
>　　Moonta toil and Moonta gain;
>And full often bless the moment,
>　　When they crossed the raging main.
>
>True it is from Mines of Moonta,
>　　World-wide wealth has oft been given;
>And from caverns dark and dismal
>　　Many a soul has passed to Heaven.
>
>Should then rich ones look complacent
>　　On those Mines of Moonta name,
>Poor may justly share the triumph,
>　　Which combined they both can claim.[1]

These lines, penned by Thomas Burtt and published in a small booklet in 1885 entitled *Moonta Musings in Rhythmic Rhyme by a Moonta-ite*, are stanzas drawn from the poem 'The Solemn Moonta Mines'. A thoughtful, melancholic composition, written by Burtt after several years absence from the district, it was, he said, a reflection inspired by the 'dirge-like sound and muffled reverberations' of the machinery as he wandered through the mines site at night. He invited his readers to 'Listen to the ceaseless throbbing,/Of those engines measured slow;/Telling many a weary spirit/How it shares a world of woe'. These readers would hear, he insisted, how 'Almost awful sounds the beating/Of those iron strokes and sounds;/Far and near the tale repeating,/ This our life with toil abounds'.

Here was sadness, tinged with resignation and even regret, and yet there was also pride – pride in achievement, in endurance, and in human triumph over adversity in an alien environment – as well as a profound appreciation of the awesome might of the mines themselves. For Burtt, a self-confessed 'Moonta-ite', these were the roots of personal identity. But, as his poem suggested, here too were the roots of a wider community consciousness. Pride, as Burtt made plain, was something that all could share in, irrespective of their social station, for it was the ordinary people, many of whom had travelled from half a world away, who had made Moonta what it was. For the Cornish, backbone of the labour force in the mines, this was further reinforcement of an already fierce identity, and over time Cornwall itself gave way to Moonta and this singular environment as the object of Cousin Jack allegiance. Indeed, stoicism in the face of the rigours and vicissitudes of the frontier was part of Cousin Jack's myth. Moonta provided just such a frontier, a harsh unforgiving landscape in which the emigrant Cornish could make their mark, stamping their transnational identity upon the locality and creating a community of which – as 'Moontaites' – they could be justly proud.

'The desert country where squatters were ruined'

Although, by Australian standards, Yorke Peninsula was no great distance from the colonial capital, it was nonetheless remote, difficult country, and remained so in the popular imagination long after Moonta, Port Wallaroo and Kadina had been proclaimed as settlements. It was the land of shipwrecks; and on occasions horrifying stories would filter through to Adelaide of emigrant vessels thrown up by wild seas onto uninhabited shores – as in 1840 when the *Marion*, from Plymouth, came to grief on a lonely stretch of Peninsula coastline.[2] In those early days Yorke Peninsula was also the land of bushrangers, or so people liked to think, and there were stories of desperate bands of escaped Tasmanian convicts on the loose, the rough uncultivated expanses of mallee scrub affording them almost impenetrable hiding places. Parts of the Peninsula had been leased as pastoral properties, which involved no land 'improvement' but allowed the lessees to graze their sheep and other stock in the wilderness. It was on one such 'run' – leased by one John Bowden, a Cornishman as it happened – that a group of convict outlaws was thought to be operating in 1848. Inspector Alexander Tolmer, a colourful figure in early Adelaide society, tracked the convicts to their camp on Bowden's run. But when Tolmer requested his assistance in carrying out the necessary arrests, Bowden 'demurred, making several paltry excuses' and would not co-operate until Tolmer had been 'compelled to impress him in the Queen's name'.[3] Such happenings were the stuff of Adelaide gossip, and in 1853 John Bowden was again the subject of whispering and innuendo when he was sued (successfully) for £960 damages in the Supreme Court over a breach of agreement concerning the sale of 4,000 sheep. Disillusioned, Bowden abandoned the Peninsula for good.

Yorke Peninsula was thought then to be so forbidding and so lacking in infrastructural support (as indeed it was), that when discoveries of copper were made there in 1847 – at the height of South Australia's 'coppermania' – the deposits were considered unworthy of development. In 1848 two celebrated local mining authorities – Francis Dutton, co-discoverer and part owner of the Kapunda mine, and Captain Richard Rodda, a well-known Cornish mine manager – visited the area, and decided that Yorke Peninsula was too remote and underdeveloped to warrant exploitation of its mineral resources.[4] Even after the significant discoveries of 1859–61, the district was slow to lose its fearsome reputation. Captain Dunstan's wife refused to join him at Wallaroo Mines: 'a whim rope wouldn't be strong enough to draw her'[5] from Cornwall to the Peninsula, he said. Another early critic thought Yorke Peninsula 'the place where there's neither water, grass nor trees – only scrub, interminable, horrible, dwarf scrub, maintaining an incessant struggle for existence in the parched, scanty, hard baked soil'. Thinking, perhaps, of John Bowden's experience, he opined that this was 'the desert country where squatters were ruined'. It was, he said, the land 'where shepherds used to grow mad in their solitary existence'.[6]

A more objective account, perhaps, was that offered by Captain Samuel Higgs, Jun., FGS, FGSC, chief captain of the Wallaroo mine. In 1872, little more than a decade after the mine was first opened, he wrote to the Royal Cornwall Geological Society (of which he was formerly Secretary) to offer 'Some Remarks on the Mining District of Yorke's Peninsula, South Australia'. His principal interest, understandably, was in the geological features of the locality – 'as a rule the rock of the district is clay-slate, overlaid by a bed of uncomfortable limestone' – but he was careful to describe the general topography, flora, fauna and climate for the benefit of his learned colleagues back home. 'Yorke's Peninsula,' he said, 'is a country entirely devoid of fresh water, except in three or four places on the sea-shore, where wells have been sunk in the sand and some brackish water found, which, for want of better, cattle drink.' In language that would have horrified emigration agents at work in Cornwall, he went on to admit that the 'climate is a most trying one ... The hot winds and dust-storms hurled along from the dry parched plains of the north are at times almost unbearable; to work is altogether out of the question. During their continuance, all nature seems gasping.' Indeed, he added, the 'only natural vegetation is a stunted mallee tree-scrub, the foliage of which is a dirty olive green'. At certain times of the year 'this somberness' (as Higgs described it) was relieved by the yellow blossom of the wattle tree or the occasional native myrtle, 'with its diminutive white flower'. After rainfall, there was also the 'spear-grass', which grew rapidly and 'for a month or two, in some places, affords fair feed for sheep'. But, Higgs observed regretfully, 'a day or two of a South Australian sirocco (north wind) dries it entirely up, and the whole country assumes the aspect of an arid wilderness'.[7]

The landscape itself was dreary. The 'country from the Hummock's range of hills, situated at the head of the peninsula, to the extreme south point, is nearly a dead level', said Higgs, and 'Of animal life there is but little'. Kangaroos were encountered in some areas, as was the occasional wallaby, and 'That extraordinary burrowing animal, the wombat, may sometimes be seen of a fine moon-light night'. There were also 'several varieties of snakes and lizards, among them the iguana', and a sprinkling of birds, among them hawks, emus, parrots and magpies: 'These constitute just the whole of the wild denizens of the district'. Only the indigenous people, Higgs concluded, had really thrived in this unpromising environment, and even then the 'native population is small, numbering, it is thought, 160 all told; their numbers never exceeded, perhaps, 350'. The smallness of the 'tribe' (as he called it) was, he thought, a result of the scarcity of water in the locality. But he had more than a sneaking regard for a people who could live their lives so successfully in what to European eyes were such harsh conditions: 'I am not inclined to speak so disparagingly of the aborigines as the writers of some books are: I see pretty much of them, and find them to be shrewd observers, with a great fund of humour, and inimitable caricaturists.'[8]

Alas, the Aboriginal people would soon be dispossessed, though some found employment around the mines, welcomed by Samuel Higgs and colleagues. Others gathered at the local Point Pearce Mission Station, established in 1868, where Methodist missionaries thought they were doing the right thing in introducing their fellow human beings to European ways and to the Christian religion. W.R. Penhall, one such Methodist – a Cornishman, and member of the Moonta Mines Wesleyan chapel – was later appointed OBE for his work as South Australia's Chief Protector of Aborigines. As incumbent in this role he had the power to confine Aboriginal people to reserves or institutions, or to remove them therefrom, or to proclaim them prohibited from certain towns or areas. The Chief Protector was also legal guardian for all Aboriginal and 'half-caste' (*sic*) children, and it was his duty to ensure that Aboriginal people from Point Pearce and other mission stations should refrain from 'profane and blasphemous' language and should not be 'dirty and untidy' or 'insubordinate in any manner whatsoever'.[9] Inevitably, the triumph of the Europeans on the Australian frontier was at the expense of the Aboriginal population.

'Vast villages ... Wallaroo Mines and Moonta Mines'

As the Aborigines were thus dispossessed, so the European – mainly Cornish – settlers consolidated their presence in the locality. They lacked the Aborigines' easy familiarity with the environment and its resources but, to a degree at least, they had modern technology on their side. The Wallaroo and Moonta mine companies erected comfortable dwellings for their senior employees but in the earliest days the miners and their families, many of whom had tramped across from Burra Burra and Kapunda, had to make do with temporary accommodation, usually tents. According to one contemporary report: 'Cornish miners and their families were living in great discomfort in a town [Wallaroo Mines] of calico amidst dust, heat and flies'.[10] Similar conditions obtained at neighbouring Moonta Mines, and before long the miners and their families had taken matters into their own hands, building their own cottages in plots amidst the mining paraphernalia of the mineral leases. This was an echo of their activities at Burra Burra, where, for example, they had hollowed dug-out cabins within the banks of the Burra creek, but it also drew upon their experiences in Cornwall. In 1831 Britton and Brayley had described how in recent times 'dreary and almost useless tract[s] of ground' which had 'remained worthless for centuries', were let out in lots of up to three acres 'to labouring miners, determinable on three lives, on condition that each occupant builds a cottage and cultivates the soil'. As they put it: 'This practice has tended to improve the appearance and condition of the county, while the industrious miner is materially benefited in health, in moral habits, and in property'.[11] Similar imperatives were apparent in South Australia, and the Yorke Peninsula mining companies, anxious to attract labour to their workings, were only too glad to let the miners and their families construct make-shift cottages on the mineral leases, land that the companies had leased from the Crown.

Single-storey, with additional rooms added on over the years as families grew and funds and time allowed, these 'Cornish cottages' (as they came to be known) were simple affairs. Oswald Pryor described the usual methods of construction: 'A few houses had wattle-and-daub walls, made by erecting a reinforcement of sticks, and then giving both sides a thick plaster of clay'. Others, Pryor continued, 'were built by placing two planks horizontally, a foot or fifteen inches apart, then filling the space between them with a mixture of loam, clay, and broken stone, which was well rammed and allowed to set before the boards were raised for a next course'.[12] But the most durable walls were those built with 'German bricks': bricks made in rough moulds from limestone rubble, wet earth and straw. Roofs consisted usually of wooden palings – though many were replaced later by galvanized iron sheeting – and a system of launders (gutters) and downpipes led generally to both an iron tank at the side of the house and a deeply sunk underground tank.

When Anthony Trollope visited the district in the early 1870s he was astonished to find that the miners had 'built habitations for themselves round the very mouths of the shafts, and in this way ... vast villages have sprung up, called Wallaroo Mines and Moonta Mines'. They were 'Very singular places', he mused, 'consisting of groups of low cottages, clustering together in streets, one street being added on to another as the need for them arises, not built with any design such as is usual in the towns of new countries'.[13] The Rev. W.H. Hosken, a Bible Christian minister from neighbouring Victoria, arrived at Moonta in 1875 and was equally surprised. He thought that the 'mines, as they are called, make a queer place. No streets, everyone builds his cottage just as fancy leads him.'[14] In the same year another observer added his own pen-picture of this striking environment. 'The most populous part of the Moonta district is in the immediate neighbourhood of Moonta Mines', he wrote, 'where the miners' cottages are clustered by hundreds. Most of them have been erected by the occupants, and are as may be supposed of an original style of architecture'. But for all their primitive attributes and coarse construction, these cabins were not unattractive, he said: 'Their appearance ... is by no means uninviting being neat and tidy, the majority of them possessing small gardens attached, properly stocked with flowers, fruit trees, and culinary vegetables.' Moreover, in 'the earlier days of the mine many of the houses were built without any regard to regularity in width or direction of public thoroughfares, and consequently the by-ways are numerous, narrow and devious'.[15]

'There is no attempt to form streets here', wrote a fourth commentator, equally amazed by the extraordinary prospect of Moonta Mines: 'houses have been built in every direction, each on its little plot of ground, with tank and fence, and often with a vine growing by the side or a cluster of fruit trees in front. To the stranger this all presents a novel and pleasing appearance.' And yet, the stranger added, this attractive scene existed in the midst of the awesome, intimidating might of the copper mines themselves. 'The noise of engines and gear, the clink of the blacksmiths' hammers on the anvils in the shops, the hoarse rattle of the chains and the escapement of steam, the sight of immense chimneys and tall engine-houses, crushing machinery and pumping machinery' would all, he said, 'combine to impress the least observant of spectators'. There were 'tramroads and skipways at your feet, overhead, and in tunnels under your feet'. But within this industrial landscape one could 'see the cottages all around, with the trim housewife waiting for her husband to come home after morning core [shift], the glimpses of the snugness and comfort within, the chapels rising up above the other buildings as if it was a great city'.[16]

'Snugness' was also a theme developed by Oswald Pryor. The cottages were 'whitewashed, inside and out, every Christmas,' he claimed, and the 'inside of a cottage was spotless – Cousin Jenny never neglected the sweeping, cleaning and dusting.' Moreover, 'No Cousin Jack miner's wife regarded her home as complete until the "best room" had a carpet on the floor, with a harmonium – a book of Wesley's hymns lying on its cover – a round table with the family album right in the centre, and half a dozen polished cedar chairs with crocheted antimacassars spread over the backs.'[17] The interior of the cottage, then, was Cousin Jenny's domain: home of the 'the trim housewife', the 'Cousin Jack miner's wife' who managed to achieve domestic order and comfort despite being surrounded on every side by the clamour and filth of deep mining, and despite her unpromising situation on the arid frontier at the end of the earth – miles from anywhere. This was a paradox that summed up the myth of Cousin Jenny. Despite everything, Cousin Jenny had triumphed over adversity – and yet, according to her myth (see p. 28), only Cousin Jenny was equipped to do so, so completely. Other, lesser women might have tried and failed, but – so the story went – Cornish women were somehow uniquely qualified for the rigours and demands of the international mining frontier.[18]

No place for a woman?

And yet, there was more; for the adversity with which Cousin Jenny was confronted was considerably more than the dirty, noisy proximity of the mines or even the unrelieved aridity of the frontier. There were real, palpable dangers that threatened her and her loved ones in her domestic sphere. Children might go missing, wandering beyond the confines of the 'snug' cottage and into the altogether more malign world of open shafts and operating machinery. In 1874, for example, six-year old William Northey fell down a shaft at the Devon Consols mine. In 1886 seven-year old Joseph Williams was killed riding a plunger pole at Hughes' shaft at the Moonta mine – even though boys had been warned time and again about the dangers of such play, and were threatened that they would be 'took to Bodmin' (gaol) if caught.[19] And beyond the bounds of the mines was a dense, bewildering, disorientating expanse of mallee scrub, home to poisonous snakes and devoid of all succour for the lost infant. Sometimes little children did wander into the wilderness, never to be seen again. At others, the hue and cry raised when a little one went missing was a chilling testament to the environment in which they all lived – featureless bush and vast horizons in which even the most alert and observant might lose his or her way. When the Simcock children, aged nine and five, were lost in the scrub beyond Cross Roads village and the Yelta mine in March 1876, the searching locals yelled 'cooey', the penetrating Australian bush call, with increasing frenzy in the vain hope of finding them.[20]

Sometimes, blinding sand-storms put a stop to all work, invading the lubricated parts of finely engineered machinery but also insinuating their ways into every corner, nook and cranny of Cousin Jenny's neat cottage and treasured possessions. This was the dreaded South Australian 'snow storm', as it was known with Cornish irony. As the *Yorke's Peninsula Advertiser* remarked with wry amusement in September 1876, recent 'new chums' had been told to imagine the full force of such a storm: 'On Tuesday our town [Kadina] was shrouded in a mantle of dust, and if our late arrivals managed to appreciate the opposite of a good old English (or rather Cornish) fall of snow, it's more than we did'.[21]

In mid-nineteenth-century Cornwall, of course, Cousin Jenny often worked considerably beyond the domestic sphere, not least as bal-maiden. Bal-maidens were female mine workers, who had created for themselves a socio-economic niche – and a source of independent means – among the otherwise overwhelmingly masculine world of the Cornish mining industry; sorting and grading ore that had been brought to surface from underground. Comparatively well-paid and usually single, these women had an independence of action, and a financial independence to back it up, that increasingly scandalized male society. The latter part of the century, therefore, saw growing male criticism of what was seen as the materialist and unfeminine excesses of Cornish bal-maidens. This was part of an increasingly assertive Victorian ideology of 'separate spheres', which insisted that women should abandon the workplace and relocate themselves within the 'domestic' sphere of the home. Indeed, it has been argued recently that the gradual disappearance of the bal-maiden from late nineteenth-/early twentieth-century Cornish mines was not so much a function of new ore-handling technologies (in which women were no longer needed) but rather the result of an assertive, male-orientated insistence that a mine was no place for a woman.[22]

Significantly, perhaps, bal-maidens, so integral to the mining scene of nineteenth-century Cornwall, were to all intents and purposes absent in Australia, certainly in South Australia. There is some evidence of women working at surface in the earliest days of the Glen Osmond mines, near Adelaide, but thereafter they are conspicuous by their absence, the work they would have performed in Cornwall done instead in Australia by 'pickey' (ore-sorting) boys and older men no longer able to work underground.[23] Very few would-be emigrants to South Australia declared themselves as bal-maidens: a notable exception (which certainly proved the rule) was that of Sukey and Jane Fletcher, female mine workers of Wheal Butson (near St Agnes) who applied for assisted passage to the colony in 1840.[24] The general absence of bal-maidens in applications for free or assisted passages suggests not so much that women who had been bal-maidens did not come to South Australia but rather, knowing that their ore-grading skills were not required (or welcomed) overseas, they presented themselves as 'female domestic servants' or members of other occupational groups that were highly sought after.[25]

Trade union pressure and governmental legislation combined to ensure that in Australia a mine was no place for a woman. At the time, and subsequently, this was taken as yet further evidence of colonial Australia's more progressive approach to social issues. In nineteenth-century Britain it was still acceptable for women to work in dirty, dangerous, back-breaking and potentially dangerous occupations and environments. But in more enlightened Australia this was no longer desirable.[26] An early twenty-first-century feminist perspective, however, might be rather different. Here, it could be argued, the men who ran colonial Australia found that, starting with a clean sheet, as it were, they could safely disregard lingering customary rights — such as those that still permitted women to work at mines in Cornwall — and attempt to create a society in which women were firmly relegated to the domestic sphere. No doubt many women willingly colluded in this process, former bal-maidens in Australia perhaps relieved that they had no longer to work in an increasingly frowned upon — not to mention strenuous — occupation, and grateful for the opportunity for feminine 'betterment'.

And yet even here there is a paradox for, as we know, however ideologically confined these women were to their domestic sphere, the reality of the colonial frontier was that the role of women was every bit as important as that of men in securing the success of new settlements in often hostile environments. For Cousin Jenny on northern Yorke Peninsula, this not only meant the daunting task of creating cosy domesticity in the midst of an unpromising industrial landscape but also required stoicism and strength of character, a determination to carry on and win through whatever the odds. Again, the suggestion was that Cousin Jenny was especially equipped for this challenging role. Indeed, the independence of spirit and physical strength that characterized the Cornish bal-maiden could be deployed to good effect at Moonta and environs. As Pryor noted, when building cottages on the mineral leases, 'Wives usually gave a hand, and some of them could use a shovel as skillfully as a man. Usually these were "bal-maidens", who had worked as ore-dressers at mines in Cornwall.'[27] This was a spirit exemplified in Phyllis Somerville's well-known novel *Not Only in Stone*, first published in 1942, the story of Mary Elizabeth 'Polly' Thomas. Born in St Ives, Cornwall, in 1838, the fictional Polly arrived in Australia in 1865. She died in Adelaide in 1927, after a long and courageous life in South Australia in which she had stood firm against all the hardships that fate had thrown against her. There was the death of her sister Ellen not long after their arrival in the colony, the loss of her life's savings in a property swindle, the growing disability of her husband Nathan – a copper miner, soon unable to work in his traditional occupation – and, worst of all, the premature deaths of two of her four children, three of whom she had born in South Australia, the other at sea during the long voyage to the colony.[28]

Polly Thomas and Cousin Jenny

Not Only in Stone is literary testament to the 'myth' of Cousin Jenny, and – notwithstanding the location of much of the story at Wallaroo Mines – it has (in the familiar paradoxical manner) also contributed strongly to the creation and perpetuation of Moonta's myth. To that extent, it has a central place in the 'invention' of Australia's Little Cornwall. Moreover, it has the ring of 'authenticity', or at least an authentic insight into life on northern Yorke Peninsula as seen through the eyes of Polly's creator, the author Phyllis Somerville, who was born at Kadina and was Cornish on both sides of her family. Somerville's fiction is, therefore, a personal testament: an evocation, if not quite a documentary record, of life on the Peninsula as she had witnessed it as a child, and as she had heard about it from her parents. It deserves to be treated in that light.

Early in the story we learn of the particular qualities that make a Cornishwoman special. 'The true Cornish heart is strong to stand the shocks of circumstance, the poverty and injustice of the world', writes Somerville. But this forbearance does not imply embitterment or a hardening of the spirit, for part of Cousin Jenny's strength is her empathy with those who suffer, where the 'tender word' can 'melt [her] into tears'.[29] This sets the mood for much that follows in the book. The ironic hand of fate in the story is also revealed early on: where Nathan, though employed happily enough in Adelaide, hankers for his old occupation as a copper miner – this had been his aim 'ever since word came home to Cornwall in 1861 of the great copper finds in South Australia'. Polly meanwhile, happy to be living near her newly-wed sister Ellen, had harboured 'a secret hope ... that Nathan might be contented in the city'. Alas he was not, and he soon moved on to find work at the Wallaroo mine, to be followed shortly to the Peninsula by the reluctant Polly. Nathan reassured her that 'his work there would be permanent. There was copper in plenty ... The mine captains were Cornishmen and knew what they were about.'[30] Thus was set in train the sequence of events, beginning with Ellen's death in childbirth and the onset of Nathan's rheumatic illness (ironically made worse by labour in the mine) that confronted Polly with the enormous challenges of her life.

At Wallaroo Mines, Nathan and Polly Thomas acquired a typical cottage: single-storey, 'made of wattle and daub ... with two rooms across the front and a skillion-room at the back'. Behind, 'the poppet-heads of the mines reared themselves into the dusk, and the tall bulks of the stone engine-houses, housing the Cornish engines, showed dark against the sunset'.[31] Nathan had bought the cottage from Ben Wilson, another miner. The miners and their families, as Somerville explained in the novel, lived rent-free in the cottages they had been allowed to build on Crown land leased to the mine companies. They could – with the company's permission – sell them on to other miners, if they so wished. Improvement and expansion were also allowed, normally following an approving nod from one of the mine captains. It was against this background that Polly decided to move the fence surrounding her newly acquired cottage to give increased space for a garden; an event that Somerville deploys as a literary device to illustrate Polly's single-minded determination and her ready adaptation to the environment in which she finds herself. Without Nathan's knowledge, or even captain's sanction, Polly takes the initiative herself, Cousin Jenny that she is, moving the fence outwards, 'sapling by sapling, and redriving each post firmly in the ground ... Nobody questioned her right to do this, but many stopped to remark upon it in a neighbourly fashion.'[32] The resultant dialogue is telling:

> Ted Polderrick, lounging at his open doorway in his shirt-sleeves early one morning, saw the little woman [Polly] in the faded pink sun-bonnet and large white apron moving the sapling fence, and he knocked the ashes out of his clay pipe on the heel of his boot and called out to his wife inside their cottage. 'Ay, mother, see 'ere, quick.'
> 'What's to do, Ted?' called back Mrs Polderrick. 'Well, well,' she exclaimed, as she stood in the doorway, with her hands spread on her hips, 'if it idden that little Miz Thomas makin' of a new fence! Go on over an' lend an 'and, Ted.'
> 'Not me,' said Ted, who was waiting for his breakfast.
> Mrs Polderrick went to her own front gate and leant her arms on the sharp points of the wattle saplings. 'Mornin', Miz Thomas. Thee's up betimes.'
> 'Mornin', Miz Polderrick,' Polly answered, straightening her back and looking across the track.
> ''Ow're 'ee doin'?'
> 'Fine, I thank 'ee.'
> 'Movin' fence?'
> 'Yes, movin' fence,' replied Polly, and calmly went on with her work.
> Joe Penworthy, coming off his shift, stopped besides her a few minutes later, put down his crib-bag and began relighting his pipe. 'Movin' fence, Miz Thomas?' he said, when the pipe was well alight.

'Yes, movin' fence, Mr Penworthy,' said Polly, and waited for him to speak again.

He picked up his crib-bag and started off towards the crossing. 'Well, thee's got a nice for 'un,' he said, with a look at the pale blue autumn sky.

When Nathan came off shift he walked in at the gate and took two stops towards the door, then stopped, looked about and opened his blue eyes wide. 'Polly,' he called, as he opened the door, 'Polly, where 'ee to?'

'Well,' said Polly, coming forward, 'what now, Nat?'

'Thees 'ave shifted the fence?'

'I 'ave!' This with a hint of pride.

'Land o' Goshen, oo gave un leave?'

'Nobody gave un, so I just took un.'

'What'll cap'n say?' said Nathan, in a hushed voice.

'If cap'n da say aught I'll up 'an tell un I 'ad to 'ave me garden an' 'twere easier to move fence than 'ouse, any day.'

Nathan rubbed a calloused hand across his chin and looked at Polly, and there was awe as well as admiration in his eyes.[33]

This was Polly Thomas as archetypal Cousin Jenny. She was equally feisty in her protection of Nathan – now 'a crippled miner' – and 'wanted to shield him from the pity of his fellows a little longer, until he should... be strong again to bear Cornish sympathy'.[34] When her son Alan was drowned accidentally in the open drain that carried away the pump water from the mine, it was Polly who found his lifeless corpse floating face-down in the muddy liquid: 'She had the strength to behold him, with only one sharp cry for expression, and, cradling his cold, stiff body in her lap, tenderly wiped the mud from his dead face'. Thereafter, she 'put her sorrow behind her' and got on with the business of life.[35]

The death of Polly's daughter, Annie, revealed similar strengths – another twist in the plot which served to illustrate still further the travails of Cornish women on the frontier, and their capacity for dealing with them. But more than this, moving beyond this literary construction, effective though it undoubtedly is, there is also in Somerville's narrative a social realism that is for us, perhaps, an authentic window to the tragedies endured by those early European settlers on northern Yorke Peninsula. Annie's death, like that of many infants in that time and place, came as if from nowhere. One evening, having gone to bed, she found that she could not sleep, and called out to her mother (Polly) for a drink, explaining that she had a sore throat: 'Me swalla da 'urt me'. Later that night Annie was delirious, calling out again for her mother and 'sitting up in bed, red-cheeked and wild-eyed'. Half awake but still living her nightmare, Annie cried out that she was about to be knocked down by a steam locomotive: 'Oh mother, save me! A big puffer-train be goin' to ride over me.' Next morning, the doctor came – 'You did well to call me, Mrs Thomas ... Membraneous croup' – and for four days and nights Polly watched over Annie's bed. On the evening of the fourth day, Annie suddenly reared up in bed, 'clutching at the air with both hands. Polly rushed to her, holding down the writhing limbs, and then, listening for the heavy sound of Annie's breathing, was terrified when it did not come.' Polly's son ran for the doctor, while Polly threw open the windows for more air and tried compressing Annie's chest, 'alternately raising and lowering her little arms and rubbing her body with swift, tireless strokes'. When the doctor arrived, he knew 'at first glance that Annie was dead ... [Polly] looked into his eyes, and she knew too.'[36]

At that point, 'something died within her [Polly's] breast, and never again as long as she lived did she know real happiness'.[37] But, resourceful to the last, Polly had already opened a successful millinery shop in Robert Street, Moonta, having moved there from Wallaroo Mines, earning her own income now that Nathan could no longer work. Young Richard, their surviving son, was taken on as a pickey-boy at the Moonta mine, adding further to the family purse. By now Polly had acquired an enviable reputation in the community for her strong-hearted resolution in the face of adversity, and was often called upon for support or advice in desperate circumstances: '"Go for Mrs Thomas!" came to be a cry for help that went out from many homes in Moonta; and Polly's stout little figure was often first to cross a troubled threshold, even before doctor or minister had been called.'[38]

There was irony in the fact that, although there was never any question of her working as a bal-maiden in South Australia, Polly had nonetheless established independence of a kind beyond the domestic sphere; unless the millinery trade – so quintessentially 'feminine' – be considered an extension of that sphere. The cry 'Go for Mrs Thomas' also indicated her stature in the community beyond the domestic sphere – or at least in the collective community of domestic spheres in which the local women operated. But above all, Polly Thomas had established herself as an exemplary Cousin Jenny, a role model for the type, as Phyllis Somerville no doubt intended.

'It had plenty of wood in en'

In the hazy middle ground between literary construction and local folklore, the myth of Cousin Jenny had proved an important component of an identity transplanted and then modified on Yorke Peninsula. As we have seen, this was demonstrated most forcefully in the 'Great Strike' of 1874, when the miners' wives, wielding their brooms, drove the blacklegs from the mines. In the words of a contemporary versifier:

> Now Cousin Jenny is no fool
>   She does not work by red-tape rule,
> But by the glorious rule of right –
>   Not recognising wealth or might,
> God bless her! She's a little Queen
>   For every one she swept out clean.³⁹

When W.G. Spence, the Amalgamated Miners' Association's representative from union headquarters in Creswick, Victoria, visited northern Yorke Peninsula in 1889 to try to resolve an industrial dispute (see pp. 126–7), he found to his surprise that memory of Cousin Jenny's exploits was still fresh, some fifteen years after the event. As Spence discovered, however, in the mythology that had grown up in the intervening period, a good deal of confusion had become apparent. Somehow the events of 1874 had been conflated with those of the earlier strike in 1864, a blurring in which the wives' action in 1874 was now also seen as responsible for the drama a decade earlier – when the Warmington brothers had been forced from their positions as Chief Captains at the mines, clearing the way for Hancock's managerial regime: first at Moonta and later at Wallaroo. Returning to his hotel at Kadina from a day's negotiations at Moonta, Spence encountered the landlord. He 'told us', Spence wrote, 'that a big Cornish-woman had just been there to borrow his stable broom because, as she said, "it had plenty of wood in en" and she "might want to sweep Captain Hancock out"'. Muddling the events of 1874 and 1864, the landlord explained to Spence 'that the Captain's predecessor had been swept out of Moonta by the women, carrying a broom each'.⁴⁰

The story may have become confused but it was already iconic, and Cousin Jenny's role in any strike action was clearly understood. As Spence recorded:

> The delivery of our report and ultimatum to the miners was a scene never to be forgotten. Excitement ran high. The brooms were ready, and their plucky owners equally so. No sooner had the signal bell rung for knock-off work at 5 p.m. than the men assembled around the platform of the tramway, from which we were to speak. All hands came just as they were. The women stood generally in the outer circle of the crowd. They left the work of decision to the men, but were prepared to loyally carry it out, whatever it might be, even if it meant going hungry in order to secure justice.⁴¹

In the end, however, the 'meeting fully accepted our recommendation [not to strike] ... and later [the miners] were specially glad that no strike had eventuated, and that there had been no need for that broom with "plenty of wood in 'en".[42]

Notwithstanding the latent – and in 1874, not so latent – violence of it all, Cousin Jenny's actions were seen by sympathetic contemporary observers to be motivated by 'the glorious rule of right', loyalty, and a desire 'to secure justice'. Here, perhaps, there is an echo of the stereotypical dichotomy of women so often apparent in colonial Australia, the duality of 'damned whores' and 'God's police' as Anne Summers once famously described it.[43] Cousin Jenny is, of course, a member of 'God's police'. To her genius as homemaker on the frontier, bringing comfort and stability to an otherwise raw and dangerous environment, has been added her inherent sense of natural justice – and her unflinching commitment to ensuring that justice is done, even by direct action if necessary.

'Young ladies halloed and hooted after'

In a strange but compelling case of the myth made flesh, the first policewoman in the British Empire hailed from Moonta – Fanny Kate Boudicea Cocks. She was usually known simply as 'Kate'. Yet the prescient choice by her Cornish-born parents of 'Boudicea' as a baptismal name spoke not only of her Cornish credentials as 'Ancient Briton' but also intimated both her strength of character and innate leadership ability: just like the formidable warrior-woman who had stood against the might of Rome. Born in 1875, Kate Cocks was to demonstrate such qualities during her remarkable career. She grew up at Moonta but in 1900 moved to Adelaide, working first as a teacher and later as a juvenile probation officer. In December 1915 she was appointed South Australia's – and the Empire's – first fully fledged woman police constable. Her principal task was to protect the moral welfare of women and children. Much of her effort initially was focused on Port Adelaide and Outer Harbour, where troops concentrating for embarkation during the Great War acted as a magnet for young women of easy virtue. Later, when she had retired from the police force, Kate Cocks collaborated with the Methodist Church (her parents had been strict Bible Christians) to establish a home in the Adelaide suburb of Brighton for young single women who were pregnant.[44]

Although the bulk of Kate Cocks' work had been performed beyond northern Yorke Peninsula, she was always claimed as Moonta's own – as indeed she continues to be – and the catch-cry 'Look out! Here comes Miss Cocks!' is remembered still.[45] The dingy backstreets of Port Adelaide, however, seemed somehow a world away from tight-knit Moonta and environs. But Port Wallaroo, much nearer to home, had its own reputation. To external observers, northern Yorke Peninsula exhibited certain unifying features but, as we have seen already, Moonta was careful to preserve

23. The mighty smelting works at Port Wallaroo, c.1910, built almost on the foreshore of Spencer's Gulf.

its exclusivity when it was in its interests to do so. Then local territorial distinctions became important. Sometimes Port Wallaroo was an integral part of 'Little Cornwall'. It had its own 'Cornwall Street', after all, alongside those of England, Ireland, Scotland, Wales, and many of the town's inhabitants were Cornish; one local recalled that the town's populace came 'mostly from Wales and Cornwall'.[46] But at other times the 'Welshness' of Port Wallaroo was emphasized.[47] Many Welsh smelters had come out to work at the mighty Wallaroo Smelting Works. Most had brought their families with them, and a local Welsh-speaking community had soon emerged. There was a Welsh chapel, where the Welsh language was used in worship, and occasionally there were Welsh-language articles in local newspapers.[48] The Welsh, like the Cornish, nurtured their reputation as pious, God-fearing folk, and guarded it jealously in their new home. But Port Wallaroo had another side. Like Port Adelaide, it was seen by some as seedy and morally dissolute, a working harbour as disreputable as any other the world over. Local young women, it was said, colloquially known as 'seagulls', gathered anxiously at the jetty to await the arrival of ships, and were so eager to share their favours with the visiting mariners that they often forgot to charge for their services.[49]

These 'seagulls' were, of course, the 'damned whores' of Australian stereotypical depiction. And if Moonta, confident of its own reputation as a Methodist heartland, felt inclined to look patronizingly at its near neighbour, with its fallen women, then it too was sometimes forced to admit the existence of 'damned whores' among it own populace. For all her upright reputation, Cousin Jenny could sometimes stumble, a moment's lapse inviting perpetual censure. As ever, it was the women – and rarely the men – who bore the brunt of public disapproval for immorality, not least because of the visible and lasting consequences of illicit pregnancy. One Methodist minister in the locality complained, probably with little exaggeration, that 90 per cent of marriages he had solemnized on northern Yorke Peninsula had 'had to take place to save dishonour'.[50] Others though took a more fatalistic view of such happenings – resigned rather than moralizing, with sexual indiscretion (on the part of men, at least) relatively far down the list of social misdemeanours – an attitude reflected in the Cousin Jack joke recorded by John Reynolds:

> Two [Moonta] miners, family men, are talking and Cousin John remarks to Cousin Thomas 'That boy of yours is a bad lad.' 'Yes,' Thomas agrees, 'he is a bad lad.' John – 'he got my Jenny in the family way down in the costeen (deep trench).' Thomas – 'Yes, he is a very bad lad: he broke the family axe twice last week, a very bad lad.'[51]

Social life revolved around the chapels, providing, ironically, the social context for young men and women to meet – the prelude all too often, critics claimed, to sexual experimentation and adventure. In March 1877 one such critic drew attention to 'the great immorality existing on the [Moonta] Mines'. He was ashamed to admit, he said, that in an area 'renowned for its Christianity, you may see sights and hear sounds that would shock the modesty of any right-feeling human being'.[52] Youthful pregnancies and early marriage were among the consequences of such behaviour but, the critic added, there were also many virtuous young women in the district who stoutly resisted the unwanted attentions of amorous males. It was not always an easy task, for 'you may see crowds of young men every evening (Sundays not excepted) standing at their rallying corners ... cursing and swearing in a manner that is disgraceful'. Moreover, he said, 'respectable young ladies [are] halloed and hooted after. I have been informed by respectable young ladies that they are almost afraid to go to Chapel on Sunday evenings on account of this.' And 'if they should pass these rowdies without speaking they are cursed and sworn at.'[53]

Such women, in their opposition to such effrontery and in their determined preservation of their own virtue, helped to maintain the carefully constructed myth of Cousin Jenny built around the likes of fictional Polly Thomas and

24. The dangerous paraphernalia of mining at surface: Wallaroo mine, c.1903, during the period of transition and modernization. Traditional Cornish engine-houses, such as Harvey's in the background, rub shoulders with new plant and giant headframes.

real-life Kate Cocks. Even the unfortunate story of Elizabeth Woolcock – the only woman to be legally executed in South Australia – somehow adds lustre to, rather than diminishes, the myth. Born of Cornish parents at the Burra in 1847, Elizabeth's childhood was 'characterised by poverty, neglect and sexual abuse'.[54] At the age of 20 she married a Cornish miner called Thomas Woolcock, and went to live with him in his cottage at the North Yelta mine, near Moonta. An alcoholic, Woolcock treated his wife appallingly, heaping new miseries upon her. Having unsuccessfully attempted suicide, Elizabeth Woolcock in her desperation poisoned her husband, who died in 1873. The cause of death (mercury poisoning) was only discovered at the inquest, and Elizabeth was duly tried and convicted of Thomas Woolcock's murder. However, the jury recommended mercy, and there was a wave of sympathy throughout South Australia as the public reflected upon Elizabeth's wretched life and the ill-treatment she had suffered at the hands of her erstwhile husband. Alas, there was no reprieve, and she was hanged. A sense of revulsion swept the colony. With wry Cornish humour, the area where she had lived at North Yelta was known thereafter as 'Poison Flat'.[55] But far more important was the enduring image of a woman wronged. There was outrage that poor Elizabeth should be have been condemned so unhesitatingly as a

25. Young children at play outside John Rowe's cottage at East Moonta in 1883.

wanton, cold-hearted and calculating murderer. Like other Cousin Jennys, she had suffered on northern Yorke Peninsula. But she had endured more than most, and had snapped under intolerable pressure. Far from being a hardened 'damned whore', Elizabeth Woolcock was a defenceless soul who, it was argued, had tried her best but had been defeated by all the disabilities that life had poured upon her. In the sentimental estimation bestowed by hindsight, she seemed an almost saintly victim of adversity amid the evil forces that were abroad on the Mines.

'And now poor Cousin Jenny thought / That her home was dearly bought'

As Captain Higgs had noted, first among these evil forces was the climate itself. Higgs had emphasized the parched nature of the Peninsula: the unrelieved summer heat and the searing dust storms caused by the northerly wind, the South Australian 'sirocco'. But, perversely, there were also on occasions monsoon-like downpours that in just a few hours deluged the locality with a considerable percentage of its annual rainfall. Mid-May usually heralded the rainy season but autumnal storms could strike as early as March, as in 1877 when there was extensive flooding on the Mines settlements as a result of heavy rain. It was reported that 'miners' houses were swamped in many instances from a depth of a few inches to a few feet'. In a matter of hours, all Cousin Jenny's homemaking was undone: her carpets ruined, furniture damaged, and cherished belongings swept away. But worse still, as 'most [cottages] are built variously of pug, German bricks, rubble limestone laid in a bedding of earth ... and stone, with a superficial jointing of lime mortar, none of these are capable of offering a resistance to long-continued rain.' Many cottages leaked like sieves, 'and whilst a few buildings have up to this time actually collapsed, it is a matter of surprise that there has not yet been wholesale destruction'. As the report explained with grim attention to detail: 'Chimneys and fowl-houses and water-closets were the first to give way; then the unfinished walls of houses fell, and in a few instances rooms "dissolved".'[56]

The 'snugness' of the Cornish cottages that had so impressed observers now seemed flimsy, even temporary: conditional upon the vagaries of the weather. Security gave way to a sense of fragility and vulnerability. Cracks had appeared in Cousin Jenny's façade – as well as in her cottages – and behind the veneer of domestic comfort and stability was revealed a more contingent existence for those who lived on the Mines. Heavy rain, when it came, was welcomed, despite its destructive power, and quickly filled the underground tanks beneath the cottages, providing a store of water to help the mineral lease dwellers through the long, hot summers. The alternative, given the absence of local spring or well water, was the purchase of water brought up from Adelaide or distilled by the mine companies or, after 1874, from the four large underground tanks built at Moonta by the government. In the dry season of 1864–65 it did not rain on the Peninsula for six months, and water was bought at 6d. per bucket. Despite the early deluge, 1877 proved to be a bad year, and in 1879 the government was reduced to carting water to the district – despite the existence of the Moonta tanks – with 11,000 hogsheads being brought in in six weeks. It was not until 1890 that water was reticulated from Beetaloo reservoir, almost a hundred miles away, ensuring at last a reliable, clean and safe supply for the locality.[57]

Even more than the alarming effects of flooding, it was the dearth of water that had frustrated the 'civilizing' influence of Cousin Jenny. As the heartfelt doggerel of the time put it:

> And now all happy might have been,
> If creek or river could be seen;
> For 'water' was the general cry;
> But none appear'd in earth or sky,
> No well or water-hole was nigh:
> All arid and intensely dry

> Was earth and air, and they, by sinking,
> Could not find water fit for drinking.
> From Adelaide the fluid came,
> A heavy price was on the same.
> And now poor Cousin Jenny thought
> That her new home was dearly bought,
> For scant was the supply brought her,
> And she'd been used to springs of water.[58]

Worse still, in the insanitary conditions that obtained in the Mines, the tanks beneath the cottages were quickly polluted and became breeding grounds for all kinds of malign bacteria. It was a situation that excited considerable anxiety. In April 1877, not long after the flooding, one horrified observer commented in detail on a typical miner's cottage at Moonta Mines. 'His earth closet, I can't find words to describe its filthy and disgusting construction,' he explained, 'but I have no hesitation in saying that it might justly be considered a disgrace to a black fellow's camp.' During the wet weather, he added, 'the drainage from all this filth flows across his fresh water drain, and passes between his back door and tank, then on to the next allotment, where it forms a large unhealthy pool.' In the dry season, 'this filth flows into the neighbouring tank'.[59] He was not alone in his criticism, another complaining in the pages of the *Yorke's Peninsula Advertiser* that 'many of the residents do not study their neighbours' interests, and are quite unscrupulous as to where

26. A miner's cottage of the better sort at Wallaroo Mines – with Cousin Jenny centre-stage.

they throw their soapsuds and filth, and if the erecting of a pigsty or closet close to their neighbour's back door will cause an annoyance, they are but too highly gratified'. Similarly, 'You may oftimes see dead cats, dogs, fowls &C lying about the streets in a state of putrefaction'.[60]

Later, in April 1884, the Central Board of Health – by now alert to the unhygienic conditions on the Peninsula – reported on a thousand cottages at Wallaroo Mines. 'They are closely crowded together,' explained the report, 'and as a consequence yards are small, closets &c in some places being erected close to a neighbour's front door.' The interiors of many cottages 'were clean and tidy', the report said, 'but the majority of them were just the reverse', although the more substantial houses constructed by the mine company were 'built in accordance with sanitary requirements, and are very comfortable'.[61] As before, earth closets were singled out for particular criticism:

> The closets are almost without exception in a foul condition. The pits are simply holes in the ground, four to six feet deep, sunk through loose limestone ground. When any of these pits are emptied – which is very seldom – the soil is taken out and buried on the premises. Sometimes the soil is thrown into an old shaft on the mines, which is also used as a receptacle for dead animals (dogs, goats, poultry &c).[62]

'Cows, pigs, goats, poultry are allowed to roam at will' in the district, the report also complained, and the very worst area was a small precinct known locally as 'Irish Town'. Here the 'houses are smaller and dirtier, with filthy pigsties and cesspits close to water tanks. On the top of several tanks in this place [were] thick layers of goats' and fowls' dung, all of which is likely to be washed into the tanks at the first rains.' Additionally, 'Soapsuds, kitchen slops, and other impurities are thrown on the surface and allowed to soak into the ground.'[63]

'Colonial fever'

Newcomers, especially, seemed susceptible to the fevers that, inevitably, stalked this unhealthy district. In May 1875, for example, John Sparnon had just arrived from Cornwall. He acquired a cottage at East Moonta and found a job in the mine but soon fell ill. A 'new chum', he had not yet paid enough into the Club & Doctor Fund to be able to draw sickness benefits. But when the trade unionists heard that 'a brother miner was sick and destitute', they sent a small delegation to investigate. 'We found the emaciated form of one who was once a hard-working, honest, quiet man', they said, 'now a perfect wreck of humanity, with an almost heart-broken wife and seven small children ... in a state of utter despair'. Had it not been for the charity of their neighbours, the whole Sparnon family 'must have died from starvation and cold, as they had not sufficient clothing to keep them warm'.[64] A decade later, and such cases were still to be found on the mineral leases. In 1884 William Bonnetta, a miner from Cornwall, had been suffering from fever for six months. He lived in a cottage on Wallaroo Mines occupied by twelve persons, seven of whom slept in a one room measuring 12 feet by 10 feet, the others sharing another of 12 feet square.[65]

Inevitably, the infant population suffered disproportionately, and there were periodic outbreaks of disease that swept through the Mines settlements. Cholera and diphtheria struck from time to time, but typhoid – also known as 'colonial fever' or 'black measles' – was the enduring enemy. The district was probably not entirely free of the fever until 1900, or even later, but the worst period of all was 1873–75. During 1873 there were 327 burials in Moonta cemetery, mostly typhoid victims, the *Register* newspaper noting up to four funerals a day in the town during June. In the single month of November 1874 there were no fewer than 119 deaths in the Moonta–Port Wallaroo–Kadina triangle. In the December, as the weather turned hot, more than 50 people died of typhoid in Moonta alone; sixteen during one twenty-four-hour period.[66]

In distant Adelaide, the Central Board of Health had become aware of the problems during 1874 and had urged the Moonta and Wallaroo companies

27. Two little girls at Wallaroo Mines, c.1916: small children were always vulnerable in the mining environment, where cottages existed check-by-jowl with the mines.

to take steps to improve conditions on the mineral leases. But the Moonta directors, in the face of all the evidence, retorted with wounded pride that 'the unhealthiness of the place [is] grossly exaggerated', and that the district 'compares favourably ... with any other locality', the company 'always having on hand a large supply of wholesome rain or distilled water available to their employees at cost price'.[67] Nonetheless, the Central Board of Health took decisive action, announcing in May 1875 that it now had the power to inspect every cottage, to have any insanitary dwelling demolished, and to determine the maximum number of people allowed to live in any one dwelling. Families on the mineral leases were to be prevented from drinking water from their own tanks, and were not allowed to keep a pig within fifty yards of their cottages.[68]

Significantly, opposition to these measures came not only from the mine companies but from the mineral lease dwellers themselves, the people they were designed to protect, one complaining that the proposals were 'uncalled for, unworkable, and illegal ... a wilful waste of public money'.[69] Offering a parodied version of 'Trelawny', the unofficial Cornish national anthem, one critic leapt into print:

> And shall th' Inspector dare,
> And will th' Inspector care,
> To brave a thousand Cornishmen
> As good as anywhere?
>
> And shall he touch our tanks
> Despite our serried ranks?
> Then all the rowdy Cornish boys
> Will give him backhand thanks!
>
> Then shall we give in so?
> Give up our right? Oh no!
> Sure all our thousand Cornishmen
> Will shout that roaring 'No!'[70]

This may have been an expression of traditional Cornish 'independence' and 'individualism', with more than a hint of anti-metropolitan sentiment, but it also showed the extent to which the Mines communities now saw themselves as separate and distinct. Here, indeed, was a profound sense of collective identity, expressed in a determination to defend a way of life and a cultural environment that they themselves had created. Paradoxically, in resisting improvements that would have enhanced their quality of life, the Mines dwellers were demonstrating their belief that they had already triumphed over adversity – they had carved their own place out of the wilderness, and they were prepared to stick up for it.

Despite this opposition, there was some improvement at the time – the typhoid epidemic was checked – but before long the situation had deteriorated once more. In 1884 the Moonta directors were again severely criticized for allowing poor conditions to continue on their leases, and in the September they were ordered to improve the cottages of William Hosking, Charles Burk and Josiah Pengelly within ninety days if they were to avoid legal action. The directors reacted, on Captain Hancock's advice, by appointing their own local health inspector (as did the Wallaroo directors), and in 1887 they created their own board of health – consisting of Captain Hancock, doctors resident in the area, and two ministers of religion.[71] They were relatively successful, but could not prevent a serious outbreak of diphtheria at Moonta Mines in 1891, the source of the disease being identified eventually as contaminated milk sold in the area.[72]

Hancock's decision to set up the directors' own board of health was shrewd. It kept the Adelaide inspectors at bay. It also responded to the local patriotism voiced so vehemently by the mineral lease dwellers, winning their approval and establishing the mine companies as the legitimate defenders of local interests and identity. There was a sense too that 'self-help', so central to Cornish Methodist ideology, was the best policy in this as in other things; an opinion that, as a Wesleyan local preacher, Hancock would undoubtedly have shared. But here the mine companies did not have it all their own way, for the local trade union was an alternative source of self-help, and indeed of authority and legitimacy, in dealing with social issues in the district. In the Sparnon case in 1875, it had been local trade unionists who had made the initial investigation. In May 1877 the Moonta miners met to discuss local poverty, the Rev. Octavius Lake, a Bible Christian minister, complaining that the poor laws were 'receiving a most harsh and illiberal interpretation'.[73] The unionists formed a committee to keep a watch on poverty, with John Prisk, veteran of the 1874 strike, suggesting that rations be handed out to the poor.

Octavius Lake and John Prisk met with A.J. Edwards, the Relieving Officer for Yorke Peninsula, who dismissed their call for additional assistance. He was already spending £1,000 per annum on relief on the Peninsula, he said, and he 'thought there was little to excite pity in seeing children shoeless. He had known plenty of Scotch children who would prefer being without shoes'. Moreover, most of the allegedly destitute women who had approached him 'were in the prime of life, and where they had children of ten years of age, these could look after the rest while the mother worked'.[74] Here he was referring to recent cases, such as that of a widow, with two children (the youngest a mere seven months old), who owned a sewing machine but pleaded that 'work was so scarce ... she could not earn 6d. a week'.[75] Another widow had explained that although she possessed a mangle, she was at present too ill to take in washing.

Cornish Methodism and Yorke Peninsula

In the presence of grinding poverty and official resistance, if not indifference, it was difficult for the trade unionists to make headway. But, as the presence of Octavius Lake attested, the unionists on the Peninsula were closely aligned with the several Methodist churches: or most of them. The Wesleyans were often thought 'the bosses' chapel' – not least because Captain Hancock was a member of the Wesleyan chapel at Moonta Mines – and occasionally the latent hostility between the competing Methodist denominations became overt, spilling over into the public domain as accusations and counter-accusations were traded between antagonists. In July 1874, for example, one local miner – presumably a Bible Christian or Primitive Methodist – wrote to the press to insist that 'the Wesleyan congregation were lovers of such display that they wore jewelry at chapel to the value of from £8,000 to £10,000'.[76] It was nonsense, of course, but it was an insight into the suspicions that existed between the different sects.

The Bible Christians were generally Radical in the old-fashioned sense – seekers of social and economic mobility and lovers of civil and religious freedom – while the Primitive Methodists were increasingly politically progressive, ready to embrace the Labor movement as it emerged and prepared to entertain new notions of social justice and social democracy. The Wesleyans in South Australia were not Tories – as much as anyone else, they rejoiced that the colony had eschewed the link between Church and State – but nonetheless they were often seen as 'establishment', not least on northern Yorke Peninsula where the subtlety of chapel membership mattered. It was not a question of whether you were 'church' (Anglican) or 'chapel' (Methodist–Nonconformist) but rather to which chapel you belonged.

Nonetheless, despite these rivalries and distinctions, competition between the denominations was on the whole a healthy thing – until the declining chapel attendances experienced towards the end of the nineteenth century – and there was an overarching Methodist culture, with norms and assumptions to which most could subscribe in principle, deriving in the first place from Cornwall. In mid-nineteenth-century Cornwall, Methodism was at its zenith – the unofficial religion of the Cornish people and a major influence on behaviour and events, from emigration to politics. It was a central plank of the culture of Cornish modernity, of Cornwall in the age of industrial prowess, an important badge of identity. Methodism was, as D.H. Luker has termed it, 'the "popular religion" of Cornwall: and the Cornish insisted that Methodism was "theirs"'.[77]

This 'Cornish Methodism' was transplanted on northern Yorke Peninsula but, an evangelical religion used to adapting to the environments in which it found itself, Methodism on the Peninsula over time developed its own particular hue. Such was the ingrained influence of Methodism, that those 'rowdies' – the threatening groups of youths who gathered on street corners and intimidated prim female chapel-goers or, after chapel, got them into trouble – were also susceptible to this wider culture. Sometimes, indeed, they seemed hardly threatening at all. Stanley Whitford recalled that at Moonta Mines it 'was a Cornish custom that after a day's work, and having had dinner, men would congregate at a certain spot or corner, and there would discuss all manner of topics and the usual gossip of the day. The boys and youths did likewise; they too had their corner.' They would play athletics, such as running, jump-backs, egg-in-hand, hoop-hoop-whistle-hollow, rounders and other games. After dark, they would play snap banker – for matches – and draughts: 'The usual romantic stories from girls to kangaroo dogs would be told'.[78] Then, said another observer, after the evening amusements were over, the youths – Methodists all, at least in name – 'clustered together and sang well-known hymns, tunefully and with the parts well maintained'.[79]

This all-pervading cultural influence was reflected in the Methodists' ubiquitous physical presence on the ground. Methodism provided social and cultural reassurance as well as spiritual support, a quality much needed as the early immigrants struggled to build communities in the harsh environment. Methodist clergy by turns soothed and inspired, finding the right words to settle and guide their flocks, and the chapels themselves – their architecture and fittings so reminiscent of Cornwall – reminded folk of home and demonstrated that the familiar House of God could be established even in this distant and forbidding land. An intensive period of construction on northern Yorke Peninsula had, therefore, resulted in a physical environment dominated by chapels. By 1862 the Wesleyans, Bible Christians and Primitive Methodists all had ordained ministers resident on the Peninsula, and in 1875 there were no fewer than fourteen Methodist chapels in and around Moonta, with twenty-four within the wider district as a whole. In Moonta township, according to one observer in August 1875, there were:

> five places of worship, including the Wesleyan Church, a handsome and capacious edifice, affording a sitting accommodation of over 700 persons, the Bible Christian Church, a newly constructed building of smaller dimensions, the Baptist, Episcopalian, and Roman Catholic Churches ... Among the buildings of note in the village termed West Moonta, are the Wesleyan Church, capable of holding about fifteen hundred persons, the Primitive Methodist Church, nearly as large, and the Bible Christian

Church, almost of equal dimensions, all built of stone, and provided with sitting accommodation.

East Moonta village contains three stone built churches, belonging respectively to the denominations mentioned [Wesleyans, Bible Christians and Primitive Methodists]. At Cross Roads, a populous village on the Yelta property, there are three or four churches, and one in course of erection; and the building of another by the Wesleyans is about to be commenced.[80]

The profusion of places of worship was impressive but also telling was the use of the word 'Church' to describe Nonconformist – Methodist and Baptist – chapels. Although many Cornish clung to the designation 'chapel', out of habit or from sentimental affection, South Australians on the whole were careful to promote the use of the term 'church'. Given that there was no Established Church in the colony, all denominations were therefore equal in law and, it was argued, should be treated as such: 'church' evoked equality, 'chapel' subordinacy. To this was added the relative strength of the Nonconformists; in South Australia generally, and on Yorke Peninsula in particular. As the above commentary demonstrated so vividly, there was nothing at all subordinate about the physical presence of Methodism at Moonta and environs. Nor was there in terms of popular adherence: in 1891 some eighty per cent of people living on northern Yorke Peninsula were Methodists.[81]

Here was institutional strength indeed. It underwrote a deep sense of ethno-religious exclusivity: in the first place a transplantation from Cornwall and an expression of Cornish identity but increasingly too a defining feature of Moonta and the regional culture of northern Yorke Peninsula. Even more than the trade unions, it was Methodism in its several denominational guises that gave institutional direction, continuity and, above all, self-confidence and self-esteem to local culture. There was mass participation in this culture, reports and obituaries in newspapers and denominational magazines shedding momentary light on the lives of countless individuals who had contributed so much to the development of Methodism on the Peninsula. There were fleeting glimpses of folk such as Rebecca Edwards from Lelant and Edward Thomas from Penzance, both devotees of Taylor Street Wesleyan chapel in Kadina, or John Cruet from St Cleer at Cross Roads chapel and John Nancarrow from Redruth at neighbouring Yelta.[82] There was the Rev. Joshua Foster, born in Cornwall in 1829, a Bible Christian who had ministered in Kilkhampton circuit before coming to Australia,[83] and the Rev. Charles Tresise, from St Erth, who at Moonta Mines 'gained much public recognition for his manliness, intelligence, and high Christian character'.[84] Then there was the Rev. G.E. Rowe who in his first sermon in the district 'thanked the

Lord he was amongst brothers and sisters from Cornwall. That set the seal of his popularity at Moonta.'[85] Rowe was, it was said, a man who 'can tell a Cornish story exceptionally well'.[86] Likewise, when the Rev. S. Trethewie Withington was appointed to the Wallaroo circuit in 1872, he was hailed locally as 'a minister long and well known in Cornwall both as a preacher and a writer of eminence'.[87]

'Souls saved every night!'

'The early days of Methodism in Moonta were great times',[88] wrote W.H. Goldsworthy in 1914, and in 1935 W. Lamshed — who had arrived in Moonta from Cornwall in 1883 — remembered that in those days the miners and their families were in 'things religious, fervid, strong in their feelings, love or hate, emotional in the extreme, passionate if you will ... Those were the days when preachers spoke of hell with an absolute belief in it as the abode of damned souls.'[89] Such sentiments came to the fore during the periodic 'Revivals' that swept the Peninsula. Of these, none was more memorable than the Revival of 1874–75, an event of extraordinary intensity that was still recalled vividly in the 1920s as part of 'the oral tradition of the region'.[90] Occurring in the aftermath of the 'Great Strike' — and at a time when deadly disease was ravaging the district and decimating the infant population — the Revival was a remarkable outburst of community affirmation and solidarity in the wake of trauma and uncertainty. It brought people onto the streets in their thousands, and the chapels were filled to overflowing night after night as individuals clamoured to assert their religious identities. Guilt, grief and angst were poured out in emotional testimonies and confessions, a cathartic process in which many found peace, hope and comfort, and were converted or re-enthused in their commitment to the Methodist cause.

The first inkling of what was to come was apparent at Jerusalem, just outside Kadina, where, according to the Bible Christian minister in August 1874, local society had sunk to a low-point: 'Dog-fighting, wombat and wallaby-hunting were the regular Sunday exercises, and sin had stamped its wretched impress upon the entire neighbourhood'. A small galvanized-iron chapel was erected there as part of an evangelical mission to improve the locality. The results were immediate, and impressive. 'On the first night there was a good attendance, and evidently a deep feeling', reported the *Bible Christian Magazine*, and on subsequent days those 'delighted ... in the happy change' they had experienced 'sought to bring their friends under the same influence'. Husbands brought their wives, and parents their children, many of whom 'were often led to surrender all to Christ in the second or third meeting. The result of this blessed work was the conversion of nearly thirty souls.'[91]

28. The plain classical lines of the Bible Christian chapel at Moonta, erected in the early 1870s.

From there the Revival spread to Moonta Mines. Here the precipitating event was the untimely death of Kate Morcombe, a young Sunday-school teacher popular in the community whose sudden loss was felt keenly. Her funeral service in the Bible Christian chapel on Sunday 4 April 1875 became a conversion experience for the attendees: 'Fifteen precious souls were brought to God'. In the following days, scores more were likewise 'brought to God', and on the following Sunday the district seemed to go wild with enthusiasm:

> Oh! What a mighty display of the saving power of God! Throughout all the services of the day, God was present among us. Crowds of people came to the chapel to hear the word of life. At the close of the evening service a leading friend at the Moonta Mines conducted the prayer meeting. Oh! What a glorious sight we were favoured to behold. Cries for mercy were heard from all parts of the chapel. One young man in great distress of soul, when asked to go down to the penitent form, cried out, 'I cannot, I cannot, the Devil has got me chained to the seat, but by God's help I will snap the chain asunder, as I am anxious to find Christ'.[92]

At the Wesleyan chapel, similar events were triggered by the tragic death of Captain Hugh Datson in a rock-fall in the Moonta mine on 15 March 1875. Curiously, a few days before the accident Datson had felt the need to confess

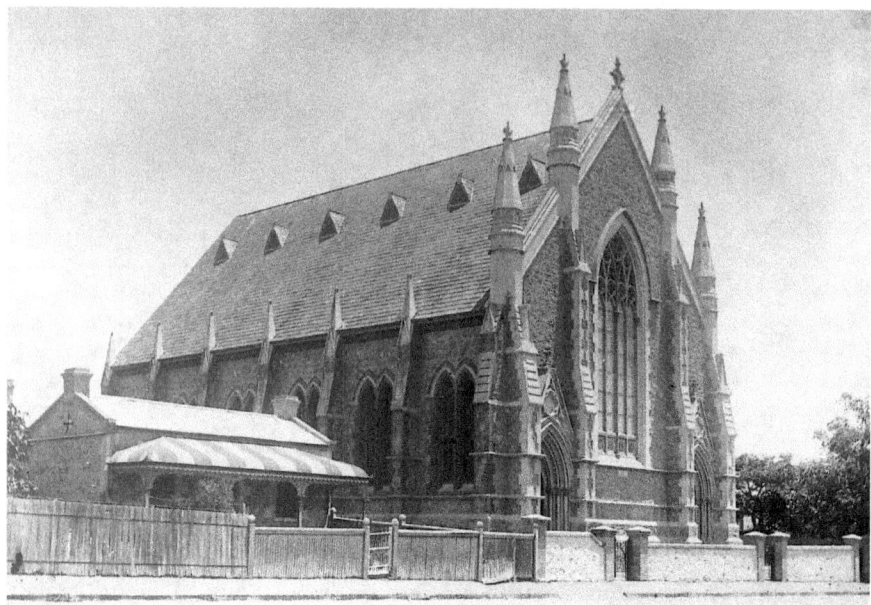

29. Robert Street Methodist Church, Moonta, as it appeared in the 1920s. Opened in 1874, its Victorian Gothic style contrasts with the less ostentatious architecture of the Bible Christians and Primitive Methodists.

to one of the circuit ministers that 'I have never retired to rest since my conversion, without a sense of God's pardon; for if I have grieved him during the day, I have sought peace again before the close'. After that, 'strange awe filled every church in Moonta', the people 'instinctively ... called to prayer'.[93] The Primitive Methodists, too, recorded a new mood abroad on the Mines. The Rev. John G. Wright, their minister at Moonta, wrote in his diary that there 'is grand work going on in all the Chapels'.[94] At Wallaroo Mines 'Many were shouting and weeping',[95] and at Moonta there were:

> Souls saved every night. At Cross Roads 30 souls in three nights. One woman 60 years of age while our people were singing 'Come to Jesus' cried out 'Yes, I am coming', she went and fell on her knees, found peace and went on her way rejoicing. How grand to see souls cast themselves on the altar. Go when you may, night or day, you hear people singing God's praise. If you see a number of boys, they are singing such hymns as 'There be no more sorrow there' or 'My all is the altar' or 'I am coming'. The work is glorious.[96]

Astonishingly, the momentum was maintained for more than a year, a religious phenomenon which culminated in a grand parade from Moonta Mines to the Wesleyan chapel in Moonta, a thousand people singing Wesley's hymns as they marched in triumph to commemorate the collective achievement of their several chapels – estimated at the time to be some 1,500 souls saved. Inevitably, there were many 'backsliders' in subsequent years, as something of the fervour was lost and individuals returned to their old ways: brandy drinking, wombat baiting, and worse. But, as Arnold Hunt has observed, there were those 'who found a new depth in their religion' as a result of their experiences during those heady months. Moreover, the intensity of this and other Revivals on the Peninsula was not mirrored generally elsewhere in South Australia: such 'movements were largely confined to Cornish settlements and owed much to the religious tradition of the people who had emigrated from [Cornwall]'.[97] But, as we have also seen, the Revivals played a major role in helping the community to come to terms with adversity at a time of strikes and epidemics, finding renewed hope and re-affirming its religious identity and social cohesion in the face of hardship and loss.

'Triumphant death'

The ever-present prospect of death – sometimes movingly tragic, as in the youthful demise of Kate Morcombe or the crushing underground of Hugh Datson – cast a perpetual shadow over the community. Disease took its toll, especially in epidemics that claimed many young lives, and there was a steady stream of mining accidents – some of them particularly grisly, as in 1893 when William Hobb of Cross Roads was killed. Descending one of the shafts at the Moonta mine, he momentarily put his head outside the skip in which he was travelling and had it dashed against the shaft wall.[98] But here again the Methodists offered comfort and support. Indeed, the 'triumphant death' – in which the dying person remained, even in his or her last moments, and despite all pain, serenely confident in the salvation of life everlasting – was something to be treasured, the Methodists insisted. At their chapels they sang Charles Wesley's words – 'Rejoice for a brother deceased, Our loss is his infinite gain'[99] – and the manner in which a person had died was the subject of endless fascination. It was important that Methodists should 'die well', as John Wesley had put it, and on the bleak frontier of northern Yorke Peninsula this stricture had especial weight. It helped people, those dying and those loved ones left behind, to bear their predicament. And, in its paradoxical way, it turned adversity *into* triumph.

When Captain Hancock's first wife, Sarah, succumbed to typhoid in June 1870 (just a few months after the *Wallaroo Times* newspaper had lambasted the Moonta company for 'the scandalous and disgraceful sanitary state of the Moonta Mines'),[100] her widower husband arranged for the headstone to be placed on her grave in Moonta cemetery. 'Shortly before the hour of dissolution', said the inscription composed by Captain Hancock, 'she calmly and distinctly expressed her humble trust in the Saviour in the following words: "Christ our wisdom, righteousness, sanctification and redemption"'.[101] Aged only thirty-two, she had 'died well': at four o'clock in the morning, as she had begun to fade, she had been 'filled with heavenly consolation', it was reported, and she joined with her husband Henry in whispering the words of 'Jesu, lover of my soul'. Shortly after seven o'clock, as it began to get light, she knew it was time to go.[102]

This was a gratifying example of 'the fullness and sweetness of Christian triumph', as the Rev. Charles Tresise described it in 1885 when commenting on the similar death of Eliza Thomas, aged only twenty, at Wallaroo. 'In her case,' said Tresise, 'the Jordan valley rang with songs of faith and joy ... There was no cessation for the whole 36 hours of this spiritual animation, except for a few minutes, when she laid her head on her mother's lap and sank to sleep saying, "I'm so tired".' Then, rallying from her slumber, she announced that she wished 'to sing all the way to heaven'. Turning to her sister, Eliza asked: 'Annie, don't the angels sing when they see another coming'. Annie replied that it was so, and Eliza answered that 'I can hear them singing beautifully now. I shall soon be through the pearly gates'.[103] It was another good death.

The miners' 'burying tune' – sung at funerals, often for those killed in the mines and who had had no time to prepare for their imminent and violent deaths – expressed similar sentiments. The mourners, though suddenly and tragically bereft, were urged to exult in the passage of their loved ones to Heaven:

> Sing from the chamber to the grave,
> I hear the dying miner say;
> A sound of melody I crave
> Upon my burial day.
>
> Sing sweetly whilst you travel on,
> And keep the funeral slow;
> The angels sing where I am gone
> And you should sing below.[104]

In 1902 the Rev. W.F. James, a Bible Christian minister, born in Cornwall at Truro in 1846 and active for many years on the Peninsula, recalled the spectacle of the old-time Cornish burial service. At Chacewater, in the heart of the Gwennap mining district in Cornwall, funerals were, he said, 'largely attended and the singing was memorable. Never shall I forget', he added, 'the sight of a funeral procession turning the corner of the street leading to the churchyard. The corpse was preceded by some twenty or thirty men, having good voices, with measured step and slow.' They were, James said, 'singing a solemn hymn to an appropriate tune. I have never heard anything like it, save at Moonta'.[105]

But death was, at best, a sombre joy. For all their fascination with the passing to the next world, the Methodists also knew how to have some fun in this. Most of all, they looked forward to their Sunday School Anniversaries or tea-treats, events which lent gaiety to otherwise drab lives and introduced a carnival atmosphere in which normal formalities were relaxed a little and people could indulge in simple pleasures. As the *Yorke's Peninsula Advertiser* remarked light-heartedly in April 1878: 'of tea-fights Cousin Jack and Cousin Jenny never seem to tire'.[106] Stanley Whitford recalled what it was like to participate in such Anniversaries at Moonta:

> The children headed by a brass band and the [Sunday] school Superintendent marched around the streets in class order, with the teachers beside their respective classes. Upon returning to the school, each child received a large bun and a packet of lollies [sweets]. Children brought their mugs for tea, and the elders would have a sit-down meal of home-made eatables, for which they paid. In the evening a big public-meeting was held in the church, and the annual report and balance-sheet of the school would be read.[107]

Saffron buns, pasties and cream-and-jam 'splits', all washed down with copious mugs-full of sugarless tea, made for an atmosphere of relaxation and care-free entertainment. But behind the innocent fun was the continuing moral pressure of self-help and mutual improvement. For the Methodists were insistent that, despite the pre-occupation with the next world, those present in this had a duty to make the best of their talents and to look continually for opportunities to improve the spiritual and moral qualities of their lives and those of their neighbours. Various mutual improvement societies sprang up on the Peninsula, as they did in Cornwall, and in the anxiety to create a model community on the frontier Temperance emerged as a major issue.

'Colonial brandy'

The locals had developed their own home-brewed herby beer, known as swanky, and 'moderate drinking' was apparent all over the Peninsula: in 1873 one visitor noted that 'ever and again you will hear sounds of singing from convivial Cornishmen who congregate together over a social glass'.[108] Such drinking was on the whole tolerated – indeed, many thought beer a wholesome working-men's beverage – and, as 'Sober Cornishman' explained in the local press in September 1878, it was the horror of 'colonial brandy' and hard spirits that really offended Methodists.[109] Nonetheless, there were those who disapproved of alcohol of any sort – Reuben Gill, Bible Christian local preacher and trade union activist, warned that 'little calves grow great cows, moderate drinkers become drunkards'[110] – and the Bands of Hope, Rechabites and other Temperance organizations active on the Mines preached total abstinence as the only means of achieving lasting improvement. In 1869 one hopeful contributor to the *Wallaroo Times* could note optimistically that 'Now, thanks to our temperance and religious institutions, there is to be seen less beer and more whitewash, less filth and dirty contagion ... less ribaldry, hubbub, and drunken rioting, and more decent, engaging, and improving conversation heard'.[111]

It was not, perhaps, the whole truth. But it was an aspiration with which many on northern Yorke Peninsula would readily identify. It reflected the familiar determination to confront conditions in this difficult environment, and it mirrored the evangelical zeal which would lie behind the periodic Revivals that would sweep the district. This zeal would also become apparent in the anxiety of the Methodists to follow the miners-turned-farmers who, as land on northern Yorke Peninsula was slowly made available for clearing and cultivation, began to turn their hands to agriculture in the country that lay beyond the mining settlements. Green's Plains, near Kadina – where, it was said, 'Farmers are struggling manfully to supplant mallee scrub with cornfields' – was producing cereals by 1870, and in June 1876 the *Yorke's Peninsula Advertiser* could report with satisfaction that 'cultivation is transforming that which was but a desert and scrubby waste'.[112] Here was the frontier re-visited, its limits pushed back once more, and the Methodists sought to play their traditional 'civilizing' role in this renewed taming of the wilderness. In 1883, for example, Reuben Gill embarked on a five-week Temperance lecturing tour of central and southern Yorke Peninsula. Nearer to home, John Prisk designed and built the modest Bible Christian chapel at the little agricultural settlement of Kulpara.[113]

'A very high opinion of themselves'

For contemporary observers, such progress was evidence that Moonta and the communities of northern Yorke Peninsula had indeed triumphed over adversity. In this triumph – wedded so closely, as it was, to the myth of Cousin Jenny and the ideology of Cornish Methodism – adversity was itself somehow a virtue. Without adversity there could be no triumph. If there had been no fearful heat, impenetrable scrub, water shortages, disease epidemics, tragic accidents and untimely deaths, then there would have been little need for the superior qualities that Cornish men and women imagined that they could bring to bear in such circumstances. If there had been no dirt, poverty, injustice, heavy drinking, sexual license, violence and other human frailties, then there would have been no requirement for self-help, mutual improvement and the search for a higher morality. The people of northern Yorke Peninsula believed that they had taken on adversity, and won.

And others believed so too, adding to the mystique that Moonta and environs had already built for itself. When May Vivienne, author of *Sunny South Australia*, visited the district at the turn of the twentieth century she seemed delighted with what she saw: for her, it was the myth made fact. She fell in love immediately with 'Moonta, or "Munta", as the old Cornishmen, of whom there are a great many, pronounce it'. 'The appearance of Moonta Mines is decidedly attractive,' she opined, its cottages 'decidedly comfortable,' and 'the majority of the Moonta miners are anything but uncouth workmen, but reading and thoughtful men; and I was quite astonished at the class of works I found on the bookshelves [of the Institute library].'[114] It was a happy and prosperous environment, she thought: 'Kadina on a Saturday night is in great form. All the miners and their wives seem to come in to do their marketing, and have a bit of amusement into the bargain ... they are sober and good-humoured, and politely make way for the stranger if he is civil.' Brass band music added to the festivity of such occasions, she added, and the local shops 'do a big trade in Cornish pasties, for the majority of the miners in this district are Cornishmen'. The hotels also 'do a big business', she said, 'but the miners, although they like a few drinks, and certainly get very jolly, are not nearly so rowdy as miners in other places I have visited'. Here was the cosy stability of 'Australia's Little Cornwall' in all its reassuring splendour. May Vivienne warmed to the myth and colluded in it unreservedly, doing her bit for its elaboration. At Moonta she thrilled at 'the wonders of the place', and she marvelled at the 'Thousands of people [who] flock the streets' to do their shopping in an array of well-stocked stores in the Peninsula towns.[115] She was impressed with what had been achieved in a place that was not so long ago a fearsome wilderness; and, she added, rather approvingly, 'the people living there have a very high opinion of themselves'.[116]

CHAPTER SIX

'Moonta's little, but she's great'
The enduring myth

'Moonta's little, but she's great.'[1] So wrote George Jose in his poem 'Moonta and the Great War', penned in 1921. A former Moonta miner, Jose had returned to his native Cornwall just after the turn of the century, retiring to the parish of Illogan in the Camborne–Redruth mining country. This was the same George Jose who coined the Kiplingesque quip 'what do they know of Cornwall, who only Cornwall know?', suggesting that those who sought to understand modern Cornwall needed first to appreciate the scale of the 'Great Emigration' and the existence of a 'greater Cornwall' beyond the seas.[2] In his retirement, Jose looked back with increasing nostalgia to what he remembered as Moonta's glory days. Sitting 'right here on Carn Brea hill', as he put it in 1921 in a letter to the Moonta *People's Weekly*, he confessed that 'I feel proud of Moonta ... Oh! how I fancy the old place and my school days at Moonta Mines.' Moonta, he said, had 'turned out Prime Ministers [he meant State Premiers: John Verran in South Australia and Jack Scaddan in Western Australia], members of Parliament, reverend ministers, and mine captains'. He yearned, he admitted, for those long-lost earlier times: 'I left Moonta in 1902, and I should like to be back in those old days again, but it's onward ever onward – no going back'.[3]

George Jose was writing in the aftermath of the Great War and on the eve, almost, of the abandonment of the Moonta and Wallaroo mines in 1923. It was clear already, as Jose must have known, that the mines were living on borrowed time: there had been a succession of temporary suspensions after the war, the first in 1919, and most observers sensed that the end was near. As Jose acknowledged, it was a moment of profound change. The Great War had transformed many things, and in its wake in the 1920s much more was to alter; often, people felt, for the worst. In Cornwall, where Jose was now living, the brief wartime upturn in the fortunes of the tin mining industry was soon left far behind, as the Cornish mines faced their worst crisis for a generation. In 1921, the year Jose wrote to the *People's Weekly*, there was but one mine active in the whole of Cornwall – Giew, part of the St Ives Consolidated group – the rest abandoned for good or lying idle in the hope of better days ahead. In South Australia, the fortunes of the copper industry mirrored those of Cornish tin, the upsurge in demand for the strategic metal during the war falling abruptly when hostilities ceased.

'The valiant stand of Moonta / With her few heroic men'

The Great War had also had profound effects upon the nature of the Cornish transnational identity. Although there was a flurry of departures from Cornwall in the mid-1920s – for the Ontario gold mines in particular, aided by the Canadian government – the demand for Cornish labour overseas had all but dried up. In such circumstances, the intimacy and immediacy in the relationship between Cornwall and her overseas communities was bound to fade. At Moonta, in any case, some forty years had passed since Captain Piper's recruiting drive in Cornwall in 1883, the last major influx of Cornish onto northern Yorke Peninsula, and Moonta and environs were now firmly the focus of 'Cousin Jack' identity – instead of distant, dimly remembered Cornwall. Moreover, the Great War itself had accelerated changing perceptions of identity. The apocryphal Billy Bray, as we saw in Chapter One (pp. 6–7), had insisted in war-torn France that Moonta was the 'hub of the universe'. Yet this was but one part of an emerging Australian national consciousness, where loyalty to King and Empire, and Cornwall too, was tempered by an increasingly vibrant, even vociferous Australian nationalism. Private J.W. Gill wrote home to Moonta from Anzac Cove soon after the landings at Gallipoli: 'Johnny Turk will never forget it. He felt the Australian bayonet then, and he has shown a great disinclination to face it ever since.'[4] Trooper Jake Roach, another Peninsula boy, thought that if 'the Empire had a few thousand more men in France and Gallipoli like the Australians I reckon they would make short work of the Germans and Turks'.[5]

George Jose appeared to recognize these changes. He welcomed the self-confident rise of Moonta and celebrated its achievements, applauding the exploits of Moonta's sons on the battlefields of the Great War. But he was also delighted when some of those sons chose to spend their leave or convalescent periods in Cornwall – searching out, as many did, friends and relations and places with family connections – hoping that this would perpetuate the link between Moonta and Cornwall:

> Many deeds of pluck and daring
>   Shine upon the roll of fame;
> Some are great, heroic, noble,
>   Bearing a thrice-honoured name.

> But a greater, nobler action
>   Ne'er was writ by any pen
> Than the valiant stand of Moonta,
>   With her few heroic men.
>
> I could doff my hat in honour
>   To the Moontas near our gate,
> And I'm proud to pen this tribute –
>   Moonta's little, but she's great.
>
> Though I'm not an aged prophet,
>   Though I'm not an honoured seer,
> I'd predict this – without question,
>   In the marriage lines so dear –
>
> There'll be many an Australian soldier
>   Linked with some sweet Cornish girl.
> Who could blame them? Not the writer.
>   He would e'er their flag unfurl.
>
> He would throw the rice and slipper,
>   And his joy would ne'er abate,
> And he writes with lasting pleasure –
>   Moonta's little, but she's great.[6]

Jose was not alone in such thoughts, and in January 1921 the enigmatic 'Oneuno' contributed an in several respects similar piece to the *People's Weekly*. Entitled 'Lest We Forget Trelawny', the composition argued that the spirit of Bishop Jonathan Trelawny – thrown into the Tower by James II in 1688 – had lived on in all the subsequent exploits of Cornish history, manifested most recently in Moonta's daring feats of arms in the Great War. It was, he suggested, a legacy that should not be forgotten on northern Yorke Peninsula:

> Trelawny was lord bishop, sir
> Of Bodmin town and Exeter,
>   When Turncoat [James II] ruled the land –
> He who forgot his Bible oath,
> Who lost his crown and sceptre both,
>   And wept, we understand.
>
> Trelawny was at Waterloo,

At Alma, Marne, the North Sea, too,
  And at Gallipoli;
With right and left he did his work,
Smiting at Bulgar, Hun and Turk,
  In air, on land, and sea.[7]

There were indeed those at Moonta who remembered 'Trelawny': both the exhilarating spirit of Cornish defiance, and the patriotic ballad so-named. In 1910, for example, 'Practical Miner' proudly recalled the opening ceremony, many years before, of Wheal Trelawny silver-lead mine at Menheniot in Cornwall: 'how the old Cornish miners heartily joined in singing – And Shall Trelawney die?'[8] There were also those who continued to proclaim the Peninsula as 'our Cornish colony'.[9] And there remained a sense that those born on the Peninsula were somehow as 'Cornish' as their forebears. Their ethnic origins were betrayed, as much as anything, by the enduring Cornish accent commonplace in the district. 'You would think', thought one observer, 'that they came direct from Cornwall when you listened to their Cornish brogue'.[10] Likewise, one Benjamin Rose was 'a native-born Australian, but coming of Cornish parents and having spent so many years in that Cornwall beneath the Southern Cross, Moonta, his speech betrayed his descent'.[11]

Nonetheless, despite the anxieties of George Jose and Oneuno or the fond remembrances of old-timers like Practical Miner, the reality was that the 'Cousin Jack' identity of northern Yorke Peninsula had acquired a life and force of its own. As we have seen already, there had been a complex process of cultural change observable in the decades since the first European settlement on northern Yorke Peninsula. 'Cornishness' had been an important resource for those constructing the new communities, the myth of Cousin Jack – and Cousin Jenny – asserting the inevitable triumph of the Cornish and their way of life in this forbidding environment. From the first, Moonta and environs had been proudly 'Cornish' but, as we have seen, the institutional life of the Peninsula – from Captain Hancock's managerial regime to the role of the trade unions and the Methodist churches – had, while drawing on this reservoir of 'Cornishness', crafted a new identity that was overtly and unmistakably 'Moonta'. It was an identity rooted in the people, places and (above all) institutions of northern Yorke Peninsula, in which Moonta and environs were thought – by both 'insiders' and 'outsiders' – to be quantifiably 'different' from other localities in South Australia. Often, this was a 'difference' that was seen to exist in cultural and geographical isolation from these other localities, the people in distant Adelaide half-jokingly imagining that Peninsula folk had 'long tails' and knowing that they were looked upon by Moontaites as 'foreigners'.

This sense of 'other' extended to the realm of politics, the United Labor Party on northern Yorke Peninsula remaining independent of its 'parent' body in Adelaide – to which it was only informally affiliated – and acting according to its own convictions and interests, as in the Federation debate, when these were at variance with the party line. However, despite this sense of cultural distance, the communities of northern Yorke Peninsula had made a strong and enduring contribution to the development of the Labor movement in South Australia as a whole. This was a legacy that was widely acknowledged across the State (as South Australia had become in 1901): so much so that, even after the swift demise of the region's copper mines, the Peninsula remained in popular imagination the heartland of the Labor movement. Moreover, even as the ULP became ever more embroiled in agendas that were distinctly Australian – the new political allegiances that had emerged after 1901, the Conscription issue of 1916, the 'Premiers' Plan' of 1933 – the public at large remembered the distinctive Moonta–Methodist inheritance. Indeed, the Labor hierarchy itself reflected this Nonconformist, mining legacy well into the 1920s and 1930s; in its membership but also in its attitudes, prejudices and preoccupations. As Donald Hopgood has noted, even into the 1920s and 1930s the cartoonist's stock stereotype of the South Australian Labor politician was a corpulent Cousin Jack complete with Moonta billy-goat beard and with a red flag hidden behind his back, the latter signifying a presumed commitment to 'advanced socialism' despite a homely and beguiling rhetoric that sounded reassuringly moderate and pragmatic.[12] And as John Lonie has concluded in his shrewd analysis of South Australian politics in the inter-war period: 'By 1930, the ALP [Australian Labor Party] itself did not mirror, in its hierarchy, the changes that had taken place in the composition of the [State's] work force since the time of the party's inception, and especially since the end of World War I'. Rather, Lonie argued, 'its composition and ideology reflected the social situation of the 1890s. Of note was the still very strong Methodist flavour which derived in the first place from the mine workers of Burra and Wallaroo who were of Cornish stock.'[13]

The first three decades of the twentieth century, then, had witnessed a weakening in the ties between Moonta and Cornwall: a process that had caused distress to some but was inexorable, indeed inevitable. Yet it was also a period that had seen the consolidation of northern Yorke Peninsula's distinctive regional identity. Nowhere was this identity more profound than in the realm of politics, where the Peninsula was imagined to be a powerhouse of the Labor movement in South Australia, a belief that survived the abrupt abandonment of the mines in 1923 and the consequent dispersal of the Peninsula's population. It was a tribute to the strength of Moonta's myth that its presumed importance in the State's popular imagination, and its continuing influence in Labor's corridors of power, should have so clearly outlasted its economic significance.

'Honest John' Verran

The symbolic triumph of Moonta's myth in this period was the Premiership of 'Honest John' Verran, the ebullient Moontaite who brought the Peninsula's particular brand of social democracy to bear on the political life of South Australia. In the April 1910 State Election the United Labor Party was swept into office for the first time, its leader, John Verran, becoming State Premier. A Cornish miner and Methodist local preacher, Verran was born at Cusgarne in the parish of Gwennap on 9 July 1856.[14] As a youngster he emigrated with his parents to South Australia, where he found work at the Kapunda copper mine as a pickey-boy (ore-sorter). Later, he moved on to the Moonta mine, where he worked underground as a tributer until his election to the Adelaide Parliament in 1901. John McConnell Black, the South Australian essayist and diarist, thought Verran 'the typical Cornish miner, with his burly frame, his goatee and general exuberance',[15] and there is little doubt that Verran's working-class, Cornish background accounted for his popularity amongst the Yorke Peninsula miners as he became involved in local trade unionism and politics. As the Adelaide *Advertiser* was to put it in 1910: 'Mr Verran is the more popular at the Peninsula towns because only nine years ago he was working with his three sons at the 360 fathom level at Taylor's Shaft at

30. 'Honest' John Verran, born in Gwennap, Cornwall, in 1856: South Australia's first Labor Premier, 1910–12.

Moonta'.[16] Indeed, Verran had shared all the exertions and dangers of those he strove to represent in politics. In April 1899 he had had a lucky escape when caught in a rock fall underground – his helmet had been smashed to pieces and he had suffered a severe gash to the head.[17]

Verran's Methodist allegiance was also important. Brought up a Primitive Methodist, he purposely mixed religious teaching with political debate. An article in the *Plain Dealer* newspaper in 1911, for example, noted how in a sermon at Wallaroo Mines Methodist Church Verran had used the parable of the 'Barren Fig Tree' to attack 'modern commercialism'.[18] On another occasion he had insisted 'that his M.P. (Membership of Parliament) was due to his P.M. (Primitive Methodism)'.[19] One observer thought that had 'not Methodism first made him a preacher, politics could not know him now as Premier',[20] while to those who argued that religion had no place in politics, Verran replied:

> Religion is citizenship, and the relationship between religion and politics is very close ... When we come to justice and righteousness and truth these are great elementary principles of religion which affect the basis of our manhood. Religion is not a question of going to heaven. It is a question of living and making the world better for having been in it.[21]

Verran had his first opportunity to put this concept of active citizenship into effect when, as President of the Moonta, Kadina and Wallaroo Branch of the Amalgamated Miners' Association (AMA), he led the miners out on strike in 1891–92 in demand for more favourable employment contracts. The strike was not a success (see pp. 127–8). But the Peninsula branch of the AMA survived the trauma of 1892, establishing itself further as an integral part of community life and continuing to put pressure on the mine company, negotiating further changes to the contract system and welcoming the company's new workers' welfare policies. It also developed an increasingly political agenda, fostering links with the United Labor Party and putting forward John Verran as a parliamentary candidate.

Verran was first elected to the State Parliament in a by-election in June 1901, having promised in his campaign to pursue 'liberal measures'.[22] He also pledged himself to reform of the Legislative Council, South Australia's conservative upper house, a commitment to which he adhered – even though it was to precipitate the collapse of his Ministry in 1912. In the State Election of 1902 he was returned with a handsome majority, and in the Elections of 1905 and 1906 he again topped the poll, the principal issue of the day being reform of the Legislative Council. A Labor–Radical Liberal coalition had been returned with increased strength in 1906 but, despite this popular mandate, the Legislative Council was successful in frustrating most of its plans. In 1909 the Premier, Tom Price, died. His death put pressure on the coalition, elements of the Labor Party arguing that – as they were the dominant coalition partner – the next Premier should also be chosen from amongst their ranks. In fact, in a sort of 'buggin's turn' power brokering, A.H. Peake, the Radical Liberal leader, was chosen. Several Labor members refused to serve under him, and so Peake, with his coalition collapsing, was forced into a new alliance with country and conservative members, a prelude to the new political allegiances that were soon to form.

Verran, in the meantime, had replaced Price as leader of the United Labor Party, and in the Election of April 1910 Labor found itself in office in its own right for the very first time.[23] Verran received a hero's welcome as he returned from Adelaide to Yorke Peninsula as Premier. The conservative *Kadina and Wallaroo Times* claimed that the demonstrations that greeted Verran were 'the most miserable specimens of his irresponsibility ... Torches and bands and wild words, and gesticulations.'[24] A more sympathetic account observed that:

There could be no doubt as to the warmth of the welcome which the Cornish miners sought to give to their President on his being raised to place and power, and the gathering will mark an epoch in the history of Moonta. Bunting was flying all over the town, and all Moonta and his wife were out to take part in the gathering. At Kadina and at Wallaroo hundreds of workers joined the train, and the scene on arrival at Moonta was an animated one. The Wallaroo town band and the combined Moonta Commonwealth and Model brass bands discoursed music as the train drew up in the platform.[25]

There followed speeches, and cheering, and even the shedding of tears. But the triumph was premature, for the Labor victory had the effect of galvanizing the hitherto disparate non-Labor factions into a new and strong Opposition force. Ironically, several of the prime movers in this progress towards Opposition were Cornishmen of long standing in the State, two of them former Labor supporters to boot. One was John George Bice, born in Callington, Cornwall, in 1853, a Methodist, trade unionist and former blacksmith at the Moonta mine. Following his marriage to Elizabeth Jane Trewenack, a Cornish woman, in 1875 he established a merchant's business in Port Augusta, becoming Mayor of that town in 1888–89 and first entering the Adelaide Parliament in 1894. He opposed 'repressive legislation,' he said, and as for women: 'I am in favour of Adult Suffrage and because I believe that women are equally as intelligent, equally as capable of studying political questions, and of recording their vote as we are, I think they should have the same privileges as men in this respect.'[26]

Such views marked out Bice as a Radical Liberal, and during the 1890s he supported the ULP (although he never formally joined its ranks), identifying with its moderate and pragmatic form of democratic socialism and the Cornish–Methodist ethos expounded by its Peninsula adherents. However, in 1906, with both 'socialists' and 'conservatives' becoming more organized, he was instrumental in the formation of the Liberal and Democratic Union, led by Peake. This, in turn, was fused with the Farmers' and Producers' Political Union and the Australian National League to form the centre-right United Liberal Union in June 1910, a little over a month since Labor's famous victory. The organizing secretary of the Farmers' and Producers' Political Union was then David Morley Charleston, another Cornishman. Born in St Erth in 1848, Charleston had been an engineer at Harvey & Co. of Hayle before emigrating to San Francisco in 1874 and arriving in Australia in 1884, in 1887 finding work in the English and Australian Copper Company's smelting works at Port Adelaide. Said to be imbued 'with characteristic Cornish fervour and enthusiasm',[27] he had won the support of the local *Christian Weekly and Methodist Journal* – which announced that 'the ideals of labour were consistent with Christianity'[28] – and he argued for a 'broad liberal Unionism', one which might somehow fuse the ideas of John Stuart Mill and Karl Marx. On the strength of such views he was elected to the Adelaide Parliament as a Labor member in 1891. However, despite his firm left-of-centre commitment, Charleston quarrelled with the parliamentary ULP. In the Election that followed, therefore, Charleston stood as an 'Independent Liberal', and was returned with a substantial majority over his ULP rival. Thereafter, he drifted gradually to the right of the political spectrum, and entered the new Federal Parliament as a centre-right Liberal Senator in 1901–03.

From triumph to disaster

The political polarization that had previously bound together hitherto like-minded men such as Verran, Bice and Charleston did not augur well for the new Labor government. As T.H. Smeaton observed in 1914: 'The path trodden by the Verran Government was not at any time a smooth one; beset as it was by snares skillfully laid by its enemies, as well as by obstacles heedlessly cast there by its friends'.[29] Indeed, the government's first year in office was characterized by industrial strife, with more than half-a-dozen major incidents in Adelaide, each one an embarrassment for Verran whose sympathies were with the trade unionists and yet who was under great pressure (not least from the Opposition) to resist what were portrayed as challenges to law and order. In December 1910 the Adelaide cart-drivers' strike erupted, an episode that proved particularly damaging for Verran. Critics suggested he was in league with the strikers, John McConnell Black writing that: 'Jack Verran took a

31. VIP visit to the Wallaroo mine, October 1910. H. Lipson Hancock is second from left. Fifth, sixth and seventh from left are, respectively, Captain James Pryor (father of Oswald Pryor), Captain Nicholas Opie and Captain Tom Tamblyn.

jovial interest in the strike and Gunn, the secretary of the union, used to stroll across Victoria Square [in the centre of Adelaide] from the Trades Hall and consult with the Premier, who sat smoking his short pipe with his legs up on the fence of his boarding house in Landrowna Terrace'.[30] Events began to turn ugly when strike-breakers (some of whom were armed) engaged by the local Tramways Trust clashed with the striking drivers, provoking a riot. The State Governor, His Majesty's representative in South Australia, summoned Verran to Government House for a dressing-down, and it was rumoured that a Naval gunboat was about to be deployed to Port Adelaide. In the end, the strike was settled peaceably enough, with the cart-drivers securing better pay and conditions, but the damage to Verran and his government had already been done.

The Opposition had been careful to exploit the situation to the full, and was given additional ammunition in the form of the State mining controversy that unfolded during 1910 and 1911. Verran had decided to acquire the near-defunct Wandilta, Yelta and Paramatta copper mines, all on northern Yorke Peninsula and located within his constituency, with a view to running them as State enterprises, for 'God had put the wealth in the earth for everyone and not just a few people'.[31] To the Opposition this 'nationalization' was seen as evidence of Verran's commitment to 'advanced socialism', though Verran retorted that it was just sound business sense. It was a great pity, he said, that promising properties 'should be languishing for want of capital'. At one of the ailing mines, he insisted, all that was needed was 'a good Cornish lift pump to get the water out'.[32] Somewhat recklessly, Verran purchased the Yelta and Paramatta mines without reference to parliament and, indeed, without reference to all the relevant officials within his own Department of Mines. As he explained angrily: 'I am not going to officers who don't know as much about mining as I do'.[33] Although the Yelta and Paramatta mines had lost £200,000 in the eight years before July 1911, Verran insisted that the Yelta had made a profit of £1,000 a month during the early 1900s and that recent reverses were merely the result of bad management. He envisaged, he said, a return of about four per cent on the capital invested, noting that the two properties had been purchased for only £6,000 while the smelting plant at the Yelta was alone worth £20,000.

In the public controversy that ensued, the Labor-sponsored *Daily Herald* supported the purchases but the Adelaide *Register* considered that Verran was 'wasting public money in a vain attempt to resurrect an abandoned property in his district'.[34] On Yorke Peninsula itself, the *Kadina and Wallaroo Times* added its voice to the condemnation of State ownership, while local experts such as Captain Richard Cowling advised that Verran's estimation of the mines' worth was unduly optimistic.[35] W.H. Trewenack (ironically, J.G. Bice's brother-in-law) was engaged to run the mines but in the event the experiment in State ownership did not last long, the incoming government in 1913 soon taking measures to close the properties.

In addition to the cart-drivers' strike and the State mining controversy, the Opposition was able to exploit the Verran government's practice of 'tacking', the attaching of provisions for new, hitherto undiscussed, public works to the Appropriation (Budget) Bill. The Opposition argued that 'tacking' was a device employed by Verran to push through legislation of a 'socialist' nature without proper parliamentary scrutiny. In the Appropriation Bill presented to the Adelaide Parliament in December 1911 there was a 'tacked' provision for the establishment of a State brickworks. This was used as a pretext by the conservative Legislative Council, the upper house, to defer the Bill, an action tantamount to refusal of the government's supply. This brought to a head a series of confrontations between Verran and the Legislative Council. In the September of 1911 the Council had rejected, for the second time, the Council Veto Bill, a measure to limit the powers of the Legislative Council, while it had also rejected, laid aside or permitted to lapse more than a dozen other Bills, all of them reformist. This was a time when there were parallel moves to restrict the powers of the House of Lords, the United Kingdom's upper house, and Verran secretly approached Asquith, asking for British intervention for 'the Constitution [of South Australia] to be so amended by an Imperial Act as to enable the matured will of the people of South Australia on these and all other questions to become law'.[36] Asquith replied that it would not be proper for him to intervene, and so, with his supply refused, Verran had little choice but to request the dissolution of Parliament and seek an election.

The election campaign that followed was described at the time as 'the most important and fiercest political battle ever fought in South Australia'.[37] Verran bitterly attacked Peake, calling him 'a political rogue' and condemning him and his 'so-called Liberals ... [for] turning from Democrat to Conservative',[38] a recognition of the threat posed to Labor by the newly coherent forces of the centre right. Indeed, in the election Labor faired badly, losing control of the House of Assembly (the lower house) and thus the government. The only constituency not to follow the anti-Labor trend was Wallaroo, Verran's own seat, showing that Verran had not yet lost his personal following in the mining communities of Yorke Peninsula. However, Verran was discredited by the defeat of February 1912, and he resigned from the Labor leadership in the following year, citing as his reason his wife's continuing ill-health.

Significantly, despite his continued popularity at Moonta, Wallaroo and Kadina, Verran had lost the unequivocal support of the Methodist establishment in South Australia. In February 1912 the *Australian Christian Commonwealth*, a Methodist magazine published in Adelaide, had warned that Verran and his cabinet colleagues had been too 'prepared to take their orders from the more violent and revolutionary forces in their party'[39] and, detecting a sinister Irish hand in this, felt that 'efforts are being made to dominate the Labour Party by the Church of Rome'.[40] This estrangement of Methodism from the Labor Party was soon perpetuated and deepened by the conscription issue which emerged during the Great War, a distancing which caused real trauma for the Moonta–Methodist tradition within Labor in South Australia.[41]

'A Britisher and a Cornishman'

The debate over whether conscription to the armed forces should be introduced raged throughout Australia. Although essentially a matter of principle and conscience, the anti-conscriptionist lobby was seen by its detractors as a Fenian, Popish and even pro-German plot.[42] In the eastern States of Victoria and New South Wales, the Irish-Catholic lobby was strong. When the Labor Party in those States adopted an anti-conscription policy, the worst fears of its critics seemed to be confirmed. Although different in make-up from its eastern States counterparts, the Labor Party in South Australia followed suit and duly adopted the anti-conscription line, immediately aggravating the tension between Methodism and the Labor movement. The Methodist Church, with its increasingly anti-Catholic rhetoric, declared in favour of conscription. The effect was traumatic, especially amongst the mining communities of northern Yorke Peninsula. Those who were Labor men first and Methodists second moved firmly behind their party, while for those for whom religion *was* politics resignation from the Labor Party was inevitable. A Moonta Anti-Conscription League sprang up but even as it was mobilizing its supporters so John Verran was announcing his resignation from the ULP and the foundation of the Moonta branch of the pro-Conscription National Labor Party.[43]

Verran managed to hold on to local support but others found a new champion in Robert Stanley (R.S.) Richards, a young trade union activist. Born at Moonta Mines in 1885, he was the son of Richard Richards of Camborne and Mary Jeffery of Tuckingmill, two Cornish emigrants. He was a Methodist local preacher but he was noticeably to the left of Verran and the earlier generation of Cornish miners. He was, therefore, an anti-Conscriptionist and he had a ready appeal for like-minded younger, second-generation Cousin Jacks. Stanley Whitford, for example, was born at Moonta in 1878. A man especially proud of his Cornish roots, Whitford, like many others from Yorke Peninsula, had been on the Western Australian goldfields in the mid-1890s where 'I was camped with a nest of Cousin Jacks from Moonta'.[44] There he had enjoyed the camaraderie of the miners, Cornish and non-Cornish, and had picked up his ideas about the relationship between bosses and workers and had acquired his Labor credentials. Come the Great War, he was 'opposed to conscription because it violated my ideals as a follower of the International Socialist movement'. He was especially critical of Verran: 'I placed him among my list of damned old humbugs, and he never reinstated himself in my estimation'. Verran was, Whitford said, 'robust, good looking, good voiced, but ignorant ... [one] in whom I had no trust'.[45] Richards was able to exploit such sentiment in the election of 1918 when, standing as the official Labor Party candidate for Wallaroo, he ousted John Verran, who had stood on the National Labor ticket.

Out of parliament for the first time since 1901, and with his local power base seriously eroded, Verran attempted to win new sources of political support. Indeed, recognizing that his support on the Peninsula was no longer solid, he had cultivated a strong anti-German stance early in the war. He argued that its was necessary for the British Empire to crush Germany so that Europe could be cleaned up, 'just as the Cornish people like their general cleaning up at Christmas'.[46] In Parliament in 1916 and 1917 he introduced Bills designed to disenfranchise South Australia's sizeable German community (both Bills narrowly failed to make their way onto the statute book), and in August 1916 he had declared in the House of Assembly: 'It is deplorable to allow those with German blood in their veins to vote in this country. No matter what they cry out, they must have a bias for Germany. I am a Britisher and a Cornishman, and no one can take away my feelings of loyalty to my country.'[47]

To some extent Verran was successful in retrieving support through his anti-German stance, one contributor to the Moonta *People's Weekly* asking, 'Who but a Hun would not say that Mr Verran is one of the most popular legislators of the State'?[48] With the end of the war, however, the German question lost its immediacy, and once again Verran found himself politically isolated. The National Labor Party tried to retain the Methodist vote by embracing the Temperance 'prohibitionist' cause but Verran failed (albeit narrowly) to regain his Wallaroo seat in 1921, and his alienation from mainstream Labor was now complete. Like Bice and Charleston before him, he was pushed further to the right of the political spectrum, and in 1924 he was contesting Wallaroo as a Liberal. In a campaign speech at Moonta he declared that:

> He could not see how any country could accept socialistic proposals of socializing all means of industry. He considered the Labor Party ideals took away a man's fundamental rights which were the basis of our civilisation. Home life went when communism came on, and he would never favour any policy which took away his right to build his home.[49]

Verran also blamed the collapse of the Wallaroo and Moonta mines in 1923 on the activities of trade union militants, although, as R.S. Richards pointed out, all this sounded very strange coming from the man who, more than anyone, had been responsible for developing the Labor movement on the Peninsula. Not surprisingly, Verran was defeated in 1924 and, with the exception of a brief spell in the Federal Senate from 1927 to 1928 when he was appointed to fill a casual vacancy, his political career was finished. He died in 1932.

The Conscription issue and its aftermath had been a personal trauma for John Verran but it had also been unsettling for the communities of northern Yorke Peninsula, presenting them with deep and bitter divisions, a marked contrast to the solidarity and cohesion they had displayed before the Great War. The estrangement of Methodism from Labor was especially painful. There was, inevitably, a generational dimension to the divisions that had emerged, the older Cornish-born population striving to preserve the Methodist–Labor link and the younger activists adopting a more militant position over conscription and other issues. There were also issues of identity at work here: the younger generation was more susceptible to a nascent Australian nationalism, and was likely to be more critical of the Imperial connection and more sensitive to Australian perspectives and Australian agendas.

It was a measure of Moonta's wider influence in Australia that its particular variant of the Conscription crisis – which forced people to chose between their Methodist and Labor affiliations – was replicated elsewhere where Moontaites had settled. Jack Scaddan, for example, born at Moonta in 1876, went to the Western Australian goldfields in the 1890s, settling there and entering the Legislative Assembly in Perth in 1904 as a Labor member and rapidly rising to become Premier. However, like Verran, the conscription issue forced him from the Labor Party and into the National Labor camp. So too with George Pearce, born 'of Cornish stock' in South Australia. He also travelled to Western Australia in the 1890s, and by 1910 was representing that State in the Federal Senate as a Labor member. Like Scaddan and Verran, he clashed with his Labor colleagues over conscription and found refuge in the National Labor ranks. Peter Heydon, his biographer and one-time personal secretary and confidante, wrote that for Pearce the conscription issue was 'the dominating, shattering political experience ... Pearce was not a bigot. A Protestant and of Cornish extraction, he tried to keep the whole conscription issue free of sectarian and Irish political issues.'[50]

'The "Bogies", the "Split", and the "Betterment Principle"'

Meanwhile, back in South Australia, the split in the Labor Party caused by the Conscription issue was mirrored in a corresponding split in the miners' union on northern Yorke Peninsula. During 1917 the Amalgamated Miners' Association held a ballot to determine whether it should merge with the Australian Workers' Union (AWU). The younger miners, such as R.S. Richards and his supporters, were in favour of the merger for 'unity is strength' but the older Cornishmen, including John Verran, opposed the move and feared that 'We will lose control of industrial matters locally'.[51] The merger went ahead, with R.S. Richards becoming President of the Moonta branch of the AWU, but Verran reacted by forming a new organization: officially the Yorke's Peninsula's Miners' and Smelters' Association but known to many local inhabitants as the 'Bogus' Union. The Wallaroo and Moonta company was accused of victimizing the militants who had engineered the AWU merger, while the 'Bogies' (members of Verran's 'Bogus' Union) were in turn victimized by the AWU men and ostracized by sections of the local community. Verran, allegedly in cahoots with the bosses, was bitterly criticized for causing 'much distress in many homes in this district'.[52] He retorted – or so it was claimed – that the AWU was 'led by Pommies who came out from England to escape conscription'.[53] R.S. Richards' electoral victory in 1918 consolidated the position of the AWU on the Peninsula but this did not prevent 'Old Cornishman' from writing to the local press to complain about the AWU's supposedly militant tactics.54

In the earlier twentieth century, in the years before 'the split' (as it was known), the AMA had enjoyed widespread support on the Peninsula, establishing a coherence and solidarity which created a certain stability within the community and lent the Union stature in dealing with external organizations, not least the bosses. Its behaviour was restrained but it was organized, competent and usually successful in its negotiations with the mine company. As the *Register* had remarked in August 1914: 'Although politically a "red hot Labour centre", the Yorke's Peninsula mines have been remarkably free from labour troubles'.55 After the strike of 1891–92, the AMA had used its influence to good effect in dealing with the mine management, co-operating with the latter's plan for rapid modernization at the mines in return for the development of an advanced welfare policy, two boom periods (1905–07 and 1911–18) creating the right conditions for this symbiotic relationship to grow.

This relationship, in turn, had been reliant upon the managerial regime of H. Lipson Hancock, who in 1898 had succeeded his father – the legendary Captain H.R. Hancock – as General Superintendent of the Wallaroo and Moonta mines. He had been born and bred on the Peninsula, spoke (it was said) with a pronounced Cornish accent, and was, despite his hybrid Devonian–Yorkshire parentage, generally considered a Cousin Jack. As one colleague put it: 'Lipson Hancock had all the Cornish virtues and only one of the vices. He was warm-hearted, hospitable, and genuinely concerned for the welfare of those under him. On Sunday afternoon he visited any old miner who was seriously ill.' And yet, 'Lipson's one limitation – and he knew it – was that of suspiciousness, characteristic of Cornishmen'.56 But despite this apparent 'Cornishness', Lipson Hancock considered himself first and foremost an Australian. This did not prevent him from making the traditional pilgrimage to Cornwall and Devon, following in the footsteps of other Wallaroo and Moonta mine captains before him, but his first impressions there were exactly congruent with the Janus-like culture from which he sprang. Acknowledging an affinity and an inheritance, he knew nonetheless that in only a very conditional sense could Cornwall – or, for that matter, Devon – be considered 'home'. He visited Launceston on market day, writing later that 'the crowds of country folk in the streets called up memories of home people at Moonta on Saturday nights. In fact,' he said, 'there is a strong feeling of being as near home in that district [the Cornwall–Devon border] as it was ever possible to be, away from the true "homeland" by the sea in sunny South Australia.'57

On taking the reins at Wallaroo and Moonta, Lipson Hancock pursued a bold and enterprising programme of development. In the space of a few years he had transformed them from being typical, but increasingly rather old-fashioned, Cornish mines into modern industrial units. The old Cornish engines and their massive stone-built engine-houses, with the flimsy 'shears' standing above the shafts, gave way to enormous galvanized-iron power-houses and gigantic head-frames. At Moonta, where only low-grade ore was left, underground work was allowed to decline, and greater attention focused on the re-treatment of wastes through the cementation process. Wallaroo now became the more important of the two mines. There was considerable movement of personnel and machinery from Moonta to Wallaroo, and much of the capital investment undertaken in the 1900s was concentrated at the latter mine. Development there, Lipson Hancock explained to the directors, would have to be 'vigorously pushed forward'.[58] By October 1900 he was pressing ahead with a new main winding shaft at Wallaroo, an enterprise which was to cost an estimated £15,000 over three years. Nearly £14,000 was expended on the cementation works at Moonta during 1900–01. Several railway locomotives were ordered, and new winding machinery was purchased from James Martin's foundry at Gawler.

Unfortunately, this rapid expansion was checked by a disastrous fire at Taylor's shaft at Wallaroo in June 1904, when the Cornish engine employed there was destroyed and much havoc was wreaked underground. Lipson Hancock estimated that it would cost £25,000 to make good the destruction. The directors were dismayed. They cautioned Lipson Hancock about the scale of his plans, and drew a response from him of which his father, the formidable 'H.R.H.', would have been proud. 'Much advantage to the Company had already accrued by the progressive policy which he had adopted,' he protested, 'and would still have accrued but for the unfortunate fire at Wallaroo Mines.' Moreover, 'in view of the skill and devotion shown by the great majority of the Company's officers, the remarks of the visiting Directors reflected on all concerned and were not warranted by the circumstances'.[59] As in earlier days, the directors backed off. By 1905 an entirely new Taylor's shaft had been sunk at Wallaroo (J. Moyle, the chief pitman, had been sent to the Great Boulder Mine, Western Australia, to observe the latest shaft-sinking techniques), complete with electrically driven underground pumps, a modern steel headframe and new winding house.[60] By 1906 there were no fewer than 2,700 men employed directly in the mines and at the smelters, with many more in the district whose livelihoods depended upon them. In 1907 the directors again warned 'Mr [Lipson] Hancock that the cost of production must be kept down' [61] but, as before, he held his ground and argued passionately for further modernization and investment. By 1911 the directors were admitting freely their indebtedness to his far-sighted planning.

Integral to this process of expansion, was the enhancement of the company's welfare provisions. Originally a transplantation of the Cornish-style Club & Doctor Fund and bal-surgeon arrangements established in the

32. New investment at the Wallaroo mine: Office Shaft, c.1900–10.

mid-nineteenth century at the Burra Burra and other major South Australian copper mines, the 'Betterment Principle' as it developed on northern Yorke Peninsula was a part of the modernization and rationalization of company practices and plant undertaken by Lipson Hancock. He felt that welfare policies were useful 'from a political point of view',[62] because they won the loyalty and appreciation of the employees and wider community. Thus when William Lathlean, a young surface worker, was badly mangled by the crusher at Moonta, Lipson Hancock recommended the payment of £90 so that the unfortunate youth might be placed in the Home for Incurables. On another occasion he organized the donation of company land to the Wallaroo Benevolent Society for their proposed old-folks' home.[63]

Lipson Hancock explained his Betterment Principle in a booklet describing the mines (first published in 1914) and in an article 'Welfare Work in the Mining Industry' which appeared in 1918.[64] The best exposition of Lipson Hancock's welfare work, however, was the report by L.C.E. Gee, Chief Registrar of Mines, in the *South Australian Department of Mines Mining Review* for the half-year ended June 1919. Gee noted that 65.5 per cent of the workforce at Wallaroo and Moonta had been with the company for a decade or more, a measure of its success in retaining its labour. Everywhere, he said, there was a general impression of 'tidiness, space and light',[65] and there were baths and changing houses for employees. At Port Wallaroo plots of company land were sold freehold to employees on easy terms. In October 1912, for example, James Henry Chynoweth secured allotment No.222 at East Wallaroo on which to build a house, while in the November Clarence William Opie acquired plot No. 212.[66] At Moonta Mines there was a vigorous tree-planting programme to improve the appearance of the place, and in addition the company supported or supplied the Moonta Mines Institute, the reference and circulating libraries, a billiards room, a recreation hall, the rotunda, tennis courts, and children's playgrounds. At Wallaroo Mines similar amenities were provided, including a pavilion, croquet lawns, a hockey-pitch, and a bowling green with 'a good club house'.[67] Additionally, the company maintained its compulsory Club & Medical Fund. A married man, for example, contributed one shilling a week to the Medical Fund and a further sixpence to the Club, while an adult employee unable to attend work through illness could claim twenty shillings per week from the Fund for six months, and then ten shillings per week for a further six months. Moreover, Gee concluded, the sliding scale of wage determination, introduced by H. Lipson Hancock in the early 1900s as an improvement to the contract system, should also be considered an integral part of the Betterment Principle because it represented a form of profit-sharing which was preferable to other types of employment.

As Lipson Hancock had intimated, there were strong pragmatic reasons why the mine company found it useful to develop such welfare policies but there was in the Betterment Principle (as even its nomenclature suggested) more than a hint of the Moonta–Methodist mutual improvement ethos that permeated the community. It was no coincidence that Hancock was himself an enthusiastic Methodist. This provided a degree of cultural common ground with his workforce – a certain mutual sympathy and understanding – and in furthering the cause of Methodism on Yorke Peninsula he adopted the Rainbow System of Sunday School instruction (already applied with success at the Marion Lawrence School, Toledo, Ohio), precipitating a re-organization which in its manner echoed both his modernization of the mines themselves and the implementation of the Betterment Principle. Methodist Union in South Australia in 1901 had rendered redundant the Primitive Methodist chapel at Moonta Mines, and after 1905 this building became the focus for the new regime. As Lipson Hancock wrote:

> This meant a complete reconstruction, necessitating careful thought and much wisdom, and involving considerable expense. The whole teaching arrangements had to be reorganized and suitable rooms provided, together with the needed apparatus for teaching. Led by the present Superintendent of the School [Lipson Hancock], the teachers undertook the reconstruction.[68]

33. Moonta Mines Methodist Sunday School in 1911. Formerly the Primitive Methodist chapel, the Sunday School – including the adjoining weatherboard huts – became the venue for H. Lipson Hancock's American-inspired 'Rainbow System' of instruction. There were ten grades, from the 'Cradle Roll' for infants to the 'Home Roll' for those too ill or aged to attend. The Rainbow course consisted of 100 lessons, which investigated every facet of the Bible, culminating in 'Lesson 100: The Call of China'.

'Scatterin' the bal'

However, behind this positive picture of benign busy-ness was the reality of increasing tension on the Peninsula, the crises of John Verran's Premiership compounded by the conscription issue and its aftermath. The estrangement of Methodism from the Labor movement, made worse locally by the split over the AMA–AWU merger, together with the growth of a new mood of Labor militancy across Australia as the war dragged on, undermined the cohesion and consensus that seemed to have marked the first decade of the new century on Yorke Peninsula. Indeed, the split of 1917, with its polarization of conservatives and militants, ushered in a new era of confrontation on the mines, the likes of which had not been seen since 1891–92. This culminated in a brief but bitter strike in 1922, when the AWU's venom was directed equally at the company and the Bogies, an antipathy reflected in the fiery words of one of R.S. Richards' pamphlets:

> Starvation may drive us back into the Mines; Man's inhumanity to Man may make countless thousands continue to mourn; but, whatever the result, we will never forget those men who aided the oppressor, we will

never forget those men who played us false, and when the Time comes to show our contempt for them, we will do so in no uncertain manner. In the meantime:

We will speak out, we will be heard, though all earth's system crack;
We will not bate one single word or take a letter back,
For the cause that lacks assistance, 'gainst the wrongs that need resistance,
For the future in the distance, and the good that we can do.

R.S. Richards, M.P.
North Moonta.[69]

When the Moonta and Wallaroo mines closed in 1923 there were some who blamed the collapse on the AWU, while there were indeed some militants who were happy to see the company go at last into liquidation. The Labor Moonta–Methodist nexus that had appeared so intact at the time of John Verran's famous victory in 1910 now seemed hardly relevant, the events immediately before, during and after the Great War having radically altered the industrial and political landscape – in South Australia in general and on Yorke Peninsula in particular. Sensing the demise of much that he had known and held dear, one contributor to the *People's Weekly* wrote sadly in 1927: 'I am not, nor have I ever been, a member of the A.W.U. that caused so much trouble and sorrow at the mining towns. I was a member of the first A.M.A., formed at Moonta Mines, and the leaders were all Cornishmen, right up to the time of the forming of the A.W.U.'[70]

Needless to say, of all the structural changes that had altered the industrial and political landscape, none was more profound nor more final than the closure of the Moonta and Wallaroo mines in November 1923. The enormity of that moment was still felt keenly some forty years on, as Oswald Pryor recalled:

Some hot-headed trade union leaders were pleased at the news. The company, they said, had kept up ornate offices in Adelaide, yet the miners had not received an adequate share of the huge profits in the early days of the field – and if an industry couldn't, or wouldn't, pay a decent wage, let it shut up shop! To the Cornish community that had lived in Wallaroo and Moonta for three generations, however, the closing of the mines was a calamity. For a while some thought that the company was only bluffing – that the announcement was just a stunt, designed to scare the miners into accepting a starvation wage. But they were faced with the fact that, for the first time in the history of the mines, the pumps were idle, water was rising steadily in the workings, and all underground gear worth salvaging was being brought to the surface.[71]

Pryor's distinction between 'hot-headed trade union leaders' and 'the Cornish community' is telling, further insight into the belief – his belief, at least – that the Labor movement on the Peninsula was now somehow less 'Cornish' than it had been hitherto, a consequence of the Great War and the turbulent post-war years, and that the Cornish inheritance had been marginalized by the militancy that characterized the new Moonta. Be that as it may, the hard fact was that the mines' closure was a result of the slump in demand for copper (and thus in its price) after the cessation of hostilities in 1918. The mines were shut down temporarily from March to September 1919, and there were further periods of inactivity from January to March 1920, January to August 1921, and February to November 1922, before the mines were abandoned finally on 23 October 1923. The company went formally into liquidation in the November, precipitating what the locals called 'scatterin' the bal',[72] the wholesale dismantling and disposal of the mines' plant and infrastructure. Like the Cornish copper industry itself in the 1860s, the South Australian mines had in the 1920s succumbed to the classic combination of low copper prices, soaring costs, and increasing impoverishment of the lodes. Anticipating this crash, many had already left the district, bands of unemployed miners gathering in Adelaide where they formed themselves into a miners' choir and created a flurry of interest, singing their Methodist hymns and Cornish carols. Thereafter, there were various forlorn attempts in the 1920s and even into the 1930s to re-establish mining but none was successful. For example, in 1936 there was a brief attempt by a Kadina Mining Company to restart the long-abandoned New Cornwall mine, while W.J.L. Polmear, born at Landrake in 1877 and a former AMA activist, worked the Poona lease on his own account without success. Slightly more fortunate was the Moonta Prospecting Syndicate, a small outfit with a capital of £3,000 which worked steadily until 1927 when, with a rise in copper prices and the help of R.S. Richards (then Minister of Mines), a form of 'subsist' (the Cornish term) was paid by the State as an advance on earnings. Richards even managed to attract Federal assistance for a time, but these modest attempts at renewal were doomed to failure and had petered out before the Second World War.[73]

In such a climate, the miners' trade union effectively disappeared, as did many of the local population. Some went to the copper mines of Bougainville,[74] near New Guinea, and in the decade after 1923 more than 3,000 people left northern Yorke Peninsula for pastures new, some 85 per cent of these migrants originating from the mineral lease settlements at Moonta Mines and Wallaroo Mines. At Wallaroo a 'strong defeatist attitude' was prevalent during the 1920s and 1930s but on the mineral leases at Moonta Mines and Wallaroo Mines, despite the continued leaching of the skilled and the restless, there was a certain stubbornness: 'when the source of employment was removed, the population proved highly resistant to migration. While many

34. New electric pumps underground at the Wallaroo mine, 1905.

left, hundreds clung on, eking out a bare living by casual labour on farms, docks and grain depots until entitled to age or incapacity pensions.'[75] Thus it was principally the younger people who departed, leaving behind 'a high proportion of aged and infirm'.[76]

R.S. Richards and the Labor hierarchy

Unpromising as the post-closure depression of Wallaroo and Moonta seemed for the further development of the Labor movement in South Australia, R.S. Richards and others continued to behave as though little had happened, insinuating themselves into the Labor Party's leadership hierarchy when the basis of their claims to power – the mines – had already vanished. This was the nub of the paradox illuminated by Lonie and Hopgood: the continued prominence of individuals of Cornish-Methodist-mining background in the Labor Party at a time when this no longer reflected the composition of the State's workforce but when popular opinion both recognized and condoned Moonta's continuing influence in the State's political culture. As Lonie intimated, a cursory glance at the composition of the Labor Party in the Adelaide Parliament in the 1920s and early 1930s revealed a block of some ten members of Cornish birth or descent, mostly Methodists. This was, from his perspective, a remarkable legacy from earlier times, these parliamentarians the physical as well as ideological embodiment of the increasingly anachronistic Moonta legacy.

Typical of this 'block' was Henry 'Harry' Kneebone, born at Kadina in 1876, the son of Henry Kneebone of Penponds (near Camborne) and Elizabeth Ann Tonkin (born in Cornwall in 1851). A journalist by training, Harry Kneebone was for a time an author and editor of some significance. He was asked, for example, to contribute to *The Wonder Book of Empire for Boys and Girls*, published shortly after the Great War in London, Melbourne and Toronto, writing a series of essays on 'Sunny Australia: The All-British Continent'. It was a revealing collection, demonstrating the importance of Methodist religious belief in shaping his political attitudes. For example, although Kneebone shared the prejudices of his contemporaries, asserting that the 'aborigines who have yielded their country to the white settlers ... are generally poor specimens of humanity', he showed a genuine – if patronizing – concern and affection for Aboriginal peoples which would have been unusual at that time. He identified qualities of selflessness and courage in the Aborigines, and observed that they 'make excellent stockmen' and that, as first-class trackers, 'they have saved the lives of many wanderers in the wilder parts'. Indeed: 'All over Australia aboriginals are attached to the country police stations so that their services may be available for tracking criminals or suspected or lost persons'. Their culture, too, was fascinating, he said, with expert spear-throwing, boomerangs and corroborees: 'Many interesting stories could be told of these folk, and for many reasons it is to be hoped that the efforts which are being made to keep them from dying out will be successful'.[77]

This essential humanity was typical of Kneebone, a committed social democrat in the old United Labor Party tradition. Like others from northern Yorke Peninsula, his political views seemed to have matured and crystallized during a spell as a miner on the Western Australian goldfields in the 1890s, providing him with a personal political catechism to which he adhered throughout his life. His daughter and biographer, Joan Tiver, in her book *Harry Kneebone: A Son of 'Little Cornwall'*, recalled that:

> He was a Socialist in the sense that he considered Jesus Christ a Socialist ... [he] was entirely democratic in outlook and did not believe that anyone can be born with 'bluer' blood than another. Although he would not have described himself as a Republican, he was not an ardent Royalist. He believed, however, that complete independence must come to Australia some day, as a child sheds its mother's apron strings. He also believed that superiority, if it need be recognised, should spring from achievement by the use and development of one's God-given talents and mental powers, never from the accident of one's birth or the inheritance of wealth.[78]

The concern for Australian independence, like concern for the future of the Aborigines, reflected the prominence of Australian preoccupations in Kneebone's political thought. And yet, the Cornish–Methodist inheritance was also plain, not least in the assumed link between religion and politics and in the Methodist commitment to self-help. Kneebone was careful to cultivate this 'Cornishness', seeking out family members during a visit to Cornwall and becoming an enthusiastic devotee of the Cornish Association of South Australia. But it was in Western Australia that he had had first decided to put his journalistic skills to work in the Labor cause, joining the pro-Labor *Coolgardie Miner* – of which newspaper he eventually became editor. In 1910 he returned to South Australia, joining the Labor-sponsored *Daily Herald* in Adelaide and becoming its editor in 1911. This was a position he held, with the exception of a brief period in London, until the paper's collapse in 1924. By now Kneebone was a key member of the State's Labor hierarchy. Following the demise of the *Herald*, therefore, he entered the Adelaide Parliament in 1925 as Labor member for the constituency of East Torrens, moving on to the Federal Senate in 1931.

Of the other members of the Labor 'block', Stanley R. Whitford – a close ally of R.S. Richards – was perhaps the most notable. His enormously long and candid autobiography (still unpublished) affords numerous insights into his career and personality, not least those experiences that helped form his Labor principles. Like Kneebone, he had been out on the Western Australian goldfields. He was also, he said, profoundly influenced by Eugene Debs – the American leader of the 'Wobblies', the International Workers of the World – and he admitted the deep impact the visit of Tom Mann to Moonta in 1910 had had upon him. But despite the attraction of Marxist thought, Whitford remained a firm Methodist all his days. He first entered the Adelaide Parliament in 1921, as Member of the House of Assembly for the constituency of North Adelaide. He lost his seat in 1927 but was back in parliament in 1929, where he remained until 1941. In 1930 he became Chief Secretary in 'Lightning Lionel' Hill's Labor government, although only a few years later, in 1934, he was dramatically expelled from the Australian Labor Party. This was because he was an advocate of the controversial and divisive 'Premiers' Plan', an economic strategy to try to beat the Depression, put together by the several State Premiers in consultation with the Federal government, a belt-tightening exercise that was bitterly opposed by much of the Labor movement.

In an echo of the damaging conscription issue years, the Premiers' Plan controversy split the Labor movement in South Australia, its parliamentary Party dividing into three mutually antagonistic camps – the Australian Labor Party, the (so-called) Parliamentary Labor Party, and 'Lang' Labor: those who supported Jack Lang, the flamboyant New South Wales Premier who opposed the Premiers' Plan and was sacked by his State Governor shortly after opening the Sydney Harbour Bridge. Whitford himself continued in Parliament as an Independent Labor member, and he recalled that 'This debacle in the ranks of the Labor movement in this State was the worst of my experience'.[79] R.S. Richards, the veteran of the conscription issue and the 'split', came at last to power in South Australia as Labor Premier at the height of this crisis in February 1933, following Hill's resignation. He was Premier for only 64 days, however, for in the State election of 1933 the Liberal Country League was swept into office, the Labor forces being in entire disarray. Only in the Wallaroo constituency did the non-Liberal forces do well, with R.S. Richards returned yet again as the darling of northern Yorke Peninsula. In his campaign he had relied skillfully on the support of local power-brokers, such as Bill 'Sponger' Tonkin, chairman of the local Unemployed Association, and his all-important policy speech at Wallaroo Town Hall was given such an easy reception that, his opponents insisted, 'the Cousin Jacks must have thought it an evening church service'.[80]

R.S. Richards continued to represent Wallaroo until 1949. It had been a remarkable performance. In his passionate and unswerving devotion to a political creed fashioned on the Peninsula in the years immediately before, during and after the Great War, he had sustained the political influence of Moonta and environs in the State's Labor hierarchy for more than twenty years since the sudden collapse of the region's copper industry. What George Jose of Illogan might have made of this astonishing legacy, we cannot know. It was hardly emblematic of the continuing intimacy between Moonta and Cornwall that Jose had sought so earnestly. But it did represent, as John Lonie recognized, the enduring influence of a distinctive political culture powerful enough to survive the demise of the mines, one derived in the first place from the State's Cornish–Methodist tradition. It also reflected the tenacity of Moonta's myth, of the enduring strength of the regional culture formulated on northern Yorke Peninsula. George Jose and R.S. Richards lived in different worlds, one in retirement in Cornwall musing whimsically on Moonta's 'golden age', the other burning bright with an indignant fury that saw the working-class heroes of northern Yorke Peninsula as the continuing victims of capitalist injustice and exploitation. And yet, if Jose and Richards had anything at all in common on which they might have agreed, it was surely commitment to the people and places of 'Australia's little Cornwall' and the firm belief, shared by both men, that 'Moonta's little, but she's great'. It was an unshakeable belief that had survived the traumas and upheavals of global conflict, international Depression, and the fracturing of the northern Yorke Peninsula community consequent upon industrial conflict and the abrupt destruction of its economic base.

CHAPTER SEVEN

'The world's largest Cornish festival'
The myth revived

The abrupt demise of the Moonta and Wallaroo mines in 1923 led to the dispersal of the younger elements of the population, who sought employment elsewhere – in the capital Adelaide, or in regional centres further north such as Port Pirie or Port Augusta, or in mining districts with long-standing local connections such as Broken Hill and Kalgoorlie, or even further afield in the mines of Bougainville. But many people proved resistant to change, especially on the old mineral lease settlements of Moonta Mines and Wallaroo Mines, the older folk determined to remain on the Peninsula and to cling to a way of life that seemed already to have been so completely overtaken by events. This tenacity was reflected in the continuing influence of Moonta and environs in the Labor Party in South Australia, where the party's hierarchy was still dominated by individuals from the Peninsula's mining–Methodist tradition – men like R.S. Richards, Stanley R. Whitford and Henry Kneebone – and where the political culture of the State's Labor movement was still thought to owe much to northern Yorke Peninsula.

Nonetheless, change there was. Attempts at small-scale mining revival proved unsuccessful, although providing work for skilled men who would have otherwise been unemployed or forced to leave the district. Instead, the region's survival was secured through a gradual broadening of its economic base. Following the introduction in the late nineteenth century of the fertilizer 'superphosphate' – which enabled agriculture to be carried on successfully in this otherwise arid, marginal land – there had been a move to farming. As land had become available, so many Cornish mining families had taken up properties in the locality, permanently exchanging the pick for the plough. After the closure of the mines, it was strategically placed Kadina that emerged as the largest and strongest of the local communities. It developed as a regional centre serving an agricultural area stretching from southern Yorke Peninsula to the towns of Crystal Brook in the north and Balaclava in the east. Kadina was also established as one of three State Storage Centres for wheat, its yards having a capacity of six million bushels. At Port Wallaroo – or plain 'Wallaroo' as it was now always known – the sulphuric acid works, originally

35. 'Scatterin the bal'. Following closure in 1923, the mining infrastructure was meticulously and efficiently dismantled for sale. In this scene (in 1924) the last Cornish boiler is being removed from the Wallaroo mine.

an appendage of the copper smelters, was purchased by the Electrolytic Zinc company in 1923 to roast zinc concentrates brought down from Broken Hill. May's Foundry continued to offer employment in the town, and the port of Wallaroo itself remained an important part of the Peninsula economy. Moonta, by contrast, found it far more difficult to survive, new roles proving elusive and old ones disappearing, its *raison d'être* now reduced to that of dormitory town serving its two more prosperous neighbours.[1]

The relative decline of Moonta had been apparent even before the closure of the mines. Under H. Lipson Hancock's regime, there had been a concentration of investment at the Wallaroo mine, at the expense of Moonta where the ore lodes were thought to be almost worked out, and personnel had been shifted from the ailing mine to the more prosperous of the two. In such circumstances, Moonta's allure might already have begun to fade, its claim to fame, like that of Cornwall, seen as increasingly hollow as its mine declined and was eventually abandoned, its younger population lost to more vibrant areas near and far, its mining–Methodist culture increasingly 'fossilized' as part of the State's Labor inheritance. The Great War had disguised signs of Moonta's sliding fall from grace, the demand for copper as a strategic metal breathing new life into the mine, the heroic exploits of 'Moonta boys' on the field of battle leading to an outpouring of local patriotism. But in the aftermath of the war and the closure of the mines in 1923, it was more difficult to assert Moonta's supposed cultural superiority with the self-confidence that had been observed only a few years before. Yet Moonta did not die. The stubborn pride inherent in the 'Cousin Jack' culture of northern Yorke Peninsula bred a tenacity that was resistant to change and refused to acknowledge defeat, perpetuating Moonta's developed sense of place even as its bedrock, the mines, had disappeared. Moreover, by the mid-1920s there was already apparent a project to re-invent Moonta anew, drawing upon the cultural resources of the Celtic Revival which at that moment was attempting just such a project in Cornwall itself.

'Moonta ... an outpost of the delectable Duchy'

In Cornwall, the Celtic Revivalists of the early twentieth century had endeavoured to look over the debris of the mining and industrial era to a time when Cornwall was more 'purely Cornish' – a golden age of Celtic Christianity, holy wells, Cornish crosses and, of course, the Cornish language. By the 1920s the project to revive the Cornish language and to reassert Cornwall's ancient Celticity was well in hand, with a Cornish Gorsedd – a college of bards modelled on those of Wales and Brittany – inaugurated in 1928. It was a project that appealed especially to the middle classes – those who understood that the enormity of the crisis facing Cornwall was cultural as well as socio-economic – and it was articulated in the Cornish press and through organizations such as the Royal Institution of Cornwall and the recently founded Federation of Old Cornwall Societies.[2] These essentially literary expressions caught the eye of the Moonta *People's Weekly*, which in a series of features, editorials and letters echoed the imperatives of the Revivalists in Cornwall. There was a piece on 'St Piran: The Patron Saint of Cornish Miners', another on the activities of the London Cornish Association, and a third on 'Cornish Nationality'. Cornwall was variously 'Trelawney Land' and the 'Land of Romance', one contributor informing readers that 'There are many traits which bring the Cornish much nearer the Welsh and Bretons than to the Anglo-Saxon English'.[3]

The 'Back to Moonta' celebrations in 1927 – when 'Moontaites' across Australia were encouraged to return home for a range of festivities – was an opportunity to apply Revivalist rhetoric to Moonta itself. An editorial in the *People's Weekly* announced: 'The Celtic spirit is deep set in folk that hail from Cornwall, and they are Celts on an equality with the Scots, Irish or Welsh. They are clannish to a marked degree, and the love of home and the clan seldom loses its hold in the individual and never in the race, and Moonta people are mainly Cornish.'[4] Six years later, the sentiment had hardly changed, although the role of Moonta had expanded to that of guardian of the Cornish spirit in Australia:

36. Back to Moonta! The excursion train, with appropriate headboard, is at Moonta on 17 September 1927 for the 'Back to Moonta' celebrations.

Our community has been in every sense a bit of old Cornwall, what with mining, agriculture and fishing. Wherever mining activities are manifest you will find some representative of Penzance or St Ives. Broken Hill and Kalgoorlie are examples of this, but they are essentially inland centres of arid regions; but Moonta, in its proximity to the sea, is able to carry the role of an outpost of the delectable Duchy.[5]

The *People's Weekly* found an important ally in the Cornish Association of South Australia, founded in 1890. In 1919 the *Cornishman* newspaper, published in Penzance, had reported earnestly that:

The Cornish Association of South Australia is, according to reports of its activities, a live institution of Cornish folk, and their Australian descendants. Distance from the 'Home Land' serves but to stimulate their love of the Duchy. In all things pertaining to Cornwall, they are the most enthusiastic. And the remarkable feature is that the love and enthusiasm for the county extends unabated to the third and fourth generations of Cornish-Australians. The Association's membership contains a long list of distinguished South Australian ... of persons who hail from Cornwall or have Cornish blood in their veins.[6]

Prominent members included David Morley Charleston, John Verran and Henry Kneebone, together with the newspaper proprietor John Langdon Bonython. Bonython was a key player and provided much of the Association's rhetoric in this period. A wealthy Adelaide businessman himself, he insisted that the 'Cornishman is not prepared to sacrifice everything for mere money-making'. The Cornish were loftier beings, he said, a principled people with a strong spiritual side to their character. Warming to his theme, he complained that the 'enemy says the Cornishman is a dreamer, he prefers to stand about and think rather than do some of things that are popular with other people'. As Bonython no doubt recognized, such a view reflected popular notions of Celticity prevalent at the time, many of them English imaginings of England's Celtic neighbours as a primitive, rustic 'other'. The Celts were, according to this construction, an unworldly, impractical, dreamy people given to 'idiosyncrasies especially their superstitions', as Bonython put it, in contrast to the hard-headed Anglo-Saxons. Yet Bonython seemed to embrace the 'enemy's' assessment: 'I admit the charge', he exclaimed, 'and should be sorry if the Cornishman lost this tendency to think ... because its wealth of imagination is one of the great assets of the Cornish race'.[7] Such rhetoric informed the attitude of the Cornish Association, with its branches on the Peninsula, and on occasions Bonython visited Moonta to speak on things Cornish, introducing his particular 'take' on 'Celtic Cornwall'.[8] For his pains, Bonython was appointed President of the Royal Institution of Cornwall in 1931, and he was elected a bard of the Cornish Gorsedd – that most Celtic Revivalist of Cornish bodies.[9]

The extent to which the *People's Weekly* and Bonython's brand of Celtic Revivalism had had an impact beyond the literati who enjoyed the newspaper articles – or the enthusiasts of the Cornish Association who willingly adopted Revivalist ideas – is open to doubt. As in Cornwall, the Revivalist project penetrated the popular consciousness but slowly. In any case, the Cornish Association was itself soon feeling the chill winds of the Depression years, with declining membership and dwindling finances. It struggled to maintain links with like Associations in New Zealand, the Transvaal and New York, and in 1931 was able to contribute one guinea to 'the agriculture centre of Ruan Minor and the fishing Lifeboat Station of Cadgwith'.[10] But an appeal from Camborne Town Band for monetary assistance had to be turned down, due to shortage of funds, while in 1930 the Association recorded its regret that 'the younger generation had no interest in the old Land or its traditions, having been born here with different surroundings'.[11] In October 1933 it was decided to 'ask other Cornish gatherings to join up with the Cornish Association' to boost its strength, approaches being made to the 'Moonta Carol Party' and the 'Kadina Carol Party', as well as the 'Back to Moonta' and 'Back to Burra' organizations.[12] The Association's membership continued to fall, however, a committee meeting in April 1935 again pointing to the twin effects of the Depression and a lack of interest among the young.[13]

The efforts of the *People's Weekly* and the Cornish Association had not constructed the new avenues of intimacy between Moonta and Cornwall for which some had hoped (see pp. 167–9). But, despite their relatively limited impact, they had provided important resources for re-inventing Moonta's myth, for perpetuating the superior sense of place into the period beyond the closure of the mines. Here it complemented the dogged survival of the Peninsula's 'Cousin Jack' identity and, in a remarkable anticipation of the fusion that would not occur in Cornwall until the 1980s, there was in subsequent years a synthesis of sorts between the old 'Cousin Jack' culture and the new notions of Celticity.[14] This was, overwhelmingly, the achievement of Oswald Pryor, who in his writings over several decades drew subtly upon the romantic vein of Celtic Revivalism to construct his own nostalgic vision of 'Australia's Little Cornwall'.

Oswald Pryor lends a hand

Born at Moonta Mines in 1881, the son of Captain James Pryor, from Wendron, Oswald Pryor was at work in the mines by the age of thirteen. From 1911 to 1923 he was Surface Manager –'grass captain' – at Moonta, with special responsibility for the cementation works. By the time the mines closed, he had already turned his hand to journalism – especially as a cartoonist. His first published cartoon had appeared in the *Quiz and the Lantern* magazine in October 1901, and by 1912 he was contributing to the Sydney *Bulletin*, his sketches reflecting the political preoccupations of the day, such as the 'Japanese threat'.[15] In the 1920s he was drawing propaganda cartoons for the Labor Party but long before that he had begun to turn to 'Cousin Jack' material. It was C.J. Dennis, Pryor's close friend and author of the hugely successful *The Songs of a Sentimental Bloke* – a book that caught the popular mood of Australian national identity when it came out in 1915 – who had first suggested that life on northern Yorke Peninsula might provide excellent raw material for cartoons and other literary work. Initially, some of these 'Cousin Jack' cartoons appeared in the *Bulletin* – gaining the attention of an Australia-wide audience – and in time they were collected together in two volumes: *Cornish Pasty* and *Cousin Jacks and Jennys*.[16]

Meanwhile, Oswald Pryor had also become a prolific contributor to the *People's Weekly*. His regular features continued to appear until the mid-1960s, just half-a-dozen years before his death in 1971.[17] His earliest memories stretched back to the days not long after Captain Piper had arrived with the last large contingent of Cornish immigrants in 1883, and he recalled it all with vivid clarity. He had an extraordinary memory for people, places and events, as well as an unparalleled gift for story-telling. The passage of time appeared unable to dim his recollection of telling incidents and amusing anecdotes. He remembered, for example, how John Verran used to call the Wesleyan chapel at Moonta Mines 'Cap'n 'Ancock's cathedral', and how when Verran was preaching there 'he used the pulpit to hit back at Authority'.[18]

Pryor wrote his compositions in a wry, humorous style, affecting a 'Cousin Jack' manner and deploying dialect phrases and sayings when appropriate, a technique that he honed over the years. He reminisced about the herds of goats that used to wander semi-wild over the mineral leases – the 'Poison Flat mob, the Karkarilla mob, and so on' – and mused that 'There has been much jesting by irreverent persons about billy-goat beards, and its is a moot point whether the goats copied the style of whiskers worn by some old Cornishmen or whether the Cornishmen copied the goats'. He knew that 'those who can't schemey must louster' – those without brains must rely on their brawn – and he wrote with authority about the 'skimp jerkers' and the 'attle jerkers': the men who worked 'with the sun as hot as Hades' to fill lines of side-tipping trucks with mine waste. He recalled the Methodist tea-treats of long ago – 'called by the irreverent a "bun struggle"' – and remembered what it was like as a boy to work on the mine. The pickey-boys, he explained, graded the ore at surface. 'To get a job as a pickey boy all one had to do was wear long pants,' he said, 'put on his age a couple of years, and way-lay Captain Skinner when he was doing his rounds on his horse.' If the lad was obviously under-age, then 'the Captain would tell the boy to go home and eat a few more pasties and come back next year'. If the youth appeared genuine, then just 'a few questions were asked about where the father worked, what chapel he attended, how many were in the family, and where they all lived'. The residence question was important because 'there was in fact, a zoning system ... East Moonta boys worked at Taylor's and Warmington's [shafts], Hamley flatters at Beddomes, and the boys from Cross Roads "down 'Ogg's".'[19]

This easy familiarity with the details of Moonta life lent Pryor's work the ring of authenticity. His skills as a raconteur ensured a ready audience when he wrote or spoke. His light-hearted, engaging manner meant that he upset few readers or listeners, and earned few critics. People warmed to Oswald Pryor. His steady stream of articles was eagerly awaited, as were the cartoons that captured so unerringly Cornish idiom and humour, and before long he had established himself as the undisputed arbiter of the life and times of Australia's Little Cornwall. By the eve of the Second World War, it was his 'composure' – his personal construction – of the history of northern Yorke Peninsula that moulded popular perceptions of the region. Like Captain Hancock in the old days, Oswald Pryor had come to personify Moonta's myth; he had become an institution in his own right. In this way, he was able to ensure that – despite the reality of the town's relative decline compared to Kadina and [Port] Wallaroo – Moonta was able to maintain its mythical place as 'the hub of the universe', or at least as the focus of the distinctive identity forged on the Peninsula. As Pryor put it: 'Moonta has produced three Premiers [Verran, Scaddan, Richards], also copper worth millions of pounds, and the only woman ever hanged in South Australia'. But, he added, there were 'other interesting facts of local history not so well remembered' – and it was as discoverer and mediator of these 'facts' that he was able to entrench his position as the unassailable authority on the region and its culture.[20]

There were endless details that confirmed his encyclopedic knowledge and his near-monopoly of those 'interesting facts'. Elderly residents confided in him, reminiscing about the 'early days' and trusting Pryor to make honest use of the stories they told him. Matt Reed, for example, imparted a graphic, horrific memory that had haunted him for years. When 'little more than the age of a schoolboy' Matt had witnessed a fatal accident underground in Taylor's shaft when a miner named Elford had been caught in a rock fall: 'he was lashed to a plank and carried up the ladder, but died before reaching the top'. But Matt remembered happier times too. 'In 1870,' he told Pryor, 'the largest "wallow" [pure concentration of ore] ever found at Moonta was uncovered at Prince Alfred Mine on the sandhill near Hancock's heap.' It was 'solid yellow ore of purest quality', and the tributers working it made hundreds of pounds between them. Pryor himself remembered characters like Bill Metherell – known innocently as 'Cousin Jack nigger' because he used to 'black up' at amateur concerts and sing ditties such as 'When tha ole man coomed 'ome sober' – and 'Jimmy' Bennett, the Bible Christian local preacher who held the first service at Moonta 'in a shed over a saw-pit in the scrub'. Sometimes there were flashes of real insight, more than mere anecdote, such as Pryor's explanation for the popularity of the Salvation Army at Moonta in the mid-1880s. The Methodist chapels, he insinuated, had by then become introspective and resistant to outsiders, so that the Salvationists were able to appeal to the disaffected and (interestingly) to newcomers; recruits were drawn from 'the swearers, blasphemers and drunkards, and from Captain Piper's new chums and others for whom the church had no attraction'.[21]

In this way, Oswald Pryor effectively reconstructed Australia's Little Cornwall – for himself, and for others.[22] It was a cosy (if sometimes tragic) and reassuring story, with a timeless quality that made the events of the 1870s or the 1890s seem like yesterday. But behind this façade, Pryor was worried that the 'real' Little Cornwall was slipping away. Correspondents who wrote to thank him for his articles and cartoons often expressed a whimsical regret that the great days had gone already. In 1932, for example, one complained that 'saffron cake is a thing of the past', admitting sorrowfully that 'I am

37. Pickey boys in the ore-sorting plant at the Moonta mine, about 1913. Oswald Pryor, who was once one of their number and later became Surface Manager at the mine, wrote sentimentally about the pickey-boys and their work.

lost for a good Cornishman to have a bit of a chat with. They are all dead and buried.'[23] Another 'old timer', again in the 1930s, wrote to say that although he was 'one of the later brigade', he could 'still tell a few Cornish yarns, and give a little entertainment, on some of their habits ... regarding the old days of S.A. copper mining'. He recalled, for example, the antics of local personalities such as the Moonta miner named Tobie, the champion euchre (card) player who would visit Huddy's pub on the mineral leases, and – when he had 'got nice and argumentative' – would stand outside and issue a challenge to all-comers: 'I stood in the crack o' the wall, and tolled the bell, I'll play any bugger, once, round the board, for a bellyful, pasties or pints'.[24]

But this was reminiscence, and Pryor fretted that the living culture was disappearing. On New Year's Day 1947 he wrote to his old friend, George A. Hicks, from his home in Adelaide to say that he had spent Christmas at Moonta – the first time he had been able to get there during the festive season for fifteen years. The visit had saddened him. 'For the first time in my memory,' he wrote, 'there were no "curls" [Cornish carols], no Christmas Night concert or Christmas music of any kind.'[25] He also dashed off an article for the *People's Weekly*, asking in Cornish idiom 'Where's Moonta's Christmas to?'. He provided the rhetorical answer himself: 'She's gone, boy'. 'Carols by Candlelight' were greeted as a novelty in Adelaide and Melbourne, he said, 'yet 80 years ago the miners at Moonta sang carols by candlelight in the flats underground'.[26] The theme of loss continued to trouble Pryor. In April 1954 he reported disappointedly that in Mexico 'Pachuca is no longer a Cornish colony', although he was cheered to hear that it 'is said that Grass Valley in California is still a mining centre for Cornishmen, and life there is still as it was in the "good old days" at Moonta, Burra Burra and Pachuca'. But by then he had already adopted the habit of ending his articles with the refrain: 'As Cousin Jack would say, "Tedden like 'e used to be"'.[27] Moonta, Pryor felt, was quietly passing into history.

In fact, Oswald Pryor had penetrated the popular consciousness in a manner that had eluded Bonython and other purveyors of 'Celtic Cornwall', his writings and cartoons acquiring an enthusiastic following at Moonta but also far beyond the confines of the Peninsula – even in Cornwall itself, where the historian A.L. Rowse and Claude Berry, editor of the *West Briton*, wrote to congratulate him on his work.[28] George A. Hicks summed up what a great many others felt, when he wrote to Pryor in December 1951: 'we as a people are greatly indebted to you for all you have done in maintaining the Celtic spirit of Cornwall in Moonta and Australia generally'.[29] The effort did not go unnoticed by the Celtic Revivalists in Cornwall, and he was duly invited to become a bard of the Gorsedd. By now, Pryor was working on the production of a manuscript, 'Little Cornwall: The Story of Moonta (South Australia) and its Cornish Miners'.[30] Much edited, this formed the basis of his book *Australia's Little Cornwall*, published in Adelaide in 1962 in his eighty-third year. It was a remarkable achievement, the culmination of a lifetime's research and writing, and was for many readers the 'definitive' account of Moonta and environs. For Pryor, it was an act of defiance as well as a labour of love, putting down a marker in the evening of his life by which people would remember the Cornish legacy. He was worried, he explained in the book, that the dispersal of local families 'meant the end of a "Little Cornwall" in Australia', and that intermarriage with other groups would dilute 'the good old Cornish strain'.[31] And yet, 'it is doubtful,' he wrote, 'if any class of pioneer has done more for Australia than the men and women from the Duchy of Cornwall.'[32] As he concluded: 'Today, the streets of "Australia's Little Cornwall" are quiet, almost sleepy. But the value to the Australian Commonwealth of the work of those who once walked them should never be forgotten.'[33]

'The largest Cornish communities beyond Land's End'

Paradoxically, even as Pryor mourned what he imagined to be the end of 'Little Cornwall', so the re-fashioning of Moonta's myth that he had undertaken with such determination and tenacity had established widespread currency. The impact was extraordinary. His book sold like hot-cakes, and ran to numerous successive editions (it is still in print in 2007). Writers as well as readers, both academic and popular, found Pryor's seductive prose utterly persuasive, and Moonta's identity was re-invigorated anew. Within a few months of its publication, Pryor's book was, despite its popular, 'folksy' tone, recognized by Australian scholars as an intriguing and possibly important contribution to Australian historiography that demanded attention. Geoffrey Blainey, for example, already alive to 'difference' in Australian history and by now the foremost authority on Australia's mining past, was enthused by the 'New Cornwalls' of northern Yorke Peninsula that Pryor had illuminated, devoting a chapter to them in his milestone volume *The Rush that Never Ended: A History of Australian Mining*, first published in 1963. Moonta and environs had been 'possibly the largest Cornish communities beyond Land's End', said Blainey: 'By the 1870s South Australia had replaced Cornwall as the largest copper region of the British Empire'.[34] Likewise, John Reynolds in his *Men and Mines*, published in 1974, marvelled at 'the singular culture' and 'unusual stability' that the Cornish had established in South Australia's mining districts in the nineteenth century.[35] Bill Peach, in his popular 1970s series of historical travel programmes, screened on the ABC, visited Moonta and munched a Cornish pasty, as did Don Dunstan, Premier of South Australia in the 1970s, who remembered his own Cornish antecedents and was careful to note in his book *Don Dunstan's Australia* (1978) the distinctive Cornish contribution to the South Australian landscape.[36] 'A prime example of the importation of a building style may be seen in "Australia's Little Cornwall"', he wrote, 'Cornish miners emigrated here to work in the copper mines, and very soon they used the local stone to build cottages and chapels which are almost exact replicas of those in their home country'.[37]

In the rush to embrace Oswald Pryor's conception of 'Australia's Little Cornwall', even serious writers could be surprisingly uncritical – both in their reluctance to deconstruct or even explain Pryor's project, and in their willing acceptance of everything that he had to say about Peninsula life. Pryor had, in short, re-worked many of the themes central to Moonta's myth, encouraging a new generation of observers to defer to them just as others had done years before. John Reynolds, for example, had freely acknowledged his debt to Pryor. But in doing so he had become ensnared by Pryor's beguiling rhetoric, falling under the spell of Moonta's myth. Pryor, for example, had projected the myth of Cousin Jenny in its entirety, arguing – as the Cornish had done before him – that Cornish women had triumphed over adversity in the Peninsula's unforgiving environment, bringing a good measure of civilization to an otherwise wild country, and themselves benefiting from a new regime in which they no longer toiled at the mines but enjoyed all the pleasures of a cosy domesticity. Reynolds was receptive to such ideas, and was entirely convinced by Pryor's warm, persuasive prose. He explained to his readers in *Men* [sic] *and Mines* that the '"Cousin Jennies" and their daughters brought new forms of domestic order and cultivation to Australia'. He argued too that their 'whitewashed stone cottages, thatched and tidy outside, clean and homely inside, contrasted greatly with the wattle daub and bark huts of most of the sheep station hands and bush workers'.[38]

There was more. In a spectacularly inaccurate description of the work bal-maidens had undertaken in Cornwall, Reynolds celebrated these women's subsequent confinement to the domestic sphere in Australia:

> In South Australia the Cousin Jennies virtually found a 'Promised Land'. The earnings of their menfolk were so much higher than in Cornwall ... that the necessity for working at the mines was absent. In Cornwall most girls and women spent much of their day recovering tin sands which had escaped the jigs ... and ran the ponds which discharged the water. The girls and women who panned the mill waters were known as Bal (ball) Maidens and their work was termed 'streaming' ... Freed from such necessity the Cousin Jennies were able to indulge their notable gifts as cooks: their contribution to the Australian diet is the well-known, popular 'Cornish' pastie.[39]

'The real glory of Moonta'

John Reynolds was not the only one to find Oswald Pryor's Moonta so irresistibly enchanting. Others were ready to succumb to Moonta's self-publicized charms, some moving considerably beyond Pryor's construction to attribute all manner of positive characteristics to the town and its environs. Graham Jenkin, in his unashamedly sentimental *Calling Me Home: The Romance of South Australia in Story and Song*, published in 1989, waxed long and lyrical about Moonta. Forgetting for a moment the severe effects of water shortages in the long, hot, dry summers of the nineteenth century, and overlooking the terrible outbreaks of 'colonial measles' (typhoid) that had decimated the infant population from time to time, and drawing a veil over the labour troubles that brought financial hardship and set workers against bosses as well as neighbour against neighbour, Jenkin recalled only the happy times:

> the real glory of Moonta ... was the *spirit* of the place pervading the city [sic] which made it such a wonderful place in which to live and which inspired such passionate devotion from its citizens. For here was an entire city at peace with itself: a city who cared for and co-operated with each;

who never had to lock their doors; who worked and played and sang together with great gusto and in perfect harmony; who actually liked each other! Was there ever another city like it?[40]

Like others before him, Jenkin also privileged Moonta in its relationships with other settlements on the Peninsula. He acknowledged that 'the whole triangular area was known as "Little Cornwall"' but argued that Moonta, with its historically larger population, was the most significant of the three towns. Indeed, 'Moonta – the largest mining town – became South Australia's second city'. Moreover, Jenkin claimed that Peninsula residents as a whole recognized and deferred to Moonta's superior status, insisting that 'Whether a person had migrated direct from Cornwall or was a third generation native of Kadina, he was likely to see Moonta as the centre of the world'.[41] This insistence echoed Pryor's belief that Moonta was 'the hub of the universe', and Jenkin also remembered that 'Thee've never travelled till thee've been to Moonta'. All this, he said, was evidence of a developed 'civic pride': for 'Moonta was, indeed, a wonderful little city – with its suburbs, its lovely stone cottages and villas, its fine schools, its town hall and other public buildings, and, of course, its splendid array of churches, practically all of them Methodist'.[42]

And yet, as Jenkin acknowledged, 'Northern Yorke Peninsula was not Cornwall'. Although there were many similarities – 'an engine house at Moonta, for instance, is scarcely distinguishable from an engine house at Penzance'– there was also 'a number of striking differences between the two districts'.[43] Forgetting for a moment Dolcoath mine at its zenith or the years when Consolidated and United were amongst the most heavily capitalized enterprises anywhere in the world, Jenkin insisted that 'there was nothing in Cornwall on such a huge scale as the operations conducted in northern Yorke Peninsula: and nothing with such an air of communal prosperity as was evident in the South Australian district in its hey-day'. But it was not just a question of size and wealth, he added, for there was something unique about Moonta's sense of place: 'Nor was there [in Cornwall] such a satisfyingly complete expression of the people, themselves, as that which was created in and around Moonta. Moonta (like the other copper towns) really did belong to the people; it was created by them in the way they wanted it, and they were immensely proud of it.'[44] The mines which had lent the district its prosperity and identity had long since disappeared but, Jenkin insisted, Moonta's special sense of place would always endure:

> The Bal be stilled and scattered wide
> And there can be no great rebirth,
> But did 'ee think we'd lose our pride

Forgetting why we're here on earth?
Not just in stone our memory be
But woven through life's tapestry
Are threads of gold bequeathed to thee
To thee and thine for all eternity.

But sometimes now, as in a dream,
The Bal begins to work again
I hear the hiss of engine steam
And see the march of Moonta men.
I hear them sing the songs they love,
Their candles light the evening sky:
While there are stars in heaven above
The soul of Moonta will not ever die! [45]

'The soul of Moonta will not ever die!'

Nonetheless, despite this conviction, Jenkin bemoaned the destruction that had attended the closure of the mines in 1923. Everything that could usefully be salvaged or sold was dismantled or broken up, he said: 'Whole suburbs, which happened to be built on the mineral leases, were flattened so that the stone in the cottage walls and the galvanized iron roofs could be sold as rubble or scrap: today there are paddocks without a trace to indicate that once a thriving community lived there.' Where infrastructure had survived – notably the massive Cornish engine houses – this was only because the cost of demolition would have outweighed the receipt from sales of the recycled building materials. Jenkin regretted that the mine company had not saved 'even a few representative pieces of mine equipment – skips, trucks, pumps, tools', symbolic items which might have 'been preserved as a memorial to the thousands of people who had made such a mighty contribution to this state and nation by creating the Moonta and extracting its buried wealth'. This was a wicked slight, Jenkin argued – 'Nothing was left; and no thought was given to the people of the copper triangle'– but even this could not diminish Moonta's spirit: 'The capitalists, in their orgy of destruction, got their money; but, there were other, infinitely more important, things which could not be taken from the Moonta or its people.' [46]

However, even as Jenkin berated those rapacious capitalists who had wrung the very last drops of profit from the mines, he applauded those 'dedicated people' who in recent years had 'been able to gather, at considerable expense and effort, the beginnings of a collection of the type which could so easily have been put aside in 1923'.[47] Here, no doubt, Jenkin was thinking of the enthusiasts who had collected together at the 'Wheal Munta' site at Moonta Mines the physical detritus and relics of the mining age found scattered across the district and beyond. He was probably thinking too of the efforts of the Moonta, Kadina and Wallaroo branches of the National Trust of South Australia, not least the remarkable collection of ephemera and artifacts housed in the museum in the old school at Moonta Mines. Perhaps he also had in mind the intervention of the State Government's Department of Mines and Energy, which by 1989 was already taking a proactive interest in the preservation and interpretation of South Australia's Cornish mining landscapes. Focused initially on the arguably more picturesque Burra Burra mine site – where Morphett's engine house was comprehensively restored [48] – the Department's interest soon expanded to encompass the old mineral lease areas of Moonta Mines and Wallaroo Mines. Engine houses were made safe and accessible with judicious repair work, and interpretation boards, many reproducing historic photographs to show the same localities in the mines' hey-day, helped visitors make sense of the landscapes and remains unfolded before them. A series of pamphlets was produced by the Department to explain the several designated 'heritage trails' in the district, inviting locals and visitors alike to understand in context the multiplicity of historic buildings and other landscape features in the area.

In 1987 the Department had collaborated with the Australasian Institute of Mining and Metallurgy to stage a conference on 'South Australia's Mining Heritage', an indication that the academic and educational aspects of that heritage were seen as being every bit as important as the touristic.[49] The previous year, the Department's Director-General, R.K. Johns, had undertaken a comparative study tour of Cornwall, and had returned to South Australia convinced that it was now vitally important to consider how the State's industrial archaeological relics 'might be recognised, interpreted and preserved for educational, historical and tourist purposes'.[50] This led to the practical activity in the mining landscape noted above but it also spawned an impressive publishing programme, the fruits of the Department's scholarly research into the technological dimension of South Australia's mining history. This culminated in the appearance in 1993 of *Cornish Beam Engines in South Australian Mines* by G.J. Drew and J.E. Connell. As Johns noted in his Foreword to the book, the 'enginehouses which were built to support these powerful machines [the Cornish beam engines] transformed the major South Australian mining fields to resemble landscapes from whence they were inspired'.[51] This was an important recognition by the Department that it was in the business of preserving and interpreting a series of mining landscapes that were quintessentially *Cornish* – of which the most extensive was the Moonta mining field. There was, therefore, considerable satisfaction in South Australia when in July 2006 the mining landscape of Cornwall itself was awarded UNESCO 'World Heritage Site' status; a sense that South Australia had somehow acted as a pathfinder in this significant endeavour and would now be associated with the wider international project that it had helped so prominently to initiate.[52]

Map Kernow

The marketing and publicity activity of the Department of Mines and Energy had the desired effect of bringing the South Australian mining landscapes to a wider public. Here Burra Burra and Kapunda vied with Moonta and northern Yorke Peninsula for the attention of the several constituencies that Johns had identified – tourist, educational and so on. But, intriguingly, while the Department had emphasized the Cornish dimension of each of these landscapes, there continued to be important cultural distinctions between them. Moonta and environs, as the myth dictated, continued to be imagined as homogeneously 'Cornish'. Burra and Kapunda, by contrast, had retained in popular imagination the 'kaleidoscopic multicultural mix' (see p. 46) that had characterised both communities in the nineteenth century, where the Cornish were seen as but one component of a more complex population.

Kapunda, for example, had always been aware of its 'Irish' identity. In the 1970s the town decided to celebrate this heritage by promoting an 'Irish and Colonial' Festival. It was another decade or so before Kapunda thought to remember its Cornish inheritance, in 1988 (Australia's Bicentenary year) erecting at the town's southern entrance – at considerable expense – a giant statue of a Cornish miner. Revealingly, the committee charged with commissioning the statue avoided the obvious name 'Cousin Jack' – redolent as it was of an assertive Cornish exclusivity – and opted instead for 'Map Kernow': 'son of Cornwall' in the Cornish language. Although the language was never spoken traditionally in South Australia, the use of Cornish – a Celtic tongue, like Irish – somehow ameliorated the worst of nineteenth-century Cornish claims to ethno-occupational superiority, as well as responding to Australia's late twentieth-century multicultural *Zeitgeist* and the town's own multi-ethnic past. As the leaflet produced by the local council explained, Map Kernow was intended as a memorial 'to all the people who are part of Kapunda's story – Cornish, Irish, German and other nationalities'.[53]

At Burra Burra a continuing 'diversity' was also apparent. As we have seen, in the nineteenth century there was an ethnic identification of sorts with the several communities that comprised 'Burra of the Five Towns': so that Redruth was Cornish, Llwchwr Welsh, Aberdeen Scottish, and so on. As time went on, the ethnic identity of these separate settlements was repeated with increasing certainty, local historians further elaborating the narrative of diversity as they noted the presence of Chilean muleteers in the early days and pointed out Hebrew headstones in the local cemetery. Ian Auhl, in his splendid succession of books on the Burra, privileged the Cornish but also went out of his way to stress the locality's multicultural credentials.[54] Auhls's *magnum opus*, for example, *The Story of the Monster Mine: The Burra Burra Mine and its Townships, 1845–1877*, published in 1986, was dedicated to 'the nameless Cornish and English miners; Welsh and German smelters; Irish teamsters and Chilean muleteers who helped to establish the Burra Burra Mine and its Townships "in the wilderness"'.[55] It was a dedication that enshrined and perpetuated the district's perceived multicultural identity, underpinning the touristic promotion of the Burra so apparent today.

In carving out subtly different identities, Kapunda and Burra had avoided direct competition with Moonta and environs, not least in the tourism stakes, allowing northern Yorke Peninsula to remain the undisputed 'Australia's Little Cornwall'. But if there was a tacit consensual division of identities within South Australia, elsewhere in the continent there was a less compliant attitude to the continuing assertion of Moonta's myth. In neighbouring Victoria, as we have seen (p. 31), Ruth Hopkins articulated a widespread and persistent irritation that that State's own considerable Cornish heritage was routinely overshadowed by the claims of Yorke Peninsula. In New South Wales, Patricia Lay offered a less strident corrective, showing that 'Cornish immigrants to New South Wales last [nineteenth] century established and maintained recognizable and cohesive groups'.[56] In Tasmania, there was a different tack. Nic Haygarth in his impressive study *Baron Bischoff: Philosopher Smith and the Birth of Tasmanian Mining* (2004) sought not so much to question the superior credentials of Moonta and environs – or even to assert those of Tasmania – but rather to challenge the myth of Cousin Jack itself, returning to contemporary nineteenth-century estimations of Cornish worth to offer, at last, a more critical assessment of the Cornish miner in Australia. In Tasmania, according to Haygarth, 'Cornish miners were as famous for their obstinacy as for their practical skill', while Ferdinand Kayser – a German miner from the Harz Mountains who was manager of the Mount Bischoff tin mine from 1875 to 1907 – thought Cornwall 'Luddite' in its apparent slowness to adopt new technologies in the years after 1850.[57] As Haygarth has noted: 'Antiquated Cornish mining methods were his favourite hobbyhorse'.[58] Others agreed – the disastrous attempts at tin-mining in the north-eastern field in Tasmania were blamed at the time on the Cornish – while Haygarth adds that the 'Mount Bischoff silver-lead debacle' (when traces of galena were wrongly assumed to indicate the existence of a payable lode) was the fault of over-confident or over-optimistic Cornishmen. The mine owners 'should have known better than to place so much trust in Cornish so-called experts who knew nothing of local conditions'.[59]

Haygarth's recent critique represents a considerable departure from the conventional wisdom but, academically important as it is in offering a more nuanced understanding of the limits of the myth of Cousin Jack, it is unlikely to affect popular imaginings of the Cornish miner in Australia – least of all in the context of Moonta and northern Yorke Peninsula. Elsewhere in Australia, there has been a different project – if not exactly to challenge the claims of Moonta and South Australia, then at least to question the State's claim to exclusive ownership of 'Australia's earliest mining era'. In 2001 Pat Banks and Ralph Thomas observed that 'Talk of Cornish migration to Australia usually centres on Moonta, Burra and Kapunda in South Australia or Ballarat and Bendigo in Victoria'. By contrast, they complained, 'Little is heard of the of the miners who emigrated to Western Australia in the 1850s'.[60] And yet, they added, even in the 1890s, Northampton, in the coastal mid-west of the colony, was still considered 'very much of a Cornish town',[61] the centre of the Murchison River mining district where galena had been discovered in 1847. Copper was also found in the locality, and, along with neighbouring Geraldton, Northampton became something of a magnet for emigrant Cornish miners in the late 1840s and into the early 1850s. Overshadowed perhaps by the might of Burra Burra and Kapunda, the Murchison River field nonetheless found its niche in the complex international web of Cornish destinations. Captain Hosken, for example, an early arrival, had already been out in Brazil mining for gold before heading for Western Australia. Further groups of Cornish miners and their families arrived during the 1860s and 1870s, the last contingent turning up in 1881, consolidating the existing Cornish community. But the mines did not last, many of the Cornish drifting to other mining districts in the continent or taking up other occupations, including farming, in the locality. However, as Banks and Thomas argued, this was a mining heritage as venerable as that of South Australia, if admittedly not on the same scale. Northampton and Geraldton were hardly likely to usurp Moonta's pre-eminent position in popular estimations of 'Cornish-Australia' but the work of Banks and Thomas showed that Australia's earliest mining era – and with it the Cornish influence in that period – was more complex than had been admitted hitherto. It was a message that filtered through to Cornwall itself, the education officers of Cornwall County Council and Geraldton Museum in 2005 seeking to develop links and exchanges between schools in the two districts, Cornwall and the Murchison River.

'Butte ... a Cornish objective'

In Australia, then, a more subtle understanding of the Cornish influence in the continent had served recently to place Moonta in a more critical, comparative context, observers probing the limits of the Cousin Jack myth and noting the previously overlooked but nonetheless competing claims of other geographical areas. On the international stage, beyond Australia, there were parallel attempts to investigate, evaluate and sometimes assert the Cornish credentials of other 'Cornish' localities. Butte, in Montana, in the United States, had been the site of extended conflict in the nineteenth and early twentieth centuries as the Cornish and the Irish struggled for supremacy in the mines and for control of the miners' trade union. More recently, rivalry of a different kind had emerged, with Butte constructed variously as an 'Irish' or 'Cornish' town. A.L. Rowse, the Cornish historian, considered Butte first and foremost 'a Cornish objective',[62] noting that his supposed biological father had settled in the district in the early 1900s, and he devoted a dozen pages to the town in his monumental *The Cornish in America*, which was published on both sides of the Atlantic in 1969. 'At home [in Cornwall] in my childhood,' Rowse recalled, 'Butte was a familiar name to us: it stood for the roughness and toughness of a mining camp still, the latest in time of all those to which the Cornish miners had flocked.'[63] Rowse found 'many hundreds' of Cornish surnames in the area in the 1960s, evidence he considered of 'how strongly concentrated the Cornish are in Butte'.[64] A.C. Todd, meanwhile, had taken a rather more measured estimation of Butte's enduring Cornish identity, opining in 1967 in his *The Cornish Miner in America* that 'Today, the Cornishman at Butte, as elsewhere, has been lost in the crowd'.[65] But Todd agreed that from the very beginning the 'Cornish were astride the mountains of Butte', as he put it, 'wrestling for survival with Welsh, Finns, Swedes, Italians, Austrians, Slavs, Mexicans, Filipinos and, above all, Irish'.[66] John Rowe, the third of Cornwall's celebrated chroniclers of the Cornish in America, added to the narrative. Writing in 1974, he insisted that by the 1880s 'Cousin Jacks and Jennies began flocking into Butte on a similar scale to that in which they had earlier come to Upper Michigan and Grass Valley [California]'. As he observed: 'To Cornishmen Montana came to mean Butte'.[67] Frequent newspaper reports indicated 'the strength of the immigrant Cornish element in the Montana mining towns',[68] said Rowe:

> Montana, of course, was not quite the 'land of pilchards and cream' [Cornwall], but there were times when pilchards, brought from Porthleven, could be bought in Butte City for thirty cents a dozen. Canned 'cream', inferior to, but a passable substitute for, the clotted cream of Cornwall cost ten cents a tin in 1893, and saffron was put up in small boxes selling at six for a dollar.[69]

Thirty years on, Alan M. Kent followed – disciple-like – in the footsteps of Rowse, Todd and Rowe, conducting research for his Brysonesque *Cousin Jack's Mouth-Organ: Travels in Cornish America* (2004). Early twenty-first-century

Butte, he found, was still 'full of stories about the Cornish', evidence of 'just how Cornish, Butte City was, *and* still is'. Butte, he said, was 'perhaps the most remarkable of all my travels and experiences in Cornish America'.[70] And yet, like Todd before him, Kent also thought Butte's Cornish identity understated, even elusive. 'I suppose I felt slightly saddened', he wrote, 'that beyond the pasty and perhaps the hard-rock mining exhibit [in the local museum], the Cornish presence there had been slightly brushed under the carpet.' He comforted himself with the thought that perhaps 'the Cornish didn't really need to stamp their identity on the town anymore. Perhaps all those head-gear frames and all those dumps stood much larger testament to our presence here.'[71] But he also knew that, in a fascinating latter-day version of the old rivalry, the Irish had gained the upper hand in twenty-first-century Butte, with its shops like 'Cavanaugh's County Celtic and Beyond', 'full of Leprechaun green Emerald Isle merchandise'.[72] For the attempts by Rowse *et al.* to assert Butte City as a predominantly Cornish town had been overtaken comprehensively by competing Irish claims. At one level, this was – as at Burra or Kapunda – a tourist device, the 'green Emerald Isle merchandise' in the gaudy gift shops appealing to romantic American conceptions of shamrockesque Irishness. But, intriguingly, there was in addition an academic dimension, in which scholarly constructions of Butte also presented the town's history as essentially 'Irish'.

In 1992 David M. Emmons investigated those 'two enduring and defining truths and half-truths of Butte and its history: it was a town with a large and important Irish enclave, and many of those Irish were from West Cork'. As he discovered, 'the reality was different from these perceptions – but not by much'. By 1900, he said, 'Butte was the most Irish town in the United States'.[73] In that year first and second-generation Irish numbered more than 8,000 out of a total population of some 30,000, a greater proportion than anywhere else in the Union. On further scrutiny, the West Cork association also turned out to have more than a grain of truth. West Cork surnames such as Sullivan, Shea, Lynch and McCarthy were commonplace in Butte, he found, and the records of local Irish societies such as the Ancient Order of Hibernians revealed that they were dominated by West Corkmen. Moreover, the majority of these West Cork folk had come from the neighbourhood of Castletownbere, near the 'Hungry Hill' copper mines of Allihies. Far from being the unskilled Irish labourers of popular fancy, these men were experienced hard-rock copper miners. As Emmons put it: 'Many West Corkmen knew how to mine; Butte had need of their skills'. Thus, between 1876 and 1900, 'Butte began to take on a West Cork character that it would never lose'.[74] Some had emigrated direct from Ireland but others had come by way of California, Nevada and Colorado, just as the Cornish had done, and in time the West Corkmen were joined by their compatriots from other parts of Ireland or from Irish enclaves in Britain, such as Glasgow and Liverpool. Nonetheless, by 1900 as many as 60 per cent of Butte's 5,300 Irish males were from Castletownbere and environs, or were the sons of West Corkmen. They constituted, Emmons explained, an 'exclusive club', an 'informal fraternity', an 'ethno-occupational enclave' which was fiercely resistant to outsiders.[75]

Although Emmons did not say so, principal among these outsiders were the Cornish – who had constructed their own ethno-occupational enclave – and, in another twist that Emmons had also missed, many of the Butte West Corkmen had already encountered the Cornish in an earlier existence: at the copper mines of Allihies.[76] As so often elsewhere, the Cornish had come to the Allihies mines as the labour aristocracy, bringing their technology (including beam engines and engine houses) with them, taking jobs as captains, engineers, tributers and tutworkmen. Initially, in the years after 1812 when the mines were first opened, the Irish were indeed restricted to the more menial tasks, a lowly status reflected in lower levels of remuneration and in poorer quality housing. In time, however, the Irish acquired the superior skills of their Cornish masters, although this was hardly reflected in better pay or sounder dwellings. Rather, the Cornish jealously maintained the wage differential, continuing to live a life apart in 'Cornish Village', a settlement of modest but well-appointed houses near the mines. Irish demands for better pay were met by insistence that they were less skilled than the Cornish – 'but this was disputed even by some Cornishmen'[77] – while the gross disparity in housing standards was obvious to all. In 1868 one newspaper report observed the 'poverty and wretchedness' of the Irish miners' existence, contrasting their 'miserable mud hovels' with the slated-roofed, whitewashed houses of the Cornish.[78] Not surprisingly, the Irish at Hungry Hill struck for better pay in 1868, as they had done before, part of a pattern of protest and resistance that these West Corkmen remembered bitterly when they had emigrated to Butte and once again found themselves rubbing shoulders with the hated Cornish.

'The carols reflected who I was'

The West Cork experience of the Irish and Cornish at Butte helps to explain both the depth and persistence of the antagonism between the two groups, as well as its reflection in competing academic constructions of the town as 'Cornish' and 'Irish'. A.L. Rowse, with all the conviction that comes of personal connection, was passionate in his belief that Butte was Cornish. David M. Emmons offered an alternative analysis, persuasively illuminating the significant Irish – particularly West Cork – influence in Butte but, in so doing, he managed to ignore the Cornish dimension altogether. Today, as Alan M. Kent discovered, it is the Irish construction of Butte that is in ascendancy. But that is hardly the point. Rather, like Kapunda and Burra Burra in Australia, Butte was never an exclusively Cornish destination, and – in marked contrast to Moonta and its myth of Cornish homogeneity – could never successfully or convincingly be portrayed as such.

Much the same could be said of Virginia City in Nevada, another mining town with both Irish and Cornish pretensions. Ronald M. James has argued in his *The Roar and the Silence: A History of Virginia City and the Comstock Lode* (1998) that 'Irish immigrants ... dominated Virginia City, where fully a third of the population claimed nativity or at least one parent from the Emerald Isle'.[79] As at Butte, more than a few were West Corkmen, skilled hard-rock miners who challenged competing Cornish claims to superiority and exclusivity. But James has also acknowledged the Cornish dimension, noting that by 1870 'immigrants from Cornwall [were] numbered in the hundreds ... claiming their place among the major ethnic groups of the district'.[80] The Cornish, like the Irish, tended to concentrate in certain localities on the Comstock – notably Gold Hill, outside Virginia City, maintaining their separate identity and distinctive cultural attributes. The same was apparent at Grass Valley in neighbouring California, where, as Ralph Mann has argued, the 'influx of Cornish miners ... contributed to another new phenomenon: the segregation of white ethnic groups. For the first time, in the late 1860s, two European-born groups, the Cornish and Irish, began to congregate in distinct areas.'[81] More so than Butte or Virginia City, Grass Valley was a Cornish town – Ralph Mann reckoned that 'the Cornish deeply influenced the town's identity' – although even here there was not the homogeneity, real or imagined, that characterized Moonta. The Cornish may have been the largest ethnic group at Grass Valley but they did not have everything their own way: 'Irish and Americans shot it out over mining claims ... Irish fought pitched battles with both Cornish and Germans.'[82]

Ironically, as we have seen, Oswald Pryor believed that Grass Valley had maintained its Cornish identity while that of Moonta had begun to wane. His perspective, no doubt, reflected the survival of Grass Valley as a mining town into the post-Second World War era. The copper mines of Moonta and Wallaroo had collapsed in 1923 but gold had remained an important metal during the Depression years, especially when President Roosevelt raised the price of gold in February 1934 as part of his 'New Deal'. At Grass Valley, several of the big mines combined during the 1930s to form the 'Empire-Star Mines', achieving various economies of scale and attracting new investment, and they were still prepared to give preferential treatment to Cornish miners: Cousins Jacks looking for work would always be pushed to the front of the queue.[83] Moreover, by the time Pryor had begun to fret about the apparent demise of the Cornish carol tradition on northern Yorke Peninsula, its equivalent phenomenon at Grass Valley had gained international exposure.

On Christmas Eve 1940, as Britain stood alone against Nazi Germany and Australia reflected with increasing nervousness on the slender military protection offered by the Mother Country, the NBC news network in North America turned its attention to more seasonal concerns. Broadcasting from the 2,000 foot level in the Idaho-Maryland mine, the wireless announcer spoke to his vast constituency across the United States and Canada. 'To all of America,' he said, 'from coast-to-coast, a merry Christmas from Grass Valley, California – where the Cornish Carol Choir is singing.' As he explained, seventy-eight years before Cornish miners had gathered in Grass Valley to sing their carols, and 'Since that Christmas so many years ago these same miners, and now their sons, have gathered each year to commemorate the birth of the Christ-Child with the singing of their beloved carols of their homeland'.[84]

These were carols that Oswald Pryor would have recognized, and would indeed have been sung at Moonta. The successful underground performance at Grass Valley was repeated again in 1941 and 1942, and news of the NBC broadcasts filtered across to South Australia. Growing American involvement in the Second World War put paid to future broadcasts, although after the war the choir regained its popularity, broadcasting once more in 1959. No wonder Oswald Pryor bemoaned the demise of Moonta's 'curls' and cast envious eyes – or ears – in the direction of Grass Valley. Here was 'another "little Cornwall" in California', he said incredulously, 'where they still bake pasties and sing "Curls"', and where the venerable Carol Choir had acquired 'an international reputation ... Good old Cousin Jacks!'[85] But by then the Grass Valley mines had themselves closed, succumbing to very different post-war conditions – the last was abandoned in 1956 – and although the choir survived for almost another decade, it suffered declining membership and waning interest, and was wound up in 1967. Paradoxically, despite the survival of the mines – and with them the Cornish choir – into the post-war era, no one of Oswald Pryor's stature or ability had emerged at Grass Valley to champion the town's Cornish identity, or to begin to reconstruct it for the post-industrial 'heritage' era. Moonta, meanwhile, as we have seen, had actively re-invented its myth, perpetuating its 'Cornish' sense of place in a way that ultimately eluded Grass Valley. Significantly, it was not until after the Cornish carol choir had been re-formed in 1990 – a result, among other things, of increasing interest in Grass Valley's mining past – that a more considered appraisal of the town's Cornish identity seemed possible. Thirty years before, Gage McKinney, then aged only nine years, had visited Grass Valley, home of his Cornish antecedents, with his parents for the festive season. He had stood in Mill Street in the freezing cold to listen to the carolers: 'Even at that age I felt it was worth it: I understood that the choir represented the heritage of a mining town, and recognized dimly that the carols reflected who

I was.'[86] Much later, in the 1990s, when the director of the choir suggested to McKinney that he might write its history, he recognized at once 'that a light trained on the choir would illuminate the history of the town'[87] itself – and with it, its Cornish past. The result was McKinney's *When Miners Sang: The Grass Valley Carol Choir*, the first sustained attempt to elucidate Grass Valley's Cornish heritage, published in 2001 – almost forty years after Oswald Pryor's *Australia's Little Cornwall*.[88]

Kernewek Lowender

Meanwhile, back in South Australia, the re-invention of 'Australia's Little Cornwall' had continued apace. In 1970 Don Dunstan's Labor Party had come to power in the State. Concerned from the first with cultural and social policy, Dunstan aimed to make South Australia a more open and self-celebratory society.[89] South Australia became 'the Festival State' – a new Festival Theatre was opened in Adelaide – and heritage tourism was actively encouraged as a means of economic diversification as well as a celebration of the State's diverse historical and natural heritage. Multiculturalism became an act of faith, pointing to the contributions by a multiplicity of different ethnic groups to the development of South Australia.

In the same year that Dunstan had assumed the Premiership, Nancy Phelan had visited northern Yorke Peninsula in search of the Cornish, raw material for her popular book on Australian immigrants. She found, she reported, that 'Little Cornwall is only a memory. A few years more, and no one will remember the miners and their Cornish ways. Only the Cornish names, and perhaps the Cornish eyes, will survive.'[90] Occasionally, what were imagined to be Cornish racial characteristics could be discerned in the local population, she said, 'you will still see unmistakable Cornish figures and faces in the streets: stocky, short-legged, with straight features, rather broad, flat-topped heads, a long upper lip and strange dark eyes and eyebrows'.[91] But for the rest, 'Australia's Little Cornwall' had all but disappeared. This was less than a decade after the appearance of Oswald Pryor's book, and if Phelan had not encountered the enthusiasm that the volume had stirred, then this suited her journalistic agenda – where the imminent demise of 'Little Cornwall' fitted the general thesis of *Some Came Early, Some Came Late*. But what Phelan could not have anticipated was the impact of Don Dunstan's reforming agenda upon the already re-invented identity of Moonta and environs. Mindful of his own Cornish descent, Dunstan had suggested that northern Yorke Peninsula might boost its cultural tourism potential and achieve greater visibility within Australia and overseas, if it were to make more of its Cornish heritage. Specifically, he proposed a Cornish festival – an idea that was immediately taken to heart by the local worthies. As Dunstan recalled: 'When I proposed

38. The Cornish Furry Dance being performed at the first 'Kernewek Lowender' festival in 1973 by members of the Cornish Association of South Australia.

the establishment of a Cornish Festival, in Australia's "Little Cornwall", people of Cornish descent came flocking. The staid citizens of the three towns were soon dancing the Furry Dance in the streets of Wallaroo.'[92]

In taking their place in Dunstan's multicultural 'Festival State', the organizers of the Cornish festival decided, wisely, to draw upon two important reservoirs of cultural capital: the Cornish heritage of northern Yorke Peninsula itself but also the iconography of the Cornish–Celtic Revival. They turned, for example, to the Cornish language, alighting upon the phrase 'Kernewek Lowender' – a slightly incorrect rendering of the words for 'Cornish festival' – establishing from the first its use as central to their marketing strategy. Although Cornish had never been spoken traditionally in Australia, the deployment of a non-English language was powerful testament to what the Kernewek Lowender organizers averred – that the Cornish on Yorke Peninsula were a distinct ethnic group. Part of their strategy was to convince observers that this remained so. Roslyn Paterson, for example, an inaugural member of the steering committee set up to launch the festival, wrote an article for the magazine *Cornish Nation*, published in Cornwall, insisting that 'Today Australia's Little Cornwall still retains its Cornish flavour'. She explained that 'Cornish pasties are still crimped, saffron cakes and buns still baked ... people use phrases that are easily identified as Cornish, with many sayings and superstitions still in active use.' Moreover, she continued, the 'miners' cottages still straggle along winding lanes, with their whitewashed walls gleaming in the sun. Smokestacks, pump houses, attle heaps, and skimp dumps bear mute reminder of a once great industry, whilst local electoral rolls list eighty different Cornish surnames.' Similarly, 'Cornish carols, "Trelawny" and typical folk songs are still performed ... and whilst there are fewer Methodist churches owing to the smaller population, Sunday school and church attendance are still high.' People from elsewhere continued to see Peninsula folk as 'different', she said: at football matches 'outsiders call the Moonta teams Cousin Jacks or C.J.s, in a derogatory way'.[93]

The first Kernewek Lowender festival was held over the bank-holiday weekend in May 1973. Conceived initially as 'a small regional celebration' – 'in many respects a pilot effort' – the festival was an instant success, surpassing the expectations of both Don Dunstan and the organizers.[94] It had, according to the local newspaper, gained 'a solid foothold in SA's festival country calendar',[95] with some 12,000 people attending the Cornish Fair at Moonta and 1,400 worshippers swelling the congregation at a special heritage service in Moonta Mines Methodist Church. Subsequent years attracted even larger crowds – the festival was held biennially – and in May 1981 the *Yorke Peninsula Country Times* announced proudly that the Kernewek Lowender was a 'unique Festival, unmatched by any other around the world, and that includes Cornwall'.[96] By 1999 the Kernewek Lowender had become 'the world's largest Cornish festival', according to its promotional literature, and in 2001 the organizers could boast that 'the Kernewek Lowender – Australia's only Cornish Festival – has blossomed into a gigantic, colourful spectacular eight-day Festival, which has won acclaim throughout Australia and overseas'.[97] Pasty-making competitions rubbed shoulders with Cornish wrestling demonstrations; there were prizes for the best-dressed 'Cousin Jack and Cousin Jenny'; there were receptions, literary events, seminars, luncheons, church services, art exhibitions, Cornish-language classes, parades, dancing, concerts, underground tours of Wheal Hughes (the local tourist mine), and a host of other activities. The emphasis, increasingly, was on family fun – 'a family festival, traditional foods, activities and celebrations', as the 2007 brochure put it – but there was also a decidedly serious dimension to the festival.

The most solemn aspect of the Kernewek Lowender was the 'Assembly of the Bards of the Gorsedd of Cornwall in Australia', a gathering of blue-robed bards who, in the symbolically profound Gorsedd ceremony, proclaimed and reaffirmed with due *gravitas* the intimate bonds of Cornwall and northern Yorke Peninsula. Conducted in the Cornish language, the ceremony explained that *Byrth an Orseth Kernow yn Australya re dhedh dhe Moonta rak bos pur gref an Kevrennow unter Kernow ha Soth-Australya, ha'agan gwaytyans yu an kevrennow-ma dhe devy creffa ha creffa y'n bledhynnow a dhe* – 'The Bards of the Gorsedd of Cornwall in Australia have come to Moonta because the links between Cornwall and South Australia are very strong, and it is our hope that these links will grow even stronger in the years to come'.[98]

Intentionally sombre, the Gorsedd ceremony hinted at deeper meanings. Behind the façade of family fun, the Kernewek Lowender was for the ideologically committed a device to perpetuate once more the myth of 'Australia's Little Cornwall', to refute firmly the assimilationist analysis put forward by the likes of Nancy Phelan and to claim a space for the Cornish in Dunstan's new multicultural construction of South Australia. As Don Dunstan had argued, there was good economic sense in such a strategy – it did indeed boost heritage tourism and raised the Peninsula's international profile – but there were also less tangible issues of identity and locality at play. In an increasingly globalized world – or the 'global village', as it was known in Dunstan's day – local identities had become ever more important to people's estimation of who they were and what they were for. Ethnicity and place had become powerful determinants of social, economic and political behaviour as individuals and communities sought to reconcile the global with the local. One result of these tensions was the emergence or re-assertion of 'complex transnational identities',[99] as the sociologist Robin Cohen termed them. One of these was the Cornish identity. At the height of the 'Great Emigration', there was, as we have seen in earlier chapters, a vibrant transnational Cornish identity, but one that lost its potency and immediacy in the changed international conditions after the Great War. By the 1970s, however, there were signs of its re-emergence – not in terms of a renewed mass emigration but as a result of a rekindled Cornish consciousness – both in Cornwall itself, and in the lands of its old diaspora. In the United States, in Canada, in New Zealand and in Australia, many people were increasingly aware of a Cornish dimension to their individual or community identities, and many were prepared to do something about it – as the burgeoning number of Cornish Associations across the globe from the late 1970s onwards was to evidence.

Here Moonta was ahead of the game. Still the acknowledged focus of 'Australia's Little Cornwall', Moonta continued to assert its supposed superiority and its sense of historic ethnic homogeneity – in marked contrast to the 'multicultural' constructions of Kapunda and Burra Burra – a stance that it was able to maintain, despite the more nuanced understandings of the Cornish in Australia that were to emerge elsewhere. On the international stage, notwithstanding the strong reassertion of a transnational Cornish identity, especially in the United States, Moonta was able to resist competing claims. There were probably more people of Cornish descent in America than there was anywhere else in the world (there were certainly more Cornish Associations) but, as we have seen, none of the great centres of

39. Moonta's myth on the eve of the new Millennium: the largest Cornish festival in the world.

Cornish concentration in the United States – Butte, Virginia City, even Grass Valley – could yet rival Moonta. The Kernewek Lowender, then, had been a timely mechanism for the renewed institutionalization of Moonta's myth. By the early twenty-first century northern Yorke Peninsula, which in other circumstances might so easily have come to be viewed as just another unremarkable tract of rural South Australian wheat country, had become ingrained in Australian national consciousness as somewhere emphatically 'different'; the spiritual home, no less, of Australia's Cornish identity. Not for the first time had Moonta seen advantage in asserting – and institutionalizing – its developed sense of place.

'The Cornish corner of Australia'

Almost inevitably, E.V. Thompson, the internationally acclaimed author of a string of popular historical fiction set in nineteenth and early twentieth century Cornwall, found it useful to place one of his novels in South Australia during the 'Great Emigration' – a story which takes the heroine first to Kadina, on Yorke Peninsula, and then on to Cornish mines in the Far North and in the Adelaide Hills. *Seek a New Dawn*, published in 2001, is the tale of Emily Boyce, who follows her lover Sam Hooper from the copper-mining area around St Cleer to the mines of South Australia. She lands, Thompson explains, at Wallaroo: 'one of the three towns marking the angles of the so-called "Copper Triangle", the others being Moonta and Kadina. A great many mines of vastly different sizes existed within this area, and most employing Cornishmen.'[100] Thompson had absorbed all the essentials of the myth but he was also an agent of its propagation – his many devotees, the world over, were now required to place South Australia and northern Yorke Peninsula within their mind's eye construction of Cornish history.

Popular perceptions of 'Australia's Little Cornwall' were reinforced by the institutionalization of the Kernewek Lowender festival. But so too were academic assessments. Not only were scholars obliged to consider the Kernewek Lowender phenomenon – where did it come from, what did it mean? – but the perpetuation of Moonta's myth meant that those who had been impressed by Oswald Pryor's work in the early 1960s were again stimulated by the continued assertion of Cornish identity. In 1994, some thirty years after *The Rush that Never Ended*, Geoffrey Blainey in his *A Shorter History of Australia* reminded readers that South Australia was 'the Cornish corner' of the continent.[101] Almost a decade later, in his *Black Kettle and Full Moon*, Blainey returned to his much earlier theme of the cultural diversity of colonial Australia, recalling the differing 'social rules for each section of society'. Germans, Jews and Irish had had their own ways of doing things, he said, and a 'Cornish funeral in South Australia was not like a Scottish funeral in Brisbane'.[102] James Jupp, doyen of Australian immigration and multicultural studies, agreed: the Cornish were 'different'. He did not, therefore, include them in his history of *The English in Australia* (2004), explaining to his readers that:

> Cornwall has only a county council, fiercely protected against amalgamation with parts of neighbouring Devon. Yet South Australia hosts the largest Cornish festival and the oldest Cornish Association in the world. Cornish emigration to Australia was at its height between 1840 and 1880 when Cornwall was exceptionally homogeneous and culturally distinct. While Cornish Australians were often imperial patriots (as were many Scots and Protestant Irish) they deserve to be treated as a distinct ethnicity at least within the Australian context.[103]

By the 1850s, he said, 'at least half of the population [of Australia] were Irish Catholics, Scottish Presbyterians or Cornish Methodists', and

'Methodist support in South Australia and Broken Hill was mainly Cornish'. South Australian immigrants generally, he observed, were 'drawn largely from England and Cornwall'.[104] These conventional wisdoms mattered, and Jupp's sensitive treatment of the Cornish, together with his willingness – like Blainey – to take the their experience in Australia seriously, was a significant influence upon a new generation of scholars. Jupp wrote with an authority that could not be ignored, and his insistence that the Cornish in Australia be treated as an ethnic group apart from the English, impressed other students of multiculturalism. Celeste Lipow MacLeod, for example, embraced the Cornish cause with alacrity, writing with enthusiasm and confidence in her *Multiethnic Australia* in 2006 that nineteenth-century 'immigrants from rural areas of Scotland, Ireland, Wales and Cornwall had little in common with the English'.[105] This was, of course, an over-simplification, an exaggeration; part of the success of the Scots, Welsh, Cornish and even Irish was that they could have it both ways, asserting 'conformity' or 'difference' by turns as the situation demanded. But, as MacLeod's book evidenced, such a belief demonstrated the extent to which the Cornish had been impressed upon contemporary practitioners of Australian studies. In the kaleidoscopic complexity of multicultural Australia, consideration of the Cornish was now *de rigueur*.[106] Moonta, it seemed, had triumphed spectacularly in its renewed assertion of 'Australia's Little Cornwall'.

Epilogue

'I spoke of Yelta, Paramatta, Wandilta and half a dozen other mines as though they were all within the parish of Calstock.'[1] So wrote Tom Cowling from Moonta, reflecting on his visit to Cornwall towards the end of the nineteenth century. It was in its simple way an eloquent commentary on the intricate relationship between Cornwall and Moonta and environs. But between the lines it also spoke much about the manner in which Moonta had in the preceding three or four decades invented itself as 'Australia's Little Cornwall', the locality establishing and then projecting far and wide an assertive identity that claimed exclusivity and superiority.

Returning to his birthplace in Calstock, Cowling had sought out Captain Edward Dunstan, who was sacked from his post at the Wallaroo mines in 1869 and had moved on to work at Cobar in New South Wales before retiring to his native Cornwall. There he had lived the life of a recluse, rarely receiving anyone into his home, brooding – perhaps – on lost opportunities and a career cut short. Dunstan's frosty exterior had repelled many a visitor but Cowling was a determined man, dropping the names one by one of Yorke Peninsula mines by way of introduction. As he heard those names of long ago, Dunstan's façade began to melt. 'Following a few more remarks on my part,' recalled Cowling, 'he became talkative and said: "Evidently young man, you must have spent time in Australia, for you have mentioned names of places not unknown to me".'[2] Forgetting for a moment any ill feelings he might still harbour, Dunstan smiled at the remembrance of his former days in South Australia, and welcomed the rare opportunity to reminisce with Tom Cowling about earlier, happier times at Moonta and Wallaroo.

As Cowling had discovered, even for difficult and disappointed Edward Dunstan, there remained an enduring bond of affection between Cornwall and the far-off land of Moonta and environs. At St Ann's Chapel, hardly a stone's throw from Dunstan's home, there was likewise a Mr Preston, who in his retirement in Cornwall acquired 'some acres' and grew strawberries, remembering fondly the years he had spent at Cross Roads, near Moonta. Not far away, at Pensilva, was a certain Mr Williams – 'an old Moonta identity', as the *People's Weekly* reminded its readers – whose return to Cornwall had not prevented him remaining in close contact with all his friends and relations on northern Yorke Peninsula.[3]

But, as we know, the majority of Cornish emigrants did not return, and for them the links of affection between Cornwall and Moonta were more complex. By the time of Cowling's visit, Moonta had already replaced Cornwall as the focus of Cousin Jack loyalty and identity on the Peninsula, so much so that in 1905 one T. Gluyas Pascoe, a Cornish settler in New Zealand, decided to 'retire among his own people' – not in Cornwall but at Moonta. It was a trend that was encouraged locally, the *People's Weekly* as late as 1929 advocating that Moonta should be regarded as a Mecca for 'our Cornish folk' in the Antipodes.[4]

'Everything connected with Old Cornwall is always of the deepest interest to Moontaites',[5] one newspaper report had insisted in November 1902. But the changing relationship between the two places was by then already apparent. In 1907 Captain Richard Cowling – Tom's brother – had also made the hallowed pilgrimage to his native Cornwall, visiting his birthplace at Calstock and contemplating the ruins of Drakewalls mine, where once his father had worked, together with the surface remains of recently abandoned Gunnislake Clitters. Richard Cowling, who had left Cornwall as a small child, pondered deeply on what he had found there. For him, it was not that Moonta was so remarkably like Cornwall but rather the reverse. If there was surprise at the similarity, then it was that Cornwall and Cornish people could be so reminiscent of his own folk and places on northern Yorke Peninsula, that 'Cousin Jack' manners in Cornwall could be so like those at home in Moonta, that the mining landscapes of both localities were so uncannily alike – Moonta, which he knew intimately, and Cornwall, which he had only now discovered. As he observed tellingly of a Cornish wrestling match he had attended at Saltash: 'Hundreds of Cousin Jacks ... came up by excursion train from different parts of Cornwall, and you would think by the remarks made, that you were at Moonta'.[6]

As Richard Cowling inferred, it was Moonta that was now the hub of his universe, as it was for other Cousin Jacks and Jennys of his generation; those who had come to South Australia as young children or, indeed, increasingly, those who had been born on the Peninsula. But there remained an understanding – sometimes unconscious, sometimes explicit – that the institutional life that defined Moonta's expansive identity owed its foundations to Cornwall. Nowhere was this more so than in Moonta's religious life, where the profound inheritance of 'Cornish Methodism' was widely acknowledged: not least in the obituary columns of newspapers in the early twentieth century, where the Methodist allegiance of those who had passed on was routinely discussed. Thus John James from Camborne was, we learn, 'a typical Cornish Methodist', while James Bennett (another Camborne man) was a 'dear old miner Methodist local preacher'.[7] Women, too, were proud standard bearers of Cornish Methodism on the harsh frontier. Elizabeth Piper, born in Roche in 1834, had 'A motherly heart, swayed by an emotional Celtic temperament'. Elizabeth Slee, from Falmouth, had turned resolutely to the Primitive Methodists on the death in South Australia of her first child: 'I stood and looked into the grave, and said "My babe has gone to heaven; but if I had been taken instead of him, where should I be now?" I resolved there and then to give my heart to God and prepare to meet my child again.'[8]

Frequent allusions to Billy Bray, the Cornish–Methodist folk-hero, emphasized the Cornish dimension in the memory of Moonta Methodism. Reuben Gill was 'the Billy Bray of South Australia', Luke Teddy was 'an ardent admirer of his eccentric countryman, Billy Bray, with whose characteristics he had much in common', and Thomas Axford was 'a Cornish Methodist of the best type', having been born 'within sound of the sweet bells of Baldhu Church, beside which lie the remains of the famous Billy Bray, whose noble spirit he seems to have emulated'.[9] When Richard Coad, the 'Cornish temperance lecturer', toured South Australia in 1890 he was met by hushed tones and deep respect wherever he preached, for he had once worked alongside Billy Bray in Hicks' Mill circuit in Cornwall. Nowhere was this appreciation more apparent than when he addressed the newly formed Cornish Association branch at Moonta, where he 'delighted his hearers with some of the quaint and funny sayings and life of that well known Cornish revivalist Billy Bray'.[10]

Although trade unions were slow to develop in Cornwall, and the Labour movement never strong, at Moonta the influence of Billy Bray was readily detected by observers in the moral courage and steadfast natures of the leaders of the local miners' union. Reuben Gill was one such leader, and so was Thomas Rodda: one of the delegates who in the 'Great Strike' of 1874 had presented the miners' grievances in Adelaide, subsequently returning in triumph to the Peninsula. In December 1908 the *Australian Christian Commonwealth* reflected on Rodda's life. Born at St Just-in-Penwith in 1832, he was 'A Cornishman with some of the finest qualities of his race, with impetuosity, fervour, strength to love, and firmness in friendship – with some very human and brotherly qualities'. These were manly attributes he had gained in chapel and put into practice in trade unionism, striving for Christian justice and equality. Thomas Rodda was, it was said, 'one of a generation of Cornish local preachers, men of the Billy Bray type, natural orators, full of the Holy Ghost and of faith ... vehement in their endeavours to serve Christ'.[11] It was no coincidence, then, that Rodda had proved so fine a leader of men, such a stalwart in the trade unionist cause.

If the Methodist-dominated trade union movement had lent a particular institutional hue to Moonta's burgeoning myth, deploying 'Cornishness' in new and sometimes startling ways, then of at least equal significance was the cult of Captain Henry Richard Hancock. He was also a Methodist local preacher – a Wesleyan – but he was born on the Devon side of the Tamar, and therefore not Cornish; a distinction that was sometimes irrelevant, at other times of deep significance. He ran his mines – Moonta at first, and then Wallaroo too – in the familiar Cornish manner, with the strict hierarchy of captains and the relative independence of tributers and tutworkmen, and took paternalism and nepotism to new heights in his management of these vast industrial plants. Long after the copper-mining industry had all but disappeared in Cornwall, Captain Hancock's mines remained significant players on the international stage, Moonta and Wallaroo the fitting inheritors of Cornwall's erstwhile industrial prowess, their miners convincing purveyors of the myth of Cousin Jack. More than anywhere else in Australia, here were Cornish copper mines run by Cornish men – and sons of Cornish men – on Cornish principles.

This strong identification with Cornish copper-mining methods gave Moonta miners the edge on the wider stage in Australia: they were, they could argue with some justification, the true heirs of Cousin Jack. But, as we have seen, this advantage could sometimes be turned on its head. At Broken Hill in the 1880s, as Bendigonians and Moontaites vied for the best jobs in the rapidly expanding lead mines, the Bendigo Cornish criticized their Moonta compatriots for being under the thumb of their captains and for knowing little beyond how to mine for copper. The Moontaites were swift to respond, of course, playing their winning 'if you haven't been to Moonta' card. Its deployment reflected Moonta's developed sense of place, and its status in the pantheon of global Cornish destinations. But it also demonstrated that Cornish ethnic consciousness in Australia had fragmented already, strong regional identifications – such as those of Moonta and Bendigo – having complemented, or perhaps even replaced, a wider sense of Cornish transnational solidarity. At Broken Hill in the 1880s, as the Moonta and Bendigo Cornish jostled for position, trading insults about their relative worths, the myth of Cousin Jack had fractured as the two competing groups deployed localized versions against each other.

The Bendigo Cornish, with their highly successful adaptation to deep gold mining in Victoria, could assert a greater versatility and a wider experience, insinuating that they were inherently more useful in new mining fields such as Broken Hill. But, whatever the relative merits of miners from Moonta or Bendigo, Moonta's myth – founded on institutional strength and a formidable and highly visible regional identity – ensured the continuing prominence (if not exactly predominance) of Moontaites in Australia's mining industry. In

September 1901, after his retirement, Captain Hancock could report with proprietorial satisfaction that 'Since he left Moonta he had visited many mining centres in Australasia, and in each place he had found miners from Moonta and Wallaroo Mines'. Moreover, he added, he 'had heard a great deal about them from those in authority over them, but in no single instance had he ever heard one word against their capacity as miners'. He had, however, 'heard a great deal in their favour ... At Kalgoorlie and other places in the West they were in the front rank as miners, while at Broken Hill they were not a whit behind. Even in far-off New Zealand he heard good concerning them.'[12]

The closure of the Moonta and Wallaroo mines in 1923 appeared to undermine fatally the intimate connection between mining prowess and Moonta's myth. How could the latter survive the catastrophic collapse of the former? R.M. Gibbs in his *A History of South Australia*, first published in 1969, wrote that it 'was the mines that were the heart of "Little Cornwall". As long as they survived, Cornishmen and Cornish life would remain.' Thus, he argued, when the mines closed and the infrastructure was summarily dismantled, it 'was the end of "Little Cornwall"'.[13] But, even as Gibbs had prepared his book, the post-mining re-invention of Moonta that Oswald Pryor had led so tenaciously since the 1920s was bursting into popular consciousness. The regional identity of northern Yorke Peninsula had proved more enduring than Gibbs had imagined, (continuing to pervade the State's Labor movement, for example). Pryor recognized this, and capitalized upon it. His *Australia's Little Cornwall*, published in 1962, was an instant best-seller: on the one hand it sounded exactly the right note at precisely the right moment as northern Yorke Peninsula began – albeit slowly at first – to ponder its heritage tourism future; on the other it prompted a new academic interest in the Cornish experience in South Australia and in the continent generally. Yet even more importantly, it demonstrated that Moonta's myth had survived the trauma of 1923, metamorphosing in the years ahead – as Cornwall's post-industrial identity had done – to become the driving force in a re-invigorated regional identity where, just as in earlier days, a conveniently subtle blurring of boundaries allowed on occasions the collective description of Moonta, Wallaroo and Kadina as 'Australia's Little Cornwall'.

The Kernewek Lowender festival, launched in 1973, happily colluded in the blurring, raising the collective consciousness of regional identity and marshalling its extensive cultural capital for the promotion of heritage tourism. At one level the festival was part of a renewed transnational Cornish identity, one element of a much wider global phenomenon. But it was also a device to perpetuate the myth of Australia's Little Cornwall into the twenty-first century. As Mel Davies has observed: 'This major tourist attraction has spread the word about "Australia's Little Cornwall" throughout the world and helped cement the Cornish identity'. Moreover, as Davies adds with telling insight: 'While drinking "swanky" and eating Cornish pasties is synonymous with the festival, Kernewek Lowender also celebrates the Cornish contribution to the social, economic and political life of South Australia'.[14]

There remains the question of the future. It is a matter of conjecture whether the renewed Cornish transnational identity will prove to be a fleeting or lasting phenomenon, and how long the Kernewek Lowender festival will survive as a major feature of the South Australian calendar is impossible to say. But an important indicator of probable future trends is the achievement in 2006 of UNESCO 'World Heritage Site' status for the mining landscapes of Cornwall. Integral to this status is recognition of the international significance of those landscapes, and an understanding that across the globe are scattered other landscapes that are inherently 'Cornish'. This is nowhere more obvious than in South Australia – most especially on northern Yorke Peninsula, and specifically at Moonta. As Cornwall moves to capitalize on its new-found status, so these other global Cornish landscapes will feature anew in consideration of the international implications of being a 'World Heritage Site', and a new inter-governmental alliance or network of transnational Cornish landscapes may well emerge. It is in this symbiotic context that Moonta's myth as 'Australia's Little Cornwall' could be comprehensively re-invented afresh during the twenty-first century.

Notes

Preface

1. Manning Clark, *Occasional Writings and Speeches* (Melbourne, 1980), p. 9.
2. Geoffrey Blainey, *Blainey – Eye on Australia: Speeches and Essays of Geoffrey Blainey* (Melbourne, 1991), p. 47.

Chapter 1. 'The largest Cornish communities beyond Land's End': Making Moonta's Cornish myth

1. Oswald Pryor, *Australia's Little Cornwall* (Adelaide, 1962), p. 7.
2. South Australian Archives (SAA), PRG 96, *Oswald Pryor Papers*, Correspondence, A.L. Rowse to Pryor, 5 December 1951.
3. See Philip Payton, 'The Cornish in South Australia: Their Influence and Experience from Immigration to Assimilation, 1836–1936', unpublished Ph.D. thesis, University of Adelaide, 1978; Philip Payton, *Pictorial History of Australia's Little Cornwall* (Adelaide, 1978); Philip Payton, *The Cornish Miner in Australia: Cousin Jack Down Under* (Redruth, 1984); Philip Payton, *The Cornish Overseas: The History of Cornwall's 'Great Emigration'* (Fowey, 2005), esp. chapter 8.
4. Mandie Robinson, *Cap'n 'Ancock: Ruler of Australia's Little Cornwall* (Adelaide, 1978).
5. Kernewek Lowender promotional leaflet, 1999.
6. *South Australian Register*, 30 April 1857.
7. (Adelaide) *Observer*, 20 December 1856, cited in J.K. Chilman, *Silver and A Trace of Gold: A History of the Aclare Mine* (Adelaide, 1982), p. 13.
8. Jan Croggon, 'Methodists and Miners: The Cornish in Ballarat, 1851–1901', in Kerry Cardell and Cliff Cumming (eds), *A World Turned Upside Down: Cultural Change on Australia's Goldfields, 1851–2001* (Canberra, 2001), p. 64.
9. R.H.B. Kearns, *Broken Hill, 1883–1893: Discovery and Development* (Broken Hill, 1973), p. 44; (Moonta) *People's Weekly*, 6 December 1896.
10. *Yorke's Peninsula Advertiser*, 4 July 1873.
11. Pryor, *Australia's Little Cornwall*, p. 148.
12. Pryor, *Australia's Little Cornwall*, pp. 148–9 (my italics).
13. Gage McKinney, *When Miners Sang: The Grass Valley Carol Choir* (Grass Valley, CA, 2001), pp. 239–43.

14. Pryor, *Australia's Little Cornwall*, p. 148.
15. Pryor, *Australia's Little Cornwall*, p. 148.
16. Robinson, *Cap'n 'Ancock*, pp. viii–ix.
17. See Payton, *The Cornish Overseas*, chapter 6.
18. Charles Fahey, 'Cornish Miners in Bendigo: An Examination of their Standard of Living', unpublished Paper, Department of History, Monash University, n.d., p. 3.
19. Pryor, *Australia's Little Cornwall*, p. 153.
20. Payton, *The Cornish Overseas*, p. 309; E.H. Coombe, *History of Gawler, 1837–1908* (Gawler, 1910), p. 295; O.H. Woodward, *A Review of the Broken Hill Lead-Silver-Zinc Industry*, 2nd edn (Sydney, 1965), p. 56; Geoffrey Blainey, *The Rush that Never Ended: A History of Australian Mining*, 2nd edn (Melbourne, 1969), p. 154.
21. R.K. Johns, *Cornish Mining Heritage* (Adelaide, 1986), p. 5.
22. For a comprehensive survey of Cornish engines and engine houses in South Australia, see: G.E. Drew and J.A. Connell, *Cornish Beam Engines in South Australia* (Adelaide, 1993).
23. J.P. McCarthy, *Cadia Conservation Study* (Adelaide, 1989); Lesley J. Morton, *The Duke of Cornwall Mine, Fryerstown, Victoria* (Melbourne, 1992).
24. Fahey, 'Cornish Miners in Bendigo', p. 3.
25. *Mining Journal*, 25 October 1873; cited in D.B. Barton, *Essays in Cornish Mining History: Volume 2* (Truro, 1970), p. 53.
26. Barton, *Essays in Cornish Mining History: Volume 2*, p. 54.
27. D.B. Barton, *Essays in Cornish Mining History: Volume I* (1968), p. 20.
28. Jim Faull, *Cornish Heritage: A Miner's Story* (Adelaide, 1980), p. 83.
29. Faull, *Cornish Heritage: A Miner's Story*, p. 83.
30. Faull, *Cornish Heritage: A Miner's Story*, p. 83.
31. Ruth Hopkins, *Where Now Cousin Jack?* (Bendigo, 1988), p. 23.
32. Hopkins, *Where Now Cousin Jack?*, p. 23.
33. Pryor, *Australia's Little Cornwall*, p. 148.
34. Robinson, *Cap'n 'Ancock*.
35. Pryor, *Australia's Little Cornwall*, p. 44.
36. Pryor, *Australia's Little Cornwall*, p. 43.
37. Pryor, *Australia's Little Cornwall*, p. 44.
38. Robinson, *Cap'n 'Ancock*, p. 160–1; *People's Weekly*, 1 March 1902.
39. Barton, *Essays in Cornish Mining History: Volume 2*, pp. 53–4; Richard D. Dawe, *Cornish Pioneers in South Africa: 'Gold and Diamonds, Copper and Blood'* (St Austell, 1998), p. 90.
40. Anon., *The Barrier Silver and Tin Fields in 1888* (1888; republished Adelaide, 1970), p. 73.
41. *Yorke's Peninsula Advertiser*, 16 October 1877.
42. Pryor, *Australia's Little Cornwall*, p. 44.
43. For the influence of Cornish nomenclature, technology and manpower in West Devon, see D.B. Barton, *A Historical Survey of The Mines and Mineral Railways of East Cornwall and West Devon* (Truro, 1964), pp. 71–102, and A.K. Hamilton Jenkin, *The Mines of Devon: Volume 1 – The Southern Area* (Newton Abbot, 1974).
44. Pryor, *Australia's Little Cornwall*, p. 40.
45. *Yorke's Peninsula Advertiser*, 3 August 1877.

46. Pryor, *Australia's Little Cornwall*, p. 44.
47. Pryor, *Australia's Little Cornwall*, p. 44.
48. *Yorke's Peninsula Advertiser*, 2 June 1874, 4 April 1876; John Rowe, *Cornish Methodists and Emigrants* (Camborne, 1967), p..24; unidentified press cutting obituary of January 1884 in SAA, Dr Charles Davies, *Biographies and Obituaries* (27 vols); G.E. Loyau, *Notable South Australians and Colonists – Past and Present* (Adelaide, 1885), pp. 61–2.
49. SAA, BRG40/543, *Moonta Mines Proprietors, Minute Books, 1861–91*, 7 February 1876.
50. Payton, 'The Cornish in South Australia', p. 564; *People's Weekly*, 16 April 1921.
51. Payton, 'The Cornish in South Australia', pp. 564–5.
52. L.L. Price, '"West Barbary": Or Notes on the System of Work and Wages in the Cornish Tin Mines' (1891), in Roger Burt (ed.), *Cornish Mining: Essays on the Organisation of Cornish Mines and the Cornish Mining Economy* (Newton Abbot, 1969), p. 154.
53. A.K. Hamilton Jenkin, *The Cornish Miner* (1927; republished Newton Abbot, 1972), p. 199.
54. Hamilton Jenkin, *The Cornish Miner*, p. 198.
55. John Rule, 'The Perfect Wage System? Tributing in the Cornish Mines', in John Rule and Roger Wells (eds), *Crime, Protest and Popular Politics in Southern England, 1740–1850* (London, 1997), pp. 53–66; see also John Rule, *Cornish Cases: Essays in Eighteenth- and Nineteenth-Century Social History* (Southampton, 2006).
56. Rule, 'The Perfect Wage System?'; John Rule, 'The Misfortunes of the Mine: Coping with Life and Death in Nineteenth-century Cornwall', in Philip Payton (ed.), *Cornish Studies: Nine* (Exeter, 2001), pp. 127–44.
57. Mel Davies, 'Collective Action and the Cornish Miner in Australia: An Early Repudiation of the "Individualistic" Thesis', in Philip Payton (ed.), *Cornish Studies: Three* (Exeter, 1995), p. 23.
58. Bernard Deacon, 'Attempts at Unionism by Cornish Metal Miners in 1866', *Cornish Studies*, first series 10 (1983), pp. 27–36.
59. Bernard Deacon, 'Heroic Individualists? The Cornish Miners and the Five Week Month, 1872–74', *Cornish Studies*, first series 14 (1986), pp. 39–52.
60. Gillian Burke, 'The Cornish Miner and the Cornish Mining Industry, 1870–1921', unpublished Ph.D. thesis, University of London, 1981, p. 383.
61. Hamilton Jenkin, *The Cornish Miner*, p. 198.
62. R.E. Lingenfelter, *The Hardrock Miners* (Berkeley, CA, 1974), p. 6.
63. *Yorke's Peninsula Advertiser*, 20 February 1877.
64. Payton, *The Cornish Overseas*, p. 155.
65. Payton, *The Cornish Overseas*, p. 251.
66. Hopkins, *Where Now Cousin Jack?*, p. 36.
67. Hopkins, *Where Now Cousin Jack?*, pp. 37–8.
68. Hopkins, *Where Now Cousin Jack?*, p. 29.
69. Hopkins, *Where Now Cousin Jack?*, p. 41.
70. Ruth Hopkins, *Cousin Jack, Man for the Times: A History of the Cornish People in Victoria*, Bendigo, 1994, p. 55.
71. *Yorke's Peninsula Advertiser*, 4 April 1876.

72. *Yorke's Peninsula Advertiser*, 2 June 1874.
73. *Australian Christian Commonwealth*, 9 May 1902.
74. *Moonta Mines Methodist Church Centenary, 1865–1965* (Moonta, 1965), p. 5.
75. *Australian Christian Commonwealth*, 5 July 1907.
76. D.H. Luker, 'Cornish Methodism, Revivalism and Popular Belief, c.1780–1870', unpublished D.Phil. thesis, University of Oxford, 1987, pp. xv, 290, 322.
77. Arnold Hunt, *This Side of Heaven: A History of Methodism in South Australia* (Adelaide, 1985), p. 173.
78. Hunt, *This Side of Heaven*, p. 117.
79. Hunt, *This Side of Heaven*, p. 169.
80. Cited in Alan M. Kent, *Pulp Methodism: The lives and Literature of Silas, Joseph and Salome Hocking* (St Austell, 2002), p. 69.
81. Hunt, *This Side of Heaven*, p. 169.
82. *Christian Weekly and Methodist Journal*, 15 December 1899.
83. Kent, *Pulp Methodism*.
84. Michael J.L. Wickes, *The Westcountry Preachers: A History of the Bible Christians* (Bideford, 1987); Jean Saxe Jolliffe (ed.), *Our Back Pages: Obituaries of Cornish and North Devonshire Settlers of Jefferson, Walworth and Wausheka Counties, Wisconsin, USA, Volume 1* (Brookfield, WI, 1992).
85. *Bible Christian Magazine*, combined volume, 1876, p. 37.
86. Cited in Hunt, *This Side of Heaven*, p. 129.
87. Hunt, *This Side of Heaven*, p. 129.
88. *People's Weekly*, 12 July 1902.
89. *People's Weekly*, 12 September 1896.
90. Pryor, *Australia's Little Cornwall*, p. 37.
91. Pryor, *Australia's Little Cornwall*, pp. 38–9.
92. See Roslyn M. Paterson, 'Kate Cocks MBE' in Cornish Association of South Australia, *Notable Cornish Women* (Kadina, 2005).
93. Payton, *The Cornish Overseas*, pp. 26–8.
94. Phyllis Somerville, *Not Only in Stone* (1947; republished Adelaide, 1973), back cover notes.
95. www.pcug.org.au/-terryg/main.html, dated 3 May 2006, p. 11.
96. See Ern Carmichael, *The Ill-Shaped Leg: A Story of the Development of Yorke Peninsula* (Adelaide, 1973).
97. *South Australian Register*, 10 June 1873.
98. *Yorke's Peninsula Advertiser*, 6 August 1875.
99. After much soul-searching, the Gorsedd ceremony was experimentally moved to Kadina in 2007: part of the restructuring of the Kernewek Lowender festival consequent upon the loss of May's bank-holiday weekend in South Australia.
100. Keith Bailey, *James Boor's Bonanza: A History of Wallaroo Mines, South Australia* (Kadina, 2002), p. iii.
101. Bailey, *James Boor's Bonanza*, p. iii.
102. Hopkins, *Where Now Cousin Jack?*, p. 12.
103. Hopkins, *Cousin Jack, Man for the Times*, p. 37.
104. Hopkins, *Cousin Jack, Man for the Times*, p. 37.
105. Hopkins, *Where Now Cousin Jack?*, p. 26.

Chapter 2. 'Wherever a hole is sunk in the ground': Moonta and Cornwall's great emigration

1. See Philip Payton, *The Cornish Overseas: A History of Cornwall's 'Great Emigration'* (Fowey, 2005).
2. See Philip Payton, 'Cornish Emigration in Response to Changes in the International Copper Market in the 1860s', in Philip Payton (ed.), *Cornish Studies: Three* (Exeter, 1995), pp. 60–82.
3. *Cornishman*, 15 March 1900; see also Richard D. Dawe, *Cornish Pioneers in South Africa: 'Gold and Diamonds, Copper and Blood'* (St Austell, 1998), p. 110.
4. For exploratory discussions of the Cornish transnational identity see Sharron P. Schwartz, 'Cornish Migration Studies: An Epistemological and Paradigmatic Critique', in Philip Payton (ed.), *Cornish Studies: Ten* (Exeter, 2002), pp. 136–65, and Sharron P. Schwartz, 'Migration Networks and the Transnationalization of Social Capital: Cornish Migration to Latin America, a Case Study', in Philip Payton (ed.), *Cornish Studies: Thirteen* (Exeter, 2005), pp. 256–87 For a recent discussion see Bernard Deacon and Sharron Schwartz, 'Cornish Identities and Migration: A Multiscalar Approach', *Global Networks: A Journal of Transnational Affairs*, 7, 3, July 2007, pp. 289–306.
5. For a general discussion of this process see 'Introduction' in Payton, *The Cornish Overseas*, pp. 9–29.
6. John Rowe, *The Hard-Rock Men: Cornish Immigrants and the North American Mining Frontier* (Liverpool, 1974), p. v.
7. A.K. Hamilton Jenkin, *The Cornish Miner* (1927; republished Newton Abbot, 1972), p. 321.
8. Hamilton Jenkin, *The Cornish Miner*, p. 321.
9. Hamilton Jenkin, *The Cornish Miner*, p. 321.
10. See Philip Payton, '"Reforming Thirties" and "Hungry Forties": The Genesis of Cornwall's Emigration Trade', in Philip Payton, *Cornish Studies: Four* (Exeter, 1996), pp. 107–27.
11. *West Briton*, 23 September 1831.
12. Payton, *The Cornish Overseas*, pp. 108–9.
13. Larry Cenotto and Robert Richards, *Foreign Money Orders: Sutter Creek Post Office*, Amador County Museum, California.
14. Gary Magee and Andrew Thompson, 'Remittances Revisited: A Case Study of South Australia and the Cornish Migrant, c.1870–1914', in Payton (ed.), *Cornish Studies: Thirteen*, pp. 288–306.
15. See Payton, *The Cornish Overseas*, chapter 1.
16. See Brian Elvins, 'Cornwall's Newspaper War: The Political Rivalry Between the *Royal Cornwall Gazette* and the *West Briton* Part Two, 1832–1855', in Philip Payton (ed.), *Cornish Studies: Eleven* (Exeter, 2003), pp. 57–86.
17. Hamilton Jenkin, *The Cornish Miner*, pp. 321–43.
18. Schwartz, 'Migration Networks', pp. 264–9.
19. See Payton, *The Cornish Overseas*, chapter 2.
20. See Payton, '"Reforming Thirties" and "Hungry Forties"'.

21. Cited in John Rowe, *Cornwall in the Age of the Industrial Revolution* (1953; republished St Austell, 1993), p. 231.
22. Cited in Piers Brendon, *Hawker of Morwenstow* (London, 1975), p. 71.
23. Bernard Deacon, 'Proto-industrialization and Potatoes: A Revised Narrative for Nineteenth-Century Cornwall', in Philip Payton (ed.), *Cornish Studies: Five* (Exeter, 1997), pp. 60–84.
24. See Sharron P. Schwartz, 'Cornish Migration to Latin America: A Global and Transnational Perspective', unpublished Ph.D. thesis, University of Exeter, 2003; see also Jim Lewis, 'Cornish Copper Mining 1795–1830: Economy, Structure and Change', in Philip Payton (ed.), *Cornish Studies: Fourteen* (Exeter, 2006), p. 178.
25. See A.C. Todd, *The Search For Silver: Cornish Miners in Mexico, 1824–1948* (Padstow, 1977).
26. *Western Luminary*, 22 February 1825.
27. *South Australian Gazette and Colonial Register*, 20 September 1845.
28. For detailed discussion of the Cornish in America, see Rowe, *The Hard-Rock Men*; A.C. Todd, *The Cornish Miner in America* (Truro, 1967); A.L. Rowse, *The Cornish in America* (London, 1969).
29. Rowe, *The Hard-Rock Men*, pp. 43–4.
30. Rowe, *The Hard-Rock Men*, p. 81.
31. Cited in Ralph Mann, *After the Gold Rush: Society in Grass Valley and Nevada City, California 1849–1870* (Stanford, CA, 1982), pp. 86–7.
32. *West Briton*, 13 September 1884.
33. Mann, *After the Gold Rush*, p. 179.
34. Rowse, *The Cornish in America*, p. 331.
35. See Payton, *The Cornish Overseas*, chapter 7.
36. For an overview of Australia, see Philip Payton, *The Cornish Miner in Australia: Cousin Jack Down Under* (Redruth, 1984); for South Africa, see Dawe, *Cornish Pioneers in South Africa*.
37. See Philip Payton, 'The Cornish in South Australia: Their Influence and Experience from Immigration to Assimilation, 1836–1936', unpublished Ph.D. thesis, University of Adelaide, 1978.
38. Francis Dutton, *South Australia and Its Mines* (London, 1846), p. 267.
39. South Australian Archives (SAA), A1118, reprinted in SAA 1384, *Pioneer Association of South Australia Publications*, No. 9, *A Holograph Memoir of Captain Charles Harvey Bagot of the 87th Regiment*, n.d., pp. 24–5.
40. Dutton, *South Australia and Its Mines*, p. 269.
41. Dutton, *South Australia and Its Mines*, p. 281.
42. For a comprehensive history of the Burra Burra mine see Ian Auhl, *The Story of the Monster Mine: The Burra Burra Mine and its Townships, 1845–1877* (Adelaide, 1986).
43. *South Australian Gazette and Colonial Register*, 20 September 1845.
44. *South Australian News*, December 1846.
45. SAA 313, *Shipping Passenger Lists*.
46. *West Briton*, 3 December 1847.
47. SAA, BRG 22/960, *South Australian Mining Association, Directors' Letter Books*, Ayers to Wilcocks, 3 November 1852.
48. SAA, BRG 22/960, Ayers to Wilcocks, 24 December 1852.

49. *South Australian Register*, 14 July 1851.
50. *South Australian Register*, 4 March 1859.
51. *South Australian*, 14 March 1848.
52. *South Australian Register*, 30 December 1859.
53. (Kapunda) *Northern Star*, 10 January 1861.
54. *South Australian Register*, 27 June 1863.
55. Michael Davitt, *Life and Progress in Australasia* p. 63.
56. *Autobiography of Thomas Cowling, junior*, unpublished MS, private collection of John Cowling (Norton Summit, South Australia), n.d., p. 75.
57. *Northern Star*, 27 July 1861.
58. See Payton, 'The Cornish in South Australia', pp. 114–21.
59. (Moonta) *People's Weekly*, 23 April 1921.
60. SAA, BRG 40/538, *Moonta Mines Proprietors, Out-letter Books, 1863–69*, McCoull to A.L. Elders, 26 April 1864; McCoull to Young, 26 April 1864. See also SAA, BRG 40/543, *Moonta Mines Proprietors, Minute Books 1861–91*, 24 April 1864.
61. See Payton, 'The Cornish in South Australia', pp. 118–21.
62. *Yorke's Peninsula Advertiser*, 9 February 1877.
63. *Yorke's Peninsula Advertiser*, 18 September 1877.
64. (Burra) *Northern Mail*, 14 July 1876.
65. *Yorke's Peninsula Advertiser*, 9 September 1879.
66. *West Briton*, 22 January 1883.
67. *Yorke's Peninsula Advertiser*, 27 April 1883.
68. *Yorke's Peninsula Advertiser*, 31 August 1883.
69. *Australian Christian Commonwealth*, 29 March 1935.
70. *Autobiography of Thomas Cowling, junior*, p. 20.
71. SAA, BRG40/543, 2 August 1869; *People's Weekly*, 24 May 1934.
72. *Wallaroo Times*, 19 April 1865.
73. *Wallaroo Times*, 29 June 1867.
74. *South Australian Register*, 25 June 1880.
75. *People's Weekly*, 24 June 1922.
76. *Yorke's Peninsula Advertiser*, 28 June 1881.
77. *Yorke's Peninsula Advertiser*, 27 June 1882.
78. *Yorke's Peninsula Advertiser*, 25 June 1886.
79. *Wallaroo Times*, 24 April 1869.
80. *Autobiography of Thomas Cowling, junior*, pp. 93–4.
81. *People's Weekly*, 26 August 1922.
82. *Wallaroo Times*, 2 September 1865.
83. *Wallaroo Times*, 31 March 1866.
84. *Wallaroo Times*, 25 March 1871; 6 November 1869.
85. *Yorke's Peninsula Advertiser*, 26 December 1873.
86. Anon., *The Christmas Welcome: A Choice Selection of Cornish Carols* (Moonta, 1893), republished as Philip Payton (ed.), *Cornish Carols from Australia* (Redruth, 1984).
87. Kenneth Pelmear, *Carols of Cornwall* (Redruth, 1982), p. 2.
88. *South Australian Primitive Methodist*, October 1896.
89. Anon., *The Christmas Welcome*, p. 4.
90. *People's Weekly*, 5 October 1907.

91. *Yorke's Peninsula Advertiser*, 27 June 1884, 25 June 1886; *People's Weekly*, 25 June 1898.
92. Keith Bailey, *Cornets on the Copper Fields: A History of Brass Bands in the Copper Triangle* (Kadina, 1998), p. 33.
93. *Yorke's Peninsula Advertiser*, 2 November 1883.
94. *Yorke's Peninsula Advertiser*, 2 November 1883.
95. *People's Weekly*, 2 April 1921.
96. See Roslyn Paterson, *Thankyou Walter Watson Hughes: Essays on Northern Yorke Peninsula* (Adelaide, 1993), pp. 72–5.
97. *Yorke's Peninsula Advertiser*, 1 April 1873.
98. Anon., *St Laurence's Priory, 1898–1973, North Adelaide, South Australia* (Camberwell (SA), n.d.), p. 11.
99. *Australian Christian Commonwealth*, 17 June 1904.
100. *Yorke's Peninsula Advertiser*, 25 February 1876, 14 April, 1876, 5 May 1876, 2 March 1877, 9 April 1878, 3 June 1887; see also Jean Fielding and W.S. Ransom, 'The English of *Australia's Little Cornwall*', *Journal of the Australasian Universities' Language and Literature Association*, No. 36, November 1991.
101. For example, *Yorke's Peninsula Advertiser*, 25 February 1876.
102. *People's Weekly*, 12 June 1902.
103. *Yorke's Peninsula Advertiser*, 15 July 1873, 29 July 1873, 5 August 1873.
104. *Yorke's Peninsula Advertiser*, 29 February 1876.
105. *Yorke's Peninsula Advertiser*, 17 December 1875, 25 January 1876.
106. *Minutes of the Yorke's Peninsula Football Association*, 4 May 1888, Kadina National Trust Museum.
107. *People's Weekly*, 19 November 1904.
108. Oswald Pryor, '8 Hours' Day in the Nineties', in *People's Weekly*, October 1943; reprinted in Liz Coole (ed.), *Writings of Oswald Pryor from the People's Weekly* (Moonta Branch of the National Trust of South Australia, 2002), p. 18.
109. *Wallaroo Times*, 7 October 1868.
110. *Yorke's Peninsula Advertiser*, 4 August 1876.
111. W.G. Spence, *Australia's Awakening: Thirty Years in the Life of an Australian Agitator* (Sydney, 1909), p. 27.
112. *People's Weekly*, 12 September 1896.
113. SAA, D3627(L), Stanley Whitford, *Autobiography*, Addendum by Sir Lennon Raws.
114. *Yorke's Peninsula Advertiser*, 28 March 1876.
115. *Yorke's Peninsula Advertiser*, 31 July 1877.
116. *Yorke's Peninsula Advertiser*, 10 April 1874.
117. *People's Weekly*, 12 July 1890; see also *South Australian Register*, 10 July 1890.

Chapter 3. The cult of Captain Hancock: The man and his mines

1. Oswald Pryor, *Cornish Pasty* (Adelaide, 1961), and *Cousin Jacks and Jennys* (Adelaide, 1966); republished as *Cornish Pasty* (Adelaide, 1976), p. 59.
2. Pryor, *Cornish Pasty*, p. 39.
3. Pryor, *Cornish Pasty*, p. 65.

4. Pryor, *Cornish Pasty*, p. 102.
5. *Moonta Mines Methodist Church Centenary, 1865–1965* (Moonta, 1965), p. 10.
6. South Australian Archives (SAA), 4959(L), *Notes on Moonta and Wallaroo*, by E. Major Senior.
7. SAA, D3217(T), *Little Cornwall: The Story of Moonta (South Australia) and Its Cornish Miners*, by Oswald Pryor (Carer Creftow).
8. (Moonta) *People's Weekly*, 12 July 1890.
9. See Mandie Robinson, *Cap'n 'Ancock: Ruler of Australia's Little Cornwall* (Adelaide, 1978), pp. 162–7.
10. For the broad biographical details of Hancock's life, see Robinson, *Cap'n 'Ancock*.
11. See A.K. Hamilton Jenkin, *Mines of Devon: Volume 1 – The Southern Area* (Newton Abbot, 1974); D.B. Barton, *A Historical Survey of the Mines and Mineral Railways of East Cornwall and West Devon* (Truro, 1964), pp. 71–102.
12. Robinson, *Cap'n 'Ancock*, pp. 21–4; Hamilton Jenkin, *Mines of Devon: Volume 1*, pp. 75–8.
13. Robinson, *Cap'n 'Ancock*, p. 26.
14. *South Australian Register*, 24 March 1849, 14 August 1854; *Mining Journal*, 16 October 1852, 23 April 1853, 21 April 1854, 17 June 1854, 17 January 1857, 14 March 1857, 12 December 1857; J.B. Austin, *The Mines of South Australia* (Adelaide, 1863), pp. 79–81; H.Y.L. Brown, *Records of the Mines of South Australia* (Adelaide, 1908), p. 191; D.B. Barton, *The Cornish Beam Engine* (Truro, 1965), p. 168.
15. SAA, D6029/97–113 (L), *Letters Written Home by Cornish Folk who Emigrated to South Australia in the Nineteenth Century*, compiled by Dr J.M. Tregenza; D6029/100 (L), William Arundel Paynter to his wife Sophia, 13 January 1859.
16. SAA, D6029/101 (L), William Arundel Paynter to his wife Sophia, 1 February 1859.
17. Barton, *The Cornish Beam Engine*, p. 168.
18. SAA, BRG40/542, *Wallaroo Mines Proprietors, Minute Books, 1860–1891*, 28 July 1862.
19. Brown, *Records of the Mines of South Australia*, p. 150.
20. Oswald Pryor, *Australia's Little Cornwall*, Adelaide, 1962, p. 26.
21. *South Australian Register*, 19 January 1861, 2 February 1861, 8 August 1861, 5 June 1862, 6 June 1862, 15 September 1862, 5 November 1862, 21 December 1865, 23 September 1867, 19 January 1870; *Wallaroo Times*, 12 July 1865, 4 November 1865, 30 December 1865, 3 March 1866, 2 March 1867; *Yorke's Peninsula Advertiser*, 16 May 1873.
22. SAA, BRG 40/542, 4 August 1862, 11 August 1862, 18 August 1862.
23. SAA, BRG 40/543, *Moonta Mines Proprietors, Minute Books, 1861–1891*, 6 October 1862; SAA, BRG 40/538, *Moonta Mines Proprietors, Out-Letter Books, 1863–69*, McCoull to Hancock, 26 June 1863.
24. SAA, BRG 40/538, McCoull to Hancock, 24 August 1863.
25. SAA, BRG 40/543, 27 June 1864.
26. Liz Coole and J.R. Harbison (eds), *Mine Captains of the Copper Triangle, Yorke Peninsula, South Australia* (Moonta, 2006), pp. 6.

27. SAA, BRG 40/538, McCoull to Hancock, 18 July 1864.
28. SAA, BRG 40/538, McCoull to Yelta Directors, 11 July 1864; SAA, BRG 40/543, 27 June 1864.
29. SAA, BRG 40/538, McCoull to Hancock, 18 July 1864; SAA, BRG 40/543, 1 August 1864.
30. *South Australian Register*, 17 January 1868; *Wallaroo Times*, 29 January 1868, 1 April 1868; *Yorke's Peninsula Advertiser*, 1 November 1872; Coole and Harbison (eds), *Mine Captains of the Copper Triangle*, p. 38.
31. SAA 4959 (L); SAA, BRG 40/538, McCoull to Hancock, 31 October 1865; Coole and Harbison (eds), *Mine Captains of the Copper Triangle*, p. 45.
32. Liz Coole (ed.), *Writings of Oswald Pryor from the People's Weekly* (Moonta, 2002), p. 71: Oswald Pryor, 'More Notable Mine Captains', *People's Weekly*, August 1957.
33. *Mining Journal*, 24 October 1863.
34. Coole and Harbison, *Mine Captains of the Copper Triangle*, p. 27.
35. SAA, BRG 40/538, McCoull to Hancock, 31 October 1865; Coole and Harbison, *Mine Captains of the Copper Triangle*, pp. 12, 36, 39, 43, 49.
36. *South Australian Register*, 18 April 1861.
37. SAA, BRG 40/538, McCoull to Hancock, 23 August 1874.
38. SAA, BRG 40/538, McCoull to Hancock, 2 August 1874.
39. SAA, BRG 40/538, McCoull to Wakefield, 2 August 1864.
40. SAA, BRG 40/538, McCoull to Wakefield, 2 August 1864.
41. SAA, BRG 40/543, 15 May 1865.
42. SAA, BRG 40/543, 22 June 1868; SAA, BRG 40/538, McCoull to Wooley & Nephew, 29 May 1868, McCoull to Wooley and Nephew, 30 June 1868, McCoull to Hancock, 16 August 1868, McCoull to Hancock, 21 August 1868; *South Australian Register*, 20 July 1868; 15 August 1868.
43. *South Australian Register*, 21 November 1872, 13 February 1873, May Vivienne, *Sunny South Australia* p. 265.
44. SAA, BRG 40/538, McCoull to Hancock, 6 June 1865.
45. SAA, BRG 40/543, 8 February 1862, 18 May 1863, 24 September 1863, 4 May 1868, 10 October 1872; SAA, BRG 40/538, McCoull to Young, 27 October 1863, McCoull to Elder, 26 January 1864, McCoull to Nicholls Williams, 26 July 1864, McCoull to Elder, 28 October 1867, McCoull to Elder, 27 March 1866; (Kapunda) *Northern Star*, 21 April 1860.
46. SAA, BRG 40/538, McCoull to Hancock, 2August 1864, McCoull to Hancock, 9 August 1864, McCoull to Hancock, 1 November 1864.
47. SAA, BRG 40/543, 30 April 1866.
48. SAA, BRG 40/538, McCoull to Elder, 28 July 1866.
49. SAA, BRG 40/543, 10 June 1867.
50. SAA, BRG 40/543, 10 June 1867.
51. SAA, BRG 40/538, McCoull to Hancock, 9 July 1867.
52. SAA, BRG 40/543, 31 July 1871.
53. SAA, BRG 40/543, 8 August 1871.
54. SAA, BRG 40/543, 5 October 1874, 29 December 1874, 18 October 1875.
55. SAA, BRG 40/543, 25 April 1877, 11 June 1877; BRG 40/542, *Wallaroo Mines Proprietors, Minute Books, 1860–91*, 23 April 1877.

56. SAA, BRG 40/543, 27 May 1878, 15 July 1878, 28 March 1881, 9 August 1882.
57. SAA, BRG 40/543, 31 May 1886.
58. SAA, BRG 40/537, *Wallaroo Mines Proprietors, Out-Letter Books, 1860–1870*, Mair to Elder, 29 November 1866, Mair to Elder, 14 June 1867, Mair to Elder, 1 February 1868, Mair to Elder, 3 March 1868.
59. SAA, BRG 40/537, Mair to Elder, 24 January 1865; SAA, BRG 40/542, 25 October 1864, 14 February 1865, 28 February 1865.
60. SAA, BRG 40/537, Mair to Roach, 7 November 1865.
61. SAA, BRG 40/537, Mair to Harvey, 23 April 1867, Mair to Elder, 3 March 1869.
62. SAA, BRG 40/542, 30 March 1869.
63. *South Australian Register*, 16 May 1870.
64. SAA, BRG 40/539, *Wallaroo Mines Proprietors, Out-Letters to Superintendent, 1875–1882*, Mair to Higgs, 23 April 1877.
65. SAA, BRG 40/542, 16 May 1877.
66. *South Australian Register*, 23 June 1879.
67. Robinson, *Cap'n 'Ancock*, p. 61.
68. Robinson, *Cap'n 'Ancock*, p. 80.
69. Anon., *The Wallaroo and Moonta Mines: Their History, Nature, and Methods, together with an Account of the Concentrating and Smelting Operations* p. 18.
70. Anon., 1914, p. 19.
71. SAA, D3217 (T), p. 36.
72. *Autobiography of Thomas Cowling, Junior*, unpublished MS in private collection of John Cowling, (Norton Summit) Adelaide, p. 128.
73. E.H. Coombes, *History of Gawler* (Adelaide, 1908), pp. 97–101.
74. John Healey (ed.), *S.A.'s Greats: The Men and Women of the North Terrace Plaques* (Adelaide, 2002), p. 83.
75. W.G. Spence, *Australia's Awakening: Thirty Years in the Life of an Australian Agitator* (Sydney, 1909), p. 31.
76. Spence, *Australia's Awakening*, p. 31.
77. Spence, *Australia's Awakening*, p. 30.
78. Spence, *Australia's Awakening*, p. 31.
79. Spence, *Australia's Awakening*, p. 31.
80. Spence, *Australia's Awakening*, p. 29.
81. Spence, *Australia's Awakening*, pp. 30–1.
82. Robinson, *Cap'n 'Ancock*, pp. 78–9.
83. SAA, BRG 40/543, 10 August 1863.
84. SAA, BRG 40/543, 13 March 1871; SAA, BRG 40/538, McCoull to Secretary of Crown Lands, 24 April 1865, McCoull to Trewin, 27 June 1865.
85. SAA, BRG 40/538, McCoull to Hancock, 15 November 1864.
86. SAA, BRG 40/538, McCoull to Magill, 8 August 1865.
87. SAA, BRG 40/543, 13 March 1871, 3 April 1871; SAA, BRG 40/538, McCoull to Allport, 5 January 1865, McCoull to Hancock, 6 August 1866.
88. *Yorke's Peninsula Advertiser*, 2 September 1873.
89. SAA, BRG 40/538, McCoull to Hancock, 6 December 1864, McCoull to Hancock, 20 December 1864; SAA, BRG 40/543, 21 August 1871, 11 November 1873.

90. Robinson, *Cap'n 'Ancock*, p. 59.
91. Arnold Hunt, *This Side of Heaven: A History of Methodism in South Australia* (Adelaide, 1985), p. 174.
92. Robinson, *Cap'n 'Ancock*, p. 85.
93. Robinson, *Cap'n 'Ancock*, p. 120.
94. Robinson, *Cap'n 'Ancock*, pp. 162–7.
95. John McConnell Black, *Memoirs* (Adelaide, 1971), p. 126.
96. Anthony Trollope, *Australia* (1873; republished St Lucia (Qld), 1967), p. 685.
97. *Yorke's Peninsula Advertiser*, 6 August 1875.
98. SAA, D3627 (L), Stanley Whitford, *An Autobiography*, addendum 'Impressions of Moonta' by Sir Lennon Raws.

Chapter 4. 'Cornwall was never conquered yet': Moonta's working-class heroes

1. *Yorke's Peninsula Advertiser*, 30 May 1873.
2. *Yorke's Peninsula Advertiser*, 14 April 1874.
3. *Yorke's Peninsula Advertiser*, 8 November 1872.
4. *Yorke's Peninsula Advertiser*, 13 May 1873, 20 May 1873, 17 June 1873.
5. *Yorke's Peninsula Advertiser*, 1 July 1873.
6. *Yorke's Peninsula Advertiser*, 13 May 1873.
7. Cited in Mark Stoyle, *West Britons: Cornish Identities and the Early Modern State* (Exeter, 2002), p. 89.
8. Stoyle, *West Britons*, p. 89.
9. Cited in Matthew Spriggs, 'William Scawen (1600–1689) – A Neglected Cornish Patriot and Father of the Cornish Language Revival' in Philip Payton (ed.), *Cornish Studies: Thirteen* (Exeter, 2005), p. 115.
10. John Langdon Bonython, *Cornwall: Interesting History and Romantic Stories, Talks at Meetings of the South Australian Cornish Association* (Adelaide, 1932), p. 17.
11. Liz Coole (ed.), *Writings of Oswald Pryor from the People's Weekly* (Moonta, 2002), p. 53 (July 1954).
12. (Adelaide) *Observer*, 25 May 1867.
13. *Yorke's Peninsula Advertiser*, 10 October 1873.
14. See, for example, *Yorke's Peninsula Advertiser*, 20 February 1877.
15. Mel Davies, 'Collective Action and the Cornish Miner in Australia: An Early Repudiation of the "Individualistic" Thesis', in Philip Payton (ed.), *Cornish Studies: Three* (Exeter, 1995), pp. 7–32.
16. *South Australian News*, August 1846.
17. *South Australian news*, October 1846.
18. South Australian Archives (SAA), BRG 22/91, *South Australian Mining Association, Letters to Burra Mines Officials (Superintendent's Letter Books)*, Ayers to Burr, 26 August 1848.
19. *South Australian Register*, 20 September 1848.
20. *South Australian Register*, 4 October 1848.
21. Davies, 'Collective Action and the Cornish Miner in Australia', p. 19.
22. *South Australian Register*, 4 November 1848.

23. Davies, 'Collective Action and the Cornish Miner in Australia', p. 22.
24. *South Australian Register*, 8 November 1848.
25. *South Australian Register*, 4 October, 1848.
26. See, for example, *West Briton*, 25 February 1831, 21 May 1847; see also Philip Payton, *The Cornish Overseas: A History of Cornwall's Great Emigration* (Fowey, 2005), pp. 132–5.
27. For a general overview of the strike, see Peter Bell, 'The Power of Respectful Remonstrance: The Wallaroo and Moonta Miners' Strike of 1864', *Journal of the Historical Society of South Australia* (1998).
28. SAA, BRG 40/543, *Moonta Mines Proprietors, Minute Books, 1861–91*, 6 October 1862.
29. SAA, BRG 40/543, 16 April 1862, 16 June 1862.
30. SAA, BRG 40/543, 14 July 1862.
31. SAA, BRG 40/543, 6 October 1862.
32. SAA, BRG 40/538, *Moonta Mines Proprietors, Out-Letter Books, 1863–69*, McCoull to Osborne, 5 May 1863.
33. SAA, BRG 40/542, *Wallaroo Mines Proprietors, Minute Books, 1860–91*, 1 February 1864.
34. *South Australian Register*, December 1862.
35. *South Australian Register*, 8 April 1862.
36. *South Australian Register*, 18 April 1864, 29 April 1864.
37. SAA 4959 (L), *Notes on Moonta and Wallaroo*, by E. Major Senior.
38. See, for example, *South Australian Register*, 8 April 1864, 29 April 1864.
39. *South Australian Register*, 7 May 1864.
40. SAA 4959 (L), *Notes on Moonta and Wallaroo*.
41. SAA, Dr Charles Davies, *Biographies and Obituaries* (27 vols), unidentified press-cutting obituary of January 1884.
42. G.E. Loyau, *Notable South Australians and Colonists – Past and Present* (Adelaide, 1885), pp. 61–2.
43. *South Australian Register*, 7 May 1864.
44. SAA, BRG 40/538, McCoull to A.L. Elders, 26 April 1864, McCoull to Young, 26 April 1864; see also BRG 40/543, 24 April 1864.
45. SAA 4959 (L), *Notes on Moonta and Wallaroo*.
46. SAA, BRG 40/538, McCoull to Warmington, 27 June 1864.
47. SAA, BRG 40/538, McCoull to Young, 28 June 1864.
48. *South Australian Register*, 1 July 1864.
49. SAA, BRG 40/543, 4 June 1864; SAA, BRG 40/538, McCoull to Young, 31 May 1864, McCoull to Trestrail, 4 June 1864, McCoull to Prisk, 8 June 1864.
50. SAA, BRG 40/537 *Wallaroo Mines Proprietors, Out-Letter Books, 1860–1870*, Miur to A.L. Elder, 27 December 1866, Miur to A.L. Elder, 29 May 1867.
51. *South Australian Register*, 4 March 1861.
52. SAA, D3217 (T), *Little Cornwall: The Story of Moonta (South Australia) and Its Cornish Miners*, by Oswald Pryor, p. 10.
53. SAA 4959 (L), *Notes on Moonta and Wallaroo*.
54. SAA, BRG 40/543, 29 August 1864; SAA, BRG 40/538, McCoull to Wakefield, 2 August 1864.

55. SAA, BRG 40/538, McCoull to Hancock, 4 October 1864.
56. SAA, BRG 40/538, McCoull to Hancock, 13 September 1865.
57. SAA, BRG 40/538, McCoull to Hancock, 31 October 1865.
58. *South Australian Register*, 17 January 1868.
59. SAA, BRG 40/538, McCoull to Hancock, 26 August 1867.
60. SAA, BRG 40/538, McCoull to Hancock, 26 August 1867.
61. SAA, BRG 40/538, McCoull to Hancock, 2 September 1867.
62. SAA, BRG 40/543, 22 January 1872.
63. Cited in Oswald Pryor, *Australia's Little Cornwall* (Adelaide, 1962), p. 160.
64. *South Australian Register*, 20 April 1872, 4 May 1872, 23 May 1872, 27 May 1872, 2 August 1872, 31 October 1872.
65. *South Australian Register*, 11 October 1872.
66. *Yorke's Peninsula Advertiser*, 27 December 1872.
67. *Yorke's Peninsula Advertiser*, 4 March 1873, 8 April 1873.
68. *Yorke's Peninsula Advertiser*, 26 December 1873, 30 December 1973.
69. *Yorke's Peninsula Advertiser*, 10 April 1874; SAA, BRG 40/543, 8 April 1874.
70. *Yorke's Peninsula Advertiser*, 10 April 1874; see also *South Australian Register*, 8 April 1874.
71. Keith Bailey, *James Boor's Bonanza: A History of Wallaroo Mines, South Australia* (Kadina, 2002), p. 31.
72. SAA, BRG 40/543, 10 April 1874.
73. *South Australian Register*, 7 April 1874.
74. *Yorke's Peninsula Advertiser*, 14 April 1874.
75. *South Australian Register*, 9 April 1874, 17 April 1874.
76. SAA, BRG 40/543, 15 April 1874.
77. SAA, BRG 40/543, 27 April 1875, 4 May 1875, 11 May 1875.
78. SAA, D4876 (Misc.), *The Great Strike*, by W. Shelley, c.1874.
79. *Yorke's Peninsula Advertiser*, 14 April 1874.
80. *South Australian Register*, 4 August 1874; *Yorke's Peninsula Advertiser*, 28 April 1874.
81. *Yorke's Peninsula Advertiser*, 14 August 1874, 31 March 1876, 9 September 1879.
82. *Yorke's Peninsula Advertiser*, 5 July 1878.
83. *Yorke's Peninsula Advertiser*, 28 April 1874.
84. *Yorke's Peninsula Advertiser*, 21 April 1874.
85. *Yorke's Peninsula Advertiser*, 17 April 1874, 19 May 1874.
86. J.J. Pascoe, *History of Adelaide and Vicinity, with a General Sketch of the Province of South Australia and Biographies of Representative Men* (Adelaide, 1901), p. 264.
87. *Bible Christian Magazine*, combined volume, 1876, p. 525.
88. J.P. Boucaut, *Letters to My Boys* (London, 1906), p. 81.
89. SAA 98u, *Boucaut Papers (Miscellaneous)*.
90. Arnold Caldicott, *The Verco Story: Hopes We Live By* (Adelaide, 1970), p. 165.
91. For details of Boucaut's parliamentary career see P.L. Edgar, 'Sir James Penn Boucaut: His Political Life, 1861–75', Department of History BA Hons thesis, University of Adelaide, 1961.
92. SAA 97/379, *Boucaut Papers (Political)*, Boucaut to McArthur, 3 August 1874, 28 August 1874, 18 September 1874; Boucaut, 1906, p. v.

93. SAA 97/379, Boucaut to McArthur, 3 August 1874, 28 August 1874, 18 September 1874.
94. *Yorke's Peninsula Advertiser*, 12 May 1874, 5 May 1874.
95. *South Australian Register*, 5 August 1874.
96. SAA, BRG 40/543, 3 May 1875, 7 February 1876.
97. SAA, BRG 40/543, 8 June 1874, 15 June 1874, 13 July 1874, 7 August 1874; SAA, BRG 40/542, 14 July 1874.
98. SAA, D3627 (L), *An Autobiography*, by Stanley Whitford, p. 400.
99. SAA, BRG 40/543, 10 August 1874, 25 August 1874, 2 November 1974.
100. SAA, BRG 40/543, 21 September 1874.
101. *Yorke's Peninsula Advertiser*, 10 November 1874.
102. *Yorke's Peninsula Advertiser*, 14 April 1874.
103. Edwin Hodder, *The History of South Australia from its Foundation to the Year of its Jubilee*, vol. 1 (London, 1893), p. 319.
104. (Kapunda) *Northern Star*, 3 May 1861, 10 May 1862.
105. *Yorke's Peninsula Advertiser*, 20 October 1874.
106. *Yorke's Peninsula Advertiser*, 31 March 1876.
107. *Yorke's Peninsula Advertiser*, 12 February 1875.
108. See L.E. Kiek, 'The History of the South Australian Labour Unions', Department of History MA thesis, University of Adelaide, 1948, pp. 26–8.
109. *People's Weekly*, 16 May 1891, 30 May 1891.
110. *Wallaroo Times*, 20 January 1866, 27 January 1876.
111. *Yorke's Peninsula Advertiser*, 20 February 1877, 6 June 1882; BRG 40/543, 27 February 1865, 5 March 1866, 12 August 1889.
112. *Yorke's Peninsula Advertiser*, 24 April 1880.
113. *Yorke's Peninsula Advertiser*, 25 January 1878, 22 February 1889.
114. *Yorke's Peninsula Advertiser*, 1 June 1877; BRG 40/543, 7 December 1885, 29 February 1888, 1 March 1888, 2 March 1888, 5 March 1888.
115. Pryor, *Australia's Little Cornwall*, p. 114.
116. SAA, BRG40/543, 11 March 1889.
117. W.G. Spence, *Australia's Awakening: Thirty Years in the Life of an Australian Agitator* (Sydney, 1909), p. 27.
118. Pryor, *Australia's Little Cornwall*, p. 120.
119. SAA, BRG 40/543, 29 July 1889, 12 August 1889, 9 December 1889, 16 December 1889; *South Australian Register*, 30 July 1891, 20 August 1891, 18 September 1891, 23 September 1891, 28 September 1891, 29 September 1891, 30 September 1891.
120. *South Australian Register*, 28 October 1891, 14 January 1892; *People's Weekly*, 10 October 1891, 21 October 1891, 14 November 1891, 28 November 1891, 12 December 1891, 28 December 1891, 30 January 1892.
121. SAA, D3627 (L), p. 118.
122. *People's Weekly*, 30 March 1895.
123. *South Australian Department of Mines Mining Review*, half-year ended December 1919, p. 12.
124. J.B. Hirst, *Adelaide and The Country, 1870–1917: Their Social and Political Relationship* (Melbourne, 1973), p. 155; Ian Craig, 'A History of the South Australian Labour Party to 1917', unpublished MA thesis, University of Adelaide, 1940, p. 53.

125. R. Norris, 'Economic Influences on the 1898 South Australian Federation Referendum', in A.W. Martin, *Essays in Australian Federation* (Melbourne, 1969), p. 150; for a broader sketch of South Australian society and politics at Federation, see P.A. Howell, *Australia and Referendum* (Adelaide, 2002).
126. Norris, 'Economic Influences', p. 150; John Hirst, *Sense and Nonsense in Australian History* (Melbourne, 2006) notes that the 'hard men' of the ULP and UTLC in Adelaide were increasingly 'disgusted' with the 'moderation' of the non-metropolitan Labour supporters; see p. 2.

Chapter 5. 'Moonta toil and Moonta gain': Women, Methodists and the triumph over adversity

1. Thomas Burtt, Moonta Musings in Rhythmic Rhyme by a Moonta-ite (Moonta, 1885), p.2.
2. W. Frederick Morrison, *The Aldine History of South Australia* (Sydney and Adelaide, 1890), p. 578.
3. Rodney Cockburn, *Pastoral Pioneers of South Australia* (Adelaide, 1925; republished 1974), vol. 1, p. 195.
4. *South Australian News*, April 1848.
5. *Wallaroo Times*, 31 March 1866.
6. *Yorke's Peninsula Advertiser*, 29 September 1974.
7. Samuel Higgs, 'Some Remarks on the Mining District of Yorke's Peninsula, South Australia', in *Transactions of the Royal Geological Society of Cornwall*, vol. ix.1 (1875), pp. 122, 123, 124.
8. Higgs, 'Some Remarks on the Mining District of Yorke's Peninsula', pp. 122, 123, 124.
9. Anon., *Moonta Mines Methodist Church Centenary, 1865–1965* (Moonta, 1965), p. 11; Wilfrid Prest (ed.), *The Wakefield Companion to South Australian History* (Adelaide, 2001), pp. 13–14.
10. (Adelaide) *Observer*, 25 January 1862.
11. J. Britton and E.W. Brayley, *Cornwall Illustrated in a Series of Views* (1831; republished Truro, 1968), p7.
12. Oswald Pryor, *Australia's Little Cornwall* (Adelaide, 1962), pp. 65–6.
13. Anthony Trollope, *Australia* (1873; republished St Lucia (Qld), 1967), pp. 680–1.
14. W.H. Hosken, 'Notes of a Tour in South Australia', *Bible Christian Magazine* (combined volume), 1876, p. 36.
15. *Yorke's Peninsula Advertiser*, 6 August 1875.
16. *South Australian Register*, 10 June 1873.
17. Pryor, *Australia's Little Cornwall*, p. 66.
18. See Philip Payton, *The Cornish Overseas: A History of Cornwall's Great Emigration* (Fowey, 2005), pp. 26–8.
19. South Australian Archives (SAA), D6010 (Misc.), *Accidental Mining Deaths (Surface and Underground) at the Wallaroo Mines at Kadina and the Moonta mines at Moonta, from 1866 to December 1900, extracted from the the Registrations of Births, Deaths and Marriages, District of Daly*, compiled by Max A. Slee, 1977; SAA, D3217 (T), *Little Cornwall: The Story of Moonta (South Australia) and its Cornish Miners*, by Oswald Pryor, p. 37.

20. *Yorke's Peninsula Advertiser*, 31 March 1876.
21. *Yorke's Peninsula Advertiser*, 15 September 1876.
22. See Sharron Schwartz, '"No Place for a Woman": Gender at Work in Cornwall's Metalliferous Mining Industry', in Philip Payton (ed.), *Cornish Studies: Eight* (Exeter, 2000), pp. 69–98; for a fuller discussion of the bal-maiden in Cornwall see Lynne Mayers, *Balmaidens: The Women and Girls of the Mines of the South West* (Penzance, 2004).
23. SAA, D3196A (T), *The Glen Osmond Mines and the Presence of Cornish Miners there, 1841–51*, by Oswald Pryor. Pryor cites an unidentified issue of the *South Australian* newspaper for 1847 to indicate that girls were employed as ore-dressers at Glen Osmond. Ian Auhl adds that 'Even the little girls of ten or so were employed as "bal-maidens" to wash and sort the ore, a Cornish custom which did not last long in South Australian mines': see Ian Auhl and Dennis Marfleet, *Australia's Earliest mining Era: South Australia, 1841–1851* (Adelaide, 1975), p. 26.
24. SAA 1529, *Alphabetical Index to Applications for Free Passage from the United Kingdom to South Australia, 1836–40*.
25. The propensity for would-be Cornish emigrants to Australia to bend the rule for free or assisted passage has been investigated convincingly in Patricia Lay, 'Not What They Seemed? Cornish Assisted Immigrants in New South Wales 1837–77, in Philip Payton (ed.), *Cornish Studies: Three* (Exeter, 1995), pp. 33–59.
26. For example, see John Reynolds, *Men and Mines: A History of Australian Mining 1788–1971* (Melbourne, 1974), pp. 16–17.
27. Pryor, *Australia's Little Cornwall*, p. 65.
28. Phyllis Somerville, *Not Only in Stone* (Sydney, 1942; republished Adelaide, 1973).
29. Somerville, *Not Only in Stone*, p. 23.
30. Somerville, *Not Only in Stone*, pp. 46, 52.
31. Somerville, *Not Only in Stone*, p. 56.
32. Somerville, *Not Only in Stone*, p. 58.
33. Somerville, *Not Only in Stone*, pp. 58–9.
34. Somerville, *Not Only in Stone*, p. 99.
35. Somerville, *Not Only in Stone*, p. 128.
36. Somerville, *Not Only in Stone*, pp. 195–7.
37. Somerville, *Not Only in Stone*, p. 197.
38. Somerville, *Not Only in Stone*, p. 199.
39. SAA, D4876 (Misc.), *The Great Strike*, by W. Shelley, c.1874.
40. W.G. Spence, *Australia's Awakening: Thirty Years in the Life of an Australia Agitator* (Sydney, 1909), p. 29.
41. Spence, *Australia's Awakening*, p. 30.
42. Spence, *Australia's Awakening*, p. 30.
43. Anne Summers, *Damned Whores and God's Police: The Colonization of Women in Australia* (Ringwood (Vic), 1975).
44. John Healy (ed.), *S.A.'s Greats: The Men and Women of the North Terrace Plaques* (Adelaide, 2002), p. 22; also see Roslyn Paterson, 'Kate Cocks MBE', in Cornish Association of South Australia, *Notable Cornish Women* (Kadina, 2002).
45. Healy (ed.), *S.A.'s Greats*, p. 22.

46. SAA, D5341 (T), *Scrap-book Relating to Kapunda, Burra, Wallaroo and Moonta Mines*, by Peter Thomas, p. 291.
47. See Bill Jones, 'Cousin Dai and Cousin Dilys?': South Australia's Nineteenth-Century Welsh Heritage', *Journal of the Historical Association of South Australia*, no. 29 (1999), pp. 28–43.
48. *Wallaroo Times*, 19 July 1865, 16 October 1867.
49. Roslyn Paterson, *Thankyou Walter Watson Hughes: Essays on Northern Yorke Peninsula* (Adelaide, 1993), p. 52.
50. *People's Weekly*, 21 February 1914.
51. Reynolds, *Men and Mines*, p. 17.
52. *Yorke's Peninsula Advertiser*, 21 February 1877.
53. *Yorke's Peninsula Advertiser*, 21 February 1877.
54. Prest (ed.), *The Wakefield Companion to South Australian History*, p. 590.
55. Pryor, *Australia's Little Cornwall*, p. 171.
56. *Yorke's Peninsula Advertiser*, 27 March 1877.
57. *South Australian Register*, 12 January 1865, 19 January 1865, 9 April 1877; Pryor, *Australia's Little Cornwall*, pp. 151–2.
58. SAA, D8476 (Misc.), *The Great Strike*.
59. *Yorke's Peninsula Advertiser*, 10 April 1877.
60. *Yorke's Peninsula Advertiser*, 10 April 1877.
61. *Yorke's Peninsula Advertiser*, 15 April 1884.
62. *Yorke's Peninsula Advertiser*, 15 April 1884.
63. *Yorke's Peninsula Advertiser*, 15 April 1884.
64. *Yorke's Peninsula Advertiser*, 11 May 1875.
65. *Yorke's Peninsula Advertiser*, 15 April 1884.
66. SAA, D5569 (T), *Historical Notes on Moonta Cemetery*, by J. Harbison; *South Australian Register*, 14 May 1873, 27 June 1873.
67. SAA, BRG 40/543, *Moonta Mines Proprietors, Minute Books, 1861–91*, 9 March 1874.
68. *Yorke's Peninsula Advertiser*, 7 May 1975.
69. *Yorke's Peninsula Advertiser*, 20 April 1875.
70. *Yorke's Peninsula Advertiser*, 15 April 1875.
71. SAA, BRG 40/543, 5 May 1884, 3 September 1884, 22 September 1894, 6 October 1884, 12 September 1887.
72. *People's Weekly*, 18 April 1891.
73. *Yorke's Peninsula Advertiser*, 18 May 1877.
74. *Yorke's Peninsula Advertiser*, 18 May 1877.
75. *Yorke's Peninsula Advertiser*, 20 July 1877.
76. *Yorke's Peninsula Advertiser*, 14 July 1874.
77. D.H. Luker, 'Cornish Methodism, Revivalism and Popular Belief', unpublished D.Phil. thesis, University of Oxford, 1987, pp. 290, 322.
78. SAA, D3627 (T), *An Autobiography*, by Stanley Whitford, p. 71.
79. SAA, D3627 (T), *An Autobiography ... Addendum by Sir Lennon Raws*.
80. *Yorke's Peninsula Advertiser*, 6 August 1875.
81. Arnold Hunt, *This Side of Heaven: A History of Methodism on Yorke Peninsula* (Adelaide, 1985), p. 117.

82. *Australian Christian Commonwealth*, 17 October 1902, 14 November 1902, 20 February 1903, 4 July 1904, 25 November 1904, 4 August 1905, 15 February 1907, 29 May 1908, 20 November 1908, 22 January 1909; *South Australian Primitive Methodist Magazine*, April 1888; *South Australian Primitive Methodist*, October 1895.
83. Phyllis Somerville, 'The Influence of Cornwall on South Australian Methodism', *Journal of the South Australian Methodist Historical Society*, vol. 4 (1974), p. 11.
84. *Minutes of the South Australian Annual Conference of the Methodist Church of Australia*, Adelaide, 1904, p. 27; see also Somerville, 1974, p. 11; *Australian Christian Commonwealth*, 11 March 1904.
85. *People's Weekly*, 10 June 1933.
86. *Australian Christian Commonwealth*, 14 November 1902.
87. *Yorke's Peninsula Advertiser*, 8 November 1872.
88. *Yorke's Peninsula Advertiser*, 28 November 1914.
89. *Australian Christian Commonwealth*, 29 March 1935.
90. Hunt, *This Side of Heaven*, p. 124.
91. *South Australian Bible Christian Magazine*, August 1874, cited in Hunt, *This Side of Heaven*, p. 124.
92. *South Australian Bible Christian Magazine*, August 1875, cited in Hunt, *This Side of Heaven*, p. 124.
93. *Australian Christian Commonwealth*, 30 August 1912.
94. SAA, SRG 4/103/1, *Diary of the Rev. John G. Wright, 1856–1901*, 25 April 1875.
95. SAA, SRG 4/103/1, 11 July 1875.
96. SAA, SRG 4/103/1, 3 June 1875.
97. Hunt, *This Side of Heaven*, p. 126.
98. SAA, D6010 (Misc), *Accidental Mining Deaths*.
99. Hunt, *This Side of Heaven*, p. 174.
100. *Wallaroo Times*, 2 March 1870.
101. Hunt, *This Side of Heaven*, p. 174.
102. Mandie Robinson, *Cap'n 'Ancock: Ruler of Australia's Little Cornwall* (Adelaide, 1978), pp. 85–6.
103. *South Australian Bible Christian Magazine*, November 1885.
104. Geoffrey Blainey, *The Rush that Never Ended: A History of Australian Mining* (Melbourne, 1963), p. 120.
105. *Burra Record*, 13 August 1902.
106. *Yorke's Peninsula Advertiser*, 9 April 1878.
107. SAA, D3627 (L), *An Autobiography*, p. 69.
108. *South Australian Register*, 9 April 1878.
109. *Yorke's Peninsula Advertiser*, 3 September 1878.
110. *Wallaroo Times*, 11 August 1869.
111. *Wallaroo Times*, 21 July 1869.
112. *Observer*, 9 July 1870; *Yorke's Peninsula Advertiser*, 13 June 1876.
113. *Yorke's Peninsula Advertiser*, 19 September 1879, 6 March 1883.
114. May Vivienne, *Sunny South Australia* (Adelaide, 1908), pp. 263–4.
115. Vivienne, *Sunny South Australia*, pp. 254–5.
116. Vivienne, *Sunny South Australia*, p. 263.

Chapter 6. 'Moonta's little, but she's great': The enduring myth

1. *People's Weekly*, 27 August 1921.
2. *People's Weekly*, 29 September 1923.
3. *People's Weekly*, 23 July 1921.
4. *People's Weekly*, 24 July 1915.
5. *People's Weekly*, 20 November 1915.
6. *People's Weekly*, 21 August 1921.
7. *People's Weekly*, 15 January 1921.
8. *People's* Weekly, 23 July 1910.
9. South Australian Archives (SAA) D3627 (L), Stanley Whitford, *Autobiography*, p. 70.
10. SAA, D3627 (L), p. 70.
11. *Australian Christian Commonwealth*, 6 December 1907.
12. Donald J. Hopgood, 'A Psephological Examination of the South Australian Labor Party from World War One to the Depression', unpublished Ph.D. thesis, Flinders University of South Australia, 1973, p. 335.
13. John Lonie, 'Conservatism and Class in South Australia during the Depression Years, 1924–1934', unpublished MA thesis, University of Adelaide, 1973, p. 173.
14. C.C. James, *A History of the Parish of Gwennap in Cornwall* (Penzance, n.d.), p. 90.
15. John McConnell Black, *Memoirs* (Adelaide, 1971), p. 66.
16. *South Australian Advertiser*, 21 June 1910.
17. *People's Weekly*, 8 April 1899.
18. *Plain Dealer*, 11 March 1911.
19. *People's Weekly*, 7 May 1910.
20. *People's Weekly*, 7 May 1910.
21. *People's Weekly*, 18 May 1917.
22. *People's Weekly*, 15 June 1901; 29 June 1901.
23. For an analysis of the fortunes of the Verran government, see R.J. Miller, 'The Fall of the Verran Government, 1911–12: The most determined attempt to abolish the Legislative Council of South Australia, and its Failure', unpublished BA (Hons) thesis, University of Adelaide, 1965.
24. Undated cutting from *Kadina and Wallaroo Times* (c.June 1910), in SAA, PRG96, *Oswald Pryor Papers*, Scrapbook: 'Electorate of Wallaroo, John Verran etc.'.
25. *People's Weekly*, 25 June 1910.
26. SAA 522, *Draft of First Hustings Speech*, by John George Bice, March 1894.
27. According to an unidentified issue of the *Cornishman* newspaper of 1919, reprinted in pamphlet form by the Cornish Association of South Australia, (Adelaide, c.1910).
28. *Christian Weekly and Methodist Union*, 5 September 1890.
29. T.M. Smeaton, *The People in Politics: A Short History of the Labor Movement in South Australia, 1891–1914* (Adelaide, 1914), p. 17.
30. McConnell Black, *Memoirs*, p. 66.
31. *South Australian Advertiser*, 2 March 1910; see also Bernard O'Neil, *In Search of Mineral Wealth: The South Australian Geological Survey and Department of Mines to 1914* (Adelaide, 1982), p. 162.

32. *People's Weekly*, 3 August 1910.
33. *Kadina and Wallaroo Times*, 1 November 1911.
34. *Daily Herald*, 26 April 1911, 18 May 1912; *South Australian Register*, 6 May 1911.
35. *Kadina and Wallaroo Times*, 13 May 1911.
36. G.D. Combe, *Responsible Government in South Australia* (Adelaide, 1957), p. 145.
37. Combe, *Responsible Government*, p. 146.
38. *People's Weekly*, 20 January 1912.
39. *Australian Christian Commonwealth*, 16 February 1912.
40. *Australian Christian Commonwealth*, 1 November 1911.
41. See Arnold Hunt, *Methodism Militant: Attitudes to the Great War* (Adelaide, 1976).
42. See Patricia Gibson, 'The Conscription Issue in South Australia, 1916–17', unpublished BA (Hons) thesis, University of Adelaide, 1959.
43. *People's Weekly*, 21 October 1916; 21 April 1917.
44. SAA, D3627(L), Stanley Whitford, *An Autobiography*, p. 252.
45. SAA, D3627(L), pp. 478, 401 & 399.
46. *People's Weekly*, 29 August 1914.
47. *South Australian Parliamentary Debates*, 30 August 1916, p. 1095.
48. *People's Weekly*, 18 August 1917.
49. *People's Weekly*, 15 March 1924.
50. Peter Heydon, *Quiet Decision: A Study of George Foster Pearce* (Melbourne, 1965), pp. 14, 79.
51. *People's Weekly*, 15 September 1917.
52. *People's Weekly*, 5 April 1918.
53. *People's Weekly*, 18 June 1921.
54. *People's Weekly*, 6 August 1921.
55. *South Australian Register*, 4 August 1914.
56. SAA, D3627, Addendum by Sir Lennon Raws.
57. *People's Weekly*, 5 December 1908.
58. SAA, BRG 40/1034, *Wallaroo and Moonta Mining and Smelting Company, Minute Books, 1895–1923*, 29 March 1898, 4 October 1898.
59. SAA, BRG 40/1034, 5 July 1904.
60. SAA, BRG 40/1034, 23 February 1904, 1 March 1904. 3 May 1904.
61. SAA, BRG 40/1034, 1 February 1905, 9 May 1906, 17 May 1906, 20 August 1907.
62. SAA, BRG 40/1034, 10 October 1899.
63. SAA, BRG 40/1034, 4 November 1902, 10 June 1908.
64. H. Lipson Hancock, *The Wallaroo and Moonta Mines* (Adelaide, 1914); H. Lipson Hancock, 'Welfare Work in the Mining Industry', *Australian Chemical Engineering and Mining Review*, October 1918.
65. *South Australian Department of Mines Mining Review*, half-year ended June 1919, p. 53.
66. SAA, BRG 40/1034, 29 October 1912; 19 November 1912.
67. *South Australian Department of Mines Mining Review*, half-year ended June 1919, p. 54.
68. H. Lipson Hancock and William Shaw, *A Sunday School of Today* (Adelaide, 1912), pp. 21–2; for further details of the 'Rainbow System' see H. Lipson Hancock,

Modern Methods in Sunday School Work (Adelaide, 1916); H. Lipson Hancock and William R. Penhall, *The Missionary Spirit in Sunday School Work* (Adelaide, 1918); H. Lipson Hancock, *The Rainbow Course of Bible Study* (Adelaide, 1919).
69. SAA, D5341(T), Peter Thomas, *Scrapbook Relating to Kapunda, Burra, Wallaroo, and Moonta Mines*, pamphlet issued by R.S. Richards, p. 124.
70. *People's Weekly*, 2 July 1927.
71. Oswald Pryor, *Australia's Little Cornwall* (Adelaide, 1962), pp. 187–8.
72. Pryor, *Australia's Little Cornwall*, p. 186.
73. *South Australian Department of Mines Mining Review*, half-year ended June 1929; half-year ended December 1931.
74. *People's Weekly*, 25 May 1935.
75. K.W. Thomson, 'The Changes in Function of Former Mining Settlements: The Wallaroo Copper Belt', *Proceedings of the Royal Geological Society of Australia, South Australian Branch*, vol. 56 (1955), p. 57.
76. Thomson, 'Changes in Function of Former Mining Settlements', p. 57.
77. H. Kneebone, 'The "Blacks" of Australia and Papua', in Harry Golding (ed.), *The Wonder Book of Empire for Boys and Girls* (London [and Melbourne and Toronto], n.d.), pp. 137–42.
78. Joan Tiver, *Harry Kneebone: A Son of 'Little Cornwall'* (Adelaide, n.d.), p. 73.
79. SAA D3627(L), p. 857.
80. Pryor, *Australia's Little Cornwall*, p. 136.

Chapter 7. 'The world's largest Cornish festival': The myth revived

1. K.W. Thomson, 'Changes in Function of Former Mining Settlements: The Wallaroo Copper Belt', *Proceedings of the Royal Geological Society of Australia, South Australian Branch*, vol. 56 (1955), pp. 50–7.
2. See Philip Payton, 'Paralysis and Revival: The Reconstruction of Celtic-Catholic Cornwall, 1890–1945', in Ella Westland, *Cornwall: The Cultural Construction of Place* (Penzance, 1997), pp. 25–39.
3. *People's Weekly*, 2 October 1920, 15 September 1923, 6 October 1923, 23 August 1924, 1 July 1926, 22 May 1926, 14 January 1928, 22 September 1943, 30 October 1934.
4. *People's Weekly*, 15 September 1927.
5. *People's Weekly*, 10 June 1933.
6. Article in unidentified edition of the *Cornishman* newspaper in 1919, reprinted in pamphlet form by the Cornish Association of South Australia and published in Adelaide c.1920.
7. John Langdon Bonython, *Cornwall: Interesting History and Romantic Stories, Talks at Meetings of the South Australian Cornish Association* (Adelaide, 1932), p. 27.
8. *People's Weekly*, 14 July 1923.
9. Fred Jones, *The Honourable Sir Langdon Bonython KCMG: An Eminent Australian* (Camborne, 1931), p. 1.
10. *Minutes of Committee Meetings of the Cornish Association of South Australia*, 27 June 1931.
11. *Minutes ... of the Cornish Association*, 30 August 1930, 27 September 1930.

12. *Minutes ... of the Cornish Association*, 28 October 1933, 29 July 1934, 29 November 1935.
13. *Minutes ... of the Cornish Association*, 26 April 1935.
14. See Bernard Deacon and Philip Payton, 'Re-inventing Cornwall: Culture Change on the European Periphery', in Philip Payton (ed.), *Cornish Studies: One* (Exeter, 1993), pp. 62–79; see also Philip Payton, 'Re-inventing Celtic Australia', in Amy Hale and Philip Payton (eds), *New Directions in Celtic Studies* (Exeter, 2000), pp. 108–25.
15. *Quiz and the Lantern*, 9 October 1901; *Bulletin*, 25 January 1912.
16. Oswald Pryor, *Cornish Pasty* (Adelaide, 1961); Oswald Pryor, *Cousin Jacks and Jennys* (Adelaide, 1966).
17. See Liz Coole (ed.), *Writings of Oswald Pryor from the People's Weekly* (Moonta, 2002).
18. Coole (ed.), *Writings of Oswald Pryor*, frontispiece: letter from Oswald Pryor to George A. Hicks, 1 January 1947.
19. Coole (ed.), *Writings of Oswald Pryor*, pp. 12 (August 1941), p. 13 (February 1942), 14 (April 1943), 15 (May 1943), 17 (July 1943).
20. Coole (ed.), *Writings of Oswald Pryor*, p. 21 (May 1944).
21. Coole (ed.), *Writings of Oswald Pryor*, p. 21 (May 1944), p. 37 (August 1949), p. 61 (November 1955), p. 64 (June 1956).
22. A glimpse of the prodigious research effort behind this construction is evident in SAA, D3668 (T), *Chronology of Wallaroo, Moonta, Kadina and the Surrounding Districts, 1860–1900, as reported in the South Australian Register and Observer*, by Oswald Pryor.
23. SAA, PRG 96, *Oswald Pryor Papers*, Correspondence, Phillips to Pryor, 22 December 1932.
24. SAA, PRG 96, Correspondence, Thomas to Pryor, n.d. c.1930.
25. Coole (ed.), *Writings of Oswald Pryor*, frontispiece, Oswald Pryor to George A. Hicks, 1 January 1947.
26. Coole (ed.), *Writings of Oswald Pryor*, p. 33 (January 1947).
27. Coole (ed.), *Writings of Oswald Pryor*, p. 52 (April 1954).
28. SAA, PRG 96, Correspondence, A.L. Rowse to Pryor, 20 September 1950; Claude Berry to Pryor, 26 August 1950.
29. SAA, PRG 96, Correspondence, Hicks to Pryor, 5 December 1951.
30. SAA, D3217 (T), *Little Cornwall: The Story of Moonta (South Australia) and its Cornish Miners*, by Oswald Pryor.
31. Oswald Pryor, *Australia's Little Cornwall* (Adelaide, 1962), p. 188.
32. Pryor, *Australia's Little Cornwall*, p. 189.
33. Pryor, *Australia's Little Cornwall*, p. 190.
34. Geoffrey Blainey, *The Rush that Never Ended: A History of Australian Mining* (Melbourne, 1963; 2nd edn, 1969), pp. 119, 124.
35. John Reynolds, *Men and Mines: A History of Australian Mining* (Melbourne, 1974), p. 16.
36. Bill Peach, *Australia Wide* (Sydney, 1977).
37. Donald Dunstan, *Don Dunstan's Australia* (Adelaide, 1977), p. 16.
38. Reynolds, *Men and Mines*, pp. 16–17.

39. Reynolds, *Men and Mines*, p. 17.
40. Graham Jenkin, *Calling Me Home: The Romance of South Australia in Story and Song* (South Australian College of Advanced Education, Adelaide, 1989), pp.136–7.
41. Jenkin, *Calling Me Home*, p. 136.
42. Jenkin, *Calling Me Home*, p. 136.
43. Jenkin, *Calling Me Home*, p. 136.
44. Jenkin, *Calling Me Home*, p. 136.
45. Jenkin, *Calling Me Home*, pp. 145–6.
46. Jenkin, *Calling Me Home*, p. 147.
47. Jenkin, *Calling Me Home*, p. 147.
48. G.J. Drew, *Morphetts Enginehouse and the Cornish Beam Engine: Burra Mine, South Australia* (Burra, 1987).
49. See Jonathan Selby (ed.), *South Australia's Mining Heritage* (Adelaide, 1987).
50. R.K. Johns, *Cornish Mining Heritage* (Adelaide, 1986), p. 5.
51. G.J. Drew and J.E. Connell, *Cornish Beam Engines in South Australian Mines* (Adelaide, 1993), p. 3.
52. Considerable enthusiasm for Cornwall's 'World Heritage Site' project was expressed at the 11th annual conference of the Australian Mining Historical Association at Kadina, South Australia, 7–10 July 2006.
53. Payton (ed.) 'Re-inventing Celtic Australia', pp. 122–3; Leaflet produced by District Council of Kapunda, c.1989.
54. See, for example, Maurice Perry and Ian Auhl, *Burra Sketchbook* (Rigby, Adelaide, 1969); Peter Finch and Ian Auhl, *Burra in Colour* (Rigby, Adelaide, 1973); Ian Auhl and Denis Marfleet, *Australia's Earliest Mining Era: South Australia, 1841–1851* (Rigby, Adelaide, 1975); Ian Auhl, *Burra and District: A Pictorial Memoir* (Lynton Publications, Cormandel Valley, 1975); Ian Auhl, *'The Story of the Monster Mine': The Burra Burra Mine and its Townships, 1845–1877* (Investigator Press, Hawthornedene, 1986).
55. Auhl, *'The Story of the Monster Mine'*, pii.
56. Patricia Lay, *One and All: The Cornish in New South Wales* (Qeanbeyan (NSW), 1998), p. 2.
57. Nic Haygarth, *Philosopher Smith and the Birth of Tasmanian Mining* (Launceston (Tas), 2004), p. 78.
58. Haygarth, *Philosopher Smith*, pp. 102, 104.
59. Haygarth, *Philosopher Smith*, pp. 122, 154.
60. Pat Banks and Ralph Thomas, 'Early Cornish Migration to Western Australia', in *The Cornish Contribution to Federation: Report of Speeches, Cornish Association of South Australia Seminar* (Kadina, 2001), n.p; see also: Martin Gibbs, 'Landscapes of Meaning: Joseph Lucas Horrocks and the Gwalla Estate, Northhampton', *Western Australian History*, 17, 1997, pp. 35–60.
61. Cited in Banks and Thomas, 'Early Cornish Migration to Western Australia', n.p.
62. Cited in Philip Payton, *A.L. Rowse and Cornwall: A Paradoxical Patriot* (Exeter, 2005), p. 64.
63. A.L. Rowse, *The Cornish in America* (London, 1969), p. 354.
64. Rowse, *The Cornish in America*, p. 362.

65. A.C. Todd, *The Cornish Miner in America* (Truro, 1967), p. 247.
66. Todd, *The Cornish Miner in America*, p. 241.
67. John Rowe, *The Hard-Rock Men: Cornish Immigrants and the North American Mining Frontier* (Liverpool, 1974), p. 239.
68. Rowe, *The Hard-Rock Men*, pp. 241–2.
69. Rowe, *The Hard-Rock Men*, pp. 248–9.
70. Alan M. Kent, *Cousin Jack's Mouth-Organ: Travels in Cornish America* (St Austell, 2004), pp. 368, 369.
71. Kent, *Cousin Jack's Mouth-Organ*, p. 380.
72. Kent, *Cousin Jack's Mouth-Organ*, p. 380.
73. David M. Emmons, 'Faction Fights: the Irish Worlds of Butte, Montana, 1875–1917', in Patrick O'Sullivan (ed.), *The Irish World Wide: History, Heritage, Identity, Volume 2, The Irish in the New Communities* (Leicester, 1992), p. 82.
74. Emmons, 'Faction Fights', pp. 83, 84.
75. Emmons, 'Faction Fights', p. 85.
76. R.A. Williams, *The Berehaven Copper Mines: Allihies, Co. Cork* (Sheffield, 1991).
77. Williams, *The Berehaven Copper Mines*, p. 153.
78. Cited in Williams, *The Berehaven Copper Mines*, p. 153.
79. Ronald M. James, *The Roar and the Silence: A History of Virginia City and the Comstock Lode* (Reno, 1998), p. 144.
80. James, *The Roar and the Silence*, p. 95.
81. Ralph Mann, *After the Gold Rush: Society in Grass Valley and Nevada City, California, 1849–1870* (Stanford, CA, 1982), p. 146.
82. Mann, *After the Gold Rush*, pp. 120, 143.
83. See Philip Payton, *The Cornish Overseas: A History of Cornwall's Great Emigration* (Fowey, 2005), pp. 24–5.
84. Cited in Gage McKinney, *When Miners Sang: The Grass Valley Carol Choir* (Grass Valley, CA, 2001), p. 1.
85. Coole (ed.), *Writings of Oswald Pryor*, p. 73 (20 December 1957).
86. McKinney, *When Miners Sang*, p. xv.
87. McKinney, *When Miners Sang*, p. xv.
88. Mention should also be made of Shirley Ewart's more modest volume *Highly Respectable Families: The Cornish of Grass Valley, California 1854–1954* (Grass Valley, CA, 1998).
89. See Wilfred Prest (ed.), *The Wakefield Companion to South Australian History* (Adelaide, 2001), p. 154.
90. Nancy Phelan, *Some Came Early, Some Came Late* (London, 1970), p. 47.
91. Phelan, *Some Came Early, Some Came Late*, p. 48.
92. Dunstan, *Don Dunstan's Australia*, p. 89.
93. Roslyn M. Paterson, 'From *Australia's Little Cornwall*', *Cornish Nation*, vol.2, no. 19, March 1975.
94. *The 2001 Kernewek Lowender Souvenir Supplement* (Kadina, 2001), p. 1; Paterson, 'From *Australia's Little Cornwall*'.
95. *Yorke Peninsula Country Times*, 24 May 1973.
96. *Yorke Peninsula Country Times*, 21 May 1981.
97. *The 2001 ... Supplement*, 2001, p. 1.

98. *Assembly of the Bards of Cornwall in Australia, Moonta, South Australia*, n.d., p. 1.
99. Robin Cohen, *Global Diasporas: An Introduction* (London, 1997), p. ii.
100. E.V. Thompson, *Seek a New Dawn* (London, 2001), p. 171; see also Rosanne Hawke, 'Jack and Jen in Oz: Cornish Identity in Australian Children's Literature', in Pamela O'Neill (ed.), *Exile and Homecoming: Papers from the Fifth Australian Conference of Celtic Studies* (Sydney, 2005), pp. 127–39.
101. Geoffrey Blainey, *A Shorter History of Australia* (Sydney, 1994), p. 50.
102. Geoffrey Blainey, *Black Kettle and Full Moon: Daily Life in Vanished Australia* (Camberwell (Vic), 2003), p. 149.
103. James Jupp, *The English in Australia* (Cambridge, 2004), p. 8.
104. Jupp, *The English in Australia*, pp. 22–3, 80.
105. Celeste Lipow MacLeod, *Multiethnic Australia: Its History and Future* (Jefferson, NC, 2006), p. 98.
106. For example, see the South Australian Migration Museum's volume *From Many Places: The History and Cultural Traditions of South Australian People* (Adelaide, 1995), pp. 96–101.

Epilogue

1. *Autobiography of Thomas Cowling Jnr*, Unpublished MS, part II, p. 1, private collection of John Cowling.
2. *Autobiography of Thomas Cowling Jnr*, part II, p. 1.
3. *People's Weekly*, 27 July 1907; 12 September 1914.
4. *People's Weekly*, 19 August, 1905; 16 November 1929.
5. *People's Weekly*, 24 May 1902.
6. *People's Weekly*, 10 August 1907.
7. *Australian Christian Commonwealth*, 18 May 1906; 17 February 1905.
8. *Australian Christian Commonwealth*, 9 December 1910; *South Australian Primitive Methodist*, July 1899.
9. SAA, Dr Charles Davies, *Biographies and Obituaries* (27 vols), unidentified newspaper cutting dated January 1884; *People's Weekly*, 10 June 1933; *Burra Record*, 20 July 1904; *Australian Christian Commonwealth*, 15 May 1908.
10. *Burra Record*, 23 September 1890; *People's Weekly*, 13 September 1890.
11. *Australian Christian Commonwealth*, 18 December 1908.
12. *People's Weekly*, 28 September 1901.
13. R.M. Gibbs, *A History of South Australia* (Adelaide, 1969), p. 105.
14. Mel Davies, 'Cornish', in Wilfrid Prest (ed.), *The Wakefield Companion to South Australian History* (Adelaide, 2001), p. 128.

Index

Aberdeen (South Australia) 45, 207
    see also Burra Burra
Aborigines, 133–4, 189–90
Adelaide, 1, 13, 25–6, 28, 42–3, 49–50,
    61–2, 70, 88, 90–2, 94, 99, 101,
    103, 106–7, 111, 114, 117–18,
    121–4, 127, 129, 131–2, 137–8,
    144, 149–50, 154, 169–71,
    173–6, 186–96, 200–1, 215, 224
Adelaide Hills, 5, 43, 220
Adelaide, Port, 44, 48, 144–5, 174–5
Amalgamated Miners' Association of
    Australia (AMA), 18, 23, 66, 87,
    123, 126, 128, 143, 172, 180,
    185–6
America, xii, 5, 12, 36, 75, 86, 102, 112,
    118, 218
    see also North America; United States
    of America
Andes, 39
Andrewartha family, 44
Anglicans, 155
Anthony, J., 60
Anthony, John, 115, 117, 123
Anzac Cove, 167
Anzac myth, 7
Appalachians, 39, 41
Arizona, 41
Asquith, Herbert, 177
Auhl, Ian, 208
Australian National League, 174
Australian Workers' Union (AWU),
    180–1, 185–6
Austrians, 210

Axford, Thomas, 224
Ayers, Henry, 44

Bagot, Charles, 42
Bailey, Keith, 30–1
Balaclava, 192
Bald Hill, 105, 107, 112, 114–15
Baldhu, 86, 224
Ballarat, 41, 52, 80, 92, 209
Ballarat School of Mines, 17
Banks, Pat, 209
Baptists, 156–7
Bargwanna, George, 56
Barkla, Captain James, 76
Barrett brothers, 24
Barrier Ranges, 42
Bartlett, Sam, 31
Beaglehole, William Henry, 123
Bedford Foundry see Nicholls, Williams
    Foundry
Beetaloo reservoir, 149
Bendigo, 8–11, 14–15, 23–4, 31, 41,
    127, 209, 225
Bendigo Miners' Association, 22–3
Bennett, John Captain, 73, 77
Bennett, James 'Jimmy', 199, 224
Bere Alston, 68, 73
Bere Ferrers, 68
Berry, Claude, 201
Berryman, James, 35
Bible Christians, 23, 26–7, 37, 45, 50,
    61, 90, 97, 105, 112, 118, 135,
    144, 154–9, 162, 164, 199
    see also Methodists

Bice, Captain Henry, 73
Bice, Captain Samuel Sandoe, 73
Bice, John George, 173–4, 176, 179
Bideford, 37
Black, John McConnell, 94, 171, 174
Blainey, Geoffrey, xii, 202, 220–1
Bodmin, 43, 76, 136, 168
Bokiddick, 71
Bolivia, 8
Bonnetta, William, 152
Bonython, Sir John Langdon, 68, 94, 99, 196, 201
Boor, James, 71
Borlase, William, 38, 88
Bosanco family, 44
Boswarva, Mr, 43
Boucaut, James Penn, 106, 115, 117–19, 121–2
Bougainville, 187, 191
Boulder (Western Australia), 42
Bowden, John, 131–2
Boyton, 37
Bradford Barton, D., 14
Bray, Billy, 224
Bray, John H. 'Dancing', 53–4
Brazil, 10, 35, 39, 209
Bremer River, 70
Bretons, 194
Broken Hill, 5, 8, 11–12, 14, 17, 31, 42, 75, 86, 124–9, 192, 193, 195, 221, 225–6
Brisbane, 220
British Columbia, 41
British Empire, 28, 144, 167, 178, 202
Brittany, 194
Browning, Samuel, 66
Bryant, Captain Matthew, 43
Bryant, Captain Thomas, 84
Bude, 37
Burk, Charles, 154
Burke, Gill, 21
Burr, Thomas, 100
Burra Burra, 5–6, 38, 45–7, 55, 57, 62, 71, 75, 101–3, 121–2, 134, 170, 183, 196, 201, 207–9, 211, 213, 218

see also mines *Australian*, Burra Burra; *also* Aberdeen (South Australia), Copperhouse (South Australia), Hampton, Kooringa, Llwchwr, Lostwithiel (South Australia), Redruth (South Australia)
Burtt, Thomas, 130–1
Butte (Montana), 210–13, 219

Cadgwith, 196
California, xiii, 6–9, 25, 35, 41, 79, 210–11, 213, 214
California Gully, 15
Callington (Cornwall), 20, 102, 118, 173
Callington (South Australia), 5, 47, 70, 74
Calstock, 52, 70, 222, 223
Camborne, 9, 14, 16, 21, 25, 37, 59, 112, 166, 178, 189, 196, 223
Camborne School of Mines, 9
Camel, River, 37
Canada, 15, 25, 37, 167, 214, 218
    see also North America
Cape Colony, 33, 34
Cape Horne, 34
Cape Town, 34
Carn Brea, 166
Carolina, North, 40
Castletownbere, 211–12
Catholics, Roman, xii, 46, 59, 156, 177–8, 220
Celts, Celtic, 20, 45, 120
Central City (Colorado), 41
Chacewater, 70, 162
Charleston, David Morley, 174, 179, 196
Charters Towers, 127
Chileans, 46
Chinese, 22, 80
Chile, 32, 39, 110, 207
Chileans, 46, 207–8
Chynoweth, Arthur, 57
Chynoweth, James Henry, 184
Clare, 62, 76
Clark, Manning, xii
Clemo, Captain, 17

Clymo, Captain Francis, 40
Coad, Richard, 224
Cobar, 6, 222
Cocks, (Fanny) Kate Boudicea, 28, 144–5, 147
Cohen, Robin, 218
Colombia, 33, 39, 43
Colorado, 41, 211
Comstock, 12, 41, 213
Congdon, John, 43, 45
Connaught, 46
Connecticut, 40
Connell, J.E., 206
Conscription issue, 170, 178–9
Coolgardie, 6, 42
Copperhouse (South Australia), 46
Copper Triangle, 29
Cork, West, 211, 213
Cornish Association of South Australia, xiii, 62, 68, 99, 190, 195–7, 220, 224
Cornish Gorseth (Gorsedd of Cornwall), 30, 196, 217–19
Cornish, John, 70
Cornish language, 59–60
Cornish mining practice in South Australia, xi, 4, 8, 11–12, 19, 45–6, 60, 74, 78, 100, 102–4, 107–8, 111, 125–6, 206, 225
Cornwall, County of (Tasmania), xi
Cornwall County Council, 209
Cornwall and Devon Society, 44
Costa Rica, 39
Cousin Jack, myth of, 6, 32, 58, 80, 131, 169, 208–9, 225
Cousin Jenny, myth of, 28, 136, 139, 142, 146, 164, 169, 202–3
Cowling, Captain Richard, 176, 223
Cowling, Captain Thomas, 52, 86
Cowling, Captain Tom, 53, 86, 222–3
Creswick, 23, 42, 143
Croats, 40
Cross Roads (Wheal Hughes settlement), 29, 53–4, 57, 136, 157, 160–1, 198, 222
Crowan, 14, 78

Cruet, John, 157
Crystal Brook, 192
Cuba, 33, 39
Cumberland, 70
Curnow, Billy, 54
Curtis, Jim, 54
Cusgarne, 171

Dartmoor, 68, 69
Datson, Captain Hugh, 159, 161
Datson, Captain James, 77, 80
Datson, Captain William, 77, 80
Davey, Lesley, 56
Davies, Mel, 20, 100–1, 226–7
Davitt, Michael, 46
Davy, Sir Humphry, 84
Deacon, Bernard, 20–1, 38
Debs, Eugene, 190
Deeble, Captain Malachi, 75–6, 101, 116, 121
Dennis, C.J., 197
Devon, 17, 20, 26–7, 32, 37, 44, 61, 68–71, 73–4, 89, 116, 181, 220, 225
Devonians, 4, 17
Dodgeville, 40
Doney, John 53
Drew, G.J., 206
Dunstan family, 23
Dunstan, Captain Edward, 83, 107, 132, 222
Dunstan, Don, 202, 215–18
Dutton, Francis, 42, 43, 132

Edwards, Martin, 115
Edyvean, David, 120
Edwards, A.J., 154
Edwards, Rebecca, 157
East, Captain Matthew, 80–1, 83, 107
Egloskerry, 37
Elphick, 100
Emmons, David M., 211–13
England, 21, 38, 97–8, 145, 196, 221
English, 25, 45–6, 98, 194, 196, 208, 221
English and Australian Copper

Company, 174
Ennor, John, 31
Euriowie, 17
Europeans, xiii, 22, 39, 43, 115, 133–4, 141, 169, 178
Eyre Peninsula, 76
Exeter, 168

Fahey, Charles, 12
Falmouth, 224
Farmers' and Producers' Political Union, 174
Faull, Christopher Captain, 14, 78, 120
Faull, Jim, 14
Federation debate, 170
Federation of Old Cornwall Societies, 194
Filipinos, 210
Finns, 40, 210
First World War *see* Great War
Fletcher, Jane, 137
Fletcher, Sukey, 137
Forest Creek, 42
Forest of Dean, 26
Foster, Rev. Joshua, 157
France, 7, 9, 167
Fryerstown, 12

Galena (Illinois), 40
Gallipoli, 7, 167, 169
Gawler, 62, 87–8, 182
Gee, L.C.E., 183–4
Georgia (USA), 40
Geraldton, 209
Germans, 46, 167, 177–9, 207–8, 220
Gibbs, R.M., 226
Gill, Private J.W., 167
Gill, Reuben, 18, 24, 105–6, 111–12, 117, 121–2, 164, 224
Glasgow, 21
Glen Osmond, 42, 137
Gold Hill, 213
Goldsworthy, Captain, 72
Goldsworthy, Captain Richard, 43
Goldsworthy, 'Uncle Joe', 127
Goldsworthy, W.H., 158

Gorsedd of Cornwall *see* Cornish Gorseth
Grass Valley, 7, 8, 41, 210, 213–14, 219
Great War (First World War), 1, 5, 7, 12, 23, 32, 40, 144, 166, 170, 177–80, 186–7, 193, 218
Green's Plains, 164
Grigg family, 23
Gunnislake, 20
Gwennap, 35, 37, 70–1, 162, 171

Hamilton Jenkin, A.K., 19–20, 21, 34, 36
Hampton, 46
Hancock, Annie Allen, 92
Hancock, Edwin, 16
Hancock, Fred, 48
Hancock, George, 68
Hancock, Captain Henry Richard:
    international reputation, 4, 15–16, 68, 86, 94–5; and Moonta's myth, 4, 18–19; 63, 74, 95; relationship with workforce, 4, 16, 18–19, 23, 63, 66–8, 81, 82, 90, 110–12, 116, 120–1, 126; as a Devonian, 4, 17–18, 63, 68, 74, 84, 92, 116, 225; fictional biography of, 9; and the 'Hancock jig', 12; relationship with management team (captains), 14, 16, 23, 73–8, 101, 110; as 'Ruler of Australia's Little Cornwall', 15; as 'H.R.H.', 15, 17, 63, 68–70, 74–5, 77–8, 81, 83–5, 89, 91, 93, 95, 182; the Moonta mine as 'Cap'n 'Ancock's White Cow', 16, 74, 95; and Horrabridge, 17–18, 68–9, 70, 73, 81, 92–4; Hancocks and Lipsons as old Devonshire families, 18, 68; his enigmatic nature, 18; tall stories about him, 18, 92, 95–6; domiciled at Moonta, 31, 92; appointed chief captain at Moonta, 49, 73, 80; develops Yorke Peninsula mines, 51, 78, 81–3, 85, 95, 110;

helps estranged families, 52; christening of new beam engines, 54; accusations of favouritism, nepotism and appropriation, 67, 85–89; relationship with mine directors, 67–8, 74–5, 79, 81–3, 89–90, 112, 120; and Cornish Association of South Australia, 68; birth, 68; parents, 68; becomes a mine captain, 69; appointed to Wheal Ellen, 70–1; temporary appointments at the Wallaroo and Yelta mines, 73; recruits Cornish miners, 75, 78–80, 108; marries Loveday Maria Jolly, 77, 92; appointed chief captain at Wallaroo, 82, 85; investigates Captains Dunstan and Roach, 84; 'Hancock jig' controversy, 85–89; paternalistic attitude, 89–91; develops welfare policies, 90–1; and free education, 91; Nalyappa property, 92; religious faith, 92, 120, 154–5, 198; marries Sarah Annie Maynard, 92; death of Sarah Annie Maynard, 92, 161–2; as family man, 92; symbiotic relationship with Moonta, 93, 169; death, 94; replaces Warmingtons, 108, 143; threats of violence, 110, 143; hostility to trade unionists, 120; appoints board of health, 154; succeeded by son H. Lipson Hancock, 181; 'Cap'n 'Ancock's Cathedral', 198; personifies Moonta's myth, 198; Hancock in retirement, 226

Hancock, H. Lipson, 16–17, 83, 92, 95, 181–4, 193
Hancock, Leigh, 16, 92
Hancock, Maria Loveday, 77, 92–3
Hancock, Robert, 68
Hancock, Sarah Annie, 92, 161–2
Hancock, Sarah Lipson, 68
Harris, Rev. D.C., 59
Harvey & Co., 45, 80, 174

Harvey, James, 84
Haygarth, Nick, 208–9
Hayle, 12, 45, 80, 174
Harz Mountains, 208
Hebrew, 208
Helston, 21, 70, 102, 123
Heydon, Peter, 180
Hicks, George A., 200–1
Hicks's Mill, 70, 224
Highlands and Islands of Scotland, 37
Higgs, Captain Samuel, 82, 84–5, 116, 132–3, 148
Hill, 'Lightning Lionel', 190–1
Hitchins, Captain Josiah, 17
Hobb, William, 161
Hocking, Joseph, 25–6
Hocking, Silas, 25–6
Hooper, Richard 'Dickie', 124
Hopgood, Donald, 170, 188
Hopkins, Ruth, 15, 23–4, 31, 208
Horrabridge, 17, 18, 68, 73, 81, 92–3
Horse Downs, 59
Hosken, Captain, 209
Hosken, James, 100–1
Hosken, Rev. W.H., 26, 135
Hosking family, 124
Hosking, William, 154
Houston, T., 24
Hughes, Walter Watson, 71–2, 81
Hummocks, the, 133
'Hungry Forties', 38
Hunt, Arnold, 25, 161

Illinois, 40
Illogan, 55, 166
Irish, xii, 7, 10, 41, 46, 59, 80, 120, 151, 177, 180, 194, 207–8, 210–13, 220–1
Irish Land League, 46
Ireland, xii, 16, 38, 97, 145, 212, 221
Isle of Man, 21
Italians, 40, 210
Iowa, 40

Jacobstowe, 37
James, John, 223

James, Rev. W.F., 162–3
James, Ronald M., 213
James II, King, 99
Japanese, 197
Jeffery, Mary, 178
Jenkin, 203–5
Jericho (South Australia), 29
Jerusalem (Kadina), 158
Jews, 220
Johannesburg, 55
Johns, R.K., 12, 206
Jolly, Joe, 77
Jolly, Captain Joseph, 70, 77, 92
Jolly, Maria Loveday see Hancock, Maria Loveday
Jose, George, 166, 169, 191
Jupp, James, 220–1

Kadina, xiii, 29–30, 52–4, 57–8, 60–1, 72, 88, 106–7, 111–12, 123, 126, 128, 131, 137, 143, 152, 157–8, 164, 165, 172–3, 177, 187, 189, 192, 196, 199, 204, 206, 220, 226
Kalgoorlie, xi, 6, 42, 192, 195, 226
Kanmantoo, 5
see also mines, Australian, Kanmantoo
Kapunda, 5, 38, 42, 45–7, 57, 62, 121, 122, 134, 207–9, 211, 213, 218
see also mines, Australian, Kapunda
Kawau, 101
Kayser, Ferdinand, 208
Kea, 112
Kempthorne, Lewis, 35
Kent, Alan M., 26, 210–12
Kentucky, 40
Kernewek Lowender festival, xiii, 5, 29, 216–17, 220, 226–7
Keweenaw Peninsula, 38, 40
Kilkhampton, 157
Kingswood (Bristol), 26
Kitto, Richard Collingwood, 105, 107
Klondike, the, 34
Kneebone, Henry, 189
Kneebone, Henry 'Harry', 189–90, 192, 196
Knowles, Mr, 105

Kooringa, 45–6
see also Burra Burra
Korea, 34
Kulpara, 164

Labor Party see United Labor Party, ULP
Ladock, 70
Laity family, 23
Lake, Rev. Octavius, 154–5
Lake Superior, 38, 40
Lamshed, W., 51, 158
Landrake, 187
Land's End, 34, 202
Lang, Jack, 190
Lansell, George, 13, 15
Lathlean, William, 183
Latin America, 37, 39, 43
Launcells, 37
Launceston (Cornwall), 181
Launceston (Tasmania), xi
Lay, Patricia, 208
Leadville, 41
Lelant, 157
Liberal and Democratic Union, 174
Linden, 40
Lingenfelter, R.E., 22
Liskeard, 20
Liverpool, 212
London, 49, 68, 106, 118, 189
London Cornish Association, 194
London, Tower of, 99, 168
Lonie, John, 170, 188
Lostwithiel (South Australia), 46
see also Burra Burra
Llwchwr, 46, 207
Ludgvan, 83–4
Luker, D.H., 24, 155
Luxulyan, 71

Macleod, Celeste Lipow, 221
Magee, Gary, 35
Magill, 107
Major, Ephraim, 66, 105, 108
Mann, Ralph, 41, 213
Map Kernow, 207

Marazion, 48, 72
Marquette Range, 40
Martin, James, 87–8, 182
Maryland, 40
Marx, Karl, 174
Massachusetts, 36
May, Alfred, 87–8
May, Frederick, 77, 80, 86–8
Maynard, Sarah Annie *see* Hancock, Sarah Annie
McArthur, J., 117, 118, 119, 120, 121
McKinney, Gage, 214–15
Melbourne, 189, 201
Menheniot, 20, 169
Menzies, Sir Robert, 23
Merritt, Thomas, 55
Metherell, Bill, 199
Methodists, xi, 5, 18, 20, 23–7, 36–7, 45, 53, 57, 59, 61, 63, 66, 74, 97, 120, 128, 133, 144, 146, 154–7, 161, 163, 164, 169–74, 177–9, 184–8, 190–3, 198–9, 217, 220–5
  see also Bible Christians; Primitive Methodists; Wesleyans
Mexicans, 210
Mexico, 10, 32, 35, 39, 41, 201
Michigan, 6, 22, 38, 40–1, 52, 210
Mill, John Stuart, 174
mines:
  Australian:
    Bald Hill, 81
    Belmont, 75
    Bingo, 73, 112
    Blinman, 98
    Block 10, 17, 86
    Boulder Central, 16
    Burnie, 16
    Burra Burra, 5, 20, 38, 43–5, 50, 71, 75–7, 84, 100, 102, 104, 107, 110, 170, 207–9
    Cadia, 12
    Cinderella, 15
    Doora, 72
    Duke of Cornwall (Victoria), 12
    Great Boulder, 182
    Great Devon Consols, 51, 72, 136
    Hamley, 72, 86, 121
    Kanmantoo, 107
    Kapunda, 38, 42–3, 83, 102, 132, 207, 209
    Karkarilla, 72
    Kurilla, 76
    Matta Matta, 114
    Matta Parra, 74
    Mid-Moonta, 72
    Mochatoona, 122
    Moonta, 1, 5, 12–19, 22–3, 31, 47, 49–50, 52, 54, 66–9, 71–7, 78, 80, 82–90, 92–5, 100, 102–12, 114–17, 120–1, 124–8, 130, 136, 142–3, 152–4, 159, 161, 166, 171–3, 179–83, 186, 192–3, 206–7, 222, 225–6
      see also Moonta and Moonta Mines
    Moonta Consols, 72
    Mount Bischoff, 208
    Nalyappa (Wilkawat), 72
    New Cornwall, 52, 54, 72, 80, 86, 107, 187
    New Moonta, 72
    North Kapunda, 42
    North Wandilta, 72
    North Yelta, 72, 147
    Old Cornwall, 72
    Paramatta, 16, 54, 72, 83, 86, 175–6, 222
    Peak Downs, 75
    Poona, 187
    Prince Alfred, 199
    South Hamley, 74
    South Kapunda, 42
    South Wallaroo, 72
    Spring Creek, 76
    Wallaroo, 30, 31, 47, 49–51, 66–7, 71–5, 78–9, 82–5, 92, 94–5, 102–7, 111–12, 114, 116–17, 120, 123–8, 132, 139, 143, 152, 154, 166, 170, 179–83, 186, 192, 193, 222, 225–6
    Wandilta, 72, 73, 107, 175, 222

Wheal Barton, 83
Wheal Ellen, 70, 71, 73, 77–8, 86
Wheal Fortune, 72
Wheal Gawler, 42
Wheal Gundry, 42
Wheal Hughes, 48, 60, 72, 86, 217
Wheal James, 83
Wheal Mixter, 71
'Wheal Munta', 206
Wheal Prosper, 72
Wheal Watkins, 42
Wilkawat (Nalyappa), 72
Yelta, 54, 73–4, 77, 80, 107, 136, 157, 175–6, 222
Yudnamutana, 122

Cornish and Devonian:
Bedford United, 17
Caradon, 20, 21, 43
Consolidated Mines, 95, 204
Cooks Kitchen, 16
Devon Great Consols, 17, 20, 68–9, 95
Devon Great United, 69
Dolcoath, 14, 16, 51, 59, 95, 204
Drakewalls, 20, 223
East Wheal Rose, 59
Fowey Consols, 95
Giew, 166
Gunnislake Clitters, 223
North Downs, 107
Sortridge mines (East Sortridge, Great Sortridge, Great Sortridge United, Great West Sortridge, Sortridge Consols), 69
South Condurrow, 21
St Ives Consolidated, 166
Tresavean, 43, 95
United Mines, 95, 204
West Wheal Robert, 69
Wheal Anna Maria, 17, 69
Wheal Basset, 21
Wheal Betsy, 69
Wheal Butson, 137
Wheal Crebor, 69

Wheal Crowndale, 69
Wheal Damsel, 35
Wheal Elizabeth, 17
Wheal Fanny, 69
Wheal Friendship, 69
Wheal Hope, 69
Wheal Jenny, 17
Wheal Josiah, 69
Wheal Margery, 84
Wheal Maria, 69
Wheal Providence, 84
Wheal Trelawney, 20, 169

Other:
Allihies (Ireland), 211–12
Bruce (Canada), 40
Calumet and Hecla (United States of America), 22, 40
Central (United States of America), 40
Cliff (United States of America), 40
Empire-Star (United States of America), 213
Gongo Soco (Brazil), 35
Idaho-Maryland (United States of America), 214
Minas Gerais (Brazil), 39
Minesota (sic) (United States of America), 40
Pewabic (United States of America), 40
Real del Monte (Mexico), 35, 39
Mineral Point, 40
Miners' Mutual Benefit Association, 20
Mississippi River, 40
Mitchell, Captain C., 77, 91
Mitchell, Captain William, 43
Mitchell, William, 53
Monmouthshire, 26
Montacute, 43
Montana, 41
Moonta: illuminated by Oswald Pryor, xii, 198; creating Moonta's myth, xii, 4, 5, 15, 18–19, 22, 24, 27, 31, 46, 52, 61, 111, 117, 128, 139, 165, 170–1, 191, 197, 204,

207, 216, 221, 225–6; National Trust branch, xiii, 216; and trade unionism, 4–5, 22–3, 76, 97, 100, 111, 117–18, 123–4, 127–8, 169, 172–3, 180, 187, 225; and 'Cousin Jacks', 5, 32, 60–1, 111, 178, 194, 225; and 'Moontaites', 5–6, 8, 31, 53, 75, 128, 131, 225; copper discovery 1861, 5; epitome of Cornish experience in Australia, 6, 42, 194, 208; 'Moonta camps' and 'Moonta towns', 6; as focus of Cousin Jack identity, 6, 7, 27–8, 51, 60, 131, 138, 167, 217, 223; as 'hub of the universe', 6–7, 28, 199, 223; and 'Moonta patriotism', 6–8, 31; and 'if you haven't been to Moonta' saying, 8–9, 31, 225; and Moonta Mines settlement, 10; international fame, 15, 32–3, 166; mines in the vicinity of Moonta, 16–17, 69, 72, 121, 147; as an emigrant destination, 21, 31, 42, 48, 70, 158, 167, 209; politics at Moonta, 24, 111, 120–2; the 'Holy Land of Moonta', 24; religion at Moonta, 24–7, 52, 59, 112, 146, 156–8, 160–1, 163, 169–70, 199; as a tourist destination, 28; as 'Australia's Little Cornwall', 29, 30, 61, 74; relationship with other northern Yorke Peninsula settlements, 29–31, 60–1, 199, 204, 220; as government township, 30, 131; entwinement with Cornish transnational identity, 33, 46, 51, 218; and Captain Piper's 'new chums', 51; Cornish wrestling at Moonta, 53–4; and local dignitaries, 54; and Cornish carols, 55; and music-making, 56–7; friendly societies and Freemasonry, 58; and Temperance movement, 59; and the Cornish Association of South Australia, 62, 68, 224; miners arrive from Victoria, 80; symbiotic relationship with Captain Hancock, 93; remembrance of 'Cornwall was never conquered yet', 99–100; remembrance of 'Trelawny', 99–100, 168–9; merchants support striking miners, 106; municipal self-government, 111; as frontier, 131; and fictional Polly Thomas, 142; first policewoman in British Empire, 144; as Methodist heartland, 146, 158; and underground water tanks, 149; and typhoid epidemics, 152, 161; chapels at Moonta, 156; funerals at Moonta, 163; Moonta and the Great War, 166–9, 193; continuing links with Cornwall, 167, 169, 170, 191, 194–5, 197, 204, 218, 222–3; Verran's popularity, 173, 177, 179; Conscription issue, 178–80; depression after closure of mines, 188, 193; continuing influence in Labor Party, 188, 192; visit by Tom Man, 190; Moonta and the Cornish-Celtic Revival, 194, 196; 'Moonta Carol Party', 196; 'Back to Moonta' celebrations, 196; Moonta myth re-invented by Oswald Pryor, 197–203, 214–15, 220, 226; myth personified by Oswald Pryor, 198; Oswald Pryor regrets decline of carol tradition, 200–1, 214–15; Graham Jenkin on Moonta, 203–6; challenges to Moonta's status, 209; compared to Grass Valley, 213; Cornish Fair at Moonta, 217; and the Kernewek Lowender festival, 219; as UNESCO Cornish mining landscape, 227

see also Moonta Mines and mines, Australian, Moonta

Moonta Anti-Conscription League, 178
Moonta Bay, 29, 92
Moonta, East, 29, 56, 58, 60, 151, 157, 198
Moonta Miners' and Mechanics' Association, 18, 22, 24, 49–50, 97, 99, 115–18, 120–3, 126
Moonta Mines, 10, 15, 24, 28, 29–31, 54–6, 58, 60–1, 63, 66–7, 77, 80, 90–1, 105, 109, 111–12, 115, 133–5, 146, 148–50, 153–7, 159, 161, 166, 178, 184, 186–7, 192, 198, 206, 217
    see also mines, Australian, Moonta; Moonta
Moonta, East, 186
Moonta West, 156
Morcombe, Kate, 159, 161
Mount Barker, 5
Mount Remarkable, 76
Moyle, J., 182
Murchison River, 209
Mylor (Cornwall), 118

Nancarrow, John, 157
Nankivell, Elias, 53
Nankivell, Ned, 54
Napoleonic Wars, 32, 39
National Labor Party, 178–80
National Trust of South Australia, 206
Nevada, 6, 12, 41, 211, 213
New Almaden, 40
New Caledonia, 8
Newfoundland, 36
New Guinea, 187
New Jersey, 40
New Jersey, West, 36
New South Wales, 6, 8, 12, 16–17, 34, 36, 41, 75, 124, 128–9, 177, 190, 208
Newtown (South Australia), 29
New York, 196
New Zealand, 31, 33–4, 42, 75, 101, 196, 218, 223, 226
Nicaragua, 39
Nicholls, Robert, 42

Nicholls, Thomas, 70
Nicholls, Williams Foundry, 70, 71, 81
North America, 8, 25, 28, 35, 40, 214
    see also America; Canada; United States of America
Northampton, 209
Northey, William, 136
Norwegians, 7
Nova Zembla, 34

O' Bryan, Mary, 26
O' Bryan, William, 26
Ohio, 184
Ontario, 26, 37, 40, 167
Opie family, 48
Opie, Clarence William, 184
Opie, John, 48
Orange Order, 59
Osborne, Samuel, Captain, 43, 75, 103
Ovens River, 42

Pachuca, 201
Padstow, 37
Pascoe family, 128
Pascoe, T. Gluyas, 223
Pascoe, William, 71
Paterson, Roslyn, 216
Paynter, Sophia, 70
Paynter, Captain William Arundel, 70–1, 78, 85–6, 89
Peach, Bill, 202
Peak Downs, 6, 14, 75, 110
    see also mines, Australian, Peak Downs
Peake A.H., 173, 174, 177
Pearce, George, 180
Pearse, Mark Guy, 25
Pengelly, Josiah, 154
Penglaze, Captain S., 43
Penhall, W.R., 133
Pennsylvania, 36, 37
Penponds, 189
Pensilva, 222
Penwith, West, 38
Penzance, 84, 157, 195
Perran Foundry, 45, 70, 71
Perranporth, 55

Perranzabuloe, 40, 77
Perth (Australia), xi
Peru, 8, 32, 39
Peter, Hugh, 98
Peters family, 126
Peters, Jimmy, 127
Phelan, Nancy, 215, 218
Phillips, Captain, 17
Phillips, Philip, 24
Phillips, Walter, 71
Piper, Captain Richard, 51, 74, 167, 197, 199
Piper, Elizabeth, 224
Plymouth, 44, 48, 51, 73, 131
Point Pearce, 133
Political Association, 118, 121, 123
Polmear, W.J.L., 187
Polperro, 55
Ponsanooth, 35
Port Augusta, 173, 191
Port Hughes, 29
Port Pirie, 191
Portreath (South Australia), 29
Poundstock, 37
Portuguese, 39
'Premiers' Plan', 170, 190–2
Presbyterianism, xii
Preston, Mr, 222
Price, Tom, 173
Primitive Methodists, 23, 26, 45, 54, 66, 114, 124, 127–8, 155–6, 160, 172, 184, 224
  see also Methodists
Prince Edward Island, 37
Prisk, Captain, 107
Prisk, John, 18, 24, 27, 50, 112, 114–16, 120, 122–3, 127–8, 154, 164
Price, L.L., 19, 20
Provis, Captain, 14
Pryor, Captain James, 78, 197
Pryor, Oswald: captures essentials of Cornish life at Moonta, xi, xii, 1, 198; cartoons, xiii, 63–4, 197; his book *Australia's Little Cornwall*, 1, 4, 86, 201, 215; as 'grass captain' at the Moonta mine, 1, 197; depicts Moonta as 'hub of the universe', 6–7; perpetuates 'if you haven't been to Moonta' saying, 8–9; describes Moonta versus Bendigo rivalry, 8–9, 11, 15; on the term 'captain', 17; on Captain Hancock, 18, 63, 198; on trade unionism at Moonta, 2, 22–3; on politics at Moonta, 24; perpetuates Moonta's myth, 24, 27–8, 31; and 'strong women', 27–8, 138; on relationship between Moonta and Moonta Mines, 30; on relationship between Moonta and other local settlements, 61; on the 'local Trevithicks', 67, 86, 89; on Captain Deeble, 76; on remembrance of 'Cornwall was never conquered yet', 99; on the Warmington crisis, 108; describes cottage construction, 134; on cottages as Cousin Jenny's domain, 136; on the closure of Moonta and Wallaroo mines, 186–7; as a journalist, 197–203; re-invents Moonta's myth, 197–203, 220, 226; on John Verran, 198; affects 'Cousin Jack' idiom and dialect, 198; personifies Moonta's myth, 198; records oral tradition, 199–200; regrets decline of Moonta 'carols', 200–1, 213–15; influences other writers, 202–3
Puritans, 36

Queensland, 6, 14, 27, 42, 75, 110

Rand, the, 16
Rapson, Captain John, 75
Redruth (Cornwall), xiii, 21, 35, 37, 43, 52, 70, 157, 166
Redruth (South Australia), 45, 46, 207
  see also Burra Burra
Reed, Matt, 199

'Reforming Thirties', 38
Renfry, W., 53, 54
Reynolds, John, 146, 202–3
Richards, James 'Fiddler Jim', 55–7
Richards, John, 123
Richards, Richard, 178
Richards, Robert Stanley, 178–80, 185–8, 190–2, 199
Rickard, Mr, 57
Rickard, T.A., 40
Roach, Captain Henry, 43, 102
Roach, Captain Paul, 83, 84
Roach, Trooper Jake, 167
Roanoke, 36
Roberts, Captain Thomas, 43
Robinson, Mandie, 8–9, 15, 85, 89
Roche, 224
Rocky Mountains, 40, 41
Rodda, Captain Richard, 132
Rodda, Thomas, 115, 122, 224
Roosevelt, President F.D., 213
Rose, Benjamin, 169
Rowe family, 23, 126
Rowe, Rev. G.E., 157–8
Rowe, John 'Mochatoona', 122
Rowe, John, 40, 210
Rowse, A.L., 201, 210, 212
Royal Geological Society of Cornwall, 84, 132
Royal Institution of Cornwall, 194, 196
Royal Navy, 36
Ruan Minor, 196
Rule, John, 20
Rundle, James, 44
Ryan, Patrick, 71

St Agnes, 35, 71, 122, 137
St Ann's Chapel, 222
St Austell, 70, 76
St Blazey, 15, 21, 70, 73, 83
St Cleer, 31, 157
St Day, 81
St Dominick, 48
St Erth, 157, 174
St Gennys, 37
St Ives, 75, 138, 195

St John's Eve, 46
St Just-in-Penwith, 21, 70, 224
St Minver, 37
St Piran, 45, 194
St Stephen-in-Brannel, 25
Saltash, 43, 118, 223
Salvation Army, 199
Sampson, John, 23
Sanders, Captain, 50
San Francisco, 174
Santo, Philip, 43, 118
Scaddan, Jack, 166, 180, 199
Scotland, 97, 145, 221
Scots, Scottish, xii, 10, 46, 71, 120, 154, 194, 207, 220
Second World War, 9, 187, 198, 213–14
Shebbear, 26, 27
ships:
  Aldinga, 80
  Britannia, 44
  Canterbury, 48
  Coorong, 80
  David Malcolm, 44
  Eliza, 44
  Gosforth, 48
  Himalaya, 44
  Hooghly, 44
  Isabella Watson, 44
  Kangaroo, 80
  Kingston, 44
  Lady Milton, 48
  Marion, 131
  Prince Regent, 44
  Princess Royal, 44
  Queen Bee, 48
  Rajah, 44
  William Money, 44
Sierra Nevada, 7, 41
Simcock family, 136
Simmons family, 125
Skinner, Captain, 78, 198
Slavs, 210
Slee, Elizabeth, 224
Sleep family, 121
Smeaton, T.H., 174
Somerset, 32

Somerville, Phyllis, 28, 138, 140–1
South Africa, 5, 28, 33, 35, 42
South America, 35
South Australia, xi, xii, 1, 4–14, 15, 20–31, 37–8, 42–4, 46–52, 55, 57, 61, 68, 70, 76, 78, 86, 92–4, 99–100, 102, 108, 111, 117–18, 123–4, 129, 132–4, 137–9, 147, 155, 157, 161, 166, 167, 170–2, 175, 177–8, 180–1, 183, 186–8, 190, 199, 202–9, 214–15, 217, 218–22, 224, 226–7
South Australian Mining Association (SAMA), 43–5, 100, 101, 102
Spanish, 37
Spargo, Peter, 43
Spargo, Stephen, 120
Sparnon, John, 151
Spence, William Guthrie, 61, 87–9, 126, 127, 143
Spencer's Gulf, 30

Stratton, 37
Stithians, 87
Stocker family, 48
Stoyle, Mark, 98
Strathalbyn, 70
Strike family, 121, 122
Sutter Creek, 35
Swedes, 40
Switzerland, 9
Sydney, 1, 197
Sydney Harbour Bridge, 191

Tamar, River (Cornwall), 17, 48, 68–9, 72, 81, 225
Tamar Valley (Cornwall-Devon), 68, 70, 73
Tamar, River (Tasmania), xi
Tasmania, xi, 7, 16, 131, 208
Tavistock, 20, 52, 68, 69, 70
Tavy, River, 68
Teddy, Luke, 224
Thomas, Captain Charles, 16–17
Thomas, Edward, 157
Thomas, Captain Ernest, 16

Thomas, Captain James, 16
Thomas, Captain J. Arthur, 16
Thomas, Captain Josiah, 14, 16, 59
Thomas, Eliza, 162
Thomas, Nathan (fictional character), 28, 139–40
Thomas, Polly (fictional character), 28, 138, 140–1, 146
Thomas, Ralph, 209
Thompson, Andrew, 35
Thompson, E.V., 219
Thorne, Rev. John, 50, 61
Thorne, Rev. Samuel, 26
Thorne, Serena, 26–7
Tiver, Joan, 189
Todd, A.C., 210
Tolmer, Inspector Alexander, 131–2
Tonkin, Bill 'Sponger', 191
Tonkin, Captain, 14
Tonkin, Mr, 116, 121
Tonkin, Elizabeth, Ann, 189
Tonkin, Thomas, 99
Toronto, 189
Torpoint, 35
Transvaal, the, 33, 196
Treais, George, 48
Trebilcock family, 125
Tredinnick, Captain, 107
Tregea, John B., 44
Tregilgas family, 124
Tregonning, E.G., 57
Trelawny, Bishop Jonathan, 99, 168
Treleaven family, 23
Tremewan family, 44
Trenoweth, 14
Trenwith family, 124
Tresise family, 91
Tresise, Rev. Charles, 157, 162
Tresize, Mr, 106
Tresmeer, 37
Trestrail, Captain, 73, 107
Trevorrow family, 44
Trevithick, Richard, 39, 67
Trewartha family, 23
Trewenack, Elizabeth Jane, 173
Trewenack, W.H., 176

Trewennack, John, 77
Trewin, Rev. James, 90
Trollope, Anthony, 94, 135
Truscott, John, 31
Truran, Richard, 71
Truro (Cornwall), 50, 162
Truro (South Australia), 47, 83
Tuckingmill, 178
Turks, 167, 169

UNESCO Cornish mining landscape 'World Heritage Site', 207, 227
United Kingdom (UK), xi, 176
United Labor Party (ULP); Labor Party, 23, 124, 128–9, 169, 171–3, 174, 177–80, 186–91, 193, 197, 215, 226
United Liberal Union, 174
United States of America, 12, 15, 34, 37, 39, 43, 52, 214, 218–19
United Trades and Labor Council (UTLC), 123–4, 127–9
Uren, J., 115
Utah, 41

Van Diemen's Land *see* Tasmania
Venning, M., 35
Vercoe, Captain George, 72
Vercoe, James Crabb, 118
Vermont, 40
Verran, John, 124, 128, 166, 171–2, 174–80, 185–6, 196, 199
Vial family, 70
Victoria, 6, 9, 10–15, 22–4, 26–7, 31, 41, 43, 44, 46–7, 60, 70, 75, 78–80, 88, 108, 110, 126, 143, 177, 209, 225
Virginia, 36, 39
Virginia City, 41, 213, 219
Virginia, West, 36
Visick, John, 18, 112, 115, 117
Vivienne, May, 80, 165

Wadebridge, 102
Wales, 21, 70, 79, 97, 99, 145, 194, 221
Wakefield, S.R., 79, 80

Wallaroo (Port), 29–30, 53, 57, 60–1, 71, 80, 84, 87, 94, 111, 115, 123–4, 126, 131, 144–5, 149, 152, 158, 172–3, 177–9, 183–4, 187–8, 191–3, 199, 206, 216, 226
Wallaroo, East, 184
Wallaroo Mines, 5, 28–30, 48, 51, 54, 58–9, 61, 79, 110, 132, 134–5, 139, 142, 148, 150–3, 160, 172, 184, 187, 191, 206
see also mines, *Australian*, Wallaroo
Walter, Richard, 71
Warbstow, 37
Warmington crisis, 49, 80, 102–8, 115–16, 124, 143
Warmington, Captain Eneder, 83, 102, 103, 104, 106–8
Warmington, Captain James, 73, 83, 102–3
Warmington, Captain William, 102–4, 105, 107
Warren, Captain John, 17, 86
Waukaringa, 88
Week St Mary, 37
Welsh, 21, 145, 194, 207–8, 210, 221
Wendron, 78, 197
Wesley, Charles, 161
Wesley, John, 161
Wesleyans, 15, 24–6, 45, 53, 63, 66, 74, 77, 90, 93, 112, 118, 120, 154–6, 159, 198, 225
see also Methodists
West, William, 83
Western Australia, xi, 5, 16, 42, 75, 128, 166, 178, 180, 182, 189–90, 209
Wheal Hughes settlement *see* Cross Roads
Williams, Mr, 222
Whinen, John, 54
Whitford, Stanley R., 120, 156, 163, 178, 190–2
Wilcocks, J.B., 44
Williams, Captain, 72
Williams, Captain Richard, 15
Williams, Joseph, 136

Wilton, William, 81
Wisconsin, 26, 37, 40, 41, 52
Withington, Rev. S. Trethewie, 158
Woolcock, Elizabeth, 147, 148
Woolcock, Thomas, 147
Worth, Tom, 48
Wright, Rev. John G., 160

Yelta settlement, 29, 157
Yorke Peninsula, 1, 5, 18, 23, 25–6, 28–9, 30, 31, 47–52, 56–63, 67, 69, 71, 73, 75–6, 78–80, 86, 94, 97, 100–3, 106, 110–12, 115, 117–18, 121, 123–29, 131–2, 134, 138, 141–2, 144, 146, 148–9, 151–8, 161, 162–5, 167–81, 183–6, 189, 191–2, 197, 199, 202, 204, 207–9, 213, 215–17, 219–20, 223, 226
Yorke's Peninsula Miners' and Smelters' Association, 180, 191

www.ingramcontent.com/pod-product-compliance
Lightning Source LLC
Chambersburg PA
CBHW050341230426
43663CB00010B/1940